The Psychoanalytic Study of the Child

VOLUME XV

The Psychoanalytic Study

of the Child

VOLUME XV

INTERNATIONAL UNIVERSITIES PRESS, INC.

New York   New York

Manufactured in the United States of America

CONTENTS

Psychoanalytic Concepts of Development

Genetic Aspects of Specific Ego and Id Pathology

Clinical Problems of the Prelatency and Latency Child

Simultaneous Analysis of Mother and Child

Problems of Psychopathology in Organically Impaired Children

PSYCHOANALYTIC CONCEPTS OF DEVELOPMENT

Editor's Note

Dr. Bowlby's paper has provoked considerable discussion. The Editors of *The Psychoanalytic Study of the Child* have therefore decided to accept this paper for publication together with the discussion remarks by Drs. Anna Freud, Max Schur, and René A. Spitz.

GRIEF AND MOURNING IN INFANCY
AND EARLY CHILDHOOD[1]

JOHN BOWLBY, M.D. (London)[2]

INTRODUCTION

In a previous paper, that on "Separation Anxiety" (1960), I sketched briefly the sequence of responses to be observed when young children are removed from their mothers and placed with strangers. After delineating the three phases—Protest, Despair, Detachment[3]— I pointed out that "the phase of Protest raises the problem of separation anxiety; Despair that of grief and mourning; Detachment that of defense. The thesis to be advanced is that the three responses— separation anxiety, grief and mourning, and defense—are phases of a single process and that when treated as such each illumines the other two." The hypothesis advanced there to account for separation anxiety was a corollary of the one advanced in an earlier paper to account for the child's tie to his mother (Bowlby, 1958b). In that paper it was suggested that the child's tie is best conceived as the outcome of a number of instinctual response systems, mostly nonoral in character, which are a part of the inherited behavior repertoire of man; when they are activated and the mother figure is available, attachment behavior results. In the paper on separation anxiety I suggested that, when they are activated and the mother figure is temporarily unavailable, separation anxiety and protest behavior follow. In this and the succeeding papers I shall advance the view that grief and mourning occur in infancy whenever the responses

---

1 Part of an earlier draft of this paper was read before the British Psycho-Analytical Society in October, 1959. Part of this version was presented as one of two Sandor Rado Lectures at Columbia University, New York, in April, 1960.

2 From the Tavistock Child Development Research Unit.

3 In earlier papers and the first drafts both of this paper and the previous one the term "Denial" had been used for the third phase. It gave rise to many difficulties, however, and is now abandoned in favor of the more purely descriptive term "detachment." It is used to indicate "lack of attachment."

mediating attachment behavior are activated and the mother figure continues to be unavailable. It is by now widely recognized that loss of the mother figure in the period between about six months and three or four or more years is an event of high pathogenic potential. The reason for this, I postulate, is that the processes of mourning to which it habitually gives rise all too readily at this age take a course unfavorable to future personality development.

This thesis does not seem to have been advanced in quite this form before. Naturally many analysts have advanced views which have features in common with it. Those, however, who have been concerned with disturbances in the child's relations with whole objects during the first few years of life, e.g., Abraham, Edith Jacobson, Spitz, Sullivan, have tended not to identify as mourning the processes set in train by disappointment and loss of love; while those who have recognized the reality of grief and mourning occurring in infancy have tended to concentrate on part objects—especially loss of breast at weaning—and events of the first year of life. Melanie Klein and her school are the outstanding example of the latter tendency. Fairbairn, Winnicott, and Erikson veer in the same direction, though, as we shall see, each is inclined to extend the vulnerable period beyond the first year. Anna Freud and Dorothy Burlingham have recorded the responses of young children to loss of mother and have recognized them as grief, but have not related their findings to the theory of mourning and melancholia.

Since the issues raised are far reaching and controversial and also have a long history in the psychoanalytic literature, five papers are required to do them justice. In this, the first, my principal aim will be to demonstrate that the responses to be observed in young children on loss of the mother figure differ in no material respect (apart probably from certain consequences) from those observed in adults on loss of a loved object. Since this is an empirical matter, I shall begin by comparing the data relevant to each age group. Only after this will the literature be reviewed; and here I shall consider among other themes the evidence on the basis of which much weight has been laid on the significance for personality development of loss of breast at weaning. In the second paper, "Processes of Mourning" it will be my aim to consider afresh the nature of the processes evoked by the loss of a loved object, and to this end attention will be paid to the responses to be observed when members of lower species are bereaved. In later papers, it will be my aim to discern what light the approach I am exploring sheds on the complex and difficult problems of psychopathology. In particular I shall give attention to the evidence that the experience of loss of mother in the early years is an antecedent of relevance in the development of personalities prone to depressive and other psychiatric illnesses and that these conditions are best understood as sequelae of pathological mourning.

Before going further it is well to define the sense in which terms will be used. "Mourning" will be used to denote the psychological processes that are set in train by the loss of a loved object and which commonly lead to the relinquishing of the object. "Grief" will denote the sequence of subjective states that follow loss and accompany mourning. Some analysts, for example, Winnicott (1954), have advocated that the term "mourning" should be restricted to those processes which have a favorable outcome. This I believe to be unsatisfactory. One of the major contributions of psychoanalysis has been to integrate psychopathology with general personality theory. To use different terms for a process or processes according to whether outcome is favorable or unfavorable seems to me to endanger this integration. Accordingly, the term "mourning" will be used to denote a fairly wide array of psychological processes set in train by the loss of a loved object irrespective of their outcome. This will enable us to discuss the different courses that mourning may take, healthy and pathological, and to relate them to each other. It is recognized, nevertheless, that there are certain responses to loss, for example, caring for a vicarious object and manic excitement, which are so unlike mourning as we ordinarily think of it that it might be confusing to include them under the term. For this reason there are times when the all-inclusive term "responses to loss" is required. In the next paper this aspect will be discussed in more detail.

The term "depression" will be used in a way which carries with it no necessary implication of pathology: this needs explanation. A normal part of the process of mourning is that the individual becomes depressed. This is both seen by others in his curtailed and disorganized behavior and experienced by himself in his own sense of inertia and purposelessness. This condition, however, although an

essential part of mourning, is not confined to the bereaved. It occurs
also following other losses and in many other circumstances. Furthermore, healthy personalities as well as sick ones are subject to it. Since
both in colloquial speech and clinical discussion the word "depression" is habitually used to describe this condition, it is in this sense
that the word will be used here. By contrast, the clinical syndrome
of which a pathological degree of depression is the main presenting
symptom will be referred to as "depressive illness" or "melancholia."
This terminology is in line with that used by Elizabeth Zetzel (1960),
in which she distinguishes between depression as "an affect integral
to psychic life," and thus comparable to anxiety, and the clinical
syndrome of which intense depression is a main presenting symptom
and which she terms "depressive illness." It differs, however, from
that of a number of psychoanalytic authors who do not make the
distinction and who use the term "depression" to denote both the
common affective state and the illness.

The terms "childhood," "early childhood," and "infancy" are
used in a progressively more limiting way. "Childhood" refers to the
whole span of life from birth to adolescence; "early childhood" to
the first three or four years, but especially to the second and third,
namely, the toddler period; "infancy" to the first twelve or fifteen
months.

In studying the literature of our subject, perhaps the most striking feature is the absence from the indexes of many standard psychoanalytic texts of both the words "grief" and "mourning." This is true
of the collected papers of Ferenczi (1916, 1926), Jones (1948), Balint
(1952), and Fairbairn (1952), of Anna Freud's *Ego and the Mechanisms of Defence* (1936), and even of a recent symposium on depression edited by Phyllis Greenacre (1953). That this is so suggests that,
despite the early work of Freud and Abraham and the constant
insistence of Melanie Klein, the significance for psychopathology of
grief and mourning, especially when they occur in infancy and early
childhood, has been and still is too little recognized. A reason for
this I believe to be the loyalty to the theory of infantile narcissism
which remains a feature of the work of many leading analysts. It
seems to me that the term "narcissism" is apt to call to mind the
picture of a self-centered egoistic individual whose demands are
exorbitant and unreasonable so that when the infant is described as

narcissistic it is easy to lack appreciation of both his expectations and his disappointments. Indeed, to describe the loss of his mother or loss of her love as "a severe injury to infantile narcissism," as Abraham and many others do, is to miss its true significance. I fear it is no accident that the reality and pathogenic implications of grief in early childhood have so frequently been overlooked.

This mistake is not made by Melanie Klein and her associates, nor by Balint, Fairbairn, Winnicott, and the many others who hold that it is in the nature of the infant's instinctual responses to be object-seeking from the first and who construct their psychopathology on this assumption. Owing, however, to the widespread tendency to identify the dynamic which binds infant to mother with orality, most of these analysts tend to see loss of breast at weaning as not only the first but by far the most pathologically significant loss suffered by the child. Furthermore, because in Western cultures weaning commonly takes place during the first year, the crucial phase during which the capacity for tolerating loss either matures or fails to mature is placed firmly in the early months of life. This is especially true of Melanie Klein.

It is my thesis that the significance of loss of breast has been exaggerated, that when it appears to be of consequence it is often because it occurs contemporaneously with separation or loss of close contact with mother, and that in consequence Melanie Klein's insistence that the processes described by her under the term "depressive position" all occur during the early months is mistaken. My view is that a principal trauma which is potentially present in the life of a young child is loss of mother, or loss of her love, and that the processes connected with the depressive position, which I conceive analogously but rather differently from Melanie Klein, are spread out over a long period, beginning at about the sixth month[4] and continuing into and beyond the fourth year. Throughout this period, I believe, there is a danger that the child may be subjected to experiences which can give rise both to separation anxiety and to grief and mourning of an intensity which can dislocate the development of his personality.

4 As I have made clear in earlier papers, I believe there is insufficient evidence to enable us to theorize with confidence about development before about six months of age.

In my view this hypothesis accounts more satisfactorily than do others for the clinical facts as we glean them in retrospect and darkly from our older patients, and their parents, and is more consonant with our present knowledge of the long phase of attachment of young child to mother and his intense distress at her loss or threatened loss. Indeed, I believe that the hypothesis now advanced would have been advocated earlier had it not happened that the phase of attachment to a mother figure was so late in being recognized and had not theory become preoccupied instead on the one hand with primary narcissism and on the other with orality.

Though in this matter I find myself differing from Melanie Klein, Fairbairn, and Winnicott, I must nonetheless express my deep indebtedness to them. In my view, in their theorizing they, more than any other living analysts except perhaps Balint and Therese Benedek, have been grappling with the crucial problems of personality development—the development of object relations and of responses, favorable or otherwise, to loss of object.

That the thesis has not been advanced in the same form hitherto may also be due to so little weight having been given in theory construction to direct observations of young children—despite Freud's having shown in one of his earliest publications[5] that they are an indispensable complement of reconstructional inferences based on data derived from older patients. In regard to this problem, as to so many others, there has been a notable failure to bring together data stemming from the two sources and to advance a unified theory as he advised should be done.

It must be emphasized that, because the purpose of this and the subsequent papers is to consider the theoretical implications of observations of grief and mourning in young children, the understanding of depression as an affect integral to psychic life and of melancholia will not be our main concern. Nevertheless, just as the discussion of separation anxiety inevitably required some consideration of the whole problem of anxiety, so in these papers we cannot escape some consideration of the wider problems. Moreover, like very many analysts from Freud and Abraham onward, I doubt if it is fruitful to consider any aspect of depression, whether normal or

5 See Freud (1905, p. 201). See also the view of Hartmann (1939).

pathological, without taking into account the experience of loss and the processes of mourning.

Comparison of Responses in Adults and Young Children

From the previous paper it will be recalled that when a healthy child of over six months is removed from the mother figure to whom he is attached and placed with strangers his initial response is to cry and seek to regain her: "He will often cry loudly, shake his cot, throw himself about, and look eagerly towards any sight or sound which might prove to be his missing mother." This, the phase of Protest, may with ups and downs continue for as long as a week or more. Throughout it the child seems buoyed up in his efforts by the hope and expectation that his mother will return.

Sooner or later, however, despair sets in. The longing for mother's return does not diminish, but the hope of its being realized fades. Ultimately the restless noisy demands cease; he becomes apathetic and withdrawn, a despair broken only perhaps by an intermittent and monotonous wail. He is in a state of unutterable misery.

Although this picture must have been known for centuries, it is only in the past two decades that it has been described in the psychological literature and called by its right name—grief.[6] This is the term used by Anna Freud and Dorothy Burlingham (1942), by Spitz (1947) in titling his film *Grief: A Peril in Infancy*, and by Robertson (1953) who during the past ten years has made a special study of its practical implications. Of the child aged from eighteen to twenty-four months Robertson writes:

> If a child is taken from his mother's care at this age, when he is so possessively and passionately attached to her, it is indeed as if his world has been shattered. His intense need of her is unsatisfied, and the frustration and longing may send him frantic with grief. It takes an exercise of imagination to sense the intensity of this distress. He is as overwhelmed as any adult who has lost

6 In the psychoanalytic literature the term "grief" is sometimes used to cover both the subjective experiences following loss and also, as in this case, the psychological processes set in train by it. Although when presenting my own ideas I shall restrict the term to the subjective experience, when describing the work of others it is often clumsy not to use it in the same way as does the author under discussion. Hence the usage in this paragraph.

a beloved person by death. To the child of two with his lack of understanding and complete inability to tolerate frustration it is really as if his mother had died. He does not know death, but only absence; and if the only person who can satisfy his imperative need is absent, she might as well be dead, so overwhelming is his sense of loss.

Despite these observations and conclusions by workers of repute, doubt has nonetheless been expressed whether we are right to equate this experience with that suffered by an adult in bereavement. Is this true grief, it is asked, and is it followed by true mourning? For instance, some years ago, before Anna Freud and Dorothy Burlingham reported their wartime observations, Helene Deutsch (1937) suggested that what in the more mature ego is experienced as grief is experienced in early childhood only as separation anxiety.[7] It is more surprising that Spitz himself, who has done so much to draw attention to these problems, in his paper on "Anaclitic Depression" (1946) rejected the view that what he was observing is a process of mourning. Furthermore, Anna Freud, while identifying the affect as grief, has recorded her belief that during the first and second years its duration extends for not more than a few days in cases where a suitable substitute is available. Because of the existence of these doubts regarding both the occurrence of grief and mourning in early childhood and its duration, it will be best, before we consider further the opinions of others, to examine the evidence. When records of the responses to loss of object by adults and young children are placed side by side, it is believed, the essential similarity of the responses will be clearly recognized.

Let us consider first descriptions of grief and mourning as they occur in adults following bereavements. One of the most comprehensive is that by Lindemann (1944) who, by a detailed clinical study of 100 cases, has been able to confirm and extend the knowledge of the usual course of events which is contained in the earlier psychoanalytic literature. Some of his cases were already under treat-

---

[7] Very recently a translation of an early paper by Helene Deutsch (1919) has appeared, in which she records in some detail the responses of a two-year-old boy to the departure of his nanny, and in which she refers both to "his despair" and to "the sixth day of his mourning" ("am sechsten Tage seines Kummers"). In view of the debate regarding length of mourning at this age it is to be noted that, despite his having familiar substitutes (including his mother) immediately available, the boy's distress lasted eight days and led to a noticeable change of personality.

ment for psychoneurotic difficulties when they were bereaved; others were ordinary people who had recently lost a relative. His method of study gave him opportunity for the first-hand observation and recording of acute grief. Another valuable study is that of Marris (1958), an investigator who combines sociological skill with clinical sensitivity. Marris interviewed a fairly representative group of seventy-two widows, aged between twenty-five and fifty-six years, at some point during the two years after they had lost their husbands. Although his initial interest had been in their social and economic circumstances, he realized that his inquiry would be worthless unless he took account of the grief and mourning from which all but a handful of his subjects were still suffering. The great merit of the descriptions of Lindemann and Marris is that they are based on observations of larger numbers and more representative samples of sufferers than is usual in the clinical literature. In regard to the common patterns of response and their usual sequence in time there is close agreement between them; there is close agreement, too, with the findings of other studies, both those by psychoanalysts and those by academic and social psychologists (e.g., Shand, 1920; Waller, 1951; Eliot, 1955). The main facts indeed are not in question.

I propose to group the psychological responses described by these different workers under five main heads:

    (a)   Thought and behavior still directed toward the lost object;

    (b)   Hostility, to whomsoever directed;

    (c)   Appeals for help;

    (d)   Despair, withdrawal, regression, and disorganization;

    (e)   Reorganization of behavior directed toward a new object.

In addition to these psychological responses, there are those of a more physiological type, including insomnia, which was present in about four fifths of Marris's cases. Lindemann has described these responses in some detail and, like Engel (1954) and others, has seen in them the origin of much psychosomatic illness. Since, however, such sequelae lie outside the scope of this paper, they will not be discussed here further.

All accounts dwell on the insistence with which behavior, thought, and feeling tend to remain oriented toward the lost person. Despite the knowledge that he will not return, there is a continuing sense that nonetheless he is present. The observations of Lindemann and Marris fully confirm Freud's well-known formulation in "Mourning and Melancholia" (1917):

> Reality-testing has shown that the loved object no longer exists, and it proceeds to demand that all libido shall be withdrawn from its attachments to that object. This demand arouses understandable opposition—it is a matter of general observation that people never willingly abandon a libidinal position, not even, indeed, when a substitute is already beckoning to them. This opposition can be so intense that a turning away from reality takes place and a clinging to the object through the medium of a hallucinatory wishful psychosis [p. 244].

Marris (1958) found that as many as half the widows interviewed had experienced after their husband's death a sense of his continuing presence, and a quarter confessed that they had been or were actually behaving as though he still lived:

> "I used to put the kettle on and make tea for him. Or when I'd come home and find him not there, I'd think he had just gone out." [A number] talked to his photograph and imagined that he advised them, clung to all his possessions and returned to places that they had frequented together [p. 15].

In these respects Queen Victoria's behavior was not unusual, even though she persisted in it unusually long.

All accounts dwell, too, on the frequency of resentment at the loss and of hostility aimed either at the lost object, others, or the self. Lindemann refers to "feelings of hostility, surprising and quite inexplicable to the patients," which appeared sometimes to be "spread out over all relationships" and, at others, to be channeled into "furious hostility against specific persons; the doctor or the surgeon are accused bitterly for neglect of duty. . . ." Marris describes one woman who "admitted ruefully that, in the first frenzy of her grief, she had assaulted the doctor for no reason whatever, and apologized to him afterwards. 'I just went berserk. Poor Dr. Roberts got a good hiding.' She added, 'afterwards depression set in and I lost interest.' " Marris comments: it was "as if her rage while it lasted had given her courage." As is well known, often these criticisms and hostile feelings are also directed against the self and manifest themselves in a profound sense of guilt and unworthiness. At other times they are directed toward the lost figure and take the form of complaints.

The tendency of the bereaved to seek consolation and help from others has been remarked upon especially by Shand (1920). "When we can resist," he remarks, "we may become angry, when we cannot there is room only for sorrow. . . . Sorrow appears to have one principal impulse—the cry for help or assistance." A great difficulty with such appeals, however, is that the bereaved either makes unreasonable demands or else seems hardly to know what he wants, and often becomes irritable and ungrateful to those who try to respond.

In the ordinary person neither appeals for help, rage at others, nor self-reproach continue indefinitely; nor does the illusion, whether accepted and encouraged or resented and discouraged, that the lost figure is still present. Sooner or later the reality of loss takes hold and with it comes an appalling "sense of the futility and emptiness of life." It was expressed to Marris in such phrases as these:

"I had nothing to live for."
"I didn't even cook myself a bit of food. I wouldn't care if I died tomorrow."
"The interest is gone, I would never have stood the house looking like this when my husband was alive. I wouldn't care if a bomb fell on the house tomorrow."

Perhaps as clinicians we sometimes fail to realize that responses of this gravity are the rule in bereavement: Marris reports them as present in no less than two thirds of his cases.

Coupled with this apathy is

. . . a tendency to withdraw from people and to reject consolation . . . Commonly it was rejected either from indifference—"I just could not be bothered with people"—or because it revived distress, or from a generalized resentment: "I hated everybody." And sometimes [because] to be in company, especially the company of married couples, only made them more than ever aware of their loneliness [Marris, 1958, pp. 20-21].

Perhaps the greatest difficulty of all for the bereaved person is the unaccountable oscillation in his feelings from one moment to the next. Eliot (1955) describes

. . . overt paroxysms of weeping, protest and . . . seizures of grief or rage [which may be followed by] temporary episodes variously described as blank, mute despair, stolidity, inability to act or even move. . . . Bereavement is full of the ambivalent conflict of despair and craving, [he remarks,] "that incomprehensible contradiction of memory and non-existence."[8]

The most striking feature about the phase of apathy is the loss of the normal organized patterns of activity. This is well described by Lindemann:

There is restlessness, inability to sit still, moving about in an aimless fashion, continually searching for something to do . . . . What is done is done with lack of zest, as though one were going through the motions. The bereaved clings to the daily routine of prescribed activities; but these activities do not proceed in the automatic, self-sustaining fashion which characterizes normal work but have to be carried on with effort, as though each fragment of the activity became a special task. The bereaved is surprised to find how large a part of his customary activity was done in some meaningful relationship to the deceased and has now lost its significance. Especially the habits of social interaction—meeting friends, making conversation, sharing enterprises with others—seem to have been lost.

Though the concept of regression is in varying degrees appropriate to explain it, I believe the more valuable concept is that of disorganization: in Lindemann's words, "there is . . . a painful lack of capacity to initiate and maintain organized patterns of activity." This is a way of conceptualizing the data in keeping with the theory advanced to account for the child's tie to his mother and one to which we shall be turning in the next paper when we come to discuss the theory of grief and mourning.

Following this phase of despair and disorganization there occurs a phase of recovery during which reorganization takes place partly in connection with the image of the lost object and partly in connection with a new object or objects. This is a transitional phase. In so far as a restructured relationship with the image of the lost object is achieved it is the final phase of mourning: in so far as a new object is found it is the first phase of a new object relationship. Being less dramatic, descriptions of this phase are less clear. One feature which is fairly common in both men and women and which is relevant to our theme is a period of promiscuity intervening between the

8 Quoted by Eliot from Proust, *Cities of the Plain.*

relinquishment of the lost object and orientation to a new one (Waller, 1951; Eliot, 1955).

Now let us compare this picture of grief and mourning in adults with what is seen in young children who have lost their mother. In making this comparison much of the evidence presented concerns the behavior of young children removed not only from their mothers but also from the whole environment with which they are familiar. In such conditions loss of mother is certainly not the only variable; and the question is sometimes asked whether it is even the main one. Are we justified, in fact, in drawing on such observations? A word of explanation is called for.

As the account given by Helene Deutsch (1919) so graphically illustrates, young children, even when they remain in their own homes and have familiar substitutes immediately available, nonetheless respond to loss of a loved figure with despair and mourning. This finding, and the fact that if left in a residential nursery or hospital ward their constant and persistent response is to scream and cry for mother, suggests that loss of mother is in fact the main variable in the situation. Nevertheless, it is clear that the fear evoked by the strangeness of the new environment greatly intensifies their responses to her loss. From comparisons such as these Robertson and I (1952) have concluded that the behavior observed in the hospital and residential nursery is not different in kind but is an intensified version of what occurs when loss of mother is the only variable. While a recognition of this warns us not to generalize too broadly, for certain purposes a magnification of what is to be studied has advantages. We believe that this is so here.

What then are young children's responses to loss of the mother figure? Typically they show a set and sequence of responses almost identical to those of adults. After the initial protest and demand for his mother's return, which often lasts many days, the child becomes quieter. It would be a mistake, however, to suppose that this means that the child has "forgotten" his parents. On the contrary, all the evidence is that as in the case of the adult he remains highly oriented toward the lost love object. Robertson has recorded many cases of young children whose longing for the absent mother was clearly apparent, even though at times so muted that it tended to be overlooked. Of Laura, the subject of his film *A Two-Year-Old Goes to*

Hospital (1952), he writes: "She would interpolate without emotion and as if irrelevantly the words 'I want my Mummy, where has my Mummy gone?' into remarks about something quite different; and when no one took up the intruded remark she would not repeat the 'irrelevance.' " The same child would sometimes let concealed feelings come through in songs and, unknown to herself, substitute the name of "Mummy" for that of a nursery-rhyme character. On one occasion she expressed an urgent wish to see the steam-roller which had just gone from the roadway below the ward in which she was confined. She cried, "I want to see the steam-roller, I want to see the steam-roller. I want to see my *Mummy*. I want to see the steam-roller."

Another child, aged three years, who had been in the hospital for ten days, was pointed out by the ward sister as being "happy." He seemed to be amusing himself with a droll game of bowing repeatedly and twisting his head. When the observer stood near, however, it was clear that, almost compulsively, the child was making the motions of looking toward a closed door and whispering, "My mummy coming soon"—though in fact his mother would not be allowed to visit for another two days (Robertson and Bowlby, 1952).

To the perceptive observer, such persistent orientation to the lost mother is apparent even in much younger children. Thus Robertson also records the case of Philip who was aged only thirteen months when placed in a residential nursery. Although he was too young to verbalize any wish for his mother, the staff reported that during the days of fretting and later, whenever frustrated or upset, he would make the motions associated with the rhyme "Round and round the garden" with which his mother used to humor him when he was out of temper at home.

Anna Freud and Dorothy Burlingham recorded many cases of persistent but muted longing for the absent mother. On a previous occasion (see Bowlby, Robertson, and Rosenbluth, 1952) we have quoted a record made in the Hampstead Nursery of a boy aged three years and two months. On being left in the nursery he had been admonished to be a good boy and not to cry—otherwise his mother would not visit him.

[On the first day] Patrick tried to keep his promise and was not seen crying. Instead he would nod his head whenever anyone looked at him and assured himself and anybody who cared to listen that his mother would come for him, she would put on his overcoat and would take him home with her again. Whenever a listener seemed to believe him he was satisfied; whenever anybody contradicted him, he would burst into violent tears.

This same state of affairs continued through the next two or three days with several additions. The nodding took on a more compulsive and automatic character: "My mother will put on my overcoat and take me home again."

Later an ever-growing list of clothes that his mother was supposed to put on him was added: "She will put on my overcoat and my leggings, she will zip up the zipper, she will put on my pixie hat."

When the repetitions of this formula became monotonous and endless, somebody asked him whether he could not stop saying it all over again. Again Patrick tried to be the good boy that his mother wanted him to be. He stopped repeating the formula aloud but his moving lips showed that he was saying it over and over to himself.

At the same time he substituted for the spoken words gestures that showed the position of his pixie hat, the putting on of an imaginary coat, the zipping of the zipper, etc. What showed as an expressive movement one day, was reduced the next to a mere abortive flicker of his fingers. While the other children were mostly busy with their toys, playing games, making music, etc., Patrick, totally uninterested, would stand somewhere in a corner, moving his hands and lips with an absolutely tragic expression on his face [p. 89].

Reading these accounts we are inevitably reminded of Freud's comment: "It is a matter of general observation that people never willingly abandon a libidinal position, not even, indeed, when a substitute is already beckoning to them."

Again as in the case of adults, the persistent longing of the young child for his lost loved object is often suffused with intense generalized hostility. This has been reported by several workers, e.g., Robertson (1953), and was one of the most striking findings in Heinicke's systematic study. Heinicke (1956) compared the behavior of two groups of children, both aged between sixteen and twenty-six months;[9] one group was in a residential nursery, the other in a day

9 Although the criterion for the sample was fifteen to thirty months, the age range for the children actually studied was narrower.

nursery. Not only did the children in the residential nursery cry for their mothers more than did the day-nursery children, but they exhibited much violent hostility of a kind hardly seen at all in those in the day nursery. The targets of this hostility were so varied that it was difficult to discern to whom it was principally directed: as in the adults whom Lindemann described, it was "spread out over all relationships."

Sometimes, however, it is evident that it is directed to the lost love object itself. Anna Freud and Dorothy Burlingham (1944) give a striking example:

> Reggie, who had come to our house as a baby of five months, went home to his mother when he was one year eight months, and has been with us ever since his return to the nursery two months later. While with us, he formed two passionate relationships to two young nurses who took care of him at different periods. The second attachment was suddenly broken at two years eight months when his "own" nurse married. He was completely lost and desperate after her departure, and refused to look at her when she visited him a fortnight later. He turned his head to the other side when she spoke to him, but stared at the door, which had closed behind her, after she had left the room. In the evening in bed he sat up and said: "My very own Mary-Ann! But I don't like her" [pp. 62-63].

As I have recorded frequently before (Bowlby, 1944, 1951, 1958a), it is my belief that there is no experience to which a young child can be subjected more prone to elicit intense and violent hatred for the mother figure than that of separation. Although often mentioned in psychoanalytic literature, I believe its significance is still gravely underestimated.

As in the case of the adult who longs for and misses a particular person and so cannot find comfort in other companions, however kind they may be, so does the separated child at first reject the ministrations of those caring for him. Although his appeals for help are clamant, often his behavior is as contradictory and frustrating to the would-be comforter as is that of the recently bereaved adult. Sometimes he rejects them. At others he combines clinging to a nurse with sobs for his lost mother. Anna Freud and Dorothy Burlingham have recorded the case of a little girl of seventeen months who said nothing but "Mum, Mum, Mum" for three days, and who, although liking to sit on the nurse's knee and to have the nurse put her arm around her, insisted throughout on having her back to the nurse so as not to see her.

Nevertheless the complete or partial rejection of the strange adult does not continue forever. After a phase of withdrawal and apathy, already described, the child begins to seek new relationships. How these develop turns on the situation in which he finds himself. Provided there is one particular mother figure to whom he can relate he will in time take to her and treat her in some respects as though she were his mother. In those situations where the child has no single person to whom he can relate, on the other hand, or where there is a succession of persons to whom he makes brief attachments, the outcome is of course different. As a rule he becomes increasingly self-centered and prone to make transient and shallow relationships with all and sundry. This condition, reminiscent of the transient sexual promiscuity of bereaved adults, bodes ill for his development if it becomes an established pattern.

There has been some debate regarding the length of the period during which young children mourn. For instance, Anna Freud and Dorothy Burlingham (1942) have expressed the view that it is "short-lived," especially in children between one and two years, and that in this respect it differs greatly from mourning in adults. This view is not supported by the observations of Robertson, made in a variety of hospitals and residential-nursery settings, including a nursery in which serious attempts were made to provide a stable mother substitute from the beginning of separation. Nor is it supported by such other evidence as is available, including that reported in the various publications deriving from work in the Hampstead Nurseries during the war.

Apart from the report by Helene Deutsch (1919), which shows that even in the most favorable conditions overt distress may continue for eight days, the most relevant study I know of so far is the one, already referred to, undertaken by Heinicke (1956). He studied six children aged between sixteen and twenty-six months who were undergoing a short stay in one of three residential nurseries. Of these, four were aged twenty months or under. In the nursery "each child belonged to a definite group of children and was cared for by a limited number of nurses. It was thus possible for each child to form attachments both to the nurses and to the children in his own particular group." This means that Heinicke was studying children of about the age with which the debate is concerned and in residential nurseries in which an attempt was made to provide for the children's need for attachment. The children were observed for a period of about one hour on one or other of each pair of days' stay (at week ends one of three days). The results are presented in statistical form.

What Heinicke's observations show is that there was a great deal of crying for mother and father during the whole of the first twelve days. During the third, fourth, and fifth days almost 17 per cent of the recorded behavior was crying, almost all of it directed toward the absent mother and father. During the tenth, eleventh, and twelfth days the children still cried, and at this period it comprised 12 per cent of the behavior recorded; again all but a small fraction was directed toward the absent parents. Autoerotic behavior and pronounced hostility, present during the first week, rose in incidence during the second; during the tenth, eleventh, and twelfth days they together comprised over 18 per cent of the behavior recorded. Thus during the middle of the second week nearly one third of the recorded behavior of these children consisted of one of three activities, all indicative of emotional disturbance, namely, crying for absent parents, autoerotic activity, and intense aggression. Even in the middle of the third week the total was still nearly one quarter of recorded behavior.

In view of the small number of children and the possible errors due to time sampling, too great weight must not be set on these figures. Moreover, studying a second sample Heinicke (personal communication) found that in the second week crying for absent parents made up a smaller proportion of recorded behavior. Nevertheless, since the general tenor of Heinicke's observations confirms the more extensive but less systematic observations of Robertson, they can be taken as demonstrating that in children of this age group mourning not uncommonly continues into the third week.

The discrepancy between these conclusions and those of Anna Freud may be due in part to the different conditions in which observations are made. Some of the differences, however, I believe to be due to the criterion which she posits for when mourning ceases.

She has suggested[10] that mourning is confined to the transient time from losing the mother to when the child is ready to accept food and comfort from a new person. In my view this criterion is likely to give a misleading impression. Children of this age, I believe, accept food and a measure of comfort from a new person long before the other signs of grief have disappeared. In other words, the duration of grief is much longer than this criterion would indicate.

There is, I believe, a further reason for the discrepancy. This lies in the expectations that Anna Freud has derived from her theoretical position regarding early ego development and which have led her to be skeptical of the view that the processes underlying the grief responses of infants and young children are similar in character to the processes underlying such responses in adults—that in fact they constitute true mourning. This is an issue which will be discussed more fully in the next section. Meanwhile, since the evidence makes it clear that at a descriptive level the responses are similar in the two age groups, I believe it to be wiser methodologically to assume that the underlying processes are similar also, and to postulate differences only when there is clear evidence for them. That certain differences between age groups exist I have little doubt, since in infants and small children the outcome of experiences of loss seem more frequently to take forms which lead to an adverse psychological outcome. In my judgment, however, these differences are best understood as being due to special variants of the mourning process itself, and not to processes of a qualitatively different kind. When so conceived, I believe, we are enabled both to see how data regarding the responses of young children to a separation experience relate to the general body of psychoanalytic theory and also to reformulate that theory in simpler terms.

REVIEW OF LITERATURE

A reading of the psychoanalytic literature on the occurrence of grief and mourning in infancy and early childhood shows that there have been two main points of controversy. The first has already been referred to. It is the crucial question whether or not, when the infant

---

10 Anna Freud advanced this criterion when a draft of this paper was discussed at a meeting of the British Psycho-Analytical Society.

or young child experiences loss of love object, he experiences grief and goes through a period of mourning. The second is contingent on the first: in so far as he does experience grief, what is the nature of the loved object, loss of which most readily evokes it? In the first half of this review, in considering the work among others of Anna Freud, Spitz, and Abraham, we shall be principally concerned with the first of these questions. In the second half, where the work of Melanie Klein, Winnicott, Fairbairn, and Erikson is discussed, we shall be mainly concerned with the second: in particular it will be necessary to review the evidence on the basis of which key significance has been attributed to weaning and the first year of life. Before embarking on these controversies, however, it is interesting to see where Freud stands.

Despite his early recognition of the role played by grief and mourning in mental illness, to which reference is made in subsequent papers, it seems that it was only toward the end of his life that Freud came within reach of appreciating the reality and significance of grief and mourning occurring in infancy and early childhood. In the final pages of *Inhibitions, Symptoms and Anxiety*, having by this time a clearer grasp of the place of the child's attachment to his mother and of separation anxiety, he takes a fresh look at the problem of mourning. Prior to this re-examination, he tells us, he had been clear that "the affective reactions to a separation . . . are pain and mourning, not anxiety" (1926, p. 131). Now, however, he discovers that after all, anxiety *is* such a reaction and he confesses himself puzzled. In a final addendum, therefore, he addresses himself to the question "When does loss of object lead to anxiety and when to mourning?" His reply, as we have seen, is that anxiety is the reaction to a danger of loss of object, pain that to actual loss of object. Mourning, therefore, has "the task of carrying out [a] retreat from the object" (p. 172).

Throughout the discussion in that book, one center of Freud's attention is the responses which young children exhibit when their mothers depart or are absent. Referring to the infant's anxiety and distress at her loss, he reflects: "That it does have anxiety there can be no doubt; but the expression of its face and its reaction of crying indicate that it is feeling pain as well." This must be, Freud thinks, because "it cannot as yet distinguish between temporary absence and permanent loss. As soon as it loses sight of its mother it behaves as if it were never going to see her again" (p. 169). From here it is but a short step to the realization that, when in fact the infant or young child does not see her again over a period of days or weeks, as we know can occur, the pain of grief becomes intense and inevitably he passes into a state of mourning. But this crucial step Freud did not take: there is no reason to think he ever fully realized the depth and gravity of grief in the very young, nor its potential pathogenic effects. Since he was already seventy at the time and had presumably never been a witness of such happenings, this need not surprise us.[11]

Among analysts Bernfeld (1925) was one of the first to recognize the reality of sadness and sorrow in infancy. Basing his views mainly on the direct observations of infants recorded in the literature he describes these emotions as common following loss of breast at weaning. His evaluation of weaning as an experience, however, seems contradictory since, although on the one hand he attaches much significance to it for future personality development, on the other he describes the response to it as "a short and mild form of sorrow" (p. 259). Nevertheless, he holds that after loss of breast the same work of mourning has to be accomplished as in all later sorrows (p. 299).

Although Bernfeld thus recognizes clearly the reality of grief and mourning in early childhood, it is to be noted that he confines his considerations to loss of breast. Although this may be partly due to the fact that his monograph is limited to development occurring during the first twelve months of the child's life, there is internal evidence suggesting that he was unaware of the long period during which the child is attached to his mother[12] and that he had given little thought to the possibility that some of the personality disturbances which he attributes to loss of breast at weaning may in fact be explained by experience of loss of mother or of her love

11 It is, however, not unlikely that Freud himself had an experience of this kind. In the biography Jones tells us that, when Freud was two and a half years old, not only was his mother preoccupied by the birth of a new baby but his Nanny was summarily dismissed after being caught stealing (Jones, 1953, p. 10).

12 For instance, Bernfeld suggests that walking is a "symbol of attained independence" and he seems to attach much importance to the achievements of walking, chewing, and speaking, which, he claims, "are acquired in a relatively short time during the end of the first year" (p. 227).

either in the first year or in a later phase. This is an issue to which we shall be returning.

It is possible that, had he made direct observations himself, Bernfeld might also have recognized grief and mourning following loss of mother. As it was it appears to have been Anna Freud, in her work with Dorothy Burlingham during the war, who was the first both to record the common responses to loss of mother as a whole object and also to have termed it grief. Spitz, whose studies were published shortly afterwards, was a close second. Nevertheless, despite their recognition of its reality, I do not find the way they have related observation to theory satisfactory. What they did was to squeeze the new observations within the framework of existing theories, especially those of primary narcissism and of the primacy of bodily needs and, in Spitz's case, of theories elaborated to account for pathological states such as melancholia. In my view it would have been better had they sought to revise theory in the light of their new observation.

First let us review the contribution of Anna Freud and Dorothy Burlingham (1942, 1944). In their experience, they state, during the phase of development starting at about six months of age and continuing until the third birthday reactions to loss of mother are

> . . . particularly violent. The child feels suddenly deserted by all the known persons in its world to whom it has learned to attach importance. Its new ability to love finds itself deprived of the accustomed objects, and its greed for affection remains unsatisfied. Its longing for its mother becomes intolerable and throws it into states of despair which are very similar to the despair and distress shown by babies who are hungry and whose food does not appear at the accustomed time. For several hours, or even for a day or two, this psychological craving of the child, the "hunger" for its mother, may over-ride all bodily sensations.
>
> There are some children of this age who will refuse to eat or to sleep. Very many of them will refuse to be handled or comforted by strangers. The children cling to some object or to some form of expression which means to them, at that moment, memory of the material presence of the mother. Some will cling to a toy which the mother has put into their hands at the moment of parting; others to some item of bedding or clothing which they have brought from home.
>
> Some will monotonously repeat the word by which they are

used to call their mothers, as, for instance, Christine, seventeen months, who said: "Mum, mum, mum, mum, mum, . . ." . . . continually in a deep voice for at least three days [1942, pp. 51-52].

In commenting on these observations, which as we have seen have subsequently been confirmed by Robertson and others, Anna Freud and Dorothy Burlingham emphasize, I believe rightly, both "the depth and seriousness of this grief of a small child" and their belief that "Mourning of equal intensity in an adult person would have to run its course throughout a year" (p. 51). Nevertheless, they also record a belief, which is at variance with their own reports, namely: "This childish grief is short-lived. . . . in the child between one and two years [it] will normally be over in thirty-six to forty-eight hours" (1942, p. 52). Furthermore, neither in this publication nor in later ones have they related an adverse development of the capacity for object relations specifically to the experience of bereavement and mourning occurring in infancy and early childhood.

In the previous section I discussed the evidence bearing on the difference of view between us regarding the length of time that responses to loss in early childhood continue and also touched upon the differences in regard to theory. Whereas the evidence points unmistakably to such responses continuing at least for a week and usually for much longer, Anna Freud has concluded that they are short-lived. However, the main reason she gives for not linking her observations of grief in infancy and early childhood to the psychology and psychopathology of mourning is because her views of ego development have led her to the belief that, before well into the second year, the infant and young child are not yet capable of mourning in its true sense. This conclusion is based on her belief that before this age the individual is unable either to accept the reality principle or to effect appropriate changes in the internal world by controlling id tendencies.[13] Up to this point, she holds, his responses to loss are governed by the pleasure-pain principle and are therefore of a much simpler kind.

What I believe to be the adverse effects of this theoretical standpoint are illustrated in the accounts, part theoretical and part empirical, that Anna Freud and Dorothy Burlingham have given of the

[13] These are the reasons given by Anna Freud in her contribution to the discussion of an earlier draft of this paper.

processes which they hold underlie the way in which a child of under three years relinquishes a loved object and adopts a new one:

> The child's life is still entirely governed by the principle which demands that it should seek pleasure and avoid pain and discomfort. A love object who does not give it immediate satisfaction is no good to it. Its memories of the past are spoilt by the disappointment which it feels at the present moment. It has no outlook into the future, and it would be of no help to it if it had. Its needs are so urgent that they [require] immediate gratification; promises of pleasure are no help.
>
> The little child will therefore, after a short while, turn away from the mother image in its mind and, though at first unwillingly, will accept the comfort which is offered [1942, pp. 52-53].

I do not think this account fits the facts as we know them. Even for children in the second half of their first year the evidence of Schaffer and Callender (1959) shows it is mistaken to suppose that the mother image is so quickly forsaken; and it is certainly so for those in their second and third year of life.

Incompatibility between a theoretical expectation and observed data inevitably calls the theory in question. How well proven, it must therefore be asked, is the theory of early ego development that Anna Freud favors? Although to discuss this thoroughly would take us too far afield, such evidence as is available hardly seems to support it. Even in the early months of life there is regulation of id demands in the light of experience and, although in the second year control is often spasmodic and unreliable, it is certainly not absent. Bearing in mind the work of Piaget (1937) and others, I believe it is safe to conclude that ego development, namely, perceptual and cognitive organization and with it the regulation of impulse, starts during the first year. For these reasons, therefore, I cannot accept as valid the objections that Anna Freud raises to the view that the processes underlying bereavement responses of infants and young children are examples of true mourning.

Because there is disagreement in regard to the psychological processes that are at work in infants and young children who have temporarily or permanently lost their mothers, it would be unfortunate if the substantial agreement between us in regard to practical implications were overlooked. Both of us hold that experiences of deprivation in the early years have adverse effects on subsequent personality development. Naturally, the way Anna Freud describes the relevant situations and the psychological processes at work is in keeping with her theoretical standpoint; in particular it is much influenced by her belief that in these years a mother's task is to provide for the satisfaction of her infant's bodily needs. The deprivation experience she specifies is that of the mother who fails to be a steady source of satisfaction to her child. The explanation she offers of the character defects that follow is that they arise from a failure in the transformation of narcissistic libido into object libido (A. Freud, 1949).

Another analyst who has recorded first-hand observations of grief and mourning in infancy following loss of mother but who, I believe, has been handicapped in his theorizing by inappropriate models is Spitz. Although he entitled his well-known film *Grief: A Peril in Infancy*, he does not use the word "grief" in the paper to which it refers ("Anaclitic Depression," 1946) and in this paper (though not in a later one) he seems to reject the view that the clinical phenomena he is describing are to be understood as due to mourning, normal or pathological. He does so on the grounds that "the process was in no way self-limiting."[14] It is because it is "a syndrome of a progressive nature which after having reached a critical point of development appears to become irreversible," he tells us, that he "call[s] the picture depression[15] and not mourning" (p. 331).

This is not a good argument. It is based on the assumption that at all ages mourning must be a self-limiting process; because the infant fails to get over it, Spitz seems to reason, it cannot be mourning. This is a mirror image of the argument once heard in regard to another diagnosis: because the patient recovered, it could not have been schizophrenia.

An examination of Spitz's clinical data makes it clear beyond reasonable doubt that what he is describing is, in fact, the process

[14] The relevant passage reads: "The main reason why . . . we feel justified in speaking of an anaclitic depression going far beyond mourning and even beyond pathological mourning is that we have observed a number of cases in which no intervention occurred and where it became only too evident that the process was in no way self-limiting" (1946, pp. 330-331).

[15] Spitz is here using the term "depression" to mean a form of pathological depression.

of mourning occurring in infants soon after the age when they have consolidated their attachment to a particular mother figure. The condition, which Spitz states is not seen in infants younger than six months, occurs only after they have lost their mothers and only when the previous mother-child relationship has been good. It is characterized by all the outward signs of grief and mourning—sadness, weepiness, lack of contact, withdrawal, dejection, loss of appetite, insomnia. Provided it does not persist too long, when mother is restored there is complete recovery.[16] It is to be noted that in a later paper (1953) Spitz himself adopts this interpretation of his observations. The children, he states there, respond "to the loss of their love object by a progressive mourning reaction." Even so by adding "if no adequate substitute is provided," he seems to suggest that if a substitute were provided the condition would not be mourning, a view that I believe would be wrong.

The views advanced in these two papers of Spitz diverge in another respect. In both papers, explicitly in 1946 and implicitly in 1953, Spitz posits that the condition present in these infants is a special form of pathological depression. This leads him to strive to frame a hypothesis which will bring it within the theoretical framework that Freud has sketched for melancholia. To do this requires him to suppose that aggression directed toward the self plays a major role, and it becomes necessary for him in consequence to explain how this comes about. Two different, though not incompatible, theories are advanced.

In 1946 he suggests that the inhibition of the infants' locomotion by confinement in their cots is the clue.

> . . . locomotion and motility [he suggests] fulfill the important task of offering a necessary channel of release for the aggressive drive. When motor activity is inhibited in infancy, all normal outlets of the aggressive drive are blocked. In this case only one alternative remains for dealing with the aggressive drive; that is,

[16] That when she is not restored it may persist and become permanent is presumably to be attributed either to the age of the children or to the conditions in which the particular infants observed by Spitz were living. Since infants of the same age observed by Schaffer and Callender (1959) undergoing a stay in a Scottish hospital, in which they received little substitute mothering, do not respond in the same way, and similar behavior has not yet been recorded by others, the particular conditions necessary to produce the Spitz syndrome remain unclear.

to direct it against the self. The resulting dynamic picture [he concludes] is identical to the one we have previously described for melancholia. The only difference is that whereas in melancholia it was the superego which made use of the aggressive drive against the ego, in the case of inhibited motor activity in infancy the intervention of the superego is unnecessary [1946, pp. 334-335].

In his 1953 paper, the topic of which is aggression, he advances another and more general explanation. He notes that at first (during what we have termed the phase of Protest) "attempts are made by these infants to regain the lost object with the help of their aggressive drive." Subsequently, however, those manifestations of aggression that are common in the normal child after the eighth month Spitz finds to be "conspicuously absent"; this leads him to the belief that there must have been a redirection of aggression inward. He therefore advances the view that "when the infant is deprived of [his] love object, the libidinal and the aggressive drives are denied the opportunity to discharge. They are dammed up and turned against the self."

There are several points of difficulty here. Some are empirical. As regards Spitz's first explanation, although Robertson and I have no first-hand experience of the conditions necessary to precipitate intense grief and despair in infants during the second half of their first year, there is no reason to suppose that confinement in a cot is one of them. It is certainly not so during the second year, though a restriction of other interests and activities seems often greatly to exacerbate the condition. The second explanation, which turns on the absence of externally directed aggression, though it may be consistent with the behavior of infants of less than twelve months, is not so with behavior in the second and later years; at this age externally directed aggression in separated children is common and often intense.

A weightier difficulty, however, lies in Spitz's assumption that the syndrome he describes can be explained only on the supposition that an essential in its dynamics is aggression directed against the self. Could it not be due simply and solely to the rupture of a key relationship and the consequent intense pain of yearning occurring in a young child? This is the view I shall be advancing when in the next paper I come to consider the nature of grief and mourning. The error into which I believe Spitz falls is that of underestimating the pain, and the disturbance of personality, to which normal mourning gives rise. Freud does not make this mistake:

> ... mourning involves grave departures from the normal attitude to life ... An exclusive devotion to mourning ... leaves nothing over for other purposes or other interests. It is really only because we know so well how to explain it that this attitude does not seem to us pathological [1917, pp. 243-244].

Once we know how to explain it, even when it occurs in very young children, I believe it will not then seem pathological either. In my judgment, the responses described by Spitz are not in them-selves pathological, or at least are not so in their earlier phases; that they may become so and can lead to grave personality disorder is, however, the burden of my thesis.

It must be noted, however, that two other child analysts con-cerned with problems of object loss, though of very different theo-retical orientations, endorse Spitz's view that what he observed is not grief or mourning. Both argue the case from a theoretical not an empirical standpoint. Rochlin (1953) recognizes that the disturbance following loss of object in the young child resembles grief in some characteristics but, like Spitz, holds that because there is failure to recover it cannot be true grief. His thinking, moreover, is strongly influenced by the theory of primary narcissism which leads him to suppose there must be major differences in the response to loss according to whether it occurs in the preoedipal or the oedipal phases. Winnicott (1954) also appears to limit his concepts of grief and mourning to examples which have a favorable outcome, and also sets a theoretical limit before which grief and mourning are not experienced. Only "if in an individual the depressive position has been achieved and fully established [is] the reaction to loss *grief*, or *sadness*." Prior to this phase, which he puts at between nine and eighteen months, it is different. This leads him to conclude that "the babies Spitz describes are depersonalized and hopeless about external contacts," and thus apparently neither grieving nor in a state of mourning. This conclusion stems, I suspect, from a confusion be-tween two distinct stages of mental development: (a) the stage after which grief is experienced and mourning processes set in train, and

(b) the stage after which mourning processes are likely to have a favorable outcome. The time elapsing between the two I believe to be a matter of years. It is an issue to which we shall be returning in a later paper.

Apart from Engel and Reichsman (1956), no other analyst appears to have recorded and theorized from the data of direct observation. Many other analysts besides Rochlin and Winnicott, however, using data derived from therapeutic sessions with older patients, have postulated that experiences of loss in early childhood are of major consequence for personality development. Nevertheless there is no agreement among them in regard to the age nor to the nature of the events which are crucial. The initiator of this immensely fruitful though inconclusive theme in psychoanalytic theorizing was Abraham.

In the years immediately before his death and before Freud's promising approach in *Inhibitions, Symptoms and Anxiety,* Abraham has given a most important role, in his theorizing about factors which need to be present if melancholia is to develop, to disappointments and deprivations occurring in the early years. In his "Short Study of the Development of the Libido" (1924) he defines one such factor as "a severe injury to infantile narcissism brought about by successive disappointments in love." After recording that "several of my melancholic cases disclosed a remarkable similarity in the scheme of significant events," he continues (evidently referring to a particular patient):

> The child had felt that he was his mother's favourite and had been secure of her love. He had then suffered a disappointment at her hands and had with difficulty recovered from its shattering effect. Later on, he had had fresh experiences of the same sort which had made him feel that his loss was an irreparable one, especially as there had been no suitable female person on to whom he could carry over his libido. Furthermore, his attempt to direct it towards his father had failed, either straight away or after some time. Thus as a child he had got the impression of being completely deserted. And it was this feeling that had given rise to his first attacks of depression [Abraham, 1924, p. 458].

An examination of this material, he tells us, led him to the conclusion that "in the last resort melancholic depression is derived from disagreeable experiences in the childhood of the patient" (p. 464). He therefore postulates that, during their childhood, melancholics have suffered from what he terms a "primal parathymia." One class of experience to which he attributes it is the oedipal situation. Referring to his findings in a particular case, he emphasizes

> . . . how much the child longed to gain his mother as an ally in his struggle against his father, and his disappointment at having his own advances repulsed combined with the violent emotions aroused in him by what he had observed going on in his parents' bedroom . . . Unable either to achieve a complete love or an unyielding hatred, he succumbed to a feeling of hopelessness [p. 469].

However, in addition to the oedipal situation, Abraham also attributes a similar significance to the child's loss of his mother following the birth of a new baby. This conclusion is reached from his analysis of another patient:

> His analysis showed that his mother had been "unfaithful" to him and had transferred her "favours" to his younger brother —*i.e.* she had nursed him at the breast. This brother occupied for him the position of father in his Oedipus complex. In each symptom of his various depressive periods he faithfully repeated all those feelings of hatred, rage, and resignation, of being abandoned and without hope, which had gone to colour the primal parathymia of his early childhood [p. 470].

In view of his pioneering work on the relation of melancholia to grief it comes as a surprise to find that in these passages Abraham never uses the words grief and mourning; nor is it clear that he recognized that for the young child the experience of losing mother (or of losing her love) is in very truth a bereavement. This failure, which I believe to have had serious and long-lasting effects on psychoanalytic theorizing, needs explanation. It is difficult not to find it in Abraham's inadequate grasp of the significance of the phase during which children are normally attached to their mothers and his postulate instead that the earliest phase is one of narcissism and egocentrism. This led him to vacillate in his theorizing and even to advance views of a contradictory kind.[17]

---

[17] In reading Abraham's work, as that of other analysts, one frequently gets the impression that, in his view, the young child's demands for love and affection are un-

It is paradoxical that most of those who, like Abraham, have postulated as pathogenic the disruption in early childhood of a *whole object* relationship have failed to identify the process set in train as that of mourning; whereas those who, like Melanie Klein and her school, have recognized mourning as central have concentrated so much attention on *part objects*, particularly the breast, and on weaning that the disruption of the whole object relationship has often been neglected. The tendency to concentrate attention on oral relationships and the breast is already present in Abraham's work and, though less so, also in that of Freud. The first suggestion that weaning is of importance seems to have been made by Stärcke (1921) (though it should be noted that he did not regard it as the first loss of a love object: instead he postulated it as a "primal castration"). Others who in the twenties came to attach crucial significance to the feeding relationship and to weaning were Bernfeld (1925), Melanie Klein (1926), and Rado (1928). It is Melanie Klein who has carried these ideas furthest.

As is well known, elaborating Abraham's views on primal parathymia, Melanie Klein has laid great emphasis on depression and mourning in infancy: "My contention is that the child goes through states of mind comparable to the mourning of the adult, or rather, that this early mourning is revived whenever grief is experienced in later life" (1940, p. 311). Furthermore, she has recognized that Abraham, in attributing such states to experiences of loss of mother occurring in the oedipal phase, had overlooked earlier experiences. Melanie Klein, however, due I believe to her tendency to identify the dynamics of the child's tie with orality, is concerned with the loss not so much of mother as of breast.

> . . . the baby experiences depressive feelings which reach a climax just before, during and after weaning. This is the state of mind in the baby which I termed the "depressive position," and I

---

fortunate aspects of human nature to be got rid of as soon and as completely as possible. In one of his last papers (1925) he tells us that "on the earlier levels of character-development the interests of the individual and those of the community ran counter to one another" (p. 410) and that "It is only by degrees that [the child] overcomes to some extent its egoistic impulses and its narcissism and takes the step towards object-love . . . The first function of [the genital] stage in the formation of character is of course *to get rid of* the remaining traces of the more primitive stages of development" (p. 408, my italics).

suggested that it is a melancholia in *statu nascendi*. The object which is being mourned is the mother's breast . . . [p. 312].

Although at times she extends the meaning of breast to become almost coterminous with that of mother, as she does in the final phrase of the sentence quoted above,[18] and also lays much store on the period when the infant is discovering that the loved and hated mother are one and the same person, throughout much of her theorizing on the depressive position in infancy the object conceived as lost and mourned is the breast. Since she believes that weaning usually takes place in the first year and that (for reasons which are not stated) the middle of it is the optimum time to undertake it (Klein et al., 1952, pp. 266-269), the whole of her theorizing about grief and mourning in infancy and early childhood concentrates attention on the first months of life.

Because of the immense importance for the child's future development that Melanie Klein and other analysts attach to weaning, and the profound effect this has had on theorizing and to a less extent on technique, it is necessary to examine the issue in some detail. First we will scrutinize the evidence on which Melanie Klein has based her view. To do so we must return to her early papers, the two most important of which are "An Obsessional Neurosis in a Six-year-old Girl," read at Würzburg in 1924, and "The Psychological Principles of Infant Analysis," dated two years later. Rewritten and expanded they form Chapters 3 and 1 respectively in her book *The Psycho-Analysis of Children* (1932).

Her first paper describes the case of Erna, who suffered from sleeplessness, phobias of burglars, head banging, rocking, obsessional thumb sucking, excessive masturbation, and depressions. Although "in her relations to her mother she was over-affectionate," it soon became clear that this was in part a defense and that she nurtured strongly hostile feelings against her. This resulted among other things in "excessive fear of her parents, especially her mother," based on "an unusual prominence of the mechanism of projection" (Klein, 1932, pp. 77, 79). The analytic material contained abundant evidence of oral and anal sadism, and Erna's anxieties were clearly connected

[18] Given in full this reads: "The object which is lost is the mother's breast and all that the breast and the milk have come to stand for in the infant's mind: namely, love, goodness and security" (p. 312).

with this. Improvement in the clinical condition followed the analysis of the anxiety and the underlying sadism.

It is an indication of the contribution that Melanie Klein has made that such clinical findings are now taken as a matter of course. As I emphasized in an earlier paper, no one has done more to call attention to the immense role of aggression in the genesis of morbid anxiety. It is when she seeks to account for Erna's intense sadism that many are more skeptical. On the basis solely of analytic material derived from a child of six she attributes it to constitutional factors and to the frustration experienced at weaning. She refers first to a "constitutionally strong anal-sadistic disposition" and proceeds: "Besides this, analysis showed that another critical phase in Erna's development had been passed through with only apparent success. She had never got over her weaning" (p. 82). This, she makes clear in a discussion in the theoretical part of her book, was due in her view to "an abnormally increased oral sadism" (p. 180).

It cannot be said that the analytic evidence points unequivocally to this conclusion. Moreover, the alternative hypothesis, that Erna's troubles stem from her experiences in relation to her mother during the second and third years as well as the first, is neither entertained nor explored. Case history material is meager, dispersed, and often relegated to footnotes. We learn that Erna had been a slow feeder and "had repeatedly injured her mother's breast by biting" (1932, p. 180 note), that her toilet-training was "accomplished without any sort of harshness and so easily that at the age of one year she was perfectly clean in her habits" (Klein, 1940, p. 148 note), and that "by the time she was between two and three years old her upbringing had become an insoluble problem, her character was already abnormal, and she was suffering from a definite obsessional neurosis" (Klein, 1932, p. 81). We are told nothing of the sources or trustworthiness of this information; nor are we given any account of Erna's mother. Although Melanie Klein claims that Erna was the subject of "excessive attention bestowed on her in her infancy" (1940, p. 149), there is a reference elsewhere to "her nurse and the other people who brought her up" (1932, p. 83). From the clinical picture and these fragments of history there must be many analytically trained child psychiatrists who, like myself, would suspect that the condition had been due in large part or wholly to lack of affection, changes of mother figure, unwise discipline, or a combination of such experiences. The main point I wish to make, however, is that the data given do not enable the reader to reach a reasoned judgment.

Similar difficulties beset us when we try to assess others of Melanie Klein's cases. Nevertheless it is on data from these cases, she states, that her theories rest. For instance, her view that a failure to obtain gratification from sucking is due to "an abnormally increased oral sadism" (1932, p. 180) seems to be attributable to the case of Erna. Similarly her view that "oral sadism reaches its climax during and after weaning" (1932, p. 185) is derived from the cases of Trude and Rita, who are first reported in 1926 (pp. 140-142).

The key place of Trude and Rita in the formulation of Melanie Klein's views on weaning is testified by the numerous references back to her 1926 paper. Yet when we come to study the evidence it is fragmentary. Trude was three and a quarter when she was brought for her first analytic session, which immediately preceded a journey abroad with her mother lasting six months. When analysis was resumed Trude recounted a dream in which she was with her mother in Italy and the waitress gave her no raspberry syrup because there was none left. "The interpretation of this dream," we are told, "showed, amongst other things, that the child was still suffering from the deprivation of the mother's breast when she was weaned." No evidence is given for this conclusion. Nor do we find any account of the child's family relationships except that a sister was born when she was two.

There is almost the same dearth of information in the case of Rita, although she is discussed further in a number of subsequent papers. At two years and nine months Rita was brought for analytic treatment as "a very neurotic child with fears of all kinds, and most difficult to bring up; her quite unchildlike depressions and feelings of guilt were very striking. She was very much tied to her mother displaying at times an exaggerated love and at others antagonism" (1936, p. 41).

In discussing this case Melanie Klein gives some weight to environmental factors, among which were that Rita's "mother suffered from a severe obsessional neurosis and had had an ambivalent attitude towards the child from the first" (1932, p. 24 note) and that a younger brother had been born nine months earlier. Despite this, however, finding both oral and sadistic material in the analysis, she concludes that the child's strong oral-sadistic impulses and low capacity to tolerate tension "were some of the *constitutional* characteristics" determining the child's relation to her mother (1945, p. 370, my italics).

Neither Trude nor Rita seem better than Erna as cases on which to base a far-reaching theory regarding the crucial roles of weaning and constitutionally excessive aggression or of the primacy of persecutory anxiety. Indeed in examining the grounds on which Melanie Klein bases her theories, we cannot help being struck by the inadequacy of the clinical data as presented and by the strong influence which her theoretical expectations played. In the years when these children were being analyzed Melanie Klein was still in Berlin and much influenced by Abraham, who was then engaged in publishing his papers on oral erotism and other aspects of the development of the libido. It is evident that, because of this, she approached her patients keenly alerted to orality, and especially to oral sadism. These she found—as we have now discovered we do in patients of every kind. Furthermore, this was a period before the publication of *Inhibitions, Symptoms and Anxiety* and when, as we have already seen, there was little understanding of the long phase during which the child is intensely attached to his mother. That Melanie Klein was herself unaware that it is usual for the child to be closely attached during his second and third years is suggested both by the absence of any reference to it and also in the way she refers to the strong attachment to their mothers of children of two as though it were itself pathological. For example, Rita, during her second year, is described as having "developed an excessive fixation to her mother" (1926, p. 142), despite the mother's ambivalent attitude and the new baby. Similarly, Trude is described as having a "fixation to her mother which, at the age of two years, was becoming particularly strong" (1926, p. 143). In place of the attachment to a real mother only the oral relationship during the first year is recognized.

As a result of this theoretical background there was evidently a strong tendency at this time to attribute all oral symptoms to disturbances *originating in the oral relationship itself*; and, since orality was thought to cease after the first year and weaning to be natural at about nine months, to the experiences of the first twelve months. This is an instance, I believe, of the pitfalls attending attempts to reconstruct phases of development from the analytic material of older patients, pitfalls to which, among others, Rickman (1951) and Kris (1956) have drawn attention. Nevertheless in the light of then-existing theory and accepted procedure her conclusions were not unreasonable. Today there is an obvious alternative. Most analysts know that oral behavior, such as thumb sucking or excessive greed, are common sequelae to an experience, short or long, of missing maternal affection. When relations between child and mother are impaired, satisfaction is sought in autoerotism: sucking, rocking, or masturbation are common alternatives. Their presence therefore tells us nothing about the age of the patient when a disappointment or a more serious deprivation may have occurred, nor does sucking point to its having been an oral deprivation in particular. Today this conclusion is not strange—indeed it has become a commonplace of the psychoanalytic literature (e.g., Fairbairn, 1941; Winnicott, 1945; Anna Freud and Sophie Dann, 1951), and is supported by observations on lower primates.[19] Yet in the early 1920's the position was different, and it is not difficult to see how Melanie Klein came to draw the conclusions she did.

Though I believe the psychological relevance of weaning to have been much exaggerated, we need not conclude that it is of no consequence. There is indeed good evidence that for some infants weaning is a distressing experience, especially when it is either premature or abrupt. However, as in the case of so much in child development that is of concern to psychoanalysis, systematic firsthand observations are scarce. "The literature on this question," wrote Albino and Thompson (1956), "is more or less restricted to reports of individual cases and lacks systematic studies." Unfortunately there is great difficulty in interpreting even such reports

[19] Rhesus monkeys brought up on the bottle and without a mother to cling to develop many autoerotic activities, including compulsive sucking of fingers and other parts, for example, nipple and penis. These activities are virtually never observed in infant monkeys cared for by a mother monkey. Similar observations have been made with chimpanzees (personal communications from Dr. William Mason and Dr. Henry Nissen). The observations of Anna Freud and Sophie Dann (1951) on the oral activities of young children who had been deprived of a mother figure bear a strong resemblance to those on infrahuman primates.

as there are: this lies in distinguishing how much of the observed behavior is a response to loss of breast and how much to loss of or rejection by mother.

It is my impression that, when the mother's attitude remains unchanged and weaning is gradual, responses to weaning are as a rule fairly mild. I am not alone in this. Bernfeld expressed surprise that there was not more disturbance. Melanie Klein herself, in discussing the histories of some of her patients, concedes that direct observation had often failed to confirm any difficulties at the time. Her explanation of the discrepancy is that "what may seem to be a success is not necessarily a complete one. Although some children appear to have gone through the weaning quite well and even for some time progress satisfactorily, deep down they have been unable to deal with the difficulties arising out of this situation; only an outward adaptation has taken place" (1936, p. 41). Nowhere does she consider the alternative hypothesis—that weaning was in fact satisfactory and that the loss which the child had failed to surmount was of another and perhaps later kind.

The difficulty of distinguishing between responses to loss of breast and to loss of mother holds for two of the most detailed studies of weaning available in the literature—that on Navaho infants by Kluckhohn (1947) and that on Zulu infants by Albino and Thompson (1956). In these two tribes, as for almost all peoples untouched by the West (see Bernfeld 1925, pp. 247-251), weaning usually occurs in the second or third years of life. In the case of the Navaho the sixty-three children studied ranged in age from eight months to over four years (average two years four months). About one third of the children weaned themselves, and the remainder were weaned by their mothers. This means that the experience of different children varies enormously, a point to which we shall be returning when considering experiences predisposing to depression. In those actively weaned the responses reported are pronounced. Temper tantrums and other signs of hostility are frequent and are commonly vented on an older sibling; attempts to find affection with another woman are also made. Is not this, it may be asked, a clear sign that weaning has traumatic effects? Unfortunately for such a thesis a main reason for weaning is the advent of a new baby and common custom is for the mother to "go off alone for a visit of some days or a week with relatives." As Kluckhohn remarks, "Deprivation of the breast is merely one visible sign of a general loss . . . weaning means less and less of the mother's attention and much sharper demands for responsible behavior."

The same difficulties occur when we come to evaluate the much fuller data of Albino and Thompson. The sixteen Zulu children that they studied were all abruptly weaned in their second year—an age range from fifteen to twenty-four months, average nineteen months. Once again, however, as the authors point out, "in addition to the weaning there is a rejection of the child by its mother" and this "may be the source of the observed effects." The behavior recorded is similar to that of Navaho children. Although the children varied greatly, without exception all sixteen showed immediate and persistent aggression. At first this was directed against the mother: "in seven children these attacks took the form of incessant fighting in which they screamed, bit, scratched and kicked their mothers and demanded the breast." Later "The child's aggression gradually extends to the whole family [and] the whole environment is attacked." Once again siblings become a favorite target. Attempts to attach himself to another woman were common but not universal. Albino and Thompson describe the successive phases of response in some detail, and it is of great interest to note how remarkably similar they are to those described for young children undergoing a separation experience without weaning. Protest and despair are both evident; later, they report, there is an increasing independence and maturity. We shall return to a consideration of this phase in a later paper.

The truth is we are still singularly ignorant of the effects on infants and young children of weaning per se. Its dispassionate evaluation has not been made easier by overconfident claims based on reconstructive theorizing. In this respect, unfortunately, Rado's 1928 paper did not set a good example. Although in fact a speculative account of events in early childhood, his conclusions are formulated more as facts than as hypotheses. The infant's need for love he describes as "narcissistic craving"; being loved is identified as oral gratification; fear of loss of love, with dread of starvation; guilt, atonement, and forgiveness are traced back to rage, hunger, and drinking at the mother's breast. That a whole object relation is present at least from the second half of the first year and that grief and mourning can result from its rupture are not recognized. Instead he suggests that the infant's feeding experience so clearly determines future development that "we surely need no further proofs." As is well known, there are many analysts who nonetheless have remained unconvinced. Some, like Winnicott and Fairbairn, go some but not all the way with Melanie Klein and Rado; others, like Balint and Edith Jacobson, frankly dissent.

Winnicott, who as we have seen is inclined to limit the term grief to what occurs after a child can mourn successfully, attaches much importance to "the careful management of weaning." In doing so, however, he extends in significant degree both the conception and the age of weaning. He explains that he uses the term weaning "in the very broad sense of the management of infants of roughly speaking 9-18 months" (Winnicott, 1952). By extending the conception of weaning in this way Winnicott takes account not only of all aspects of infant management and relations with mother but also of events up to at least eighteen months of age. Whether, however, it is wise to use the term "mother's breast" to "include the whole technique of mothering" (Winnicott, 1951), and "weaning" to cover all aspects of management may be doubted. There is a real danger not only of misunderstanding resulting from such usage but of the broader considerations with which Winnicott is so rightly concerned being overlooked.

Since Fairbairn bases the whole of his psychopathology on object relations and attaches the utmost importance to the psychological sequelae of loss of object, it is surprising that he hardly ever invokes explicitly the concepts of grief and mourning. Nevertheless his thinking bears much in common with that of Melanie Klein and Winnicott and, apart from the nature of the object lost and the age scale, with that advanced here. At least until recently, for Fairbairn "infantile dependence is equivalent to oral dependence," and he is therefore led to place the most crucial phases of development in the first year of life. Nevertheless he has concluded from clinical experience that it is "when object-relationships continue to be unsatisfactory during the succeeding years of early childhood" that ill effects are likely to result. This finding he seeks to account for by postulat-

ing that during later childhood there may be "a regressive reactivation . . . of situations arising respectively during the early and late
oral phases" (1941, pp. 47, 55). It is to be noted, however, that such
a postulate is unnecessary if we see infantile dependence as more
than oral dependence and, instead of being confined to the first year,
as stretching over a number of the early years of life.

Erikson's position is not unlike that of Melanie Klein and Fairbairn: he too sees the child's tie to his mother in terms of orality and
regards weaning as of much importance. Nevertheless, like Winnicott, he recognizes that there is more to a mother than a pair of
breasts and advises that "weaning, therefore, should not mean sudden
loss of the breast and loss of the mother's reassuring presence too."
He continues, with reference to Spitz's work on anaclitic depression,
"A drastic loss of accustomed mother love without proper substitution at this time can lead (under otherwise aggravating conditions)
to acute infantile depression or to a mild but chronic state of mourning which may give a depressive undertone to the whole remainder
of life" (Erikson, 1950, p. 75). To what extent he recognizes that
loss of mother occurring after the first year of life can lead to the
same result is unclear.

Two analysts who have attributed major significance in psychosis
to events occurring *after* the first year of life are Edith Jacobson
(1946) and Searles (1958). Like Fairbairn, however, neither has in-
voked explicitly the concepts of bereavement and mourning; instead
both use the terms "disappointment" and "disillusionment" to
describe experiences which they believe can be pathogenic for a
child. Edith Jacobson criticizes Melanie Klein's reconstructions on
grounds similar to those advanced here. She believes that "Klein
loses sight of the realistic conflict history throughout later infantile
phases" and that her focus "seems unduly shifted onto the pathogenic
significance of the first year of life."

This completes our review of the literature as it relates to the
occurrence in infancy of grief and mourning. Very many analysts,
it will be seen, recognize either explicitly or implicitly both their
reality and their significance for personality development. This
conclusion is in many ways more striking than that there is still much
controversy both over the nature of the relevant losses and the
period of life which is most crucial.

CONCLUSION

In writing this paper I have had in view two main objectives. The first has been to demonstrate the reality and duration of grief and of the psychological processes of mourning in even very young children, certainly from six months of age onward, and the intimate relationship that grief has to separation anxiety. This part of the paper is in many respects an expansion and elaboration of the viewpoint reached by Freud in the final pages of *Inhibitions, Symptoms and Anxiety*.

The second objective has been to call in question the common assumption that in regard to future capacity to make object relations loss of breast at weaning is the most significant loss sustained by the infant and young child. On scrutiny the evidence advanced to support this view is found to be unconvincing. In contrast, evidence that loss of mother in the three or four years from about six months of age onward can be of consequence is seen to be weighty. This does not mean that loss of breast at weaning is never of importance. What it does mean is that the role of weaning needs to be evaluated afresh in the light of more systematic evidence and that, in the meantime, the hypothetical significance of loss of breast during the early months should not be allowed to obscure the much clearer significance of loss of the mother figure during a number of the early years.

So far the issues raised in the discussion are largely empirical; that is to say, the correctness or otherwise of most of the conclusions reached can in principle be tested by further empirical studies. At the same time, however, they touch on a number of theoretical questions concerning responses to loss of object that have long been regarded as central to psychopathology. What, for instance, are the processes comprising mourning, and how do we conceptualize them? In what ways do such processes vary with the age of the individual and with his previous experiences? What are the criteria that lead us to judge that certain forms of mourning are pathological? And are there responses to loss which deviate so far from mourning as we ordinarily think of it that they seem to fall outside the range even of pathological mourning? What are the conditions which influence the selection and course of responses to loss; and, in particular, what do we know of those that lead them to take a pathological turn? Finally, to what sorts of personality disturbance and psychiatric symptom does an experience of loss in childhood commonly lead? It is to these and related problems that the following papers will be directed.

Acknowledgments

I am much indebted to James Robertson for the observations on which I have drawn. The inquiry was undertaken as part of the work of the Tavistock Child Development Research Unit, which is supported by the National Health Service and by grants from the Josiah Macy Junior Foundation, the Foundations' Fund for Research in Psychiatry, and the Ford Foundation, to all of which our thanks are due. A draft of the paper was prepared while I held a Fellowship at the Center for Advanced Study in the Behavioral Sciences, Stanford, California.

BIBLIOGRAPHY

Abraham, K. (1916), The First Pregenital Stage of the Libido. *Selected Papers on Psycho-Analysis*. London: Hogarth Press, 1927.
—— (1924), A Short Study of the Development of the Libido, Viewed in the Light of Mental Disorders. *Selected Papers on Psycho-Analysis*. London: Hogarth Press, 1927.
—— (1925), Character-Formation on the Genital Level of Libido-Development. *Selected Papers on Psycho-Analysis*. London: Hogarth Press, 1927.
Albino, R. C. & Thompson, V. J. (1956), The Effects of Sudden Weaning on Zulu Children. *Brit. J. Med. Psychol.*, XXIX.
Balint, M. (1952), New Beginning and the Paranoid and the Depressive Syndromes. *Primary Love and Psycho-Analytic Technique*. London: Hogarth Press, 1953.
Bernfeld, S. (1925), *The Psychology of the Infant*. London: Kegan Paul, 1929.
Bowlby, J. (1944), Forty-four Juvenile Thieves: Their Characters and Home Life. *Int. J. Psa.*, XXV.
—— (1951), *Maternal Care and Mental Health*. Geneva: World Health Organization Monograph.
—— (1958a), Psycho-Analysis and Child Care. In *Psycho-Analysis and Contemporary Thought*, ed. J. D. Sutherland. London: Hogarth Press.
—— (1958b), The Nature of the Child's Tie to His Mother. *Int. J. Psa.*, XXXIX.
—— (1960), Separation Anxiety. *Int. J. Psa.*, XLI.
—— & Robertson, J., Rosenbluth, D. (1952), A Two-Year-Old Goes to Hospital. *This Annual*, VII.
Deutsch, H. (1919), A Two-Year-Old Boy's First Love Comes to Grief. In *Dynamics of Psychopathology in Childhood*, ed. L. Jessner & E. Pavenstedt. New York: Grune & Stratton, 1959.
—— (1937), Absence of Grief. *Psa. Quart.*, VI.
Eliot, T. D. (1955), Bereavement: Inevitable But Not Insurmountable. In *Family, Marriage, and Parenthood*, ed. H. Becker & R. Hill. Boston: Heath.
Engel, G. L. (1954), Selection of Clinical Material in Psychosomatic Medicine: The Need for a New Physiology. *Psychosom. Med.*, XXVI.

Engel, G. L. & Reichsman, F. (1956), Spontaneous and Experimentally Induced Depressions in an Infant with a Gastric Fistula. *J. Am. Psa. Assn.*, IV.

Erikson, E. H. (1950), *Childhood and Society*. New York: Norton.

Fairbairn, W. R. D. (1941), A Revised Psychopathology of the Psychoses and Psychoneuroses. *Psycho-Analytic Studies of the Personality*. London: Tavistock, 1952.

—— (1952), *Psycho-Analytic Studies of the Personality*. London: Tavistock.

Ferenczi, S. (1916), *Contributions to Psychoanalysis*. Boston: Badger.

—— (1926), *Further Contributions to the Theory and Technique of Psycho-Analysis*. London: Hogarth Press.

Freud, A. (1936), *The Ego and the Mechanisms of Defence*. New York: International Universities Press, 1946.

—— (1949), Certain Types and Stages of Social Maladjustment. In *Searchlights on Delinquency*, ed. K. R. Eissler. New York: International Universities Press.

—— & Burlingham, D. (1942), *War and Children*. New York: International Universities Press, 1943.

—— —— (1944), *Infants Without Families*. New York: International Universities Press.

—— & Dann, S. (1951), An Experiment in Group Upbringing. *This Annual*, VI.

Freud, S. (1905), Three Essays on the Theory of Sexuality. *Standard Edition*, VII. London: Hogarth Press, 1953.

—— (1917), Mourning and Melancholia. *Standard Edition*, XIV. London: Hogarth Press, 1957.

—— (1926), Inhibitions, Symptoms and Anxiety. *Standard Edition*, XX. London: Hogarth Press, 1959.

Greenacre, P., ed. (1953), *Affective Disorders*. New York: International Universities Press.

Hartmann, H. (1939), *Ego Psychology and the Problem of Adaptation*. New York: International Universities Press, 1958.

Heinicke, C. M. (1956). Some Effects of Separating Two-Year-Old Children from Their Parents: A Comparative Study. *Human Relations*, IX.

Jacobson, E. (1946), The Effect of Disappointment on Ego and Super-ego Formation in Normal and Depressive Development. *Psa. Rev.*, XXXIII.

Jones, E. (1948), *Papers on Psycho-Analysis*, 5th ed. London: Baillière, Tindall & Cox.

—— (1953), *Sigmund Freud: Life and Work*. Vol. I. London: Hogarth Press.

Klein, M. (1926), The Psychological Principles of Infant Analysis. *Contributions to Psycho-Analysis 1921-1945*. London: Hogarth Press, 1948.

—— (1932), *The Psycho-Analysis of Children*. London: Hogarth Press.

—— (1936), Weaning. In *On the Bringing Up of Children*, ed. J. Rickman. London: Kegan Paul.

—— (1940), Mourning and Its Relation to Manic-Depressive States. *Contributions to Psycho-Analysis 1921-1945*. London: Hogarth Press, 1948.

—— (1945), The Oedipus Complex in the Light of Early Anxieties. *Contributions to Psycho-Analysis 1921-1945*. London: Hogarth Press, 1948.

—— & Heimann, P., Isaacs, S., Riviere, J. (1952), *Developments in Psycho-Analysis*. London: Hogarth Press.

Kluckhohn, C. (1947), Some Aspects of Navaho Infancy and Early Childhood. In *Psychoanalysis and the Social Sciences*, Vol. I. New York: International Universities Press.

Kris, E. (1956), The Recovery of Childhood Memories in Psychoanalysis. *This Annual*, XI.

Lindemann, E. (1944), Symptomatology and Management of Acute Grief. *Am. J. Psychiat.*, CI.

Marris, P. (1958), *Widows and Their Families*. London: Routledge & Kegan Paul.

Piaget, J. (1937), *The Child's Construction of Reality*. New York: Basic Books, 1955.

Rado, S. (1928), The Problem of Melancholia. *Int. J. Psa.*, IX.

Rickman, J. (1951), Methodology and Research in Psychopathology. *Brit. J. Med. Psychol.*, XXIV.

Robertson, J. (1952), Film: *A Two-Year-Old Goes to Hospital*. London: Tavistock Child Development Research Unit. New York: New York University Film Library.

—— (1953), Some Responses of Young Children to the Loss of Maternal Care. *Nursing Times*, XLIX.

—— & Bowlby, J. (1952), Responses of Young Children to Separation from Their Mothers. *Courrier Centre Internationale de l'Enfance*, II.

Rochlin, G. (1953), Loss and Restitution. *This Annual*, VIII.

Schaffer, H. R. & Callender, W. M. (1959), Psychological Effects of Hospitalization in Infancy. *Pediatrics*, XXIV.

Searles, H. E. (1958), Positive Feelings Between a Schizophrenic and His Mother. *Int. J. Psa.*, XXXIX.

Shand, A. F. (1920), *The Foundations of Character*. London: Macmillan.

Spitz, R. A. (1945), Hospitalism. An Inquiry Into the Genesis of Psychiatric Conditions in Early Childhood. *This Annual*, I.

—— (1946), Anaclitic Depression. *This Annual*, II.

—— (1947), Film: *Grief: A Peril in Infancy*. New York: New York University Film Library.

—— (1953), Aggression: Its Role in the Establishment of Object Relations. In *Drives, Affects, Behavior*, ed. R. M. Loewenstein. New York: International Universities Press.

Stärcke, A. (1921), Castration Complex. *Int. J. Psa.*, II.

Waller, W. W. (1951), *The Family; a Dynamic Interpretation*. New York: Dryden.

Winnicott, D. W. (1945), Primitive Emotional Development. *Collected Papers*. London: Tavistock, 1958.

—— (1951), Transitional Objects and Transitional Phenomena. *Collected Papers*. London: Tavistock, 1958.

—— (1952), Psychoses and Child Care. *Collected Papers*. London: Tavistock, 1958.

—— (1954), The Depressive Position in Normal Emotional Development. *Collected Papers*. London: Tavistock, 1958.

Zetzel, E. R. (1960), Depressive Illness. *Int. J. Psa.*, XLI.

DISCUSSION OF DR. JOHN BOWLBY'S PAPER

ANNA FREUD, LL.D. (London)

Dr. Bowlby's paper on "Grief and Mourning in Infancy" offers to analysts a number of controversial points for discussion, amplification or refutation. The following comments apply partly to the wider issues raised by his article, partly to those specific points in it where he makes direct reference to Dorothy Burlingham's and my account (1942) of the observations collected in the Hampstead Nurseries.

IDENTITY OF OBSERVATIONS

There is little difference in the observed material collected during the war by the Hampstead Nursery team with regard to separated children and the observations made later in connection with Dr. Bowlby's study of separation anxiety by a Tavistock Clinic team with regard to hospitalized children. Actually, James Robertson on whose observational studies Dr. Bowlby relies predominantly, was, and is, a valued and important member of both teams. With this identity of material, and partly of observers, in mind, explanation is needed not only why the theoretical interpretations of the data on our two sides are divergent but also why misunderstandings in the discussion of the divergencies are persistent.

DIFFERENCE IN THEORETICAL ORIENTATION

Referring back also to Dr. Bowlby's earlier papers on "Separation Anxiety" (1960a), and "The Nature of the Child's Tie to His Mother" (1958), it becomes possible to point to a basic difference in orientation between his and our theoretical approach. Dr. Bowlby is concerned on the one hand with a biological theory in which an inborn urge is assumed which ties an infant to the mother, on the other hand with the behavior resulting from this tie ("attachment behavior") or from the untimely disruption of the tie (separation

53

anxiety, grief, mourning). The gap between biological urge and manifest affect and behavior is bridged for him by certain actions and events occurring in the external world which activate inherited responses.

If this description of Dr. Bowlby's position can be accepted as correct, it may serve to explain some of our dissatisfaction when following his line of argumentation. Not that, as analysts, we do not share Dr. Bowlby's regard for biological and behavioral considerations. But taken by themselves, not in conjunction with metapsychological thinking, these two types of data do not fulfill the analyst's requirements. As analysts we do not deal with drive activity as such but with the mental representations of the drives. In the case of the biological tie of infant to mother this representation has to be recognized, I believe, in the infant's inborn readiness to cathect objects with libido. Equally, we do not deal with the happenings in the external world as such but with their repercussions in the mind, i.e., with the form in which they are registered by the child. In the case of the activating events it seems to me that they are experienced as events in the pleasure-pain series. It is true that this translation into psychological terms interferes with the simplicity and straight-forwardness of Dr. Bowlby's scheme and introduces numberless complications. But these complications seem to me no more than a true reflection of the complexity of mental life, built, as we know it to be, on the drive derivatives and the dynamic interplay between them; on the sensations and perceptions arriving from the internal and external world; on the pleasure-pain experiences; on mental imagery and fantasies. Since Dr. Bowlby in his present paper extends his material on separated children far beyond the first year of life, we have to add as complicating factors to the enumerated primary manifestations all the later elaborations which are known as secondary mental processes, such as verbal and logical thinking and the structural conflicts with their specific anxieties, guilt reactions and defensive activities.

Theoretical Misconceptions

There are two points in Dr. Bowlby's paper which I find more suited than any others to highlight the misconceptions which arise due to the described difference in viewpoint.

(i) *Mother Attachment versus Pleasure Principle*

When discussing the problem of need satisfaction in the first year of life, Dr. Bowlby queries the role which we ascribe to this factor. He sets up a controversy between the tie to the mother and the action of the pleasure principle in terms of "primary and secondary drive" and criticizes us for reversing their order of importance, i.e., for regarding the tie to the mother as a secondary, the search for pleasure as a primary instinctual urge. To my mind, this objection of his is based on a theoretical misunderstanding. We agree with Dr. Bowlby that the infant's attachment to the mother is the result of primary biological urges and ensures survival. But although the search for gratification is a tendency inherent in all drive activity, in our view the pleasure principle as such is not a drive representation at all, neither a primary nor a secondary one. In its metapsychological sense it is conceived as a principle which governs all mental activity in the immature and insufficiently structured personality. Since it embraces all mental processes, the tie to the mother is governed by it as well. But to assume a struggle for priority or first place between mother attachment and pleasure principle as if they were mental phenomena of the same order does not seem to me to apply.

Once this particular misunderstanding is removed, Dr. Bowlby's and our treatment of this subject are nearer to each other than appears at first glance. As suggested above, his conception of a biological tie resulting in certain patterns of behavior when activated by nursing care is paralleled in our way of thinking by the conception of an inborn readiness to cathect with libido a person who provides pleasurable experiences. It becomes evident that this latter theory is no more nor less than the classical psychoanalytic assumption of a first "anaclitic" relationship to the mother, i.e., a phase in which the pleasurable sensations derived from the gratification of major needs are instrumental in determining which person in the external world is selected for libidinal cathexis.

Moreover, in both theories, in Dr. Bowlby's as well as in the classical one, the mother is not chosen for attachment by virtue of her having given birth to the infant but by virtue of her ministering to the infant's needs.

(ii) *Infantile Narcissism*

A second area where controversy seems to be based on misconceptions is the problem of infantile narcissism. Dr. Bowlby denies that narcissism can exist or does exist in infancy, i.e., at the period when he sees the child as wholly attached to the mother. Argumentation concerning this point is made difficult by the fact that Dr. Bowlby's use of the term differs from ours in important respects. He understands narcissism in the descriptive sense, as a state in which the infant is supposed to be withdrawn, self-sufficient, and independent of the object world, and he maintains that no normal infant displays behavior of this kind. While agreeing with this last assertion, we disagree on our side with his definition of the term. Metapsychologically speaking, the concept of infantile narcissism refers not to behavior but to an early phase of libido distribution and organization. There exists in this phase, according to this assumption, a state of libidinal equilibrium, similar to the equilibrium obtaining during intrauterine existence. The infant himself is unable to maintain this state and dependent for its upkeep on the presence and nursing care of the mother who becomes the first object in the external world. It is characteristic for this phase that there is no libidinal exchange with the object as there will be in the later stages of true object love (loving and being loved). Instead, one-sided use is made of the mother for purposes of satisfaction. The object—to use an expression introduced by W. Hoffer—is drawn wholly into the internal narcissistic milieu and treated as part of it to the extent that self and object merge into one.

There is no other point where the clash between metapsychological and descriptive thinking becomes as obvious as it is here. It leads to the apparently paradoxical result that what in terms of the libido theory is the apex of infantile narcissism, appears in Dr. Bowlby's descriptive terms as the height of "attachment behavior." But we agree with him, of course, that never again in his life will the child be found to be more clinging to the mother or more dependent on her presence.

DISAGREEMENT ON CLINICAL POINTS

With the above-named major differences in theoretical outlook in mind, it becomes easier to discuss minor disagreements in clinical observations, their description, and their interpretation.

(i) *The Three Phases of Behavior after Separation from the Mother*

In his exposition of the child's reaction after separation, Dr. Bowlby isolates three main phases which can be easily distinguished from each other by observation: a first phase of loud, angry, tearful behavior which he calls *Protest*; a second one of acute pain, misery, and diminishing hope which he calls *Despair*; and a third one in which the child behaves as if he had ceased to care, which he calls *Denial*.[1] As regards the description of this sequence, there is no disagreement between observers such as the Tavistock or Hampstead teams or René Spitz. As regards the interpretation of the observed data, argumentation centers around the third and last phase. The question arises in which sense Dr. Bowlby uses the term denial. If it is purely descriptive, it might imply no more than absence of manifest bereavement behavior; if used in the analytic dynamic sense, it would imply a defensive process directed either against the recognition of external reality (i.e., the absence of the mother), or against the affect itself (i.e., an intolerably painful sense of bereavement). In neither case does it include the purely libidinal aspect which seems of the greatest importance to us. If we see the trauma of separation from the mother in terms of what happens to the libidinal cathexis of her image, we take the phases of protest and despair as manifestations of the child's attempt to maintain the libidinal tie with the absent object, the third phase as a sign that cathexis is not denied but actually withdrawn from the object.

I suggest therefore the use of the term *"withdrawal"* for Dr. Bowlby's third phase of bereavement behavior. It has the advantage of covering the manifest withdrawn behavior of the child as well as the internal process of libido withdrawal by which we believe this behavior to be caused.

[1] This discussion was prepared before Dr. Bowlby, in the final version of the present paper, adopted the term "Detachment" in favor of "Denial."

(ii) *Duration of Bereavement Reactions*

In his paper Dr. Bowlby emphasizes the identity of the young child's grief and mourning with the reactions shown by the normal adult after object loss. While taking a similar view so far as the overt manifestations are concerned, we have been reluctant to assume a corresponding identity of the underlying processes in infants and adults. The process of mourning (*Trauerarbeit*) taken in its analytic sense means to us the individual's effort to accept a fact in the external world (the loss of the cathected object) and to effect corresponding changes in the inner world (withdrawal of libido from the lost object, identification with the lost object). At least the former half of this task presupposes certain capacities of the mental apparatus such as reality testing, the acceptance of the reality principle, partial control of id tendencies by the ego, etc., i.e., capacities which are still undeveloped in the infant according to all other evidence. We have hesitated therefore to apply the term mourning in its technical sense to the bereavement reactions of the infant. Before the mental apparatus has matured and before, on the libidinal side, the stage of object constancy has been reached, the child's reactions to loss seem to us to be governed by the more primitive and direct dictates of the pleasure-pain principle.

Considerations such as these were significant for our attempts to understand the most outstanding difference between the bereavement reactions of young children and adults. While the term of mourning traditionally assumed for normal adults is one year, such loyalty to the lost object would be considered abnormal in a young child. We stated, on the basis of what we saw in the Hampstead Nurseries, that we expected bereavement behavior to last any length of time "from a few hours to several weeks or even a few months." On the basis of more systematic observations undertaken by James Robertson and Chris. Heinecke, Dr. Bowlby queries the possibility of the "few hours" or similarly short periods and endorses the validity of the longer periods. But he agrees with us, seemingly, that the child's grief reactions do not normally approximate the duration usual for the adult.

In our minds we linked the time needed to adjust to a substitute object less with the chronological age of the child, and more with the level of object relationship and ego maturity reached by him before separation: the nearer to object constancy, the longer the duration of grief reactions with corresponding approximation to the adult internal processes of mourning.[2]

There is a further point which seems to me worth noting. Neither the Hampstead Nurseries nor hospitals and other residential homes have offered ideal conditions for studying the length of time needed by young children to displace attachment from one person to another. We, as well as Dr. Bowlby, used data collected under circumstances where the children had to adapt not only to the loss of the mother but also to the change from family to group life, a transition very difficult to achieve for any young child. Whereas the mother herself had been the undisputed possession of the child in many cases, the nurse as substitute mother had to be shared inevitably with a number of contemporaries; also, inevitably, it is never one single nurse who substitutes for the all-day and all-night care of the mother.

If we wish to determine how long an infant needs to transfer cathexis from one mother figure to a substitute mother in the full sense of the word, we need to supplement our observations, excluding group or ward conditions. For all we know, duration of grief might then be found to be either shorter or longer. Also, in the circumstances which we studied, the infants were separated not only from their mothers but from their home background which included separation from the other parent, possible siblings, all the inanimate familiar objects, sights, sounds, etc. From direct observation we know little or nothing about the duration of grief in those instances where the mother has to leave temporarily or permanently while the child remains at home.

(iii) Pathological Aftereffects of Separation

As regards the pathology following on early separations, Dr. Bowlby remarks quite rightly that we made no attempts to link these with later states of depressive or melancholic illness. Actually,

2 Homesickness of older children is not included in this category. We reserve this term for a neurotic symptom to be found in latency children who cannot bear separation from their oedipal objects owing to a highly ambivalent attitude toward them. With them the repressed negative side of the ambivalent relationship is responsible in separation for guilt reactions, fear of death of the parents, intolerable longing, etc.

at the time of writing our study we had no access to material of this kind. Since then, observational and analytic contact with a group of young concentration-camp victims has provided additional data of some relevance. These children who had undergone repeated traumatic separations from birth or infancy onward achieved comparatively stable relationships during their latency period; but from preadolescence onward they displayed almost without exception withdrawn, depressive, self-accusatory or hostile mood swings. We expect that those among them who are now undergoing therapeutic analyses will supply us in time with more detailed information concerning the links between their early losses and their later pathology. Meanwhile, to avoid the impression that we underestimated the pathogenic potentialities inherent in the separation trauma, I summarize in what follows some of our earlier findings.

Our wartime efforts concerning this subject did not go beyond a rough division between immediate and delayed, transitory and permanent consequences. Among the permanent damage done to the child we emphasized above all the impairment in the capacity for and quality of object relationships which can be observed in cases where repeated changes of mother figure have taken place. Under such circumstances the child either becomes withdrawn (disinclined to cathect objects) or shallow and superficial in his object relations (i.e., never reaches or recaptures object constancy). On this point agreement between Dr. Bowlby and us is complete.

As regards some of the immediate pathological effects of separation, we were inclined to group them under headings such as the following:

Psychosomatic Conditions: These were frequent especially with the youngest children in the form of sleeping disturbances, feeding troubles, digestive upsets especially constipation, an increased readiness to develop sore throats or succumb to respiratory infections.

Regression in Instinct Development: On the libidinal side this consisted of a return to earlier levels, the more primitive manifestations being displayed toward the new objects (clinging, domineering, querulous anal or greedy, insatiable, dependent oral behavior) and in autoerotic activities (sucking, rocking). On the aggressive side it resulted in the earlier, cruder forms of aggression coming to the fore (biting, spitting, hitting) or, worse still, in a diffusion of libidinal and aggressive elements which allowed the latter to dominate the picture.

Regression in Ego Development: One of the most impressive and unexpected consequences of separation was undoubtedly the loss of ego functions such as speech, bowel and bladder control, and of the beginning of social adaptation. According to our observations, the functions most endangered in this respect were those that had been most recently acquired.

Upsets in Libido Distribution: We have always considered the interval between loss of contact with the mother ("withdrawal," see above) and attachment to a substitute mother as the period most productive of pathology, especially if this interval is prolonged either for external reasons (lack of suitable substitute mother) or for internal reasons (inability to transfer cathexis). For the form of the pathological outcome it is decisive what happens during the interval to the libido withdrawn from the mother. It may be used to cathect (or recathect) the child's own body, resulting in disturbances of a psychosomatic or hypochondriacal nature; or it may be used for cathexis of the self-image where it may cause a variety of disturbances such as increased self-love, omnipotence, ideas of grandeur, all due to narcissistic imbalance; or it may be employed to overcathect a crude inner fantasy world with the result that the child may become autistic, cut off from the environment, and wholly immersed in himself. The longer the interval lasts, the more difficult will it be to reverse these pathological developments.

Any assessment of the eventual pathological consequences of a separation trauma is inseparable, in our belief, from the assessment of the level of libido development at the time of its occurrence. Results vary according to the fact whether at the moment of separation the tie to the mother was still of a narcissistic nature, dominated by the search for instinctual satisfactions; or whether in the relationship to the mother the personal and affectionate elements had begun to predominate, transforming the attachment into object love; or whether the child had attained the level of so-called object constancy. In this last instance the image of a cathected person can be maintained internally for longer periods of time, irrespective of the real object's presence or absence in the external world, and much internal effort will be needed before the libido is withdrawn. Such withdrawal happens gradually by means of the painful disengagement process known to us as mourning.

Conclusion

One more concluding remark: in a last section of his paper on "The Occurrence of Mourning Behaviour in Animals" (1960b), Dr. Bowlby suggests tentatively that there are three main features which are specific to human as distinct from animal behavior: the long-drawn-out persistence of reactions oriented toward the lost object; the presence of hostility toward the self (which, I suppose, includes the guilt reactions); and the tendency to identify with the lost object. I should like to offer the suggestion that this useful distinction lends itself also to a sharper differentiation between the bereavement reactions of the youngest infants on the one hand and, on the other hand, the reactions to the separation trauma of young children with more highly developed and, accordingly, more complex mental processes and personality structures.

BIBLIOGRAPHY

Bowlby, J. (1958), The Nature of the Child's Tie to His Mother. *Int. J. Psa.*, XXXIX.
—— (1960a), Separation Anxiety. *Int. J. Psa.*, XLI.
—— (1960b), The Occurrence of Mourning Behaviour in Animals. No press.
Freud, A. & Burlingham, D. (1942), *War and Children*. New York: International Universities Press, 1943.

DISCUSSION OF DR. JOHN BOWLBY'S PAPER

MAX SCHUR, M.D. (New York)[1]

Dr. Bowlby refers throughout his article on "Grief and Mourning in Infancy and Early Childhood" to a series of his other papers, both published and unpublished. My discussion must therefore deal with all of them. In his previous papers (1958, 1959, 1960) Dr. Bowlby discusses the development of the infant's tie with the mother and separation anxiety, and emphasizes the crucial importance of this tie and the intensity of the child's reaction to separation. There can be no disagreement with Bowlby on this score.

However, Bowlby also found it necessary to propose in each of these papers a set of explanatory formulations which by their very nature are at complete variance with basic concepts of both psychoanalysis and most animal researchers who are engaged in the study of developmental psychology. In addition, Bowlby directly attacks many psychoanalytic concepts and extensively reshuffles present-day psychoanalytic terminology.

For these reasons my discussion will touch upon—and, I hope, also will help to clarify—a number of complex theoretical problems. The latter part seems to me to be the main justification for my paper.

"INNATE" VS. "ACQUIRED"

The cornerstone of Bowlby's formulation is the assumption that human infants are "starting with a number of *highly structuralized responses* (some of which are *active at birth and some of which mature later*")" (1958, pp. 364-365; my italics). Bowlby claims that five "instinctual response systems" (IRS's), as he calls them—sucking, crying, smiling, clinging, following—supply the "positive dynamic"

[1] From the Department of Psychoanalytic Education of the New York State University, Downstate Medical Center.

(1958, p. 365) for the child-mother tie. To emphasize their innate, preformed character he calls these responses "primary." Bowlby considers it a mistake to "give pre-eminence to sucking and feeding" (1958, p. 366). To him, clinging and following are all-important, although he assumes that they "become activated" by *maturation* at a later date.

In justification of these sweeping assumptions Bowlby draws heavily on certain aspects of the "instinct" concept of ethology, which originated as a branch of comparative zoology under the influence of Darwin's theory of selective evolution. Ethologists, many of whom started as naturalists, collected a wealth of highly sophisticated observations which confirmed, for instance, (a) that behavior patterns of animals may have the same value for taxonomic differentiation as anatomical structures; and (b) that many complex behavior patterns of animals are beyond their actual "intelligence" and have one thing in common: they have developed under the pressure of selective evolution, and serve the preservation of the species.

These generally acknowledged facts, which provided an important stimulus for the comparative study of animal behavior, were supplemented by a set of controversial theoretical propositions claiming that (a) instinctive behavior patterns are *entirely* innate, subject to *maturation* but not to *learning*; (b) they are based on a specific drive element which generates an "action-specific energy," and which causes the animal to seek for the "consummating act"; if the act is blocked, the animal may resort to "vacuum or displacement activities";[2] (c) animals are equipped with "innate releasing mechanisms" (IRM's) anchored in some unknown way in the central nervous system. Such IRM's are "tuned in" to specific releasers.

Bowlby's concept is therefore mainly based on that part of the instinct theory of ethology which assumes the *fully innate, unlearned character of most complex behavior patterns.*

Most of these theoretical constructs met with valid criticism. What I have in mind is not the fully negative criticism of strict adherents to stimulus-response psychology, but the debate between ethologists and what one could call "biopsychologists" represented

---

[2] It can easily be seen that these concepts have been influenced by the "hydrodynamic model" (*damming up of energy*) of early psychoanalytic formulations.

in the United States, for instance, by Schneirla, Lehrman, Beach, and others. This debate centers mainly on the problems "innate," "unlearned," "maturational," versus "acquired," "learned," "developmental" origin of species-specific (*instinctive*) behavior patterns.

This debate was carried on in various publications and in a series of interdisciplinary conferences—among them the Paris Conference on "L'instinct dans le comportement des animaux et de l'homme" (1956); The Macy Foundation Conferences on "Group Processes" (1954-1957), "The Nebraska Symposia on Motivation" (1959, 1960) and a "Symposium on Animal Research" of the American Orthopsychiatric Association (Schneirla, 1960; Schur, 1960b).

Under the impact of this debate most ethologists, e.g., Thorpe, Tinbergen, and others, have abandoned the rigid insistence on the *entirely innate* origin of instinctive behavior, on the specificity of the drive element and of action-specific energy, and on the "hydrodynamic model"—all of which play such a great role in Bowlby's formulations.

Moreover, these biopsychologists are engaged in highly sophisticated studies of animal behavior under normal and experimental conditions. It is most pertinent here that, for instance, such investigations as Schneirla's studies on cats (1960) show both the *early impact of learning* and the great intricacy of the interaction between mother and litter. This interaction starts at birth, involves a great variety of percepts, and leads eventually to what Schneirla (1954) called a "biopsychological" child-mother relationship.

Biopsychologists and ethologists also agree that selective evolution has resulted, especially among higher vertebrates, in an ever-widening scope of learning potentialities. With it goes an increasing range of the ontogenetic development of each phenotype. Even Lorenz, the foremost exponent of the innate character of instinctive behavior, emphasizes (1935, 1937, 1950) that phylogenetically under the impact of selective evolution curtailment of instinctive behavior and development of acquired, learned, "insightful" behavior go hand in hand. Introducing the concept of *interlocking*, Lorenz assumes that with evolution more and more "rigid instinctive links of a reaction chain" are being replaced by "conditioned and intelligent behavior patterns." Lorenz explains the preservation of certain instinctive links in intelligent behavior of higher animals and man with this mechanism of interlocking.

The critics of the instinct concept as originally proposed by ethologists do not, of course, disclaim that "instinctive," species-specific behavior patterns are based on innate givens. I have recently (1960b) proposed the following common-ground formulations which, as will be discussed later, also conform with psychoanalytic concepts: every species is endowed with an innate equipment which consists of a specific set of perceptive and executive apparatuses; with the Anlage to develop a specific set of needs; an Anlage for specific growth, maturation, and development, and for a specific type of learning. Under the influence of both maturation and development, and in constant interaction with an "average expectable environment" (Hartmann, 1939, 1958) any phenotype will develop (with considerable variations) a set of drives (in higher animals and man also *wishes*) and a species-specific type of behavior pattern, some of which guarantee the survival of the individual and of the species. Such behavior patterns are called "instinctive behavior."

The range of interaction with the environment grows with evolution. Lower animals respond to a limited set of environmental stimuli. The development of more or less specific "releasers" and the more direct relationship between specific behavior patterns and specific perceptive and executive apparatuses are expressive of this limited range in lower animals.

We can apply to the problem of the relative importance of "innate" versus "acquired" (learned) the concept of a *complementary series*. We will postulate that on the one hand in lower animals certain behavior patterns can to a lesser degree be modified by learning and that on the other hand in a species with a wider ontogenetic range of development the influence of learning will be comparatively greater.

Man has, of course, the widest range of ontogenetic development. The prevalence of learning makes it therefore extremely difficult to unravel the remaining "instinctive" links in human behavior.

I tried in previous papers (1958, 1960a) to speculate on the various ways in which "instinctive patterns" may be utilized in affect and structure formation and in what Hartmann (1939, 1958) called "preconscious automatisms."

With his assumption that human infants "are starting with a number of *highly structuralized responses* (some of which are active at birth and some of which mature later), Bowlby applies to *human behavior* an instinct concept which neglects the factor of development and learning far beyond even the position taken by Lorenz in his early propositions. It is therefore not surprising that Bowlby engages in criticism of psychoanalytic instinct theory. His criticism culminates in the rejection of this theory because it "conceive[s] of the organism as starting with a quantum of unstructured psychic energy which during development becomes progressively more structured" (1958, p. 364). Bowlby's criticism of Freud's "instinct" concept is based on a series of misconceptions which are not limited to psychoanalytic instinct theory:

1. Bowlby actually backtracks the development of the "instinct" theory which changed it from a "biophysiological" to a psychological concept.

Bowlby compares his assumptions of "instinctual response systems" (IRS's) with Freud's theory of "partial instinctual drives" (*"Partialtriebe"*) as expressed in the *Three Essays* (1905). However, when in his essay on "Instincts and Their Vicissitudes" (1915) Freud defined the instinctual drive as "the psychical representative of the stimuli originating from within the organism and reaching the mind" he made the decisive transition from a "peripheral," biophysiological to a psychological concept of instinctual drive. This psychological concept is the basis of any psychoanalytic theory of motivation (see Rapaport, 1960).

Actually this psychological concept of instinctual drive can already be detected in Chapter VII of *The Interpretation of Dreams* (1900) where Freud describes how a *"wish"* develops under the influence of the memory traces of the perception of need satisfaction. With the emergence of a "wish" begins what we call psychic structure, and the pleasure-unpleasure principle[3] becomes a psychological concept in contrast to need satisfaction which is a physiological concept.

The development of instinctual drives in the course of evolution is part of what Hartmann called the internalization of the mental apparatus (1939, 1948, 1958).

[3] See Anna Freud's discussion in this volume.

Inherent in Freud's discussion of the development of a wish is already the concept of an undifferentiated phase—Spitz (1959) calls it the phase of nondifferentiation—which was later broadened by Hartmann and his co-workers (Hartmann, 1939, 1950, 1958; Hartmann, Kris, and Loewenstein, 1946).

It is pertinent that many of Freud's genetic formulations—e.g., the development of the mental apparatus, of a "wish" (1900); his suggestion that instinctual drive may be the eventual precipitate of external stimulation (1915)—have both a phylogenetic-evolutional and an ontogenetic implication (Schur, 1959). The development of a "wish" in Freud's meaning corresponds to the phylogenetic-evolutional transition from what Schneirla (1954) calls a "biosocial" to a "psychosocial" pattern, a transition which is being repeated during ontogenesis. In my subsequent discussion of Bowlby's ideas about anxiety and depression I will try to show how this genetic approach can be applied also to these affective states.

2. Bowlby alludes to the fact that the translation of the German word "*Trieb*" with "instinct" has been the source of many misunderstandings. Hartmann (1939, 1948, 1958), Rapaport (1958a), myself (1959, 1960a, 1960b) and many others have pointed this out. To avoid such misunderstandings I have suggested the use of the term "instinctive" as pertaining to the instinct concept of ethology and to reserve the term "instinctual" as pertaining to the psychoanalytic concept of instinctual drive, a term which should exclusively be used in translation of the German word *Trieb*.[4]

Bowlby compares and contrasts the two concepts "instinct" and "instinctual drive." While ethologists speak about the internal drive element which they conceptualize as the force which activates "instinctive behavior," their main emphasis is on "systems of coordination" which are the basis of "instinctive behavior" (Thorpe, 1956). Any comparison of the psychoanalytic theory of "instinctual drive" and the instinct theory of ethologists must restrict itself to the "internal drive" element (Hartmann, 1948; Schur, 1958, 1960a), and cannot be extended to the modes of drive execution which characterize behavior.

3. Psychoanalytic theory does not assume that "the organism [is]

---

[4] It is unfortunate that the Standard Edition which is in most instances so excellent, uses the term "instinct" for the German word "*Trieb*."

starting with a quantum of instructed psychic energy which during development becomes progressively more structured." It assumes that it starts *ab ovo* with an Anlage. Anlage is of course not just a "quantum of psychic energy" (see p. 66 above). Already at birth the development of this Anlage has reached a stage where we can assume the presence of a mental apparatus equipped with energy which is probably undifferentiated. Psychoanalytic theory further assumes that this energy forms the matrix out of which, under the influence of certain experiences, and therefore in interaction with the environment, develop what we call the instinctual drives.

Freud (1937) and especially Hartmann (1939, 1950, 1958) have extended the concept of Anlage to the development of that part of the mental apparatus which psychoanalytic theory calls the ego.

The newborn is already equipped with a set of perceptive and executive apparatuses and with innate "discharge channels" (Rapaport, 1953), all of which form the basis of what Hartmann (1950) calls primary ego autonomy. The five responses designated by Bowlby as IRS's are using such inborn apparatuses. The concept *Anlage* implies that eventually, under the motivational stimulation of the instinctual drives and in constant interaction with the environment, the human phenotype develops its individual, highly complex ego structures which enable the ego to become what Hartmann calls the organ of adaptation (1939, 1958).

This—very sketchy—presentation shows the analogy of psychoanalytic concepts of development and of the common-ground formulations which I proposed for the biological concepts "innate" versus "acquired" (see p. 66 above).

Bowlby, however, endows "instincts" with such qualities of structure that we usually attribute to the ego—after a considerable stretch of its development.

Bowlby's concepts are therefore at variance with the concepts of biophysiologists and of most ethologists. They are not only at variance with Freud's psychological concept of instinctual drives, they also express a misconception of the concept Anlage, and they completely neglect all achievements of ego psychology.[5]

Bowlby polemicizes against what he calls the "secondary drive

[5] It is pertinent in this connection that the name Hartmann is absent from the bibliography of all the papers to which this discussion refers.

theory" of Freud and other analysts. He uses the semantic designation "secondary drive" in a somewhat similar manner as, for instance, Hull (1943). Bowlby assumes that (a) psychoanalysis distinguishes between primary (innate) and secondary (acquired) "drives"; (b) psychoanalysis claims that the child's relationship to the mother is based on a "drive"; and (c) psychoanalysis attributes, to such secondary (learned) drives, the motivation for the development of this relationship.

Psychoanalytic theory does not distinguish between "primary" and "secondary drives." Nor can, therefore, psychoanalytic theory assume that there exists either a "primary" or a "secondary" drive responsible for the child's ties to the mother. Psychoanalytic theory assumes that the child is endowed with instinctual drives which become expressed as wishes; that instinctual drives are seeking for an object; that the child is born with an Anlage to develop under average expectable environmental stimulation an object relationship to a mother figure. Psychoanalytic theory assumes that this vitally important relationship is the result of a long, immensely complex development, of an interaction which takes place at every psychological and physiological level (see also p. 65 above).

As to the assumption of a "primary drive," in his paper on "The Child's Ties to the Mother" (1958), Bowlby was still somewhat hesitant in claiming a primary "instinctive" tie to the mother and spoke only about "monotropy." When I reminded him at the 21st International Psycho-Analytical Congress at Copenhagen (1959), that the claim of a "superordinated drive" in the sense of McDougall would run counter to most biological and ethological concepts, he stated that his concept of monotropy does not imply a superordinated instinct. However, in his paper on "Separation Anxiety" (1960), he comes even closer to this claim. In discussing my anxiety papers he says: "Although he [Schur] discusses various dangers which he thinks may be based on innate givens, nowhere does he consider the possibility that loss of mother may be one of them." This criticism of Bowlby expresses implicitly that to him (as will be discussed later) this danger *is* based on innate givens; it implies also that according to Bowlby the tie itself is also present at birth in a preformed, "structuralized" way. Elsewhere in this paper he says, "As soon as the instinctual response systems mediating such behavior (meaning "attachment behavior") have matured and, by a process of *learning of a simple kind* [my italics] become oriented towards any object." This too implies Bowlby's assumption of the pre-existence of an instinctive drive requiring little learning.

"Orality" and "The Oral Phase"

Bowlby is intensively preoccupied in all his papers with orality— or rather with the denial of its importance. This goes so far that in his paper for the Symposium on Ethology and Psychoanalysis at the 21st Congress of the International Psycho-Analytical Association at Copenhagen (1959), Bowlby speculated that oral phenomena in neurosis and psychosis could be interpreted not as regressive but as "displacement phenomena" in the meaning of ethologists (for instance, Tinbergen, 1951). This de-emphasis of orality is paralleled by a lack of emphasis on the great importance of the first few months of the infant's life. Bowlby's reasoning is in a way quite simple: the child-mother relationship is based on fully structuralized, instinctive response mechanisms, *mainly* clinging and following. These responses mature only later—*ergo* the preceding period must be relatively unimportant. In his underestimation of the relative importance of the first year of the infant's life, Bowlby finds himself in conflict not only with the results of reconstructive analysis of adults and children but especially with the results of longitudinal observation which is mushrooming, for instance, all over the United States. He finds himself also at variance with such longitudinal animal observations as, for instance, the already cited study of Schneirla on newborn cats. It is not quite understandable that Bowlby, who describes so poignantly his and Robertson's observations of the protest of children against separation, should disregard the most violent of all protests—the protest of the hungry infant screaming for food. In his preoccupation with "dethroning" the concept of orality, Bowlby overlooks that neither Freud nor most of the psychoanalytic theoreticians have concentrated on the concept "orality" exclusively from the point of view of satisfaction of the infant's *hunger*.

A *most sketchy* historical review might show best the many

aspects of "orality" which describe a *specific phase* of human development.

1. In Chapter VII of *The Interpretation of Dreams*, Freud introduces the example of the infant, hungry, screaming, and kicking helplessly (pp. 565-566), as a *prototype* situation to illustrate his theory about the following psychoanalytic concepts: (a) the development of the first memory structures and their relationship to special percepts, connected with tension and tension relief; out of these concepts grew the concept of the pleasure-unpleasure principle as a regulating principle of the mental apparatus;[6] (b) the psychoanalytic concepts of the relationship of, and the transitions between, discharge, action, hallucination, thinking, wishes; (c) the maturation and development of inhibitory structures which eventually permit delay and later the transition to the secondary process and the reality principle.

2. With the recognition of the importance of infantile sexuality and of certain phases of psychosexual development (Freud, 1905) the oral phase came to represent a definite phase. (a) During this phase oral and tactual stimulation were the leading zones of sexual stimulation. (b) During this phase various perceptions utilizing innate apparatuses on which primary ego autonomy is based (Hartmann, 1950) stimulate the beginnings of structure formation. During this phase certain percepts may follow what Erikson (1959) has called the oral "mode." The processes incorporation and introjection which lead to the first identifications may also during this phase follow the same "modes." (c) Oral perceptions initiate the differentiation between inside and outside (Hoffer, 1950).

3. Direct infant observation *and* reconstruction in analysis of children and adults have enriched our knowledge. (a) They indicate that the infant during this phase needs a great deal of perceptual stimulation apart from feeding. Spitz's "hospitalism" is of course the extreme example (1945). Perceptual stimulations of various kinds play an important role in structure formation (learning). The counterpart of this fact can be seen from the experimental production of psychosis through stimulus deprivation (Rapaport, 1958b). (b) The observations of the violent reaction of infants to rigid feeding

[6] See Anna Freud's discussion in this volume.

schedules and abrupt weaning led to a "revolution" in the nursery and the introduction of "self-demand feeding."[7]

4. When Freud introduced in his *Inhibitions, Symptoms and Anxiety* (1926), as one of his main contributions (more about this later), the concept of a hierarchy of traumatic and danger situations —he used again the model of the hungry infant as one of the prototypes of a traumatic situation. For this reason and others Rapaport (1951) described this prototype situation as "the conceptual model of psychoanalysis."

All this and more we understand now when we speak of orality or rather of the "oral phase." All through this phase the mother is the source of all these stimulations, stimulations which represent "food and vitamins," but also pain and danger. The percept mother initiates also the Gestalt "familiar," in contrast to "unfamiliar"; it initiates the gradual development of the concepts "I" and "non-I," the crucial differentiation between self and object. The mother is initiator and receiver of this most miraculous instrument: language.

The development of the tie to the mother is therefore the result of an Anlage, its maturation and development in an unbelievably complex interaction. It is revealing that longitudinal observations on animals, as Schneirla's study on cats (1960), confirm this complexity and the very early beginnings of learning. Schneirla states also that whatever the variety of stimuli—"feeding provides a functional center for the socialization of kittens."

It is hard to understand how and why Bowlby tries not to see the importance of what we call the oral phase for the development of the child-mother relationship. When the child enters the phase in which, according to Bowlby, clinging and following would be "activated," this tie is already well established. Clinging and following become then some of the many functions which *utilize innate executive apparatuses* and help the child to prevent separation.

---

[7] I am treating a patient who entered analysis because of an addiction to Dexedrine (90 mg.!) and thyroid (more than one gram!) daily. Reconstruction in her analysis led to the assumption that this patient had suffered very early, severe "oral" frustration. On the very day when this part of my article was written she heard from her mother that at the age of one month her pediatrician declared that night feeding had to be stopped abruptly. The baby screamed through several nights. She then started to vomit each feeding and had to be spoon-fed mainly solids and water for many months.

SEPARATION ANXIETY

We can now come to Bowlby's formulations about anxiety in general and "separation anxiety" in particular which are the direct outgrowth of his formulations about the nature of the infant's tie to the mother.

Bowlby refers liberally to Freud's *Inhibitions, Symptoms and Anxiety*, especially to such passages which deal with the importance of the child's separation from the mother. Bowlby also mentions my various papers on anxiety; but apart from calling them "carefully reasoned studies," he completely disregards my attempts to arrive at a unitary, genetic concept of anxiety and singles out for criticism only my failure to consider that the danger of loss of mother may be based on innate givens. Here I could just refer to my papers. However, in order to clarify why I object to Bowlby's formulations and also to his terminology, I have to repeat in a few sentences what I have already said so often.

In *Inhibitions, Symptoms and Anxiety*, Freud formulated the main metapsychological points of view about anxiety: its structural, genetic, economic, dynamic, and adaptive aspects. He introduced the simple definition that anxiety is always a *response* in a *given situation*, and he established a hierarchy of such situations. He defined the difference between a traumatic situation and a danger situation. He described several prototypes of such situations—the situation of the hungry infant being one such prototype. Among his main contributions were also the formulation that anxiety is an ego response and the concept of "signal anxiety." For these reasons *Inhibitions, Symptoms and Anxiety* became a turning point in the theory and practice of psychoanalysis.

My own studies (1953, 1955, 1958, 1960a) were devoted mainly to the closer examination of the ego's role in various gradations of anxiety and in the various, especially economic, consequences of ego regression. I applied the genetic point of view to pre-ego stages of the anxiety response, and eventually included phylogenetic-evolutional considerations. My definition—that anxiety is a response of the ego or its precursors to a traumatic situation or to danger, present or anticipated—tried to eliminate Freud's distinction between "automatic" and "signal anxiety."

I traced the precursors of the affect anxiety to biophysiological responses, which change in the course of evolution, to follow Schneirla's terminology (1958) from "withdrawal" to "avoidance." The *ontogenetic* development proceeds from various species-specific responses of the infant to various changes of the homeostatic equilibrium, responses which utilize inborn discharge channels, to the development of the affect anxiety, which is an ego response. According to my formulation, primary anxiety (and I use the term in a genetic sense) in the traumatic situation and the thoughtlike awareness of anticipated danger represent the two extremes in a complementary series of responses. Between these extremes are the innumerable gradations of anxiety for which our language has designated such varied terms as awareness of danger, apprehension, fear, fright, panic, etc.

Bowlby's ideas about anxiety have turned the clock back to Freud's concepts of 1894, with some modification by his special interpretation of the instinct concept. Bowlby could have followed Freud's concepts of 1926 and described the consequences of the child's reaction to a crucial *danger* situation, namely, to separation from the mother. However, for Bowlby, "separation anxiety" is "the inescapable corollary of attachment behavior—the other side of the coin." Accordingly, Bowlby assumes that "a blind and automatic type of anxiety results if an instinctual response system"[8] is not satisfied, and is unable to reach termination. This anxiety Bowlby calls "primary anxiety." Especially nontermination of the "clinging" and "following" IRS's are, according to him, such sources of primary anxiety. Bowlby is not quite sure about the relative importance of "nontermination" of the "sucking" and "crying response systems."

Bowlby then adds two additional IRS's which are released by certain external stimulations and result in "escape behavior and/or freezing." The subjective experience of these responses which "does not presuppose any conscious awareness of danger," Bowlby designates as fright. He emphasizes that the instinctual escape response includes not only "escape from" but also "escape to." *Secondary* to

[8] Instinctive in the terminology proposed by me.

these IRS's is, according to Bowlby, a certain amount of "simple learning—mainly conditioning."[9]

According to Bowlby, the main "ingredients" of separation anxiety are the various "IRS's" with "some learning" added. It is in line with Bowlby's attempts to eliminate the concept of orality that he does not consider the infant's violent reaction to hunger and to delay of its satisfaction as an important genetic source of separation anxiety. Despite his preoccupation with "biology" and "survival value," Bowlby negates the importance of physiological-homeostatic needs—and *their* survival value.

According to Bowlby—and here he follows certain ethological observations on some lower animals—the infant eats because it has to suck. But this is true only for the very first moments of its life. We know how soon even a chicken learns, partly by habituation, what to eat and what to avoid pecking.[10]

We can now summarize Bowlby's concepts as follows: the child develops the tie to the mother because it is *directed* by certain IRS's; it develops separation anxiety if these responses cannot be terminated. To this regulation by preformed IRS's is added "a process of learning of a simple kind." To summarize this theory in a form which may sound drastic but is not exaggerated: the infant eats because it has to suck; it develops a tie to the mother because it *has* to cling, follow, and escape *to*; it develops separation anxiety if it cannot "terminate" these responses.

All this is a determined and extremely systematic effort to show that the tail is wagging the dog and not vice versa.

I have tried to describe in a very cursory way how complex the development of the tie to mother is. Our "other side of the coin," the explanation of separation anxiety, is equally complex. I will represent it in an equally cursory way:

[9] Bowlby calls the experience which then develops not as one would expect "anticipatory anxiety" but "expectant anxiety." This semantic distinction is indicative of Bowlby's *need* for *new* terminology and of his neglect of Freud's danger concept. Anticipating anxiety means that we anticipate danger and experience some shade of anxiety. It is the phobic patient who *expects* to experience anxiety when he anticipates danger.

[10] It was fascinating to watch how during imprinting experiments shown to me through the courtesy of Dr. Charles Tidd at the University of Southern California, newly hatched chickens within a few minutes learned *not* to peck at their own excrements, but to circle around them.

1. The human infant is an altricial creature *par excellence*. It is utterly dependent (a term Bowlby frowns upon) on external help for any satisfaction of its needs which cannot be satisfied by automatic homeostatic regulations.

2. Its structure formation is dependent on a steady stream of stimuli (Piaget [1936] calls them nutriments).

3. It learns to connect a "mother" figure with the source of all these "physiological" and psychological "nutriments." It enters the "symbiotic" phase (Benedek, 1956; Jacobson, 1954; Mahler, 1958) where self-awareness and body image start to develop—where, however, self and objects are not really differentiated.

4. The capacity to tolerate delay depends on the development of such complex ego faculties as differentiation between present and future, neutralization, beginnings of abstraction of an object which is temporarily beyond perceptual grasp, etc.

5. With locomotion and increasing regard for the environment the infant becomes aware of all kinds of external dangers, and now confuses internal, instinctual with external danger. The child develops also the recognition of his own helplessness, which is the core of any traumatic situation. This helplessness is the expression of the weakness of his own rudimentary ego which can be overcome only through his "external executive" ego (Spitz, 1951, 1959), the mother. It enters a phase in which it experiences various needs of his pregenital sexuality and also various restrictions (weaning, toilet training, the various do's and don't's). It becomes aware of its ambivalence. All through these phases the mother is the supplier of need satisfactions and nutriments, the savior from inner and outer danger. Separation remains traumatic until ego development can give the child the capacity to tolerate delay with all its implications (time, spacing, etc.).[11] For all these and many more *developmental* reasons the child experiences anxiety in the absence of the mother.

Bowlby remains true to his ideas when he finally states that the gradual disappearance of separation anxiety might be due to a "waxing and waning of 'IRS's' at a time when they are not bio-

---

[11] Beres said in a recent paper (1960): ". . . only with the development of the imaginative process, of the capacity to create a mental representation of the absent object, does the child progress from the syncretic, sensory, motor-affective, immediate response, to the delayed, abstract, conceptualized response that is characteristically human."

logically necessary any more." Here he concedes that "experience and learning certainly play a considerable part also." *We* would say that ego development eventually guarantees an increased stability of what Mahler (1958) calls the separation-individuation phase.

Before finally discussing Bowlby's ideas about grief and mourning, a few words about a point which is not only of theoretical but also of practical import:

Bowlby assumes on the basis of a few random quotations, mainly from Freud's *Three Essays*, that Freud saw in the element of "spoiling" the cause of excessive separation anxiety. Bowlby claims that Freud's hypothesis of spoiling has been built deep into psychoanalytic theory. Bowlby uses this contention to establish *his* priority for having pointed out the importance of separation, of threats of separation and/or loss of love, rejection by the mother, etc. The following remarks may help to correct this assumption of Bowlby. During Freud's first "environmental" orientation he blamed mainly two factors for the etiology of neurosis—early seduction and sexual frustration. We know why Freud had to give up this simplified theory. However, for decades education was plagued by a misinterpretation of psychoanalytic concepts: "Protect a child from 'trauma' and 'frustration' and everything will be fine." Freud had to issue a warning. He expresses this dilemma best when he says in his *New Introductory Lectures* (1932, p. 204):

> Education has . . . to steer its way between the Scylla of giving the instincts free play and the Charybdis of frustrating them. . . . It is a matter of finding out how much one may forbid, at which times and by what methods.

This warning did not help too much. The "rejecting mother" became the scapegoat for every mental illness, and permissiveness became the cornerstone of "modern" education—especially in the United States. For this reason Anna Freud (1954) and many others had to repeat the warning. The ideal safe channel between Scylla and Charybdis has not been found. However, most analysts agree that avoidance of frustration is especially important during that very phase which seems to Bowlby so relatively unimportant for the development of separation anxiety: the first few months of the infant's life. Hence the general acceptance of self-demand feeding, etc.

But even during this phase overanxious mothers overfeed and over-stimulate their infants. Most analysts agree also on the fact that every phase can be "critical" for the ability to handle the next one.[12] Analysts agree also that with the beginning of ego formation infants should be progressively *helped* in building their adaptive, inhibiting mechanisms. This, however, is not spoiling.

"Depression" or "Grief and Mourning"

We can now finally turn to the formulations which Bowlby first expressed in the paper appearing in this volume. Bowlby's clinical thesis is relatively simple: he claims that the infant's reaction to actual separation from the mother, especially between the ages of six months and three years, is longer-lasting and of more profound consequence than had been assumed—according to him—in psycho-analytic literature. Bowlby then announces that he will deal with the pathological consequences in future papers.

Bowlby seems to think that the pathological consequences of separation from the mother can be better understood when he describes them in terms of grief and mourning rather than by using the concept of depression.

Bowlby calls upon the authority of Zetzel and her paper on "Depressive Illness" (1960) to support what he calls his "far-reaching and controversial" conclusions. However, Bowlby utilizes from Zetzel's review only the distinction she made between depression as an affective state and depressive illness.

Zetzel's paper is a continuation and elaboration of the work on depression by E. Bibring.[13] Zetzel emphasizes rightly that the key word of Bibring's thesis is the word "ego." According to Bibring, both anxiety and depression are basic ego reactions. As affective states both can be experienced only by the ego.

Expressed in terms of relationship to the object: anxiety is the reaction to danger of losing the object; depression is the reaction to having lost it. (See also Greenson, 1959.)

The affective anxiety reaction in a traumatic situation and the

---

[12] See also Schneirla's discussion (1960) of the concept "critical phase"; and Erikson (1959).

[13] Another name which is missing from Bowlby's bibliography.

affect, depression, share the ego's experience of complete helplessness. Helplessness and inhibition of ego functions are, according to Bibring, ubiquitous characteristics of depressive ego states—and accordingly also of depressive illness.

Zetzel suggested that my concepts of "controlled" and "uncontrolled" anxiety (1953), which are based on the importance of ego regression for the various phenomena of anxiety, should be extended to the study of depression. She speaks therefore of depressive illness as a "regressive clinical phenomenon." In other words, Zetzel applies to the problem of depression among others also the genetic point of view of metapsychology (Rapaport and Gill, 1959).

In a recent paper on "Bibring's Theory of Depression" (1959), Rapaport also emphasizes that depressive illness is not simply an id regression, but "primarily a regression to an ego state, which is not produced *a novo* . . . , but is a reactivation of a primal state."

We can extend the analogy between anxiety and depression to the assumption that genetically both affects must have their precursors in pre-ego states. Both the affects, which are ego responses, and their precursors have their specific discharge phenomena. My concepts of "desomatization" and "resomatization" (1955) may also apply to depression, and might explain the economic consequences of various types of depression.

While anxiety results in a mobilization of defenses, depression induces inhibition and eventually paralysis of ego functions. This process is paralleled by an inhibition of vital somatic functions. These considerations apply also to pre-ego states, where both the precursors of anxiety and of depression are truly "psychosomatic."[14]

The toleration of object loss and the ability to re-establish ego control, and thereby to limit the reaction to a "controlled" depression, are a measure of well-established ego autonomy (Hartmann, 1950; Rapaport, 1958b). It is obvious that the budding ego of the infant has not yet reached this stage of development.

I have pointed out earlier in my discussion that the mother provides the necessary "nutriments" (Piaget, 1936) for structure formation. Her absence makes the child literally wilt away. This process has been vividly described by Spitz (1945) and Engel and Reichsman

---

[14] See also A. Freud's discussion in this volume.

(1956). Spitz (1956) used the analogy to Selye's concept of the exhaustion phase of the stress reaction. We may speak even more appropriately of a deficiency syndrome, which is truly "psychosomatic." It might be pertinent here that on the one hand depressive illness results in hormonal inhibition, and that on the other hand both avitaminosis and certain hormone deficiencies may simulate depressive illness.

Anna Freud mentions in her discussion the frequency of psychosomatic conditions in children after separation from their mother. I would assume that some somatic phenomena must be present in every case of bereavement.

I have brought all this up to show that the concept "depression" is—if we use the metapsychological approach—broad enough to describe all responses of reaction to the accomplished loss of an object. The process of mourning could then be seen not as an especially severe type of depression, but rather as an attempt at restitution, which may or may not succeed.[15]

SUMMARY

Staying within the framework of psychoanalytic concepts and terminology, which are broad enough for the expression of the pertinent problems, Bowlby justly considers the child's relationship to his first object, the mother, as an essential, vital part of his development. He rightly considers separation from mother as one of the basic danger situations, and his and Robertson's observations bring beautiful illustrations of it.

To the danger of separation from the mother, the child responds with various gradations of anxiety. The child responds to the actual, temporary, or permanent loss of the mother, among other reactions, with various shades of depression.

Bowlby then assumes that this response is longer-lasting and has deeper pathological consequences than—as he claims—had been assumed, and with these consequences he wants to deal in future papers.

In order to reach these conclusions, which are not "controversial," Bowlby felt compelled to revamp, more or less, some of the

[15] See A. Freud's discussion in this volume.

most fundamental concepts and formulations of psychoanalysis, reached in the last decades by reconstruction in analysis and by direct observation. Among these basic concepts, to mention only a few, are ego development; interdependence of drive, ego development, and environment; orality; narcissism; the metapsychological approach to the problem of the affects anxiety and depression, etc.

Bowlby tries to base this very extensive—and, in my opinion, not constructive—reformulation on *his* application of the instinct concepts of ethology, an application in which he goes far beyond the claims of even Lorenz. His application contradicts also all the evidence accumulated by research on animal behavior and the development of human structure, which prove the importance of learning for the development of the species-specific Anlage.

I hope that this critical discussion has contributed toward the clarification of some of these issues.

BIBLIOGRAPHY

Benedek, T. F. (1956), Toward the Biology of Depressive Constellation. *J. Am. Psa. Assn.*, IV.

Beres, D. (1960), Perception, Imagination and Reality. Paper read at the New York Psychoanalytic Society, May 31, 1960.

Bibring, E. (1953), The Mechanism of Depression. In: *Affective Disorders*, ed. P. Greenacre. New York: International Universities Press.

Bowlby, J. (1958), The Nature of the Child's Tie to the Mother. *Int. J. Psa.*, XXXIX.

—— (1959), Psychoanalysis and Ethology. Paper given at the Symposium on Ethology and Psychoanalysis at the 21st International Psycho-Analytical Congress, Copenhagen, July, 1959.

—— (1960), Separation Anxiety. *Int. J. Psa.*, XLI.

Engel, G. L. & Reichsman, F. (1956), Spontaneous and Experimentally Induced Depressions in an Infant with a Gastric Fistula. *J. Am. Psa. Assn.*, IV.

Erikson, E. H. (1959), Identity and the Life Cycle. *Psychological Issues*, Vol. I, No. 1. New York: International Universities Press.

Freud, A. (1954), Psychoanalysis and Education. *This Annual*, IX.

Freud, S. (1894), The Justification for Detaching from Neurasthenia a Particular Syndrome: The Anxiety-Neurosis. *Collected Papers*, I. London: Hogarth Press, 1949.

—— (1900), The Interpretation of Dreams. *Standard Edition*, IV & V. London: Hogarth Press, 1953.

—— (1905), Three Essays on the Theory of Sexuality. *Standard Edition*, VII. London: Hogarth Press, 1949.

—— (1915), Instincts and Their Vicissitudes. *Standard Edition*, XIV. London: Hogarth Press, 1957.

—— (1926), Inhibitions, Symptoms and Anxiety. *Standard Edition*, XX. London: Hogarth Press, 1959.

—— (1932), *New Introductory Lectures on Psychoanalysis*. New York: Norton, 1933.

—— (1937), Analysis Terminable and Interminable. *Collected Papers*, V. London: Hogarth Press, 1950.

Greenson, R. (1959), Phobia, Anxiety and Depression. *J. Am. Psa. Assn.*, VII.

Hartmann, H. (1939), *Ego Psychology and the Problem of Adaptation*. New York: International Universities Press, 1958.

—— (1948), Comments on the Psychoanalytic Theory of Instinctual Drives. *Psa. Quart.*, XVII.

—— (1950), Psychoanalysis and Developmental Psychology. *This Annual*, V.

—— (1958), Comments on the Scientific Aspects of Psychoanalysis. *This Annual*, XIII.

—— & Kris, E., Loewenstein, R. M. (1946), Comments on the Formation of Psychic Structure. *This Annual*, II.

Hoffer, W. (1950), Development of the Body Ego. *This Annual*, V.

Hull, C. L. (1943), *Principles of Behavior*. New York: Appleton.

Jacobson, E. (1954), The Self and the Object World. *This Annual*, IX.

Lorenz, K. (1935), Companionship in Bird Life. In: *Instinctive Behavior*, ed. C. Schiller. New York: International Universities Press, 1957.

—— (1937), The Nature of Instinct. In: *Instinctive Behavior*, ed. C. Schiller. New York: International Universities Press, 1957.

—— (1950), The Comparative Method in Studying Innate Behavior Patterns. *Symposium of the Society for Experimental Biology*, IV. Cambridge: Cambridge University Press.

Mahler, M. S. (1958), Autism and Symbiosis: Two Extreme Disturbances of Identity *Int. J. Psa.*, XXXIX.

Piaget, J. (1936), *The Origins of Intelligence in Children*. New York: International Universities Press, 1952.

Rapaport, D. (1951), The Conceptual Model of Psychoanalysis. In: *Psychoanalytic Psychiatry and Psychology*, ed. R. P. Knight and C. Friedman. New York: International Universities Press, 1954.

—— (1953), On the Psychoanalytic Theory of Affects. *Int. J. Psa.*, XXXIV.

—— (1958a), Editorial footnote in: Hartmann, H., *Ego Psychology and the Problem of Adaptation*. New York: International Universities Press, p. 29.

—— (1958b), The Theory of Ego Autonomy: A Generalization. *Bull. Menninger Clin.*, XXII.

——(1959), Edward Bibring's Theory of Depression. Paper read at the Boston Psychoanalytic Society, April, 1959.

—— (1960), On the Psychoanalytic Theory of Motivation. In: *Nebraska Symposium on Motivation*, ed. M. R. Jones. Lincoln: University of Nebraska Press.

—— & Gill, M. (1959), The Points of View and Assumptions of Metapsychology. *Int. J. Psa.*, XL.

Schneirla, T. C. (1954), Discussion in: *Group Processes. Transactions of the First Conference*, ed. B. Schaffner. University Seminar on Communications. New York: Columbia University.

—— (1958), An Evolutionary and Developmental Theory of Biphasic Processes Underlying Approach and Withdrawal. In: *Nebraska Symposium on Motivation, 1958*, ed. M. R. Jones. Lincoln: University of Nebraska Press, 1959.

—— (1960), Analysis of Socialization in a Mammal. *Am. J. Orthopsychiat.*, to be published.

Schur, M. (1953), The Ego in Anxiety. In: *Drives, Affects, Behavior*, ed. R. M. Loewenstein. New York: International Universities Press.

—— (1955), Comments on the Metapsychology of Somatization. *This Annual*, X.

—— (1958), The Ego and the Id in Anxiety. *This Annual*, XIII.

—— (1959), Chairman's Introduction to the Panel on Ethology and Psychoanalysis at the Fall Meeting of the American Psychoanalytic Association, New York, December, 1959. For a report of this Panel, see *J. Am. Psa. Assn.*, VIII, 1960.

—— (1960a), Ontogenesis and Phylogenesis of Affect and Structure Formation and the Concept of Repetition Compulsion. *Int. J. Psa.*, to be published.

—— (1960b), A Psychoanalyst's Comments at the Symposium on Animal Research at the 37th Annual Meeting of the American Orthopsychiatric Association, Chicago, February, 1960. *Am. J. Orthopsychiat.*, to be published.

Spitz, R. (1945), Hospitalism. *This Annual*, I.

—— (1951), The Psychogenic Diseases in Infancy. *This Annual*, VI.

—— (1956), Some Observations on Psychiatric Stress in Infancy. In: *Fifth Annual Report on Stress, 1955-1956*, ed. H. Selye & G. Heuser. New York: M. D. Publications, pp. 193-204.

—— (1959), *A Genetic Field Theory of Ego Formation*. New York: International Universities Press.

Thorpe, W. (1956), *Learning and Instinct in Animals*. Cambridge: Harvard University Press.

Tinbergen, N. (1951), *The Study of Instincts*. London: Oxford University Press.

Zetzel, E. R. (1960), Depressive Illness. *Int. J. Psa.*, to be published.

DISCUSSION OF DR. BOWLBY'S PAPER

RENÉ A. SPITZ, M.D. (Denver)

Dr. Bowlby's paper "Grief and Mourning in Infancy and Early Childhood" is one of a series of articles of which two have already appeared (1958, 1960) and several others are to be published in the future. In what follows I will limit my considerations to his present paper, in which he reopens the discussion concerning infantile responses to loss of object and redefines some psychoanalytic terms and concepts. His thesis is that the responses of infants to loss of object do not differ from that of adults and that these responses are grief and mourning. His crucial question is "Whether or not, when the infant experiences the loss of the love object, he experiences grief and goes through a period of mourning."

A second part of the paper consists in an extensive review of the literature which he quotes to document the thesis advanced by him.

Dr. Bowlby's paper stresses the need for a more exact, clear, and consistent use of terms and concepts, which in many writings have been used carelessly. I am particularly referring to terms like "weaning," also spoken of as "loss of breast." We rarely mention that weaning, as Bowlby states, is not only the loss of the breast, but necessarily represents also the interposition of a greater distance between mother and child, and a reduction of the opportunities for physical closeness between the two.

Furthermore, Bowlby points out that weaning coincides frequently with a separation experience from the mother (for instance, with the birth of a younger sibling), or with an actual loss of the mother figure; this has always been my view (Spitz, 1948).

Bowlby states that in the normal child the manifest consequences of weaning are as a rule fairly mild. I have gone even further: in my opinion, the experience of weaning is actually one of the necessary and beneficial frustrations; it not only accelerates but redirects the development of the infant on his road to becoming a human being (Spitz, 1948).

One reservation I have is that to speak of "loss of the mother figure" is an undynamic formulation; it does not do justice to the extraordinary richness of exchanges and interrelations between mother and child in the course of the first year of life. I have made a first and, to my mind, barely sufficient attempt to describe these exchanges and interrelations (Spitz and Wolf, 1946; Spitz, 1954, 1957).

We are also indebted to Bowlby for pointing out that it is confusing to use the term "breast" in some instances in its dictionary meaning, namely, to designate the organ which the infant perceives, and in others as a psychoanalytic concept which has a variety of meanings, in some of which the term "breast" becomes practically "coterminous with the mother figure." The meaning in which the term "breast" is used should be specifically defined in the given case. For instance, in the first months of life, the breast is the relevant central experience in the infant's world. For this stage in particular, it was demonstrated (Spitz, 1955), that the mother's breast and her face are inseparably fused in the "cavity experience." By that is meant the perceptual combination of the tactile sensation of the nipple in the mouth, plus the cutaneous sensation of being cradled at the breast, and the simultaneous visual perception of the face. With the help of a variety of regressive phenomena in the grownup it could be shown that this fusion retains its effectiveness from earliest infancy into adult life (Isakower, 1938). When discussing such regressive phenomena, we will have to specify whether we are actually speaking of the "cavity experience" as a whole or of a part of this experience. The same caution applies when we speak of "the loss of the mother figure" in the case of the child.

Another of Bowlby's contributions in this paper is his emphasis on the fact that the inherited behavior repertoire of man includes a number of nonoral instinctual response systems. These must, however, not be mistaken for the instinctual drives of which psychoanalysis speaks. The innate preformed response patterns are partly effective at birth, partly they will become so at later stages; they represent, together with the oral responses, the physiological and behavioral foundation on which the child's earliest object relations (that is, his first interchanges with the human environment) are established. Examples of such inherited response patterns are rooting and the sucking response (Spitz, 1957); the "turning toward" response to warmth and cutaneous stimulation; probably, in part, the smiling response; and others which have not yet been sufficiently investigated.

One might say that these innate response patterns are necessary, but not sufficient, conditions for the formation of object relations. These earliest interchanges provide the child with experiences that partake at the same time of the physiological and of the psychological. They trigger the first psychological processes and thus endow object relations with psychological content and meaning. This process transforms the object relations: at their inception they were essentially biological and mechanical. But in the process of development they gradually and increasingly assume the nature of an interaction that is primarily of a psychological nature (Spitz, 1957).

Without the intervention of psychological processes, no object relations would ever be formed. We might have reflex behavior, but not interrelations of a reciprocal nature which ultimately lead to social relations. It is the loss of such psychological relations to which the child responds with pain and with the grief of which Bowlby speaks. As long as the innate responses are the sole carriers of the relations between mother and child, the loss of the mother will be responded to primarily in a physiological manner and not by psychological pain, not by the affect grief. To experience these affects, the infant has to develop a psychological organization, an occurrence which, in my opinion, takes place around the sixth month of life.

I believe that this explains, though not completely, my observation that the critical period for the emergence of the grief reaction begins after the sixth month of life, a finding confirmed by others and most recently by Schaffer and Callender (1959).

Neither emotions and affects nor perceptions are available or differentiated at birth; they are developed interdependently, step by step (Malrieux, 1952, 1958). And a certain level of perceptual as well as emotional maturation and differentiation is the prerequisite for the maintenance of object relations, and therefore for the experience of grief (Spitz, 1947, 1950, 1954).

I concur with the emphasis which Bowlby places on the need to distinguish between "depression" as a nosological concept from depression as an affective state. The two are frequently confused in the literature. Throughout my work I have tried to use "depression," together with a qualifying adjective, in the sense of a *nosological* entity.

Bowlby discusses extensively the violent manifest hostility arising in mourning after object loss. This seems to me a most important observational finding, supported by numerous investigations, like those of Anna Freud on children, as well as observations made on adults and reports on preliterate societies. In children *under* one year of age, I never observed such hostility (Spitz, 1953, 1954). The aggressiveness, often combined with hostility, was regularly manifested *after* the object had returned, the depression had lifted, and the child appeared to function normally or even better.[1]

This difference between Bowlby's statements and my observations has its reason in the fact that the observations quoted by him refer exclusively to children older than eighteen months, while the children observed by me were with a few exceptions under one year of age; the oldest children in the group were around fifteen months.

This is where Bowlby and I part company. Bowlby rejects my proposition that the damage in the object-deprived infants is caused by their incapacity to turn aggression toward the outside and that, in order to deal with it, they are forced to turn it against the self. Instead, Bowlby explains the syndrome of anaclitic depression and hospitalism by the "rupture of a key relationship and the consequent intense pain of yearning." As a description of the observable phenomena, this is quite correct, and I have actually so stated;[2] however, this is not an explanation in terms of underlying dynamics.

Furthermore, it is rather surprising to find Bowlby (in quoting Lindemann and Marris) speaking of hostility aimed either at others or *at the self*, and on another page rejecting as improbable my con-

---

[1] I often observed that children show a spectacular advance in every sector of their personality after the object had been returned to them. I have never been able to explain this phenomenon satisfactorily. Perhaps it is the release of aggression, previously turned against the self, which now becomes available for mastery and for use against the outer world.

[2] By describing the infant's reactions of weeping, of wailing, and, in the progressed stages, of whimpering, as well as by illustrating the expression of suffering in my films.

clusions that in infants who have lost their love object aggression is turned back on the self.

It is also somewhat puzzling when Bowlby states that "the particular conditions necessary to produce the Spitz syndrome remain unclear" because Schaffer and Callender (1959) did not observe it in similarly deprived infants.

In contrast to the *total* deprivation suffered by the children which I have studied, the deprivation of the children observed by Schaffer and Callender was only *partial*, for, after all, as the authors state, the children were visited almost daily by their mothers or relatives. Moreover, Schaffer and Callender state that none of their children were deprived of the mother figure for more than seven weeks; one half of them were deprived one month or less.

I have explicitly stated that the serious (and often fatal) consequences of loss of love object begin *after* the third month of deprivation; the damage inflicted is still reversible in separations lasting three to five months but probably becomes irreversible thereafter (Spitz, 1945, 1946, 1954).[3]

The fundamental difference between Bowlby's approach and mine is that Bowlby disregards the difference of developmental levels which obviously exists between infants aged six months and children between three to four years of age. Bowlby assumes that there is practically no psychological, particularly emotional growth, maturation, and development of the child in the period between six months and four years of age. There is just the barest hint that perhaps the infant who is in the process of acquiring the rudiments of an ego at "less than twelve months" may react differently from the child at the age of twelve to eighteen months who goes through the process of firmly integrating and establishing his ego.

[3] The symptoms resulting from loss of the mother figure in the course of the first seven weeks of separation, referred to by Schaffer and Callender, are essentially the same which I have described. Any difference is a semantic one: Schaffer and Callender use a so-called "objective-behavioristic" terminology, whereas we use clinical-diagnostic categories. Schaffer and Callender believe that "hospitalism" is the result of special, and nowadays infrequent, conditions of infant care and ask that an account of reactions to such care be accompanied by precise description of the conditions applying to the populations studied. In this respect, I refer them to pages 60 to 64 of my article "Hospitalism" (1945), where the background, housing conditions, food, clothing, medical care, toys, personnel, and radius of locomotion are described; in addition, the visual radius, including the measurements of the cots in which the children are housed, for both Foundling home and Nursery are given.

Nor is the next, equally great step in development given any consideration, the step which comes in the latter half of the second year, when speech in the adult sense is acquired and language is used in thought processes. This step in the personality development makes the infant as different from what he was at the previous stages as if he now belonged to a different species (Spitz, 1957).

Instead there is in Bowlby's article great emphasis on the assumption that the loss of the love object causes pain in the infant, and grief, and results in mourning, as it does in the adult.

The psychoanalyst is far more interested in the *nature* of the psychological organization which experiences this pain; what *means* are available to the infant or adult for dealing with traumatic experience; and *how*- the traumatic experience is dealt with. If these circumstances are taken into account, it becomes evident that the more inadequate the personality organization is in terms of defense, the greater will be the impact of psychological trauma, for the ego is that organization to which devolve the tasks of defense and mastery.

It follows that below the age of one year when the ego is in the process of being established (Hartmann, Kris, and Loewenstein, 1946; Hartmann, 1950), the consequences of loss of object will not only be different, but also more severe than at a later age. Bowlby admits that he has not yet had occasion to observe the responses to prolonged loss of the mother figure in infants less than twelve months old. Perhaps the observation of the consequences of *complete* loss of love object at this earlier age might alter his evaluation. This is, however, doubtful, for it appears that Bowlby has excluded from his theorizing the structural viewpoint, that is the assumption of a division of the psychic apparatus into id, ego, and superego, which is indispensable for any psychoanalytic interpretation of the responses of infants (Freud, 1923; Spitz, 1954).

One also misses in his arguments any references to the dynamic viewpoint, that is, to the existence of aggressive and libidinal energies in the psyche and their respective cathexis. When Bowlby speaks of dynamics, it is mostly in terms of hostility, hate, pain, love, etc., i.e., in descriptive terms. It is as if Bowlby were unwilling to go further than Freud did in *Beyond the Pleasure Principle* (1920) in which for the first time Freud uses the term "hate" and "aggressive instinct" interchangeably (although he speaks of "aggressiveness" already earlier). Bowlby offers no discussion of the instinctual drives in terms of libido and aggression; he speaks of hostility and of object relations and limits himself to the behavioral level.

That is a legitimate approach and, like other psychoanalytic authors, I have endeavored to follow it for the observational and descriptive part of my work. But for the purpose of explaining empirical data in terms of psychoanalytic theory, this approach is inadequate. Behavioral description has to be combined with the explication of observational facts from the economic, the dynamic, and the structural viewpoint; in some cases, the topographic viewpoint and the genetic approach should be added.

If Bowlby wishes to do without this kind of explanation, he is entirely within his rights. However, it then ceases to be a psychoanalytic explanation, and the quotations from Freud, which Bowlby uses here, do not really apply.

If we examine Bowlby's article from the theoretical point of view, he appears to have excluded from his considerations the structural principle, the dynamic viewpoint, and the developmental stages leading to the establishment and unfolding of the ego. As far as observational data are concerned, he fails to take into account that, for the formation of object relations, the development of the perceptual apparatus and of directed neuromuscular functioning on the one hand, emotional development and differentiation on the other, are prerequisites. In his arguments Bowlby therefore takes it for granted that the infant and the toddler both have a personality quite comparable to that of the grownup; both are therefore presumed to go through the same kind of mourning process as the adult when losing a love object. But it would appear that for *one* particular item Bowlby rejects this similarity which he otherwise postulates between the infant and the adult: for the adult he accepts Freud's (1926) proposition that aggression turned back against the self is operative in depression; for the infant, he claims that this is not so.

Against all evidence in the literature[4] proving the vast differences

4 Two recent articles by J. Weidemann (1959a, b) present a methodologically impeccable investigation of 121 children institutionalized from the first month of life to their sixth year and a control group of 62 family children of comparable age, with an extraordinary wealth of data and an extensive statistical work-up. In this investigation he arrived at quite similar results as had earlier investigators, including myself, in regard to the damaging influence of institutionalization. One would hope that the

between the infantile personality at successive age levels, Bowlby disregards the developmental approach to the point that for the sake of argument he belittles even the significance of neuromuscular maturation. He considers unimportant the role of muscular activity in providing a discharge for at least part of the aggressive drive in the nine- to twelve-month-old infant. On the other hand he does not seem to realize that when he speaks of a reaction of "protest" to object loss in the somewhat older child, consisting of the child crying loudly, shaking his cot, and throwing himself about, Bowlby is describing just such an attempt at a neuromuscular discharge of the aggressive drive.

As a psychiatrist Bowlby would be the first to recognize that loud and violent manifestations of grief are more therapeutic than its silent suppression. Yet he belittles the idea that the discharge function would be better served if grieving children were not confined to their cots, as were the infants described by me. Confinement to the cot makes extensive muscular discharge difficult and ineffectual.

This statement should not be construed, as Bowlby seems to do, as if I were placing the responsibility for the consequences of the loss of object solely on the inhibition of the discharge of the aggressive drive through the neuromuscular system. On the contrary, I found, and have so stated repeatedly (Spitz, 1945, 1946, 1950, 1953, 1954, etc.), that it is specifically the loss of the love object, the deprivation of emotional interchange, which is to be held responsible. At the risk of repetition I have to stress once again that in the emotional interchanges with the love object *both* the libidinal *and* the aggressive drive find their discharge. This must be evident to anyone observing an infant with his mother; how else is the picture of the infant snuggling to his mother's cheek while tearing her hair or slapping her, to be explained. (Examples could be multiplied; the psychoanalytic cliche is that of the infant sucking at the mother's breast and biting it at the same time.) The loss of the love object interrupts the discharge of both drives. It certainly is no *cure* to afford discharge for at least part of the aggressive drive; but it helps—

---

huge amount of data assembled in Weidemann's research, the sophisticated statistical devices, the extraordinary precautions taken to cancel out possible sources of error would finally put an end to the ever repeated specious objections of improper methodology, insufficient data, hasty generalizations, etc., raised against earlier investigations.

and no discharge at all obviously makes the consequences of object loss worse.

In summing up I can say that I am in agreement with Bowlby on the need for conceptual clarification in general and with some of his efforts to implement it in the present paper. I agree with him that loss of the mother figure—or, as I prefer to call it for the age below one year, loss of love object—is responded to by the infant with grief.

However, on the observational level, Bowlby has passed under silence in his present article a number of psychological differences that mark the successive stages of infant development and which can be observed and measured. On the theoretical level he disregards the structural and dynamic viewpoints which for quite some time have been accepted as cornerstones of psychoanalytic theory. On the other hand, Bowlby assumes the existence of certain selectively specified psychological differences between infant, child, and adult for which there is no empirical evidence and no logical need.

I do not wish to enter into a discussion of the merits of Bowlby's assumption that the infant shows a mourning reaction following the loss of the love object. This is more or less a matter of semantics. But if we do use the term "mourning," we should remain aware that this is a term reserved in psychoanalysis for a precisely defined dynamic process that has also pathological forms.

When submitting new theories we should not violate the principle of parsimony in science by offering hypotheses which in contrast to existing theory becloud the observational facts, are oversimplified, and make no contribution to the better understanding of observed phenomena (Beck, 1950).

BIBLIOGRAPHY

Beck, L. W. (1950), Constructions and Inferred Entities. In *Readings in the Philosophy of Science*, ed. H. Feigl & M. Brodbeck. New York: Appleton-Century-Crofts, 1953.
Bowlby, J. (1958), The Nature of the Child's Tie to His Mother. *Int. J. Psa.*, XXXIX.
—— (1960), Separation Anxiety, *Int. J. Psa.*, XLI.
Freud, S. (1917), Mourning and Melancholia. *Standard Edition*, XIV. London: Hogarth Press, 1957.
—— (1920), Beyond the Pleasure Principle. *Standard Edition*, XVIII. London: Hogarth Press, 1955.
—— (1923), *The Ego and the Id*. London: Hogarth Press, 1949.
—— (1926), Inhibitions, Symptoms and Anxiety. *Standard Edition*, XX. London: Hogarth Press, 1959.

Hartmann, H. (1950), Comments on the Psychoanalytic Theory of the Ego. *This Annual*, V.
—— & Kris, E., Loewenstein, R. M. (1946), Comments on the Formation of Psychic Structure. *This Annual*, II.
Heinicke, C. M. (1956), Some Effects of Separating Two-Year-Old Children from Their Parents: A Comparative Study. *Human Relations*, IX.
Isakower, O. (1938), A Contribution to the Pathopsychology of Phenomena Associated with Falling Asleep. *Int. J. Psa.*, XIX.
Malrieux, P. (1952), *Les Émotions et la Personnalité de l'Enfant*. Paris: Librairie Philosophique.
—— (1958), L'étude génétique des émotions. *Psych. Franç.*, III.
Robertson, J. (1952), Film: *A Two-Year-Old Goes to Hospital*. London: Tavistock Clinic.
Schaffer, H. R. & Callender, W. M. (1959), Psychological Effects of Hospitalization in Infancy. *Pediatrics*, XXIV.
Spitz, R. A. (1945), Hospitalism: An Inquiry Into the Genesis of Psychiatric Conditions in Early Childhood. *This Annual*, I.
—— (1946), Anaclitic Depression. *This Annual*, II.
—— (1947), Emotional Growth in the First Year. *Child Study*, Spring, 1947.
—— (1948), The Importance of Mother-Child Relationship During the First Year of Life. *Mental Health Today*, VII.
—— (1950), Psychiatric Therapy in Infancy. *Am. J. Orthopsychiat.*, XX.
—— (1953), Aggression: Its Role in the Establishment of Object Relations. In *Drives, Affects, Behavior*, ed. R. M. Loewenstein. New York: International Universities Press.
—— (1954), Genèse des Premières Relations Objectales. *Rev. Franç. Psa.*, XXVIII.
—— (1955), The Primal Cavity. A Contribution to the Genesis of Perception and Its Role for Psychoanalytic Theory. *This Annual*, X.
—— (1957), *No and Yes: On the Genesis of Human Communication*. New York: International Universities Press.
—— & Wolf, K. M. (1946), The Smiling Response: A Contribution to the Ontogenesis of Social Relations. *Genet. Psychol. Mon.*, XXXIV.
Weidemann, J. (1959a), Das Kind im Heim. *Ztschr. Kinderpsychiat.*, XXVI.
—— (1959b), Heimkind und Heimmilieu. *Ztschr. Kinderpsychiat.*, XXVI.

ON ADOLESCENCE[1]

JEANNE LAMPL-DE GROOT, M.D. (Amsterdam)

Adolescence is often regarded as a "stepchild" in psychoanalysis, in a theoretical as well as in a practical sense. A number of analysts consider the treatment of adolescent boys and girls to be very difficult, sometimes even impossible, though in some cases good results have been achieved, especially with inhibited, depressive, and compulsive-neurotic patients.

Many authors stress that our theoretical knowledge of adolescence is incomplete. I shall not review the literature in detail, but refer to the surveys of this subject by Leo Spiegel in 1951 and by Anna Freud in 1958.

Out of the many problems of adolescence, my paper will focus on two points: (1) a practical experience; and (2) some theoretical considerations, especially in connection with the formation of superego and ego ideal.

I

Anna Freud (1958) has reminded us of the fact that "our knowledge of the mental processes of infancy has been derived from reconstructions in the analyses of adults and was merely confirmed and enlarged later on by analyses or observations carried out in childhood." It is Anna Freud's opinion that in the treatment of adult cases one seldom succeeds in reviving their adolescent experiences in full force.

I think most authors will agree with this statement, and I have done so myself. However, a number of years ago two adult patients came to me for analytic treatment, a man and a woman, both in their early thirties, in whose analyses a wealth of adolescent experi-

1 Read before the 21st Congress of the International Psycho-Analytic Association in Copenhagen, July, 1959.

ences, real events as well as fantasies and impulses, came to the fore with remarkable liveliness and were accompanied by strong emotions and impulses. I hasten to add that this re-experiencing only emerged in the later phases of the analyses. In the beginning of treatment the adolescent material was brought forward merely as an account of the patient's life history in the way described by Anna Freud. The most interesting point was that the reliving of affects connected with this material did not become possible until the patient's childhood had been uncovered and reconstructed. Confronted with these observations, I recalled a statement which Freud made to me some thirty years ago. Freud told me about a young woman, who had cooperated well in her analysis and whose childhood development had been fairly well reconstructed—however, without a therapeutic result. Most of the patient's symptoms had persisted until she suddenly and vividly recollected a traumatic experience that had occurred in her fifteenth year of life. After this traumatic situation and all the emotions involved had been worked through, the patient was cured.

My own observations led me to review a number of other cases, and I gained the impression that in some of them the failure or incompleteness of success might have been due to the lack of revival of the adolescent experiences. Of course I now had to ask myself what causes might have been responsible for the fact that in these cases childhood development could be reconstructed without difficulty and re-experienced with full emotional force, whereas the adolescent period remained deprived of a full affective conviction.

From the direct study of adolescent cases we all are familiar with the charged atmosphere in which the adolescent lives, with the intensity and depth of his feelings, the sudden and unexpected mood swings, the strength of his impulses, and the force of anxiety and despair. However, are we really entitled to assume that in small children their feelings, impulses, demands, their unforeseen swings from complete happiness toward deepest sorrow and desperation are less intense than similar phenomena in adolescence?

There is indeed a difference in the demands of the instinctual drives in childhood and in adolescence, because infantile sexuality is different from genitality, which has to become the leading factor in the adolescent and adult love life.

I have the impression, however, that it is not merely the intensity of feelings, impulses, and mood swings but other factors which are more responsible for the difficulties of reviving the adolescent mental processes. These factors seem to be ego and superego development.

The little child's ego, undeveloped as it is, has to rely upon the auxiliary ego borrowed from the mother in order to master outer and inner conflicts. The superego is not yet established as an independent mental agency in infancy. Norms and restrictions are imposed upon the child by the parents. Only in the oedipal phase a structuration of the personality takes place. In latency the child develops into a more or less individual personality, though he is still dependent upon the parents. A wealth of ego capacities is established and matures during this period. In the sphere which is relatively free from conflict, intelligence, knowledge, special talents and abilities are developed, whereas in the conflictual sphere, adaptations, reaction formations, and defense mechanisms gradually become character traits. The superego as an inner institution supervises the latency child's behavior to a large extent.

This brief outline of a child's development is very sketchy and incomplete, but it may suffice as a prelude for our considerations about adolescence.

When in puberty the instinctual drives make their new and intensified demands upon the youngster, they meet with a different personality than they did in childhood. The adolescent ego has many more ways and means of coping with the drives; in a certain sense, we could call this ego stronger. However, on the other hand, it lacks the support of the parents' auxiliary ego because the adolescent turns away from the parents. The loosening of the ties with the parents is a difficult and protracted process, often accompanied by genuine mourning, as Root (1957) and Anna Freud (1958) have pointed out. In this respect, the adolescent ego presents itself as much weaker than the child's ego. A similar process is going on with the superego. On the one hand the adolescent superego is now established as an inner conscience, on the other hand it is shaken in its foundation by the very process of turning away from the parents and the parental norms and morals. The adolescent has to rely upon his own superego. The adult, looking back upon his life history, feels more responsible for his adolescent than for his infantile behavior; he feels more guilty and more ashamed about his adolescent conflicts, disharmonies, and oddities. As he usually remembers the factual events of adolescence, he tries to escape the revival of the accompanying guilt- and shame-burdened emotions, either by suppressing and denying every emotion of that period or by retreating to infantile experiences.

This is precisely what we often observe in analytic treatment. The patient brings us a wealth of infantile material, more and more, in different forms and associations, even when the childhood history has already been fairly well reconstructed and re-experienced. He clings tenaciously to infantile material; yet when we look at this material closely we realize that adolescent features have entered into the picture. The patient has used the infantile material in order to ward off adolescent experiences. The analyst then must analyze the defensive character of, and the underlying anxiety in regard to, this material and confront the patient with his adolescent feelings of shame, guilt, hurt pride, etc. In a number of cases the result will be a real revival of the patient's adolescence in full force.

In trying to accomplish this task we meet with difficulties, not exclusively due to the patient's reluctance to face his own adolescent problems, his unbalanced behavior, his extreme feelings, his extravagant emotions, and his oddities. We also have to cope with the analyst's reactions to it. The analyst is prepared to meet with the patient's acting out in the transference. When the patient transfers impulses upon the analyst from his childhood period and in an infantile form, it is much easier for the latter to keep to his attitude of friendly understanding and neutrality. The adolescent has made use of all of his intelligence, capacities, and special gifts to ward off his intolerable impulses, his disappointments, and his conflicts. This is especially true in connection with his hostility toward parents, and toward adults in general. Hence, in encouraging an adult patient to relive his adolescent experiences, the analyst must cope with a refined form of the patient's aggression.

One can smile at a little child's direct form of aggressive behavior, but an adolescent's aggression is clothed in a much more irritating, tormenting, and sometimes nearly intolerable shape. It might happen that the analyst, being a human creature himself, is (unconsciously) inclined to follow the patient in his flight toward infancy in order to escape the patient's refined criticisms, reproaches, and hostile demands. In every adult, traits not only from the little child but also from the adolescent persist. This is especially true for our patients. They tend to excuse themselves for their accusations and tormenting attacks in taking for granted that the analyst is an omnipotent and therefore invulnerable person. The interplay between the patient's anxiety to relive his adolescent emotions and conflicts and the analyst's unconscious shyness to bear the adolescent forms of aggression might be one of the causes of the difficulties we encounter in analyzing and working through an adult patient's adolescence.

II

I now come to my second point: some theoretical considerations, which, I hope, will contribute to our understanding of the practical difficulties just mentioned as well as of the adolescent psychic life in general. In the scope of this presentation I can only throw light upon a few points. My assumptions are based partly on material gained in the treatment of adolescents, mainly, however, on reconstruction of adolescent experiences in adult cases.

A youngster's ego can react in an infinite variety of ways to the newly flourishing demands of his instinctual drives and to the newly arising social demands which are so different from those made upon the little child. The adolescent has on the one hand the ardent wish to be grown up because he usually imagines adults to be free, independent, and self-supporting, and he tries to use all his faculties in order to equal or even to better them. On the other hand, however, he wants to remain a little child, in order not to have to relinquish his infantile ties with the parental objects. It is very well known how difficult a task this is. Having lost a beloved person or even having renounced the love of a still existing object is followed by a certain amount of "work of mourning" ("*Trauerarbeit*") (see Anna Freud, 1958). Whether the outcome of the mourning process will be a relatively normal or a pathological one depends upon a wealth of factors, among them upon the amount of aggression originally directed toward the parents. We know that the little child holds the parents responsible for his distress and losses, and he responds to all sorts of pain with hatred and death wishes toward his parents. When in puberty the infantile object relationships are revived, the adolescent begins to react in a similar way. The more intense his archaic hostility was, the more difficulties he will have in dealing with his death wishes. The mourning processes are colored by the aggression turned inward. The result may be a depressive neurotic disorder, psychotic reactions, acting out or antisocial behavior, or a combination of these various disturbances. Many authors have described several outcomes in clinical and theoretical papers.

I shall now turn to another problem of adolescence which is very different from childhood processes and nevertheless very closely dependent upon them. I mean the superego problems. I have already mentioned that in adolescence the superego has become an inner agency, whereas in early childhood behavior was directed by the parents' demands, prohibitions, and morals. The little child cooperates with them mainly in order to avoid loss of love or punishment. Only gradually does he internalize the parental norms, which subsequently become the content of the superego. Now in adolescence he must give up his old incestuous ties to the parents—a process partly equivalent to losing the love object. But in addition he must also give up a fundamental part of his superego content—that part of the restrictions, norms, and ideals which, though internalized, are still closely linked to the incestuous object. But the very fact that these superego contents are internalized implies that the adolescent must give up something that is essentially a part of his self. To turn away from a love object is a hard and painful process; to disengage oneself from a part of one's own personality is still more difficult to achieve.

In order to examine these events more closely I propose once more to distinguish between the superego in a narrower sense as the restricting and prohibiting instance and the ego ideal as comprising norms, ethics, ideals. I have made this distinction in previous papers and it has, in my opinion, some advantages. The compliance with parental restrictions and prohibitions requires renunciation of direct pleasure, but this compliance is rewarded with love and approval from the side of the parents. The formation of ideals, however, has an additional function and has already been on the way long before parental restrictions have become internal demands. The little child idealizes the parents and conceives of them as perfect, omnipotent creatures. He clings tenaciously to these ideas because he feels himself so extremely powerless. The introjection of the almighty and faultless parental images is a compensation for the feelings of helplessness; it begins in very early childhood and is a narcissistic satisfaction *par excellence*. These introjected images give rise to fantasies of grandeur and omnipotence, which in the magic phase of development are among the fundamentals of the child's self-esteem and self-maintenance. It is well known that part of the feelings of grandeur continue to exist, though unconsciously, throughout life.

The adolescent must bear not only the pain of losing love objects, of coping with the attending mourning, and of revising old patterns of restriction and prohibition. In addition to all these hard tasks, he must endure the narcissistic injuries caused by his self-esteem being shaken in its fundamentals and therefore more or less lost. We know too well that a certain amount of narcissistic cathexis of the personality is indispensable for a healthy development. When the basis of the ideal formation has gone to pieces, the youngster is utterly helpless. I hasten to add that the loss of love is of course partly felt as a narcissistic injury as well. The finding of a new love object raises the person's self-esteem, too. However, it seems to make a considerable difference when an essential part of the ego (ego ideal) is damaged or lost and has to be newly built up. New love objects are relatively easily found in adolescence in teachers, leaders, companions, etc. New ideals that compensate for the essential helplessness of human beings are more difficult to acquire (at least in our civilization). The youngster very well knows, and feels, that adults are not omnipotent but vulnerable creatures. We find a confirmation of this assumption in studying those adolescents who do not respond to offers of love and guidance from a new object (relative, teacher, therapist, companion, etc.). These youngsters could not overcome the depth of their inner narcissistic injuries; consequently they are indifferent to supplies of love from the outer world. It is possible that a number of strange reactions, of unexpected attitudes and unpredictable mood swings are due to this basic disturbance in the economy of narcissistic libido and the ego's failure to restore it. Moreover, it is just the narcissistic injuries that are pre-eminently apt to give rise to aggression, and this hostility in its turn diminishes a person's susceptibility to another person's loving assistance or the offer of new ideals and norms.

In the transference during treatment we can observe that a patient's deep and refined hostility, severe criticisms of the analyst, reproaches that the analyst is impotent and worthless go side by side with an unconscious, archaic conviction of the analyst's omnipotence. The ideal image of almighty parents and analysts not only is indispensable for the youngster's maintenance of narcissistic cathexis, but it is secondarily used in order to diminish the guilt feelings aroused by precisely this same hostile and aggressive behavior. It is as if the youngster says to himself: "Parents and analyst are omnipotent, consequently they are invulnerable; so I can scold, torment, and act out every aggression without having to feel guilty or reproach myself."

It would be tempting to illustrate these assumptions with detailed analytic material. However, in this paper, I merely wanted to emphasize the importance of the problems around the ego ideal in adolescence. The adolescent's clinging to the very archaic, idealized parental images makes it so difficult for him to cope with the narcissistic injuries occasioned by the necessity of having to give them up and finding new ideals in a more reality-adapted form. Furthermore, they need to hold on to this idealized picture because it also serves as a defense against guilt and shame engendered by the intense hostility.

When many analysts agree that adolescent patients are often not suitable for analytic treatment, we must, in our attempts to understand adolescent psychology, rely mainly on observations and reconstructions of adolescence in adult cases. But even these reconstructions, as has been pointed out, are extremely difficult to achieve. This paper has endeavored to investigate some of the obstacles in the way of such reconstruction and to indicate means of overcoming them.

I believe that we might be successful in reviving adolescence in a number of cases if we make an effort to overcome our own resistance against the patient's adolescent forms of aggression, if we focus our and the patient's attention upon his hidden ideals and fantasies of omnipotence attributed to his parents and later on internalized, and if we support the patient in enduring his narcissistic hurts and in giving up the defensive character of his archaic ideal. I believe that this effort is worth while.

BIBLIOGRAPHY

Freud, A. (1958), Adolescence. *This Annual*, XIII.
Root, N. N. (1957), A Neurosis in Adolescence. *This Annual*, XII.
Spiegel, L. A. (1951), A Review of Contributions to a Psychoanalytic Theory of Adolescence: Individual Aspects. *This Annual*, VI.

INTRAUTERINE AND EARLY INFANTILE MOTILITY[1]

BELA MITTELMANN, M.D. (New York)[2]

In previous communications (1954, 1958), I have advanced the thesis that there is a period in infantile development in which motility predominates both as an urge and source of pleasure and as a form of reality testing and integration. This period is ushered in by the development of locomotion; the psychological characteristics and pathological implications of this phase are closely connected with various aspects of motility as the dominant function.

In this communication I will focus on motility development and its psychological corollaries in the period of intrauterine life and the first year of life.

The constructions to be presented, while all based on observations, range from reasonable assumptions through extrapolations to conclusions supported by an impressive array of data. Thus their convincing value varies; e.g., the assumption that the infant's gazing at his hands held aloft at three months of age is connected with development of self-image is more convincing than the assumption that the fetus is rhythmically being moved by the mother's movements, which thus contribute to the infant's rocking at six or seven months of age.

INTRAUTERINE MOTILITY

It is a moot question to what extent, if at all, one may speak of a psychological significance of any intrauterine happening. One possibility is that intrauterine events are physiological antecedents of later happenings, leaving traces that in some way are equivalents of

[1] Supported in part by a research grant (M-2069) from the National Institute of Mental Health, Public Health Service.
[2] From Albert Einstein College of Medicine, Yeshiva University, New York.

later memory traces, but which, of course, cannot be recovered in conscious form. Another way of saying this is that the intrauterine events have aspects of "conditionings" or "learning."

Passive Intrauterine Motility

By "passive motility" is meant being moved or being held in a given posture. "Active" and "passive" motility often appear in combination, e.g., during the earlier months the fetus initiates a movement and then is passively carried by inertia.

Intrauterine passive motility has two aspects. (1) Intrauterine posture is, as is generally known, characterized by flexion in all joints. This position is of course imposed on the infant, but the traces it leaves are clearly visible in postnatal life in which the infant has a tendency to resume the intrauterine position. This is effected by the relative functional shortening and lengthening of the respective muscles and by the conditioning through afferent impulses in the joint and muscle nerves. (2) The other form of passive posture is experienced through the muscle and the joint sense, whereas being moved is probably experienced through the labyrinth and, to a lesser extent, through the skin.

All aspects of intrauterine motility are affected by the mother: the rhythmic passive motility by the nature and frequency of her movements; the posture by the relative ampleness of her uterus and amniotic fluid, and, to anticipate, the active movements by the fetus's reactions to the stimuli furnished by the mother. Thus the fetus may be influenced by the mother's temperament and, possibly, neurosis.

Intrauterine posture becomes equated with a passive, blissful state of being taken care of by a benevolent power, and is related to the fantasy of return to the womb.

The experience of being moved rhythmically is the precursor of rhythmic experience in infancy, and will carry the connotation of being soothed and being cared for by a superior benevolent force, which the infant for some time cannot possibly distinguish from himself. The rhythmic experience, in addition to remaining passive, becomes also active in infancy, as in rocking, and acquires a variety of psychological connotations to be discussed later.

The most obvious pathological manifestation that can be linked up with intrauterine motility is the regressive recurrence of the fetal posture, seen at times in catatonic schizophrenics. A tendency to resume the intrauterine posture appears in many normals and may be accentuated in some psychoneurotics. A brief illustration follows.

A thirty-five-year-old male patient whose main symptom was fatigue ("neurasthenia") stated in the course of his analysis that his almost exclusive sleeping position was on the side, in the intrauterine position. He suffered from insomnia, at times having difficulty falling or staying asleep. He needed ten hours of sleep to feel completely rested. He felt this "intrauterine" position definitely pleasurable, showing thus postural muscle erotism. His emotional life was characterized by a severe conflict between activity and self-assertion on the one hand, and passivity, a tendency to lean on a powerful person on the other, with an undercurrent of unconscious passive homosexuality. He suffered from an intense masturbation conflict with severe guilt during adolescence.

As this example illustrates, the regressive symptom has multiple meanings (passivity, withdrawal, autoerotism) and is part of a complex psychopathology.

Active Intrauterine Motility

"Quickening" usually occurs about the fourth or fifth month of pregnancy. The movements may involve the whole body, the limbs or mainly the torso and head. For several months after their beginning the movements are rather free, e.g., the infant may change from breech to occipital presentation. During the latter months the uterus restricts the movements of the now larger fetus and the movements are more limited. The movements seem to occur largely spontaneously, e.g., while the mother is lying motionless on her back; but they can also be elicited "reflexly," e.g., by the pressure of a stethoscope. In general, multiparas perceive movements earlier and better than primiparas. But it is to be noted that apart from this, the amount of movement reported by the mother varies with the fetus. One may say that the amount of activity, the intensity of the motor urge, differs with the individual fetus.

The spontaneous intrauterine activity is the precursor of postpartum random movements, and the reactive intrauterine activity is the precursor of later attempts to cope with stimuli.

In general, one may differentiate between adaptive and nonadaptive motility (Gesell) or between movement and goal-directed activity (Freud). Nonadaptive motility dominates intrauterine life and the first six months of postpartum life. (Some goal-directed activity is often present *in utero* in the form of hand-mouth movement obviously in connection with sucking. The proof of this is that the hand moves to the mouth in many infants soon after birth.)

The circumstances of movement in the fifth, sixth, and seventh months are unique in that gravity in the amniotic fluid is negligible and space is relatively ample. Whether the fetus's nervous system is sufficiently developed for this experience to leave any traces, along with the subsequent restriction during the eighth and ninth months, is questionable. This prenatal sequence of freedom of movement superseded by restriction would be the precursor of two later similar sequences: (1) If the infant is allowed free motility during the first eight months of life, he begins to react with rage and anxiety to restraint usually during the ninth month. (2) Even after this period, he retains his inner freedom of motility, but at about one year of age, he begins to manifest inner restriction of movement (inhibition) in response to parental taboos. As was discussed in connection with intrauterine posture, the intrauterine restriction, at least once it is established, is "satisfying" to the fetus.

Motility is the first one of the "urges" to make its appearance genetically, although orality and vision will predominate over it during the first year of postnatal life.[3] The tendency to total body musculature reaction characteristic of intrauterine movements will persist during the first year of life and will recur later in strong affective and instinctual situations.

PASSIVE MOTILITY DURING THE FIRST YEAR OF LIFE

Being Moved

The soothing aspect of being carried or rocked is characteristic of the first six months of postnatal life. The movements had their intrauterine precursors and will persist in some form, often with an active component, e.g., the rocking chair, throughout life. These movements have the connotation of being looked after by a benevo-

[3] It is clear on direct observation that "looking" and later "moving"—considered primary ego functions (Hartmann, 1939, 1952)—have the attributes of absorption, drivenness, and pleasure for the infant and toddler. Hence, they are referred to here as "urges." The bearing of this on instinct theory and "neutralized energy" will be discussed in a future publication.

lent power, as yet not differentiated from the infant; therefore the experience may also have an omnipotent, autoerotic quality. After the first few months these passive movements contribute to the differentiation between the self and the environment. In later years conflicts over dependency, submission, and autoerotism, along with fear of the superior power (parents), may contribute to a reaction against such rhythmic experiences, as in motion sickness.

Some mothers and many fathers playfully move infants with rhythmic vigor, starting about the sixth month. The infant reacts to this with pleasure, tinged with anxiety. "Dropping" and "tossing" elicit similar responses. This is the precursor of later normal and pathological utilization of anxiety for pleasure.

The other aspect of passive motility in infancy is the limbs being moved. This is part of the daily care and is fused with the stimulation of the skin and of the erotogenic zones, particularly the anal and genital regions in the process of cleaning (Freud, 1905). These aspects equate this type of passive motility with being taken care of, and with obtaining relief from discomfort. They further make these experiences precursors of erotic stimulation by the object, with attendant fantasies.

A common form of contact of the mother with the smiling, kicking baby is her moving of the infant's limbs. These passive movements acquire the connotation of joyous contact with the early object. Being carried and being held in the arm represent being loved and cared for and are ego-syntonic, regressive elements in adult love-making. Pathologically, this need may predominate to the exclusion of genital contact because of excessive fear of genital injury.

Postural Passivity

There are considerable cultural differences in regard to postural passivity, depending upon the prevailing practices of infant care. If the infant is swaddled or carried on the mother's back or the cradle board is used, the respective passive posture has a similar significance as in intrauterine life. Infants reared with such methods develop motorically somewhat more slowly than infants reared with greater motor freedom. Yet if they have adequate physical and emotional care, they quickly catch up once motor freedom is provided. Nevertheless, we may assume that the prolonged continuation of the intrauterine type of restriction leaves an increased tendency toward passivity, longing for care, and readiness for submission.

The customary position of the infant with free motility, whether supine, prone, or on the side, depends upon the mother's preference and is at times identical with the mother's favorite sleeping position. This can be impressive, e.g., if the mother favors the prone position. When the infant is uncomfortable on his back, getting into the prone position requires being moved. Here again, passive motility becomes equated with relief from distress. Lying prone is a distinctly infantile posture, but may, as in the mother mentioned above, continue into adulthood.

In the foregoing, the feeling of dependency and the sense of being taken care of were connected with various forms of passive motility. Equally relevant is the fact that, apart from temporary gratification through autoerotic activity, the infant can get relief only through the mother's intervention. Thus the limitation of the infant's active motility and someone else's "unlimited" motility underlies the infant's experience of motor dependence and feeling of care. This is vaguely fused with the infant's concept of his own and of the parents' omnipotence. However, passive motility acquires also a hostile (directed against the infant) meaning either when the mother does not bring relief, or when the infant is subject to an impersonal force, i.e., gravity, when he falls. Sudden loss of support is one of the standard ways of eliciting the startle response in the newborn. In the infant's daily experience, however, actual, though passive falling starts to occur when he begins to sit up. One may conclude that passive motility contributes to the image of the "good" and "bad" mother or to the antecedents of ambivalence, and to the later fear of passive, motor-aggressive retribution.

Active Motility in Infancy[4]

Complex Reflex Reactions

The two characteristic reflexes are the grasp reflex and the startle pattern. By grasp is meant automatic grasping if a small object, e.g.,

---

[4] Reflex, random, and nonadaptive motility together with the initial forms of motility aiming at gratification of instinctual urges may be called primary-process motility. All forms of voluntary adaptive motility, including the learned aspects of behavior aiming at instinctual gratification, may be called secondary-process motility.

a finger, is put into the infant's palm. This is present at birth and continues up to the age of six months. The startle pattern is likewise present at birth and occurs in response to sudden loss of support or to a loud noise. The arms are abducted suddenly, frequently with a secondary abduction and flexion at the elbow. Neither of these reflexes has any adaptive value in the human infant. The adaptive value of the grasp reflex can phylogenetically be seen in the clinging of monkeys to the furry mother. The startle pattern is suggestive of an attempt to break a fall by contact with some object.

The grasp reflex is the precursor of later voluntary grasping. It is thus the antecedent of the later handling of objects, which is an avenue of reality testing, and is a security measure in anxiety. It is also the antecedent of the embracing movement appearing about the middle of the first year which turns into clinging in anxiety. Clinging is object directed, whereas grasp is often self-directed. The infant may grasp the erect penis beginning with about the sixth month of life. (Frictional masturbation usually does not occur until the second year of life.) Some infants grasp the nonerect penis beginning with the ninth month in states of frustration. This represents a double form of reassurance: the experience of grasping as well as the sensations coming from the penis.

Some form of the startle pattern is retained throughout life, although the character of it is different from the infantile pattern: a sudden patterned contraction of all muscles of the body (Landis and Hunt, 1939). The startle reaction may increase in any anxiety state, but it is particularly characteristic of traumatic neurosis (here usually in response to sudden noises—one characteristic eliciting stimulus of startle in the infant). This represents a regression to the infantile reactiveness also in the sense that the vulnerable ego is being flooded by excessive stimuli in the infantile startle reaction as in the traumatic neurosis.

Random Movements

"Random" movements are movements particularly of the limbs and, to a lesser extent, of the head and the torso, which do not serve any apparent purpose and do not follow a clearly discernible sustained pattern. Like their intrauterine antecedent, they are a manifestation of a motor urge and seem pleasurable. With the infant's development, random movements are crowded out by shifting patterns, e.g., turning the head to look, manipulating an object, engaging in expressive movements. Random movements are among the precursors of the tendency to "discharge" tension through diffuse motor activity.

Expressive Movements

Expressive movements referred to here are changes in the state of the skeletal muscles during varieties of pleasure and displeasure. The following statements can be made about the expressive patterns.

a. Expressive movements show maturational changes. The crying pattern is present at birth and it is characterized, apart from facial expression and vocalization, by windmill movements of the upper extremities, and by sudden alternate or symmetrical rhythmic pulling up of the lower extremities. This pattern will be discussed again in the section on aggression. The smiling pattern appears at about the third month and is characterized by a variety of motor patterns such as bicycle movement of the lower extremities and a characteristic position of the upper extremities such as bending the elbows and raising the hands somewhat. It should be added that the total smiling motor pattern and, after the third month, the crying pattern show considerable individual variations. Although in the individual infant it is usually possible to differentiate, at least in movies, the crying motor pattern from the smiling pattern, there is a considerable overlap between the two, e.g., extension of the extremities may occur in both. Beginning with about the tenth month, waving the hand, reaching for, or withdrawing from the stimulus, and jumping up and down become predominant.

b. If the stimulus is sustained long enough, expressive movements represent the liveliest activities of the infant up to about ten months when locomotion (crawling) and manipulation of objects take over. The expressive motor responses represent neuromuscular patterns, semi-reflex in character, or, in the ethologists' terminology, "innate releasing mechanisms," and can be very pleasurable. In addition, they have great interpersonal significance in that they spontaneously affect the mother. Further, the infant learns that his crying and moving leads to appropriate action by the mother, and his smiling and kicking elicit a pleased response in her.

c. Affectomotor patterns, while not intentionally serving this purpose, seem to be precursors of more adaptive forms of coping with stimuli: the windmill movements of the crying infant are the precursors of pushing away the noxious stimulus. The sudden pulling up of the extremities represents pulling away from the stimulus. The affectomotor arm position, after three months of age, occurring both in smiling and in crying, seems preparatory to dealing with the stimulus positively or negatively. The bicycle movement of the lower extremities during smiling represents a response to the stimulus by recurring contact. The extension during crying represents a pushing away of the stimulus; during smiling an attempt at closer contact with the stimulus. Where extension as a pattern predominates, usually around the seventh month, one can frequently observe the infant in a "swan-dive" position. This certainly does not get the infant closer to the agreeable stimulus or farther away from the disagreeable stimulus. It looks more like a phylogenetic phase suggesting swimming, with the possibility of either moving toward or away from the stimulus.

These early expressive patterns are the precursors of later expressive movements, i.e., gestures. An excessive amount of the latter represents a tendency toward infantile type of motor discharge. Infantile types of expressive movements largely subside during the second through fourth years of life. They may persist or reappear, however, particularly the jumping up and down with hand flapping under certain circumstances and in certain types of pathology. These will be discussed together with the autoerotic movements to which they are closely related.

Anxiety is clearly distinguishable as a separate affect about the eighth to tenth month, e.g., in response to a stranger. If locomotion has already developed, the infant crawls or toddles to the mother, and then there is immobilization of the body with intensive staring. If the way between the infant and the mother is barred, the infant becomes immobilized and the affect of anxiety seems to merge into panic with an element of depression while he turns away from the stranger. This immobilization in anxiety is the antecedent of later nightmares of "being rooted to the ground."

Autoerotic Movements

Autoerotic movements such as rocking, bouncing or jumping up and down appear in three or four out of ten physically and emotionally well-cared-for infants. They may rock so hard on being put to bed or after waking that the crib gets propelled across the room. In a lesser and more fleeting form, such movements are observable in another four out of ten infants, making a total of about 80 per cent (Mittelmann, Malkenson and Munroe, 1959). Of course, the infants must have reached a certain level of motor development before these patterns can be manifest. For example, jumping up and down requires the infant to be able to stand and propel himself into the air. These autoerotic movements merge with some of the expressive patterns in that the former may occur fleetingly in joy and the latter may become secondary sources of motor pleasure. While potentially nearly all infants may manifest autoerotic movements, e.g., in institutions, the ease and intensity of occurrence have a strong constitutional determinant. These movements usually disappear between the ages of a year and a half and three. They may reappear during excitement combined with sustained tension, even in seven- or eight-year-olds or in adults. When their team wins the World Series, the fans may jump up and down. These movements are important manifestations of the motor urge and forms of motor pleasure. While these patterns represent predominantly active motility, they contain passive motor pleasure also. Thus rocking on hands and knees has a slow (forward) and a fast (backward) component. The child actively starts the vigorous backward movement and lets his body (the buttocks) slam against his heels. In jumping up and down the passive element is obvious. Both the rhythmic and the passive aspect are a continuation of the experience of being rhythmically moved in the uterus and in the cradle.

In these movements motor pleasure is primary, but secondary anal and genital sensations or actual excitement are elicited. Vigorous and sustained rocking may lead to erection. Some of these patterns become incorporated into adult intercourse movements. This applies particularly to the expressive or motor autoerotic movement consisting of rapid pelvic thrusts against the surface in a prone infant. As previously mentioned, institutionalized infants show these autoerotic motor patterns frequently and in a sustained and vigorous manner. This is due to an accent on motor autoerotism in the absence of adequate interpersonal contact and limitation of manipulative motor activity in the crib. It may be added that at least certain forms of head banging may occur in well-cared-for infants. Usually this is the same movement as rocking, but with the fast component forward so that the head (instead of the buttocks) gets slammed against a hard surface. This may not be pathological to begin with, but even then it facilitates a masochistic development. Other times head banging clearly represents masochistic motor autoerotism with aggression directed simultaneously toward a substitute inanimate object and the self.

The expressive and the autoerotic infantile rhythmic movements along with diffuse motor discharge may appear in the course of the treatment of neurotic children, e.g., during anger over frustration, rejection and sexual excitement. They may be retained and narcissistically elaborated in severely neurotic, borderline, blind and schizophrenic children. About 80 per cent of the last two show some form of it, at least up to the age of eleven. These movements in the male infant may causatively contribute to the development of foot fetishism, both via interest in the feet and through the kinesthetic sensations produced in the feet in the process of jumping up and down.

Adaptive Motility

Adaptive motility comprises: (a) active posture, (b) manipulation, (c) active locomotion. It is the sudden spurt in these three functions, particularly locomotion, that ushers in the period of development to which one may refer as the motor phase of ego and libido organization (Mittelmann, 1954, 1958). Characteristic of this motor period, starting with the second year, are dominance of motor urge, motor pleasure, motor communication, increase in self-assertion, independence and self-esteem, motor reality testing, motor aggression, and fear of passive motor-aggressive retribution. It should be mentioned here that a degree of object relations seems indispensable for adequate adaptive motor development. For details of this development the reader is referred to Gesell's publication (1941).

Posture and manipulation show progress within the early months, e.g., ability to raise the head and to reach for an object. Locomotion, while it has early antecedent patterns in the form of alternate leg movements, for practical purposes makes its first appearance about the tenth month in the form of crawling, and really becomes dominant after one year, with walking. Manipulation of objects contributes to reality testing and to the ability to differentiate between the self and nonself as well as to mastery and thus to the feeling of independence, self-esteem, and self-assertion. The development of posture likewise contributes to reality testing and to the differentiation of the "I" and "not-I," because with the change of posture the infant perceives different aspects and connections of the identical environment. Furthermore, the sitting or the erect posture facilitates the manipulation and the mastery of objects. All three functions have important effects on the relationship with the parents because of parental help and participation needed in the early execution of adaptive motor tasks. In addition, with the development of locomotion, the infant now can get to the parents for affection or protection, or can get away from them in pursuit of his own goals which, because of improved postural and manipulative ability, he now can reach better.

Posture has some additional connotations. Lying down is equated in later periods with being taken care of, being fed, but also with being powerless and dead. In a previous publication (1954) I mentioned that children for several years usually lie down horizontally when they are given bottles, as is customary now even until the age of three or four. Further, the illustration was given of a dream of an adult in which the ability to sit up was equated with survival, acquiring the same significance for survival as being fed. Stating it in another way, the inability to sit up was equated with starving to death. Inability to sit up becomes also equated with being forced to lie down, about the eighth to tenth month, when many infants become both anxious and resentful when they are put into the supine position or are restricted in their free motility. This statement also illustrates the fact that with the development of motility new anxieties appear. Thus, after the infant learns to climb up steps in the eleventh or twelfth month, the task of climbing down evokes a fear of falling and the infant bursts into tears. This fear persists throughout life and may undergo pathological intensification and symbolic

elaboration, as in nightmares, or further combined with motor failure, plea of helplessness, and aggression directed toward the self
may lead to hysterical astasia-abasia. The uncertainty of the toddler's
footing in the powerful, at times threatening adult world may appear
as an expression of anxiety in the dream of the adult. This, together
with other infantile active (e.g., whirling) and passive retributive
and symbolic motor phenomena is illustrated in Descartes' repetitive
dream:

> Descartes tells us that, on November 10, 1619, having re-
> turned to rest full of enthusiasm and entirely taken up with the
> thought of having discovered the foundations of a science so
> marvelous, he had in a single night three consecutive dreams
> which he imagined could only have come from on high. After he
> had fallen asleep, his imagination was strongly impressed with
> certain phantoms which appeared before him and terrified him
> in such wise that, while walking, as he fancied, through the
> streets, he was obliged to turn himself over to his left side so as
> to be able to advance to the place where he wished to go, feeling,
> as he did, a great weakness in his right side which disabled him
> from leaning on it. Ashamed of walking in that manner, he made
> an effort to straighten himself, but felt an impetuous wind which,
> catching him up in a kind of whirlwind, made him revolve three
> or four times on his left foot. But what really frightened him was
> something more; the difficulty he had in dragging himself along
> made him think he was falling at every step . . . He tried to reach
> the church of the college, . . . he was flung violently against the
> church by the wind . . . those who were gathering round him for
> conversations stood on their feet straight and steady, whereas he
> himself on this same ground was still bowed and staggering
> [Lewin, 1958].

The natural infantile tendency to stumble and fall, to handle
dangerous objects and to overestimate one's own strength, combined
with aggression directed toward the self may later result in accident
proneness.

The fear of lying down may appear as a result of anxiety in
analysis where the respective motivations include the fear of being
totally overwhelmed and genitally attacked in a helpless position.
This fear may be reinforced by the fear of abandonment, again on
the infantile pattern, when lying down may have meant loss of the
object because of lack of visual contact. Fear and rage in connection

with restraint and forced supine position will increase during the motor phase of development and, in the case of excessive traumatization, may contribute later to neurotic or psychotic development.

Motility in Relation to Vision, Touch, and Equilibrium

The connection between motility and vision has five aspects: (a) total body musculature reaction in response to vision; (b) following objects with the eyes and turning the head; (c) eye-hand coordination; (d) gazing at one's own body with simultaneous active position or manipulation; and (e) orientation and motility in space, guided by vision.

Following objects with the eyes and head is the beginning of the organization of motility under the guidance of vision, so characteristic of seeing people. The absence of this guidance and the reliance on tactile and auditory clues, together with the attendant anxious caution, make the motility of blind people appear less integrated.

Eye-hand coordination and orientation in space contribute to reality testing, development of concepts of self and not-self, and a more independent self-image. The other two aspects will be discussed in greater detail. While the phenomenon appears earlier in a transitory manner, by the end of the first month the infant fixes his gaze on the human face and simultaneously there is "inactivation," i.e., cessation of random movements. This "inactivation" on looking at the human face is present through the first year of life as a response preceding activity. It may be mentioned here that gazing at his hands held aloft (often with slow finger movements), and at objects is a very absorbing activity for the infant. The looking at the hands combined with their being held actively in position contributes to the development of the body image and its differentiation from the environment. This is furthered by a common activity of the sixteen-week-old infant: he holds his hands together on his chest playing with his fingers. This combines active motility with a double sensation of touch.

The interest in looking in conjunction with "inactivation" is the precursor of the general interest in looking and being looked at. Thus, there is a motor element in this process. The absorbed gazing at the hands is a further phase in this development. An equally absorbed, but more complicated, preoccupation is the infant's tendency at about six or seven months of age of holding on to his feet with his hand, possibly putting his big toe into his mouth and sucking on it, while also looking at his feet. This activity occurs during the period when many infants have a tendency to hold their legs up, bent at the hip joint about 90 degrees. They also engage in manipulative exploration of the lower abdomen, the inguinal region, the knees and the feet. This is the period when most male infants discover and manipulate the unexcited genitals, both the scrotum and the penis. This gazing also contributes to the evaluation of the concept of the self, particularly the body image. They also illustrate that the initial self is a part self, the same way as the initial object is a part object (Klein, 1932; Mittelmann, 1955).

All of the visuomotor phenomena mentioned contribute to the development of voyeurism and exhibitionism. Further, these phenomena are among the precursors of hysterical displacement from the genital to the feet, because the feet are explored, discovered, and invested with interest at the same period of development as the inguinal and genital regions. Both of these represent the normal precursors of the later development of foot fetishism. Displacement from below upward, i.e., to the hands, prepared at an earlier period, likewise takes place at this time. The inactivation on looking at the adult's face, the staring at the hands and feet, the interest in looking and being looked at, combined with intense staring and immobilization in anxiety, mentioned earlier, form the precursors of the kind of anxiety that is revealed in the Wolf Man's dream. There, the Wolf Man is lying motionless; suddenly the window opens and six wolves sitting on a tree gaze at him intently, obviously with him gazing at them too.

> The only piece of action in the dream was the opening of the window; for the wolves sat quite still and without making any movement on the branches of the tree, to the right and left of the trunk, and looked at me. It seemed as though they had riveted their whole attention upon me (Freud, 1918).

The device of expression by the opposite, which Freud assumes in the interpretation, to the effect that immobility really means violent movement (primal scene) is also forecast in infancy. It is not an uncommon observation that if the infant comes to grief as a result of vigorous activity, e.g., harmless falling while crawling upstairs, a well-developed function, e.g., crawling, may become inhibited for a few days or weeks. Thus expression by the opposite may have as a background the feeling of punitive retribution.

The labyrinth, while regulating adaptive motility, plays perhaps an even greater role in passive motility, or in active-passive motility. The occurrence of the startle pattern with the loss of support; the loss of equilibrium in falling from the sitting or standing posture; and the combined pleasure and anxiety when the infant is being swung, "dropped," or "tossed" have been mentioned. They are among the precursors of the fear of motor retribution, resulting from the toddler's motor aggression. These experiences become elaborated in such amusements as rides in the roller coaster; and in the case of sexual, aggressive, and hostility conflicts, the anxiety may be expressed and the problem neurotically solved in such pathological states as psychogenic dizziness.

MANIPULATIVE MOTILITY SUBSERVING LIBIDINAL GOALS

As pointed out in a previous article (1954), there is a striped muscle aspect to all libidinal activities (e.g., the mouth muscles) and the gratification is a combination of motor pleasure, the sensations from the mucous membrane and skin, and autonomic responses. This aspect of motility is not discussed here, although there are skeletal muscles involved, with learning, in the process.

Oral Motility

The most important of these is the mouth-hand coordination which for a long time manifests itself only in finger or hand sucking, and only at later periods, at about four months and thereafter, in carrying objects to the mouth. Infants differ with respect to their hand-mouth behavior. Some are "born with the hand in their mouths," i.e., they put their hands into their mouths soon after birth, indicating that they must have done the same *in utero*. Others do this later. There is always a maturational improvement in the function (Hoffer, 1949) on the basis of a more complex neuromuscular organization several months later.

It would be tempting to consider all the motility during most of the first year of life oral motility, particularly if one considered vision essentially "oral" in the sense of the infant's wanting to incorporate objects via the eyes, and the affectomotor responses and crying and smiling "oral," because of the facial expression and vocalization. This approach is too one-sided. First, motility is present in some form *in utero* when oral activity could hardly be considered dominant; secondly, infantile expressive movements are not oriented toward the mouth. Thirdly, long periods of the infant's gazing at his hands instead of carrying them to his mouth speak against such an interpretation of both vision and motility. Nevertheless, the oral aspect of motility is very significant during the first year of life.

Any mouth function has varying degrees of passive and active aspects. Things arriving at the mouth (by the mother's efforts) lead to a passive receptive experience. In so far as the infant tastes, sucks, bites, chews, swallows, the mouth is active. One of the first postnatal activities on the part of the rest of the body subserving oral needs is "rooting behavior," i.e., searching for the orally need-gratifying object with rhythmic head movements. This involves the neck muscles. Spitz (1957) assumes that the horizontal rooting behavior is the prototype of the head movement, saying "no," and the vertical searching, i.e., head nodding, appearing at about the third month, of saying "yes." An analysis of the component movements in head shaking shows, however, that the end points at which they aim is the side position, i.e., the head is turned away. In nodding, the head is raised for the purpose of the downward movement. Thus it seems that the rotating behavior is the most primitive antecedent, followed by one closer in meaning, namely, turning the mouth (head) away from the offered food in "no" and seizing the food with the mouth in "yes." In either case "oral" motility seems an important step in the development of communication. It may also be an antecedent of the side-to-side movements of the head in some institutionalized infants; in the autoerotic head rolling of infants and schizophrenic and blind children; and in patients with tics.

The hand-mouth movements temporarily preceding, or simultaneous with, "rooting" are at first circumscribed activities. Later posture and locomotion are added for the purpose of more effective reaching and carrying food and objects to the mouth. It was shown that if the infant is allowed free use of his hand during feeding (even if food gets wasted), his general motor mastery and independence proceed faster than if, as nurses often do, a sheet is wrapped around him and food is being carried to his mouth.

Hand-to-mouth movements also contribute one of the important nuclei to the development of the image of the self, because the hand in the mouth produces a double sensation, and is also under the infant's control. When the infant carries objects to his mouth, then looks at them and shakes them alternately, we may speak of oral, combined with visual and manipulative reality testing. Lastly, with the aid of the neck and torso, the infant uses his mouth in a somewhat similar manner as animals. Seriously disturbed children are apt to chew almost anything, such as pencils or candle grease—which would be libidinal and aggressive activity—but they also use the mouth as a manipulative organ such as holding fast an object while they master it with their hands. They keep nails in their mouths or bite off part of an object which they are unable to break with their hands, or remove the cork of a bottle.

Incorporation, identification, and introjection, along with the corresponding fantasies in later years, likewise present a mixture of activity and passivity. At one extreme the objects are presented to or pushed into the subject's mouth; at the other, the subject is seizing and devouring them.

Excretory Functions and Motility

It is implied in some of the foregoing that the motor executive aspects of all libidinal urges, as of all adaptive motor activities, depend upon the time and method of training and learning. Sphincter training in most sections of the United States is usually initiated after the first year of life. The following statements may therefore apply in the beginning of the second year of life. The training itself has two motor aspects. Retention is handled by the sphincters, but the later expelling of urine and feces requires a rather complicated relaxation of the sphincter and the activation of other (mainly abdominal) muscles, usually in the sitting or the standing position. The characteristic motility of compulsive neurotics is characterized by a general muscular tension and repetitiveness. The general tension comes partly from anxiety on the pattern of "freezing" in the first year of life, from restrained aggression and the general tension of the musculature during bowel movement. The repetitiveness is the motor repetitiveness characteristic of the period of "the motor phase of ego and libido development." During this period the toddler repeats the complex movements he has partly or just mastered, e.g., opening a box, endlessly. Thus the repetitiveness has the implication of problem (conflict) solving.

Genital Function and Motility

The connection between the two functions in infancy may consist of (a) the handling of the genitals; (b) the arousal of the genitals concurrently with, or as a result of, generalized rhythmic body movements; and (c) body movements resulting from genital excitement. If infants are allowed relatively free motility, the genital function can undergo a complex motor development in the first year of life. Most well-cared-for boys discover their genitals during the first year of life. When the arms have grown somewhat and motor functions have reached a certain maturity, the infant begins to explore the lower abdomen, the inguinal region, and the lower extremities. This coincides with the preoccupation with the feet previously mentioned. In the exploratory process the scrotum is handled before the penis, and, as a rule, without the presence of erection. Starting between the sixth and twelfth months, the reaction to genital excitement, e.g., if erection occurs during bathing, takes the form of further stimulation by grasping. As previously mentioned, this has its antecedent in the grasping reflex, although now it occurs on a higher level of motor organization. The erection and grasping are as a rule relatively transient. Sustained genital excitement and stimulation with bodily writhing, pelvic thrusts, flushing, and sweating, and what seems final orgasm, may occur in the first year of life, but then it seems to be the result of sustained masturbatory stimulation by the adult (Kinsey, Pomeroy, and Martin, 1948; Mittelmann, Malkenson, and Munroe, 1959). In the second year of life, although rarely, the male or female infant may develop this pattern without such obvious adult intervention. The expressive and autoerotic movements previously mentioned lead to genital and anal sensations, and if sustained long enough, at times to erection. Erection during crying or startle may occur soon after birth. "Intercourse movements," i.e., rapid pelvic thrusts, may be observable in later months if the infant is inclined to autoerotic motor activity in a prone position—although mostly without observable signs of genital excitement. If the rhythmic patterns are markedly developed in infancy and are later combined with a taboo against touching the genitals, there may be a preference to stimulate the genitals in subsequent years by total movements. A five-year-old foot fetishist, described in a previous paper (1955), used to hug the pillow, as a substitute for the mother, with the upper extremities while performing writhing and rhythmic body movements as a method of masturbation. The masturbatory use of the total body, although often combined with manual handling of the genitals, is observable in schizophrenic and blind children with marked rhythmic motor patterns. Needless to say that in comparison with the initial pattern there is a considerable amount of learning in the later use of these body movements for genital stimulation. The occurrence in infancy of the "intercourse movements" together with the rhythmic expressive and muscle autoerotic patterns implies that there is an ego-syntonic regressive element in the rhythmic total body movement dominated by pelvic thrusts during adult intercourse. This regressive nucleus is present in the motor pattern as well as in total bodily and psychological absorption in the activity. The ease of occurrence of genital excitement in infancy; its appearance simultaneously with, or arousal by, generalized body movements (including generalized motor extension); and the lack or vagueness of differentiation of parts of the body—these form some of the precursors of the symbolic use of body as a phallus (Lewin, 1933).

AGGRESSION AND MOTILITY

The problem of the relationship between aggression and motility in the first year of life is a complex one. Movements with clearly aggressive intent occur only toward the end of the first year of life, mainly, if not exclusively, in the form of striking. But this movement has its antecedents in two other types of movements, namely, affectomotor waving of the hands and the shaking of objects; the first one appears at about the seventh—rarely, as early as the third—month. The combination of these two often leads to an affectionate grasping and shaking of the furry skin of a pet animal or to a vigorous rhythmic slamming of a person. These movements have no hostile intent, but they hurt the living creature involved. The objections—or countermeasures—of the living being sooner or later anger the infant.

Taking a broader—and debatable—approach, one may consider the affectomotor crying pattern of the infant as a primitive form of motor aggression. Crying is considered to be the equivalent of the precursors of rage and anxiety. In indirect support of the rage component we may mention that many mothers, seeing the windmill movements of the infant's arms and the vigorous pulling up and extension of his legs, coupled at times with the throwing around of the whole body, exclaim: "Is he mad (angry)!" If the windmill movements carry the hands and fingers close to the face, the infant actually scratches himself. This may be considered the primitive precursor of aggression directed toward the self. Supportive evidence for considering some of these rhythmic movements as precursors of aggression is seen in the fact that they may recur at later periods as a part of the temper outburst of the child or of the adult. The matter is complicated by the fact that from the third to the tenth month these rhythmic movements may be more characteristic of the joyous response of the infant. It is definite, however, that beginning with about the seventh month, many infants slam their thighs with their hands rhythmically during crying, but not during smiling. This autoaggressive action may receive reinforcement later from the relatively uncommon head banging.

Infantile rage is a very diffuse process without a clear goal and object. Regression to this diffuse type of rage may occur in later years, combined with infantile movements. It is to be noted that distinct frustration with an assumed mixture of anxiety and rage occurs earlier than the distinct expression of pleasure. The experience of "satisfaction" occurs, of course, very early. The onset of distinct pleasure (smile) as considered here is a definitely established, predictable—not just fleeting—pattern. As such it appears at about the third month of life.

The regressive fusion in later years of (muscle) autoerotism, adaptive locomotion (with attendant pride), aggressive and genital activity is illustrated in three brief sketches.

A twenty-eight-year-old man used to jump from furniture to furniture in a "Tarzan" fashion after intercourse.

A thirty-eight-year-old man used to ask muscular women, to whom he was impulsively attracted, to struggle with him during love-making (Mittelmann, 1954).

A twenty-six-year-old woman used to engage in a playful boxing bout with her sex partner after intercourse.

SUMMARY

Dynamically, we may differentiate between motility (1) as an urge, a factor in object relations, and a source of pleasure (id aspects); (2) as a form of reality testing, mastery, communication, and integration (ego); and (3) as relating to the ultimate formation of conscience and ideals (superego aspects).

From the point of view of maturation and relation to the environment, we may differentiate between movement and action. The former predominates in the intrauterine or pregravitational period as well as in the first six months of the postnatal or gravitational period.

The study of motility suggests that later motor and related psychological phenomena have successive precursors in intrauterine and early infantile motility. The time of the appearance and the quality of the pattern vary with environmental circumstances, and immediate or later pathology may arise because of trauma to motility proper, e.g., being hurt while crawling, or through motility being involved in other traumatic situations, e.g., affect starvation.

Passive motility, i.e., intrauterine posture and being moved rhythmically, reinforced by the similar postnatal experiences and by being cared for, stand for unlimited care and protection. Later horizontality may also mean helplessness and death.

Active motility involves, at first *non-adaptive* varieties. *Reflex grasping* is the antecedent of later voluntary grasping, of clinging, of grasping for manipulation, and therefore of later adaptation and reality testing. It is antecedent to the manifestations of dependent longings, anxious dependency, affection, adult love-making, particularly dependent love-making. *Random movements*, with the antecedent "quickening" *in utero*, are the first manifestations of the motor urge, and are precursors of regressive diffuse discharge via motility.

Affectomotor patterns are antecedents of interpersonal communication, and adaptive handling of objects; together with *autoerotic rhythmic patterns*, they are the precursors of adult intercourse movements, of excess discharge through hypermotility, and via kinesthetic sensation of foot fetishism. They are retained and narcissistically elaborated in blind and schizophrenic children.

Adaptive motility (manipulative, postural, and locomotor) is one of the main avenues of the development of mastery, reality testing, motor urge, object relations, and later, aggression, self-esteem (with possible later self-depreciation) and of the concept of the self and not-self. Fear of falling and of failure of motor function now appear. Restriction arouses anxiety and rage which in excessive amounts raise the possibility of later neurosis or psychosis.

Sensory motility (visual), together with tactile motor exploration of the body, contributes to reality testing and mastery, differentiation of part self, self, and not-self, and displacement from the genitals to the extremities.

Generalized inactivation when looking at the faces, combined later with inactivation and staring during anxiety while being looked at, is the precursor of voyeurism and exhibitionism, a paralyzing fear, e.g., in the Wolf Man's nightmare, or in hysterical paralysis.

Oral motility, i.e., hand-to-mouth movement and support of mouth activity by posture and locomotion, is an element in self-differentiation, reality testing, passive or active aggressive devouring fantasies, and use of the mouth as a manipulative and aggressive organ.

Excretory motility combined with "freezing" in anxiety and restrained aggression contributes to the general muscle tension in obsessive-compulsive states.

Genital motility, as manual handling or grasping, results in incorporation of the male genitals in the body image, and in the relief of anxiety. Rhythmic pelvic thrusts are the precursor of adult intercourse. The ease of occurrence of erection, often combined with general motor responses, is the precursor of the symbolic use of the body as a phallus.

The early motor crying pattern, reinforced later by slamming of the thighs and head banging, is the antecedent of *aggression* directed outward and toward the self, and therefore of masochism and conscience. Combined later with the general motor-rage response to restriction, it is the prototype of diffuse outburst of hostility.

BIBLIOGRAPHY

Freud, S. (1905), Three Essays on the Theory of Sexuality. *Standard Edition*, VII. London: Hogarth Press, 1953.
—— (1918), From the History of an Infantile Neurosis. *Standard Edition*, XVII. London: Hogarth Press, 1955.
Gesell, A. & Amatruda, C. S. (1941), *Developmental Diagnosis*. New York: Paul B. Hoeber, 2nd ed., 1947.
Hartmann, H. (1939), *Ego Psychology and the Problem of Adaptation*. New York: International Universities Press, 1958.
—— (1952), The Mutual Influences in the Development of Ego and Id. *This Annual*, VII.
Hoffer, W. (1949), Mouth, Hand and Ego-Integration. *This Annual*, III/IV.
Kinsey, A. C., Pomeroy, W. B. & Martin, C. E. (1948), *Sexual Behavior in the Human Male*. Philadelphia: Saunders.
Klein, M. (1932), *The Psycho-Analysis of Children*. London: Hogarth Press, 2nd ed., 1937.
Landis, C. & Hunt, W. A. (1939), *The Startle Pattern*. New York: Farrar & Rinehart.
Lewin, D. B. (1933), The Body as Phallus. *Psa. Quart.*, II.
—— (1958), *Dreams and the Uses of Regression*. New York: International Universities Press.
Mittelmann, B. (1954), Motility in Infants, Children, and Adults: Patterning and Psychodynamics. *This Annual*, IX.
—— (1955), Motor Patterns and Genital Behavior: Fetishism. *This Annual*, X.
-—— (1958), Psychodynamics of Motility. *Int. J. Psa.*, XXXIX.
—— & Malkenson, L., Munroe, R. L. (1959), Mannerisms in Blindness and Childhood Schizophrenia: A Preliminary Report. *Am. J. Orthopsychiat.*, in press.
Spitz, R. A. (1957), *No and Yes: On the Genesis of Human Communication*. New York: International Universities Press.

ON THE CONCEPT OF SUPEREGO[1]

JOSEPH SANDLER, Ph.D. (London)

INTRODUCTION

The theory of psychoanalysis represents the common matrix with-in which the many different aspects of our work at The Hampstead Clinic are conceived. We continually apply psychoanalytic theory as a frame of reference through which observations can be made and assessed, be it in diagnosis, therapy, education, or research. But this is far from being a one-way process, and we have learned from Freud the necessity to pause and to return, every now and then, to take stock of and to re-examine our theory in the light of experience, so that the understanding of our material can be more incisive and precise.

The work reported in this paper is in part the outcome of such a pause for taking stock, and it has been prompted by a specific and practical problem connected with the handling of analytic data which have accumulated over a number of years in therapists' regular reports and in the Index.

The Index

The Index project was begun several years ago with the aim of categorizing and classifying on index cards the abundant clinical

[1] This investigation has been aided by a joint grant from the Foundations' Fund for Research in Psychiatry, New Haven, Connecticut, and the Psychoanalytic Research and Development Fund, Inc., New York.

The material used has been taken from The Hampstead Child-Therapy Clinic, a therapeutic and research center financed by the following Foundations: The Field Foundation, Inc., New York; The Ford Foundation, New York; The Foundations' Fund for Research in Psychiatry, New Haven, Connecticut; The Anna Freud Foundation, New York; The Grant Foundation, Inc., New York; The Estate of Flora Haas, New York; The Old Dominion Foundation, U.S.A.; The Psychoanalytic Research and Development Fund, Inc., New York.

The author is also indebted to Anna Freud and members of her Metapsychology Study Group for many helpful ideas and criticisms; and to those analysts, therapists, and students who have been concerned with the collection and handling of superego material in the Index project.

case material in the weekly and bimonthly reports of cases in analytic treatment at the Clinic. It represents an attempt to keep these data "alive" and to provide a pool of case material within reach of any interested research worker (de Monchaux, 1958; Anna Freud, 1959). The construction of a comprehensive set of headings to encompass this material has proved a formidable task, presenting many difficulties and taking much time. Although the whole process of categorization is rooted in psychoanalytic theory, individual therapists have largely been left to classify their observations in the ways which seemed most meaningful to them, although the choice of Index headings has often been the outcome of joint discussions between therapists and advisors from one or other of the Index committees. Indexing is thus to some extent a compromise between the respective therapist's free choice of data and headings, and a structure imposed by the common psychoanalytic framework, and by the recommendations of the Index committees. The final integration of these different sources has found expression in the set of Index manuals now being prepared. It has always been recognized that a piece of clinical material may be viewed from a number of directions (e.g., from the transference aspect, or from a structural point of view), and the therapists' own preferences have been respected.

The Problem

It follows from what has been said above that certain headings and subheadings must inevitably receive more attention than others, and this has indeed proved to be the case. Whereas material is classified in great and fruitful detail in certain areas, others appear to have received a minimum of attention. A quite striking example of an understocked section of this sort is that relating to the superego. Now even the slightest acquaintance with the details of cases treated at the Clinic is sufficient to show that the role of the superego is implicitly, if not explicitly, appreciated, and it is necessary to ask why this has not been equally reflected in the Index, and why the tendency to veer away from the conceptualization of material in superego terms has occurred. Examination of the way in which cases have been indexed shows quite clearly that therapists have preferred to sort their clinical material in terms of object relationships, ego activities, and the transference, rather than in terms of the participation of the superego. It is partly the purpose of this study to investigate some of the reasons for this phenomenon, a phenomenon all the more surprising in view of the advantages which have accrued to psychoanalytic theory and practice from the adoption of the structural point of view.

Once attention had been drawn to the problem, it was not difficult to see that two interrelated factors were operating in producing the tendency to formulate material in other-than-superego terms. The first is what I shall call the apparent "conceptual dissolution" of the superego, and which can be regarded, in part at least, as a consequence of advances in the understanding of the superego's genetic roots. The second is the lack of theoretical precision which exists in the differentiation of superego content from content of the ego, and the confusion which still exists among psychoanalysts in regard to the mechanisms of superego formation. In the latter half of this paper, a provisional restatement of the superego concept will be put forward, a formulation which has followed directly from the difficulties experienced in indexing our observations, and which may provide a useful basis for a more systematic ordering of the relevant clinical material.[2]

The Apparent "Conceptual Dissolution" of the Superego[3]

Freud's View of the Superego (Ego Ideal)

Although it is possible to find, when looking back, germs of the superego concept in Freud's Project (see Freud, 1887-1902) and in *The Interpretation of Dreams* (1900), the notion of an ego ideal was first explicitly presented by Freud in his paper "On Narcissism"

[2] The difficulty which exists in integrating the superego concept into the psychoanalytic model does not appear to be only a Hampstead idiosyncrasy. Thus Rapaport, in his discussion of the conceptual model of psychoanalysis (1951), mentions the superego very briefly, and then only to say that he leaves it undefined. Hartmann has traced, in an illuminating paper (1950), the development of the ego concept in Freud's work, but he explicitly puts the concept of superego to one side. In contrast, there are many papers which refer, either directly or indirectly or in passing, to the superego. But on the whole, the more theoretical these papers are, the more complicated and intricate they appear to be, in contrast to the relatively simple formulations of Freud (cf. Jones's paper on the superego, 1926).

[3] The account of trends in the development of the superego concept given here is a selective one, influenced by a number of factors—not the least of which is the need to emphasize points which will be taken up later in this paper.

(1914). There he put forward the idea of an institution in the mind which watches the ego and which compares it with an ideal standard—an ideal which is derived from standards of behavior set by the parents.

Starting from the observation that libidinal impulses are repressed if they are in conflict with the subject's ethical ideas, he suggested that the formation of this ideal, against which the subject assesses himself, would be a necessary precondition for such repression. He speaks in this context of the self-respect of the ego. In the ideal image the child embodies all the feelings of perfection which he felt himself to possess in his early childhood. If he can conform to it, he regains this early state of narcissistic perfection.

The conscience is formed as an institution in the mind which sees to it that the ego gains narcissistic gratification from the ego ideal, and which watches the real ego and constantly compares it with the ideal standard.

The main impetus to the formation of the ideal, Freud felt, stems from parental criticism, and this is later reinforced by further training and education. He points out that what has previously been spoken of as the dream censor is in fact the ego ideal. It is worth noting that he uses the same term to include both the ideal image and that organized part of the ego which constantly observes the ego and matches it up against the ideal standard.

In this paper, Freud discusses the role of the self-regarding attitude and of the vicissitudes of the libido in the development of the ego ideal. He saw the development of the ego as consisting in "a departure from primary narcissism" and this development "gives rise to a vigorous attempt to recover that state." He adds: "This departure is brought about by means of the displacement of libido on to an ego ideal imposed from without; and satisfaction is brought about from fulfilling this ideal."

In Group Psychology and the Analysis of the Ego (1921), Freud expanded somewhat on his concept. He saw it as embodying "the sum of all the limitations in which the ego has to acquiesce . . . ," and he noted that "all the interplay between the external object and the ego as a whole . . . may possibly be repeated upon this new scene of action within the ego." He emphasized again the positive rewarding aspect of the relationship between the ego and its ideal.

When some thought or activity in the ego coincides with the standards of the ideal there results a feeling of triumph and release—a return to the state of primary narcissistic union with the parents.

In joining a group, the subject may give up his ego ideal and substitute for it the group ideal as embodied in the leader. The leader becomes invested with all the individual's idealized qualities, and the fact that other members of the group are doing the same thing leads to a reinforcement of this process by an identification of the group members with one another. The ego in turn is experienced as an object to the ego ideal.

In the condition of mania, we find the extreme and pathological instance of the feeling of narcissistic union with the parents, in which ego and ego ideal are completely at one, and the subject can blithely disregard feelings of social responsibility. Conversely, the sense of guilt and feelings of inferiority represent an expression of tension between the ego and the ideal, finding its extreme expression in the abject misery of the melancholic.

Freud makes an explicit distinction between identification of the ego with an object (which results, for example, in the pleasure of being one of a group in such organizations as the army), and the embodiment of the ego ideal in an external person, in external authority (as in the Church).

Two years later Freud presented the structural point of view in *The Ego and the Id* (1923). The term ego ideal is replaced by superego, but Freud did not imply by this change of term that he was dealing with two separate organizations. He saw the superego, as he had seen the ego ideal before, as constituting a modification of the ego. The superego—a structural precipitate within it—comes into existence at the time of the resolution of the oedipus complex and, through its formation, becomes the main agent in bringing about a solution to the oedipal conflicts which occur so intensely during the phallic phase of instinctual development. He saw it as the vehicle of morality, reflecting the "higher nature" of man, and as such being a representative of the child's relation to his parents and to society. It exercises the function of self-judgment, and preserves throughout life the capacity to stand apart from the ego and to rule it. In the same way as the child had no choice but to obey his parents, so the ego later submits to the imperative demands of the superego. It exercises the "censorship of morals," and tension between ego and superego is manifest as a sense of guilt and worthlessness.

The superego is for the most part unconscious, and in analysis its critical functions can produce certain special forms of resistance. It can be hypermoral and even tyrannical toward the ego; but it is capable of modification to the extent that the standards and moral injunctions of other external authorities (such as teachers) may be absorbed into it.

Freud regarded the superego as being formed on the basis of identifications with the parents, such replacement of object cathexes by identifications being an important part of character development, though superego identifications can be distinguished from those which enrich the ego. The decisive superego identifications take place as a consequence of the necessity to deal with both positive and negative oedipus complexes. The parents are introjected after the fashion described in "Mourning and Melancholia" (1917), and the child erects, in the superego, the same barrier to instinctual expression as existed outside in the shape of the parents. The superego represents, however, a definite structure within the ego, and it is more than the simple sum of the parental identifications—it is a consistent organization which stands apart from the other constituents of the ego. The more intense the oedipus complex and the more rapidly it is repressed under the influence of external measures, the stricter becomes the superego.

Freud repeatedly stressed the fact that the superego is not only a product of parental identifications, but it functions also as a mode of expression of the most powerful id drives. By constructing the superego, the ego places itself in subjection to the id. Indeed, he says "the ego forms its superego out of the id," and it is the unhindered traffic between the id and the superego which accounts for its largely unconscious nature. Thus, the more a child controls his aggressive impulses toward another, the more tyrannical does his subsequent superego become. The dread of the superego persists from the earlier fear of castration, a fear which is reinforced, as we know, by the child's own aggressive impulses.

Thus the id finds a path through the ego in two ways: directly, to the extent to which its impulses are ego-syntonic; and indirectly, through the superego.

With every identification, Freud points out, there is a desexualization and at the same time an instinctual defusion. The libidinal cathexis no longer binds the destructive tendences which now find expression in the severity and punitiveness of the superego. This defusion is particularly evident in melancholia.

The superego has also elements in it which represent *reactions* against the id. Thus it not only contains the precept "be like your father," but it also contains prohibitions—certain things are father's prerogatives.

In 1926 Freud published *Inhibitions, Symptoms and Anxiety*, in which he put forward his new theory of anxiety and stimulated the many subsequent developments in ego psychology. From this time he made no modification of the superego concept, though he recognized that it was by no means as clear and as uncomplicated as one might wish it to be. Nor did he feel the need to revise the theory of narcissism, which had played so important a role in the earliest delineations of the ego ideal.

Freud made subsequently, however, a number of statements which are relevant to our understanding of the superego. In *Inhibitions, Symptoms and Anxiety* itself, he refers to the many situations in which ego and superego are merged, and in which no distinction can be made between the two. He speaks of the ego acting "in obedience to the superego" (though in the *New Introductory Lectures* [1932] he spoke of repression being "the work of the superego," which it either carried out directly or "ordered" the ego to do). Freud saw the threat of the superego as being an extension of castration threat, which is in itself a development (by way of the danger of loss of object) from the earliest and primary danger, that of being helplessly overwhelmed by excitation. The little boy's penis has an immense narcissistic investment, and the threat to the penis becomes also a threat to his narcissism.

In the *New Introductory Lectures*, Freud refers, as he had done earlier, to the superego as a "function" in the ego, but adds that it is to a certain extent independent, pursuing its own ends. He reiterates the superego's role as a replacement of parental authority, as an inner agent which now dominates the ego by granting proofs of affection and by threats of punishment which in turn mean loss of love. He contrasts the harshness of the superego in many people with the kindness and gentleness of their real parents, and attributes this disproportion to the "transmutation of instincts" which occurs at the time of the resolution of the oedipus complex.

In *The Future of an Illusion* (1927), Freud draws attention to the role of the superego in the perpetuation of culture, and much of what he has to say about the transmission of culture (in particular, the cultural illusions of religion) is pertinent to our understanding of the superego, which is, after all, the most effective agent of cultural transmission. He says, "Every individual is virtually an enemy of culture," and culture must protect man against his own hostile impulses. He goes on to say that the satisfaction provided by the attainment of a cultural ideal is essentially a narcissistic one.

In *Civilization and Its Discontents* (1930), Freud amplified the connection between the superego and the aggressive instinct. The child's dread of the parents, which had manifested itself as social anxiety, is, as he had previously described, felt as guilt, once the parents have been replaced by conscience. But over and above this the aggressiveness of the superego is reinforced every time the child renounces its own aggressive wishes on account of the demands of society. Indeed, frustration heightens the aggressiveness inherent in the child's ambivalence, and it is deflected into the superego, its strength now being seen to be a measure of the child's own hostility toward the prohibiting and restraining parent. Masochistic behavior can then be seen to be a function of the ego's erotic attachment to a sadistic superego.

In his first presentation of the concept of ego ideal (1914), Freud had stressed the importance of the libidinal, erotic aspects of the tie to the parents, especially the mother, in the formation of the ego ideal. Later, and most explicitly, in *Civilization and Its Discontents*, he emphasized the aggressive, sadistic side. Yet he did not fail to point out that the setting up of high ideals and standards is a function of the superego, as is also the punishment meted out to the ego by the conscience, for failure to fulfill these ideals.

As late as 1938, in the *Outline of Psychoanalysis*, Freud reiterated his views on the superego, describing it as "a special agency in which

... parental influence is prolonged." He adds that "the details of the relation between the ego and the superego become completely intelligible if they are carried back to the child's attitude toward his parents"; and the parents' influence includes also the traditions of the larger group as well as the family.

Freud always related the development of the superego specifically to the resolution of oedipal conflict, and he saw its development as being the outcome of two factors: the long period of helplessness in the human infant, and the occurrence of the oedipus complex.

The earliest relationship of the child to the mother is an anaclitic one—based, that is, on the mother's real capacity for gratifying the infant's instinctual needs. The father is dealt with, Freud suggests, through identification—not identification of the sort which leads to superego formation, but rather "a direct and immediate identification . . . [which] . . . takes place earlier than any object cathexis."

This early state of affairs persists until intense phallic sexual wishes arise toward the mother. The father is now perceived (we are speaking of the little boy) as an obstacle to these sexual aims, and the child's feelings toward him become marked by ambivalence.

The cathexis of the mother as a sexual object must now be given up and it may be replaced either by identification with the mother, or by an intensified identification with the father. The latter identification endorses and consolidates the masculinity of the little boy and permits him an affectionate relation with the mother. The relative predominance of these identifications is also influenced by the negative oedipus complex, and by the constitutional bisexuality of the child.

These identifications coincide with, and are an essential ingredient of, the oedipus complex. The father identification preserves the object relationship to the mother, and replaces the sexual relation to the father which belonged to the negative oedipus complex. Similarly, the mother identification retains the object tie to the father, and replaces the normal phallic sexual relation to the mother. The child erects, in the superego, the same obstacle to instinctual expression as existed outside in the shape of the parents. The strength to do this was, as Freud puts it, "borrowed from the father" through the boy's prior identification with him.

Further Developments

Although Freud made a number of references to the complexity of the superego concept, there can be little doubt that the difficulties which he saw were for the most part peripheral rather than central to the concept. In tracing his references to the ego ideal and super-ego, particularly in the fifteen years following *The Ego and the Id*, one cannot fail to be struck by the internal consistency of his formulations.

We know that the development of psychoanalysis has not taken place with equal speed in all directions; and following the publication of *The Ego and the Id*, the main advances in psychoanalysis have been concentrated on a few related fronts, and I should like to mention particularly ego psychology and child analysis.

The revision of the theory of anxiety in 1926 (in *Inhibitions, Symptoms and Anxiety*) with its insistence on the ego as the only seat of anxiety led, as Hartmann and Kris (1945) have shown, to far-reaching theoretical developments in the psychology of the ego. They say: "If we turn to the ego as the psychic system that controls perception, achieves solutions, and directs actions, we have to insist on distinctions that seemed irrelevant when Freud first formulated his genetic propositions." Anna Freud's *The Ego and the Mechanisms of Defence* (1936) deepened and systematized our knowledge of the ego's defenses and elaborated the concept of defenses to include the idea of defense against "pain" arising from the real world. Hartmann's *Ego Psychology and the Problem of Adaptation* (1939) introduced the concepts of the undifferentiated phase, conflict-free ego development, and primary and secondary autonomy. Ego functions such as reality testing, perception, memory, control of motility, and the synthetic function have all received increased attention,[4] and the concept of neutralized energy has been introduced (Hartmann, Kris, and Loewenstein, 1949). Attention has been paid to the development of ego apparatuses, particularly those concerned with thought and cognition (cf. Rapaport, 1957), and psychoanalytic theory seems to be moving rapidly toward becoming a general psychology, and the findings of academic laboratory psychologists are tending to be absorbed into it.

[4] The list of postulated ego functions is continually growing, including recently even the function of consciousness (George Klein, 1959).

Progress in ego psychology has highlighted certain areas which are particularly relevant to our conception of the superego. Functions of the superego have gradually been absorbed into our model of the ego. This is a continuation of a tendency which was evident even in Freud's own writings, for in 1914 (and again in 1921) he ascribed the function of reality testing to the ego ideal, only to allocate it, quite explicitly, to the ego in 1923. The self-observing function of the superego has, however, not so readily been yielded up to the ego (cf. Nunberg, 1932), and the question of structure versus function of the ego in relation to the superego itself has not yet been satisfactorily investigated (Freud, on more than one occasion, referred to the superego as a "function" of the ego).

Developments in ego psychology have also shown up a large area of theory, fundamental to a consideration of the genesis of the superego, which is still unclear. Although the concepts of identification, introjection, and internalization are of the utmost clinical value, their metapsychological status is at present complicated and often confused, even though numerous attempts have been made to disentangle them (e.g., Fenichel, 1926, 1945; Foulkes, 1937; Knight, 1940; Glover, 1949; Hendrick, 1951; Jacobson, 1953; and Greenson, 1954). Freud uses the term "identification" in a large number of different senses, to include identification into the ego and into the superego, and he speaks of an identification (with the father) which precedes object relations. In addition we must take into account the fact that some identifications appear to be ego-dystonic (Greenson, 1954). Furthermore, identification as a defense is frequently not differentiated from the defensive use of introjection. This latter term is often also used in the same sense as incorporation in relation to the processes of inner enrichment, even though, strictly speaking, the term incorporation should be used only to refer to the oral instinctual activity of physical "taking in," and introjection to the psychical counterpart of that activity (Glover, 1949; Greenson, 1954). One may also ask whether introjection is wholly an instinctual activity, and to what degree it represents an autonomous ego function, related, for example, to perceptual organization. The term internalization is used by Hartmann (1939) to denote the set of processes whereby internal regulation substitutes for external trial-and-error activity, but it is also often used synonymously with incorporation, introjection, and identification.

To these problems we must add another which has arisen as a result of the growth of ego psychology. It seems to have become necessary to differentiate a part of the personality from the ego proper, a part nevertheless which is intimately associated with it; viz., the *self*. Consequent on a proposal of Hartmann's (1950), Edith Jacobson (1953, 1954a, b, c) has put forward a concept of self-representation which has the same status within the ego as have object representations. It is then the self, the "endopsychic representation of our bodily and mental self in the system ego" (Hartmann), which receives the cathexis withdrawn from external objects and directed toward the ego. This concept, which appears to be not only of theoretical but of clinical value as well, has had a number of repercussions on the theory of narcissism and of masochism, and on our understanding of the processes of introjection, projection, and identification (which would then be seen to be a fusion of representations of object and self). It also affects our view of superego development, which Jacobson sees as the outcome of widespread reaction formations to the child's oedipal and narcissistic strivings, to sexual desires as well as aggressive impulses.

Certain authors have increased the conceptual differentiation between the libidinal (ego ideal) and the aggressive (superego "proper") aspects of the superego, to the extent of postulating, implicitly or explicitly, two separate structures. This tendency is evident in the work of a number of different authors. Piers and Singer, in their recent monograph on *Shame and Guilt* (1953), ascribe guilt to the tension between ego and superego, and shame to tension between ego and ego ideal. Nunberg (1932) speaks of two concepts, but goes on to say that it is difficult in practice to separate them sharply from each other.

Perhaps the most potent stimulus to further understanding of the superego concept has come from the experiences and insights of those engaged in child analysis. This is particularly true in relation to superego precursors and to the whole problem of the ontogenesis of the mature superego. Indeed, the genetic perspective may well prove, as Hartmann and Kris (1945) have suggested, the most illuminating and useful one from which to view this difficult concept from both its structural and functional aspects.

As long ago as 1926, Anna Freud in a series of lectures to the Vienna Institute of Psychoanalysis (later published in *The Psycho-Analysis of Children*, 1946) put forward a number of considerations regarding the superego which represented an amplification of the description given by Freud in *The Ego and the Id*. She drew attention to the relative importance of the influence of the outer world, of the real parents in particular, in the mental life of the small child. Whereas in the mature superego the detachment from the parents and superego identification with them has led to a marked degree of independence, in the small child the detachment from the parents is far from complete. Although a superego does indeed exist, following the oedipal phase, its importance to the child is still correlated with the relationships actually obtaining between the child and its real parents. The child's control of its excretory activities, for example, although reflecting an inner prompting to cleanliness, is, in the early years, largely dependent on the state of its relations to the real objects. If the object relationship to the mother is at all disturbed, a regression to soiling can easily take place. Even in latency, changes in the real object relationship can affect the established but immature superego of the child. This tie to the parents reveals itself in a double standard of morality—one for grownups and another for the child itself and for other children. This has important implications for analytic work with children, and Anna Freud went on to suggest that the analyst must take over the role of the child's ego ideal during the course of analysis. The modification of the child's superego was thus seen, because of the child's dependence on real objects, to be easier with the child than with adult patients.[5]

In 1927, in a symposium on child analysis held in London, Melanie Klein presented a vigorous attack on the technical and theoretical views which Anna Freud had expressed, and I want to describe her ideas in so far as they refer to the formation of the superego. Melanie Klein took the view that the superego of even the

---

[5] Later Anna Freud (1946) pointed out that the guiding and educative functions could be left to educators and others from the child's environment, leaving the analyst free to concentrate on the analytic work proper.

very young child closely resembles that of the adult, and is not greatly modified during the course of later development. This infantile superego can be of the highest degree of severity and, in this respect, can often stand in sharp distinction to the real parents; indeed, the objects introjected into the superego can on no account be identified with the real parents.

Melanie Klein expressed the view that the oedipus complex occurs toward the end of the first year of life, following weaning, and that its early occurrence is associated with the beginnings of superego formation; a process which terminates with the onset of latency. The resulting superego is "at heart unalterable," and she distinguishes a true inner superego (as distinct from various other superegos set up by the child) which is not identical with that which Anna Freud described as still operative in the person of the real parents.

Some years later, in a paper on "The Early Development of Conscience" (1933), Melanie Klein reiterated her view that there exists in the child a full superego of the utmost harshness and cruelty, before the resolution of the oedipus complex. The fears of the external world which the small child displays are due to the fact that the child views the world fantastically under the influence of the superego. The child's first imagos are endowed with tremendous sadism, stemming from the death instinct, and in childhood fears these terrifying imagos are reprojected. The early function of the superego is to arouse anxiety, but as its severity is reduced, during the phallic phase, by the positive side of the child's attachment to the mother, so anxiety is transformed into guilt. The sense of guilt arises from the child's feeling that in sadistically attacking its mother's body, it is attacking its father and brothers and sisters contained in her body. Social feeling develops from the urge to reconstruct and to repair the damage. It is of some interest, however, that Melanie Klein differentiates the conscience from the superego, the conscience being established only after the resolution of the phallic oedipus complex.

In a recent paper "On the Development of Mental Functioning" (1958), Melanie Klein places the beginnings of the superego in the second quarter of the first year, and her account of its formation is as follows: The self-destructive (death instinct) impulses of the infant have to be projected outward as they would otherwise over-whelm him. Introjection, being largely in the service of the life instincts, serves to bind the death instincts, and these two sets of forces attach themselves to the mother's breast, which is then felt to be good or bad at different times. From this we get the primal "good" and "bad" objects, split from each other through the need to master persecutory anxiety. Melanie Klein relates the division into ego and superego to the polarity of the two sets of instincts. The internalized good object supports the ego which is strengthened by an identifica-tion with it; a split-off portion of the death instinct, fused with a certain part of the life instincts, then becomes the basis of the super-ego. Because of the fusion with the life instincts, the superego acquires protective qualities as well as destructive ones. Melanie Klein points out now, however, that not all internalized objects are integrated into the superego, but they can be split off in a non-superego way and pushed into the deep unconscious. These nonsu-perego objects are characterized by instinctual defusion, while it is the dominance of instinctual fusion in the superego which allows the ego to accept it, as the two institutions now share aspects of the same good object. As latency approaches, the organized part of the superego becomes more isolated from the unconscious, unorganized part.

These views of Melanie Klein, in spite of discrepancies which might be attributed to semantic differences, are very far removed from what we understand by ego psychology (Rapaport [1959] refers to them as an "id mythology"). Her assumption of an intricate psychic system elaborated soon after birth, capable of highly sophis-ticated fantasy activities; her equation of memory images, uncon-scious fantasies, introjections, and "internal objects"; her lack of distinction between affect and ideation; and so on—are all at vari-ance with our metapsychological thinking. Yet there can be little doubt that the controversial propositions of Melanie Klein regarding superego development have stimulated others to direct more atten-tion to superego precursors in the preoedipal phases.

In addition to the earlier work on "precursors" of the superego, such as that of Aichhorn (1925), who was specially interested in the superego of delinquents, and Ferenczi (1925), who had described the way in which a child complies with the demands of the parents in the anal phase through the development of "sphincter morality," attention has been paid in recent years to forerunners of the superego. Thus Annie Reich (1954) has shown the existence of early "superego-type" identifications which represent archaic elements in the superego; and more recently David Beres, in an illuminating paper (1958), has reviewed the whole problem. The work of Spitz is particularly relevant (1945, 1946, 1950, 1957), and in a recent study (1958) he has discussed the development of superego "primordia" in the child's earliest years.

It is particularly the work of those engaged in direct observation of normal and disturbed children which has thrown light on early stages of superego formation, as the growth of the child's social sense and the appearance of an internal morality can be seen to have a close connection with the state of its object relationships in the first years of life; and disturbance in these relationships has been found to have a marked influence on later object relationships and on ego and superego development. Apart from the work on children separated from their parents carried out at the Hampstead Nurseries during the last war, the prevailing theoretical outlook at the Hampstead Clinic has been influenced by the studies of Ribble (1944), Fries (1946), and Ernst and Marianne Kris at the Child Study Center at Yale University (Marianne Kris, 1957). And to these may perhaps be added the unpublished recorded observations on superego precursors at the present Hampstead Nursery.

Repercussions of Advances in Knowledge on the Superego Concept

We have seen that since Freud outlined his original views on the superego, a considerable amount of work has been done on various aspects of this concept. What is striking about this work is, however, that it has been very largely analytic—analytic in the sense that superego elements have been put under the microscope, so to speak, and broken down into their structural, dynamic, economic, and genetic components; analytic, that is, in a sense opposite to synthetic. In the course of this process, much of what might be called superego territory has been yielded up to the ego. Other areas have been traced in greater details to their origins in the id, and still more has been connected with real experiences of the child in his early life. This process has gone on without any real regathering of the pieces into a coherent framework, so that some of the original power of the construct as a theoretical unity has been lost. The very process of examining the superego in detail in order to clarify it has blurred it to some extent, at any rate from the point of view of theoretical lucidity and simplicity. As we can regard the superego as being formed out of the interaction of id, ego, and the real world, so theoretical dissection of it, particularly dissection of its origins, has tended to some extent to diffuse it conceptually back into the ego, id, and the real world. In a sense the superego has thus lost some of its theoretical identity as a compact and coherent organization, as a thing-in-itself and an agency in the production of psychic conflict. In striking contrast, developments in ego psychology have served to enrich our view of the ego, for our examination of ego functions has not led us out of the ego (except perhaps to the notion of an undifferentiated state).

In the same way as increased theoretical interest in the superego has tended to complicate what was a relatively simple concept, so does a parallel process occur in relation to clinical psychoanalytic work. We aim in analysis to deal, in part at any rate, with the outcome of the oedipal conflict; yet it is the very resolution of the oedipus complex which brings the superego into being. If we analyze superego conflict, we find that, in the course of the analysis, what we might call an apparent *conceptual dissolution* has taken place. The object relationships and conflicts which entered into superego formation have unfolded themselves onto the person of the analyst; the transformed id drives, which form so important a part of the superego, have been traced back to their origins in direct instinctual wishes and fantasies; and the introjective and identificatory processes which have contributed so much to superego genesis have been seen as defensive or adaptive ego mechanisms which were called into play during critical phases of oedipal and preoedipal development. This process may cause us temporarily to lose sight of the superego as a coherent organization with properties of its own; and it seems clear that this apparent conceptual dissolution has been a potent factor in determining therapists' preferences in approaching their clinical material for purposes of indexing. In a sense the Index has functioned rather like a microscope, and as in the examination of physical tissues, increasing magnification may cause grosser structures to disappear from sight—but this by no means implies that they cease to exist.

A View of the Superego

The apparent "dissolution" of the superego concept, as a result of increased knowledge of its origins and as a consequence of the regressive processes which occur in the course of psychoanalytic work, by no means accounts for all the reluctance shown by therapists to conceptualize their clinical material in superego terms. The concept itself, even when used at a relatively low level of molecularity, is one which is indistinct, and it has become increasingly so with the absorption into our day-to-day thinking of advances in ego psychology. In particular, the distinction between identifications which enrich the ego, and those which can be regarded as leading to superego formation, is vague and ill defined. Similarly, the lack of clear differentiation between processes of internalization, introjection, and identification (Freud often used the terms introjection and identification synonymously) has led to further confusion, in spite of the efforts of a number of authors to clarify some of the issues involved.

Faced with the practical problem of devising a basis for classifying material in the superego section of the Index, it has been necessary to formulate our view of the superego and its development in such a way that both the tendency to "dissolution" and some of the theoretical problems which obscure its definition are overcome. Such a reformulation must of necessity fit well with theory and knowledge in other areas, but equally it must inevitably cut across a number of established ideas. The formulation presented here is a tentative and incomplete one, representing more an attempt at defining a theoretical framework rather than the presentation of a comprehensive statement.

A Framework for Viewing Superego Development

The development of the ego, from the earliest weeks of life onward, is marked by the construction, within the mind of the child, of organized frames of reference or schemata which subserve adaptation. These schemata or mental models revolve at first around experiences of need satisfaction, and no distinction is made by the child between sensations which arise from inside its own body and those which occur as a result of the activities of the mother. With development, these schemata gradually extend to include aspects of the external world other than those intimately associated with immediate need satisfaction. Essentially they enable the child to assess the properties of the outer world with increasing efficiency, and to predict the pleasurable or unpleasurable consequences of his behavior.

The term *internalization* has been used in regard to these processes, but as its current usage is such as to include processes of introjection and identification as well, it seems preferable to think in terms of an *organizing activity* to describe the construction of these inner models. The concept of an organizing activity seems a particularly appropriate one as the schemata of the child embrace not only data gained through sensory impressions arising from the outer world, but sense data (including affect data) arising from instinctual tensions as well. In addition, it will be necessary, as I hope to show later, to *contrast* organizing activities with those of introjection and identification, and to dissociate them from processes of "taking in" traditionally associated with oral instinctual aims. Indeed, organizing is primary to and must precede introjection and identification, in the sense in which these latter two processes will be used in this presentation. One can neither identify with nor introject aspects of another person unless one's ego has previously constructed some sort of mental model of that person. Organizing activity embraces those activities grouped by Piaget (1936, 1937) under the headings of "assimilation" and "accommodation," by Hartmann (1939) as "fitting together," the construction of "perceptual" and "effector" worlds (Uexküll's *Umwelt* [1920]), "differentiation" and "integration" (Werner, 1940), and is a reflection of the synthetic function of the ego.

Organizing activity begins to occur extremely early in life, from the moment when the child's experience of the present can be said to be modified by what has been experienced in the past; from the moment sensations begin to be transformed into percepts, however primitive these percepts may be; from the moment that differential cathexis of aspects of the child's world can be said to occur. Clearly, it is those experiences which are directly concerned with need satisfaction that are first registered and organized by the child, under the dominance of the pleasure principle, and the child's first models of the world (and the term "world" includes, of course, the child's own body) are extremely scanty, primitive, and self-centered. The child's inner world, Hartmann (1939) points out, arises as "a central regulating factor . . . interpolated between the receptors and the effectors."

Organizing activity is much more than the mere taking in of impressions from the outside, but is intimately connected with the development of all organized ego functions and secondary processes. It includes the construction of frames of reference, schemata, and all the techniques by which the child controls his perceptions (arising from the id or the outside world) and activities. It includes also the development of ego functions such as memory, thinking, imagination, and the capacity for purposive action, functions which in turn foster further organizing activity. Part of the child's inner world consists of models of his objects (or aspects of his objects) and of the self, models[6] which are composites and abstractions created[7] by the child out of its multiple experiences. The self-schema can also be classed as a type of object schema, cathected by instinctual energy as are the other object models of the child.

In the normal child, object relationships develop out of the child's first experiences of satisfaction and dissatisfaction, and their development is associated, in the inner world of the child, with the construction of a libidinally cathected mother schema or imago, although this is limited at first to qualities of experience associated by the child with need satisfaction. Initially these need-satisfying experiences are not differentiated from the self, but as time goes on a distinct mother schema is organized. It consists, in essence, of a set of expectations relating to the mother's appearance and activities, and when the mother conforms to these expectations (which vary according to the state of instinctual tension within the child), the

6 The use of the term "schema" or "model" in this context by no means implies a static conception. The "models" are, in a sense, "working models," and include all the sequences of behavior on the part of the object which can be predicted by the child on the basis of its past experiences.

7 The term "introjection," which has been used to describe this process, is reserved in this paper for a very special sort of ego activity, a mechanism which is associated with unique and important changes in the disposition of instinctual energies.

child experiences satisfaction. When the mother's behavior does not in fact correspond to the cathected internal mother imago, the child experiences frustration, unpleasure, and anger. Later the response of the child becomes more and more removed from the original gratifying situations, so that the presence of the mother, or even the knowledge of the mother's readiness to attend to the child, becomes a source of satisfaction in itself.

The internal imago of the mother is thus not a substitute for an object relationship, but is itself an indispensable part of the relationship. Without it no object relationship (in the psychological sense) exists. It is not in itself a source of real gratification to the child, although it may temporarily achieve a diminution of an instinctual tension through hallucination. The real source of gratification is the mother or any other object who can conform to the child's mother schema.

The child's inner world enables him to distinguish, localize, and interpret his sensory impressions; but it also functions to provide him with warning or guiding signals which regulate his behavior. Thus his developing body schema gives him a means of identifying sensations and experiences in his own body, and also assists him to coordinate his bodily activities, as, for example, in learning to walk. Similarly his mother and father schemata gradually enable him to recognize and interpret the activities of his parents, and at the same time allow him to predict what behavior will evoke their love and approval, and what their disapproval, and to control his behavior accordingly. I want to draw particular attention to these two functions of the child's inner world, the function of *representing* and the function of *guiding*, for they will ultimately be reflected in that specialized part of the inner world which later becomes the superego.

The growth of the inner world goes hand in hand with the partial abandonment of the pleasure principle in favor of the reality principle. The notion of "reality" in this context includes the reactions of the parents to the child's behavior, and no essential distinction can be made till relatively late in development between the "real world" as adults know it and the culturally determined or idiosyncratic commands, wishes, and precepts of the parents. There is as yet no distinction in kind between frustrations imposed by the parents and those which are a consequence of the resistance of other aspects of the "real world" to the demands of the child. Indeed, the child gains much of its knowledge of the properties of the real world, with consequent benefit to ego development, through parental interpretations of reality. It is largely through the agency of the parents that the reality principle replaces the pleasure principle.

Now we know that the needs of the child progress from the need for bodily satisfaction and comfort to a need to feel loved in a variety of other ways as well. With increasing discrimination between the self and other schemata, the child comes to realize that his early pleasurable, narcissistic state of union with the mother is threatened. He suffers a lowering of the level of libidinal cathexis of the self, with consequent narcissistic depletion, and, as Freud puts it (1914), he needs to restore the state of "a real happy love [which] corresponds to the primal condition in which object-libido and ego-libido [we would now say self-cathexis] cannot be distinguished."

The child's many attempts to restore this original narcissistic state provide an enormous impetus to ego development. Freud (1914) says: "The development of the ego consists in a departure from primary narcissism and gives rise to a vigorous attempt to recover that state."[8]

The child has a number of techniques at its disposal for the restoration of this original state of well-being, and of these I want to consider only two which are relevant here:

1. *Obedience* to and compliance with the demands of the parents.
2. *Identification* with and imitation of the parents.

The term *identification*, which refers both to a process and to the end product of that process, has been used by psychoanalysts

---

[8] The problem of what it means to "feel loved," or to "restore narcissistic cathexis," is one which has as yet been insufficiently explored. What the child is attempting to restore is an affective state of well-being which we can correlate, in terms of energy, with the level of narcissistic cathexis of the self. Initially this affective state, which normally forms a background to everyday experience, must be the state of bodily well-being which the infant experiences when his instinctual needs have been satisfied (as distinct from the pleasure in their satisfaction). This affective state later becomes localized in the self, and we see aspects of it in feelings of self-esteem as well as in normal background feelings of safety (Sandler, 1959). The maintenance of this *central affective state* is perhaps the most powerful motive for ego development, and we must regard the young child (and later the adult) as seeking well-being as well as pleasure-seeking; the two are by no means the same, and in analysis we can often observe a conflict between the two.

in a variety of ways, and attempts to differentiate ego identifications from superego identifications have led to much confusion. In the present formulation the term will be used only in respect of identifications which modify the ego; so-called superego identifications will be seen as a combination of *introjection* on the one hand, and a corresponding "ego" identification on the other.

The observation of very young children has taught us that identifications with parents and others are an aspect of normal development, and that identification is by no means always a substitute for an object relationship, nor is it always used defensively. Transient identifications may later become a permanent feature of the child's personality, but the capacity to make temporary identifications remains after childhood, and is a particular feature of adolescence. We can define identification by saying that it represents a process of modifying the self-schema on the basis of a present or past perception of an object, and that such modification may be temporary or permanent, whole or partial, ego enriching or ego restrictive, depending on what is identified with and whether the need for such an identification is of short or long duration.

Whereas in primary identification the child fuses or confuses the rudimentary schema of the self with that of another person, so that the distinction between self and not-self does not exist, in secondary identification the self-schema is modified so that it becomes *like* that of the object, and some of the libidinal cathexis of the object is transferred to the self. Secondary identification is a later acquisition of the child, and grows out of the more primitive mechanism, which remains, in a controlled way, within the ego as a constituent of the capacity for empathy. Primary identification also reappears as a feature of ego functioning in deteriorated schizophrenics, when the capacity for distinguishing between self and not-self has broken down. We might say that secondary identification represents an attempt to create the illusion of primary identification. Secondary identification is not very different from imitation in the small child, though conscious intent is more prominent in the latter. For present purposes we need not make a fundamental distinction between the two.

Identification is a means of feeling the same as the admired and idealized object, and therefore at one with it; and, as Freud has pointed out, it can exist side by side with object relationships. If we recall the joy with which the very young child imitates, consciously or unconsciously, a parent or an older sibling, we can see that identification represents an important technique whereby the child feels loved and obtains an inner state of well-being. We might say that the esteem in which the omnipotent and admired object is held is duplicated in the self and gives rise to self-esteem. The child feels at one with the object and close to it, and temporarily regains the feeling of happiness which he experienced during the earliest days of life. Identificatory behavior is further reinforced by the love, approval, and praise of the real object, and it is quite striking to observe the extent to which the education of the child progresses through the reward, not only of feeling omnipotent like the idealized parent, but also through the very positive signs of love and approval granted by parents and educators to the child. The sources of "feeling loved," and of self-esteem, are the real figures in the child's environment; and in these first years identificatory behavior is directed by the child toward enhancing, via these real figures, his feeling of inner well-being.

Identification may also be used for the purposes of defense, particularly where the child is faced with a problem of resolving a conflict between its need for an object's love and its hostility to that object. In the familiar "identification with the aggressor" the child deals with his fear of a threatening person by identifying with his omnipotent, powerful, and terrifying qualities. It may also be called into play in an attempt to deal with a loss or a withdrawal from a loving object. In this latter case it is usually accompanied by an introjection of the object, a process which I shall discuss presently; but identification is not the same as introjection as it will be defined here, and the distinction between the two is, as we shall see, of supreme importance in understanding the formation of the superego.

The two *techniques* of restoring a feeling of being loved (of increasing the level of libidinal cathexis of the self) which I have mentioned, identification and obedience, make use of the two functions of the child's parental schemata which I have described earlier, the function of representing and the function of guiding respectively. But the mechanisms of identification and obedience by no means operate in isolation from each other. In many activities the child obtains what amounts to a double gain through behaving in such a way as to identify with the parents and at the same time obey their wishes. Thus the toddler who seriously washes his hands after playing with dirt gains both from "doing what mother wants" and from "being like mother."

The Preautonomous Superego Schema

What develops in the ego of the child in the preoedipal years is an organization which reflects the idealized and desirable qualities of the parents on the one hand and which prompts the child to suitable object-related behavior on the other (behavior, that is, which will gain for the child a feeling of being loved). It contains approving and permissive as well as prohibiting and restraining features. It is not yet a structure (in the sense in which Freud used the term in *The Ego and the Id*), for the introjection of parental authority which will elevate it to autonomous superego status has not yet taken place. It is a preautonomous superego schema, a "plan" for the later superego. It is a sort of undergraduate superego which only works under the supervision of the parents, and is a differentiated part of the child's own "reality," influenced as is all the child's inner world by instinctual drives and fantasies. It has not yet gained a license for independent practice, so to speak, and it will only do so with the decisive introjections which go with the resolution of oedipal conflict. What might appear to be conflict between ego and "superego" in the preoedipal stages is based on the child's predictions, often distorted, of parental reaction.

We know that the child's view of his parents is objective only to a limited degree. His parental schemata will be colored by his fantasies, and in particular by the projection of unwanted qualities of his own onto them. The child may not be able to tolerate the aggressive and sadistic parts of his self, and transfers these features from one part of his inner world to another—from his model of his self to his model of his parents. In this sense, projection is the opposite of identification.

The warning signal of impending punishment or loss of love provided by the preautonomous superego schema does not yet deserve the name of guilt, though the affective state it produces in the ego may be identical with that which we refer to as guilt, later in the child's development.

I do not need to describe here the ways in which the child's conflict between his instinctual urges and his need to preserve his narcissism are intensified when the child enters the phallic stage. His positive and negative oedipus complexes, the ambivalence inherent in them, the impossibility of really fulfilling his instinctual wishes, the fear of punishment and castration (which is correlated with a father image distorted by the projection of the child's own aggression)—all of these combine to create a situation of unbearable tension in the child. During the phallic phase the superego schema is much elaborated and modified, although it will always bear the stamp of his pregenital relationships to his parents. This schema, not yet the superego, has the function of representing (albeit in a distorted way) the admired and feared qualities of the parents. But it also functions to indicate to the ego which piece of behavior will evoke the love and admiration of the parents, and which will cause their displeasure, with consequent lowering of the narcissistic level in the self.

We link the development of the superego proper with the resolution of the oedipus complex. Freud regarded this development not only as the outcome of oedipal conflict, but also as the very means whereby the child effects a resolution of this conflict. The superego is formed, as Freud puts it, as a precipitate within the ego, and its formation is correlated with a partial and relative reduction of interest in and dependence on the real parents. The major source of self-esteem is no longer the real parents, but the superego. *Introjection* of the parents has taken place, and a structure has been formed which did not exist in this form before.

At this point it is necessary to indicate the meaning given to the term introjection in this context; for, after all, have not the functions which we call superego previously existed in the mind of the child in the shape of the parental schemata? What distinguishes the introject from the internal schema is precisely the capacity of the introject to substitute, in whole or in part, for the real object as a source of narcissistic gratification. This implies that the introject must somehow be developed out of the schema, crystallized and structuralized within the ego, so that it can be given the power to satisfy, and be felt by the ego to be a sufficient substitute for the objects. The construction of an introject is thus the sequel of a complete or partial dissolution of the relationship to the real object. Through introjection the *relationship* to the object is maintained and perpetuated, but the real object is no longer so vital to the relationship. It follows that what is introjected is neither the personality nor the behavior of the parents, but their *authority*. (This view of introjection is therefore different from that of Ferenczi—who introduced the term—and that of Melanie Klein.)

With this elevation of the superego schema to autonomous status —with its structuralization, in the sense described by Freud in *The Ego and the Id* (1923)—what was previously experienced as the threat of parental disapproval becomes guilt, though the affective experience is probably the same in both; and an essential component of this affective state is the drop in self-esteem. This differentiates guilt from anxiety, and links it with feelings of inferiority and inadequacy as well as with the affect which is experienced in pathological states of depression. An *opposite* and equally important affective state is also experienced by the ego, a state which occurs when the ego and superego are functioning together in a smooth and harmonious fashion; that is, when the feeling of being loved is restored by the approval of the superego. Perhaps this is best described as a state of mental comfort and well-being, of *eupathy*. It is the counterpart of the affect experienced by the child when his parents show signs of approval and pleasure at his performance, when the earliest state of being at one with his mother is temporarily regained. It is related to the affective background of self-confidence and self-assurance, as well as to the pathological state of mania.

Freud has described the way in which both superego formation and identification are associated with a desexualization of the child's libidinal aims, and with an instinctual defusion. This defusion enables the child to retain his tender feelings toward his parents, and to divert his destructive urges into his now structuralized schema of parental attributes and behavior—that is, into his superego. The degree to which his hostile wishes cannot find expression through his ego will determine the degree of severity or even savagery of his superego. This may occur to such a degree that the superego may be a much-distorted representative of the real parents of childhood. In this way, as Freud has frequently pointed out, the superego is also a representative of the id, in close and constant touch with it.

There has been a strong tendency in psychoanalytic writings to overlook the very positive side of the child's relationship to his superego; a relation based on the fact that it can also be a splendid source of love and well-being. It functions to approve as well as to disapprove; and the relative understressing by psychoanalysts of the former may be due to the fact that they are primarily concerned as therapists, rather than as educators, with situations of conflict and inner disharmony.

It will be noticed that superego formation has been linked throughout with introjection, and has been separated conceptually from processes of identification. That the reinforcement of identifications with the parents is something which occurs concurrently with superego formation and progression into latency, is something which cannot be questioned. Freud himself did not always distinguish identification with the parents, particularly with the father, from their introjection and the consequent setting up of an internal authority which can act in opposition to the ego; but in view of recent developments, particularly the increasing theoretical importance of the concept of "self," such a distinction appears to be essential.

Identification is a technique whereby the self is modified so that it corresponds, to a greater or lesser extent, with an object as perceived by the ego. The model for the ego may be a real person, or an introject. Thus we have a state of affairs in which the ego can use its capacity for identification to obtain a libidinal gain through being at one either with another person who is idealized or feared (or both), or through feeling at one with the introject which contains a representation of the behavior, appearance, and attitudes of the parents. Thus we can replace the notion of superego identification with that of *identification with the introject*.[9] It changes and modifies the *content* of the self, but does not result in the formation of psychic structure. Where ego and superego work together harmoniously, the harmony may be achieved by such an identification on the part of the ego, and also by direct obedience to or compliance

9 Anna Freud has suggested that this is essentially similar to the mechanism of identification with the aggressor.

with superego precepts and demands. This harmonious working together does not represent a merging of the superego into the self (which we see in manic states and which is associated with primary identification), but a modification of the self on the basis of a model of the idealized qualities of the parents, or their demands and prohibitions, as embodied in the superego. Furthermore, if the child can both identify with and obey the introjected parents at one and the same time (as in the example I gave earlier of the child washing his hands "to be like mother" and "to please mother"), a double gain is effected.

We can also see, particularly in the course of an analysis, how guilt feelings may be dealt with by identification with the introject, an identification which shows itself through the adoption of a strict and moralizing attitude to another. The child who tells a doll or the analyst not to be naughty deals with his feelings of guilt and gains a feeling of well-being by identifying with the critical aspects of his superego, projecting his self-imago onto another. In this extremely common mechanism there is also a double gain. We know that those who most vocally proclaim moral precepts are often those who feel most guilty about their own unconscious wish to do that which they criticize in others.

That dependence on the superego is so long-lasting, and often results in more or less permanent changes in the ego, is a reflection of the child's dependence on his real parents as a source of narcissistic gain in the earliest years of life. But the superego is only supported by the ego as long as it functions, in its turn, to support the ego; and situations do exist in which the ego can and will totally disregard the standards and precepts of the superego, if it can gain a sufficient quantity of narcissistic support elsewhere. We see this impressive phenomenon in the striking changes in ideals, character, and morality which may result from the donning of a uniform and the feeling of identity with a group. If narcissistic support is available in sufficient quantity from an identification with the ideals of a group, or with the ideals of a leader, then the superego may be completely disregarded, and its functions taken over by the group ideals, precepts, and behavior. If these group ideals permit a direct gratification of instinctual wishes, then a complete character transformation may occur; and the extent to which the superego can be abandoned in this way is evident in the appalling atrocities committed by the Nazis before and during the last war. Changes in morality can sometimes be seen when a person becomes much loved by another; the superego is then not as necessary as before as a provider of love and as a source of well-being.

Many examples exist in ordinary life of the way in which group morality and group ideals may replace personal morality; these include religious conversion, and the gang formation and hero worship of adolescence. In psychotherapy or in analysis, the supporting role of the analyst, who may be invested with the authority of the parents, can permit the ego's dependence on its superego to be sufficiently reduced to enable forbidden and repressed material to be brought into consciousness and inner conflict worked through.

Similar phenomena occur when the feeling of well-being in the self can be obtained by means of drugs, and drug addiction can then replace what might be termed normal superego addiction. Indeed, the superego has been facetiously defined as that part of the mental apparatus which is soluble in alcohol.

Anna Freud has pointed out that the establishment of the superego does not entirely remove the child's dependence on the real parents and parental figures as a source of love, and when we speak of the latency child's independence we use a relative term. To some extent this reliance on others as a source of self-esteem persists throughout life, and we all know how the support and reassurance of a friend can mitigate unhappiness in oneself.

Lampl-de Groot, in two interesting papers (1936, 1947), has drawn attention to the importance for the child, and later for the adult, of maintaining a sufficient level of self-esteem, and to the ways in which threats to the self-esteem can give rise to disturbances of ego functioning. For the ego to operate well, it is necessary that one be in receipt of regular narcissistic supplies, and a study of the sources of an individual's self-esteem can enable much of his behavior, neurotic or otherwise, to be understood. Alfred Adler has taken one source of lowered self-esteem (organic inferiority) and embroidered it into a whole system. And although we reject Adler's highly oversimplified views, the techniques by which the ego can restore its self-esteem and the ways in which these techniques enter into character have been insufficiently studied.

In its dealings with its superego the ego may involve other persons as well. It may do so when it has the need to force others to reinforce the superego through the provocation of approval, forgiveness, or punishment. In so-called superego projection (or externalization), we can observe an attempt by the ego to restore the existence of the original superego objects in the external world. In one sense, this is an attempt at regression, and it is particularly fostered by the analytic situation, where it appears in the form of a superego transference. The involvement of others in superego conflict also appears in moral masochism. (When the ego has a masochistic attitude to the superego, this is a reflection of an earlier masochistic tie to the parents.)

The problem of delinquent behavior has been studied by Aichhorn and other psychoanalysts, and it does seem that their findings, particularly in relation to the superego, can be integrated into the conceptual framework outlined in this paper. This applies in particular to the well-known distinction between those who are delinquent because of the introjection of a delinquent parental morality, those whose delinquency is a result of structural faults in the superego, and those neurotic delinquents who are hounded by an inordinate sense of guilt.

The tentative formulation of superego development given here leaves a number of crucial gaps unbridged. One of these gaps is in our knowledge of what the transfer of parental authority from the real parent to the superego schema in the process of introjection really implies. Nevertheless, the concept of superego, when approached from this point of view, has made it possible to categorize superego material in the Index (and therefore in our thoughts) in a more meaningful way. The basic ideas expressed here are to be found in Freud's paper "On Narcissism," and it is precisely the role of narcissism in the development and function of the superego which needs to be stressed. Threats to the narcissistic cathexis of the self exist from birth, and stem from the interaction of the instinctual life of the child, in both its libidinal and aggressive aspects, with the demands and frustrations of the real world. The factors which ultimately determine the superego operate from the beginning, yet what we tend to call superego precursors are an integral part of the development of the ego itself; the superego as a structure comes into existence only with the resolution of the oedipus complex. And although it is often the agent of pain and destruction, its existence appears to be brought about by the child's attempts to transform paradise lost into paradise regained.

Freud sums up the function of the superego, appropriately in the last chapter of his last book, *An Outline of Psychoanalysis* (1938), as follows. He says:

> The torments caused by the reproaches of conscience correspond precisely to a child's dread of losing his parents' love, a dread which has been replaced in him by the moral agency. On the other hand, if the ego has successfully resisted a temptation to do something that would be objectionable to the superego, it feels its self-respect raised and its pride increased, as though it had made some precious acquisition. In this way the superego continues to act the rôle of an external world toward the ego, although it has become part of the internal world. During the whole of a man's later life it represents the influence of his childhood, of the care and education given to him by his parents, of his dependence on them—of the childhood which is so greatly prolonged in human beings by a common family life. And in all of this what is operating is not only the personal qualities of these parents but also everything that produced a determining effect upon them themselves, the tastes and standards of the social class in which they live and the characteristics and traditions of the race from which they spring [pp. 122-123].

APPLICATIONS TO CLINICAL MATERIAL

On the basis of the formulations presented here it has been found possible to devise a system of classification of superego-related material. This will form the basis of a later paper, which will include examples of clinical observations classified in the Index.

Because of the inevitable "dissolution" or regression of the superego in the course of treatment, it has been necessary to consider the child's relationships to authority, without making, in the first instance, a distinction between inner and outer authority. These relationships can be categorized according, for example, to types of control—the ways in which the child gains or loses narcissistic supplies from his superego, its representatives, or other external persons. A large subsection deals with the responses of the ego in the face of the fear of or wish to please internal or external authority. This includes all the attempts made by the child to restore his narcissistic equilibrium as a result of conflict with authority. "Identification with the superego," and certain aspects of the construction of a system of ideals, fall into this subsection.

Parallel with this, it has been possible to classify statements by therapists relating to the nature and extent of structuralization (including stages of development) and to qualities and characteristics of the superego. (Both object and instinct sources have been categorized, together with special contents of behavior and fantasy which evoke tension with inner or outer authority. Special characteristics of the superego [e.g., severity or inconsistency] have also been indexed; and a number of further subsections deal with other aspects.)

It seems clear that the construction of a comprehensive framework for classifying clinical observations, in the area of the superego as well as in other areas, will inevitably have repercussions on the actual observations made by therapists; this in turn must lead to further theoretical reconsideration. In all of this, the formal process of indexing data assists the healthy interaction between practice and theory.

BIBLIOGRAPHY

Aichhorn, A. (1925), *Wayward Youth*. New York: Viking Press, 1935.
Beres, D. (1958), Vicissitudes of Superego Functions and Superego Precursors in Childhood. *This Annual*, XIII.
de Monchaux, C. (1958), Pooling of Case Material: A Methodological Project. In: Clinical Studies in Psycho-Analysis: Research Project of the Hampstead Child-Therapy Clinic, by A. Freud. *Proc. Roy. Soc. Med.*, LI.
Fenichel, O. (1926), Identification. *The Collected Papers of Otto Fenichel*, I. New York: Norton, 1953.
—— (1945), *The Psychoanalytic Theory of Neurosis*. New York: Norton.
Ferenczi, S. (1925), Psycho-Analysis of Sexual Habits. *Further Contributions to the Theory and Technique of Psycho-Analysis*. London: Hogarth Press, 1927.
Foulkes, S. H. (1937), On Introjection. *Int. J. Psa.*, XVIII.
Freud, A. (1926), *The Psycho-Analytical Treatment of Children*. London: Imago Publ. Co., 1946; New York: International Universities Press, 1959.
—— (1936), *The Ego and the Mechanisms of Defence*. New York: International Universities Press.
—— (1959), Clinical Studies in Psychoanalysis: Research Project of the Hampstead Child-Therapy Clinic. *This Annual*, XIV.
Freud, S. (1887-1902), *The Origins of Psychoanalysis*. New York: Basic Books, 1954.
—— (1900), The Interpretation of Dreams. *Standard Edition*, IV & V. London: Hogarth Press, 1953.
—— (1914), On Narcissism: An Introduction. *Standard Edition*, XIV. London: Hogarth Press, 1957.

—— (1917), Mourning and Melancholia. *Standard Edition*, XIV. London: Hogarth Press, 1957.

—— (1921), Group Psychology and the Analysis of the Ego. *Standard Edition*, XVIII. London: Hogarth Press, 1955.

—— (1923), *The Ego and the Id*. London: Hogarth Press, 1927.

—— (1926), Inhibitions, Symptoms and Anxiety. *Standard Edition*, XX. London: Hogarth Press, 1959.

—— (1927), *The Future of an Illusion*. London: Hogarth Press, 1928.

—— (1930), *Civilization and Its Discontents*. London: Hogarth Press, 1946.

—— (1932), *New Introductory Lectures on Psychoanalysis*. New York: Norton, 1933.

—— (1938), *An Outline of Psychoanalysis*. New York: Norton, 1949.

Fries, M. E. (1946), The Child's Ego Development and the Training of Adults in His Environment. *This Annual*, II.

Glover, E. (1949), *Psycho-Analysis*. London: Staples Press.

Greenson, R. R. (1954), The Struggle Against Identification. *J. Am. Psa. Assn.*, II.

Hartmann, H. (1939), *Ego Psychology and the Problem of Adaptation*. New York: International Universities Press, 1958.

—— (1950), Comments on the Psychoanalytic Theory of the Ego. *This Annual*, V.

—— & Kris, E. (1945), The Genetic Approach in Psychoanalysis. *This Annual*, I.

—— —— & Loewenstein, R. M. (1949), Notes on the Theory of Aggression. *This Annual*, III/IV.

Hendrick, I. (1951), Early Development of the Ego: Identification in Infancy. *Psa. Quart.*, XX.

Jacobson, E. (1953), Contribution to the Metapsychology of Cyclothymic Depression. In: *Affective Disorders*, ed. P. Greenacre. New York: International Universities Press.

—— (1954a), Contribution to the Metapsychology of Psychotic Identifications. *J. Am. Psa. Assn.*, II.

—— (1954b), The Self and the Object World: Vicissitudes of Their Infantile Cathexes and Their Influence on Ideational and Affective Development. *This Annual*, IX.

—— (1954c), On Psychotic Identifications. *Int. J. Psa.*, XXXV.

Jones, E. (1926), The Origin and Structure of the Superego. *Int. J. Psa.*, VII.

Klein, G. (1959), Consciousness in Psychoanalytic Theory. *J. Am. Psa. Assn.*, VII.

Klein, M. (1927), Symposium on Child Analysis. In: *Contributions to Psycho-Analysis, 1921-1945*. London: Hogarth Press, 1948.

—— (1933), The Early Development of Conscience in the Child. In: *Contributions to Psycho-Analysis, 1921-1945*. London: Hogarth Press, 1948.

—— (1958), On the Development of Mental Functioning. *Int. J. Psa.*, XXXIX.

Knight, R. P. (1940), Introjection, Projection and Identification. *Psa. Quart.*, IX.

Kris, M. (1957), The Use of Prediction in a Longitudinal Study. *This Annual*, XII.

Lampl-de Groot, J. (1936), Hemmung und Narzissmus. *Int. Ztschr. Psa.*, XXII.

—— (1947), On the Development of the Ego and Superego. *Int. J. Psa.*, XXVIII.

Nunberg, H. (1932), *Principles of Psychoanalysis*. New York: International Universities Press, 1955.

Piaget, J. (1936), *The Origins of Intelligence in Children*. New York: International Universities Press, 1952.

—— (1937), *The Construction of Reality in the Child*. New York: Basic Books, 1954.

Piers, G. & Singer, M. B. (1953), *Shame and Guilt: A Psychoanalytic and a Cultural Study*. Springfield, Ill.: Charles C Thomas.

Rapaport, D. (1951), The Conceptual Model of Psychoanalysis. *J. Personal.*, XX.

—— (1957), Cognitive Structures. In *Contemporary Approaches to Cognition*, ed. J. S. Bruner et al. Cambridge, Mass.: Harvard University Press.

—— (1959), A Historical Survey of Psychoanalytic Ego Psychology. In: *Identity and the Life Cycle*, by E. H. Erikson. *Psychological Issues*, I. New York: International Universities Press.

Reich, A. (1954), Early Identifications as Archaic Elements in the Superego. *J. Am. Psa. Assn.*, II.

Ribble, M. (1944), *The Rights of Infants*. New York: Columbia University Press.

Sandler, J. (1959), The Background of Safety. Paper read to 21st International Psycho-Analytical Congress in Copenhagen.

Spitz, R. A. (1945), Hospitalism. An Inquiry into the Genesis of Psychiatric Conditions in Early Childhood. *This Annual*, I.

—— (1946), Hospitalism. A Follow-up Report. *This Annual*, II.

—— (1950), Anxiety in Infancy. A study of Its Manifestations in the First Year of Life. *Int. J. Psa.*, XXXI.

—— (1957), *No and Yes: On the Genesis of Human Communication*. New York: International Universities Press.

—— (1958), On the Genesis of Superego Components. *This Annual*, XIII.

Uexküll, J. (1920), *Theoretical Biology*. New York: Harcourt Brace, 1926.

Werner, H. (1940), *Comparative Psychology of Mental Development*. New York: International Universities Press, 1957.

THE LOVING AND BELOVED SUPEREGO IN FREUD'S STRUCTURAL THEORY[1]

ROY SCHAFER, Ph.D. (New Haven)[2]

In an inspired, highly condensed passage, near the end of *The Ego and the Id* (1923), Freud stated:

> The fear of death in melancholia only admits of one explanation: that the ego gives itself up because it feels itself hated and persecuted by the super-ego, instead of loved. To the ego, therefore, living means the same as being loved—being loved by the super-ego, which here again appears as the representative of the id. The super-ego fulfils the same function of protecting and saving that was fulfilled in earlier days by the father and later by Providence or destiny. But, when the ego finds itself in overwhelming danger of a real order which it believes itself unable to overcome by its own strength, it is bound to draw the same conclusion. It sees itself deserted by all the forces of protection and lets itself die. Here, moreover, is once again the same situation as that which underlay the first great anxiety-state of birth and the infantile anxiety of longing for an absent person—the anxiety of separation from the protecting mother [pp. 86-87].

Freud concluded the monograph very soon after this passage and in his later writings never developed this complex of themes. Considering its importance, one cannot escape the impression that a train of thought had been interrupted. In fact, consequently Freud again broke off the same train of thought, once at the end of his paper "Humour" (1928a), and the second time at the end of *An Outline of Psychoanalysis* (1938). In other places, as in *The Problem of Anxiety* (1926) and the *New Introductory Lectures* (1932), he referred to this important subject only briefly though most significantly. These references will be considered below.

[1] Presented before The Western New England Psychoanalytic Society, March 19, 1960.
[2] From Yale University School of Medicine.

It seems, therefore, that Freud was not prepared to pursue to its end the line of thought leading to a loving and beloved superego or to integrate such a conception with his decisive treatment of the criticizing and feared superego. Later writers, for example, Fenichel (1945), take it for granted that the superego has a loving, protective role. It remains to be better understood, however, why Freud could not or did not develop this idea systematically. A biographer might seek reasons for this in Freud's character and life experience. I shall approach the problem only from the standpoint of Freud's theoretical and technical preoccupations and commitments. It also remains to be seen whether, when Freud's various unsystematic comments are assembled and analyzed, they add up to a consistent and useful formulation of a benign superego. To this end, I have re-examined all of Freud's writings since 1923, beginning with *The Ego and the Id*, together with those earlier works most obviously presaging and paving the way for his superego theory.[3] From these sources I have abstracted all the points bearing either directly or by implication on the present subject, and have attempted to explicate and, to a degree, to amplify and synthesize their meaning.

METHODOLOGICAL CONSIDERATIONS

My emphasis on the superego as a whole and on the benign superego in particular should not be mistaken for special pleading. None is intended, neither for the superego vis-à-vis the ego, the id, and external reality, nor for the benign superego vis-à-vis the hostile superego. In all structural analyses, the principle of multiple function, as set forth by Waelder (1930), is the necessary guide. Yet, part of understanding and developing a concept consists of viewing everything else through it, as through a special lens.

No attempt will be made in what follows to formulate a complete metapsychology of the superego. Such a formulation would require a detailed analysis of the precursors of the superego; of the processes of internalization, identification, and structure formation; and of the place of values in psychic functioning.

---

[3] The latter works are *Totem and Taboo* (1912), "On Narcissism" (1914), "Mourning and Melancholia" (1917), *Beyond the Pleasure Principle* (1920), and *Group Psychology and the Analysis of the Ego* (1921).

Inevitably, in such a survey as this, one must take it upon himself to decide whether Freud meant to retain, minimize, or discard some of his formulations, especially those preceding the appearance of *The Ego and the Id*. In different places he discussed the superego (or ego ideal)in varying terms and with varying emphases. In making these decisions, one must obviously rely on criteria of frequency and emphasis of formulation. Additionally, one must spell out the implications of these formulations and apply to the formulations and their implications the additional criteria of theoretical necessity, internal consistency, and conformity with prevailing clinical findings. For this reason the presentation changes from a survey to a synthesizing interpretation of Freud's scientific preconscious.

There is an additional consideration. Many incidental references to this or that aspect of the superego never appeared in Freud's major formulations. Were they unimportant to him, or too obvious to need further elaboration, or just lacking a context, a broad conception, into which they could be fitted? In any event, I believe they should not be neglected, and I shall try to show that the superego as a loving and beloved institution in the mind, as well as a hateful and feared one, provides a context for many of these undeveloped or unintegrated comments.

I must note one other methodological problem before proceeding. Freud frequently used the term *ego* where he appeared to mean *superego* alone or superego and ego simultaneously. This was especially so when he discussed the identifications that form the core of superego.[4] For Freud, the superego was "a differentiating grade in the ego" (1921, pp. 101-109), a "precipitate in the ego" (1923, p. 44), and a "function" of the ego (1923, p. 73; 1932, pp. 85-86), and sometimes he used *ego* in the comprehensive sense without so specifying. Accordingly, I have had to infer his meaning in certain ambiguous instances.

I shall begin with a brief summary of what is generally more familiar, Freud's conception of the hostile superego. Against this summary as background, the benign superego should emerge later in sharp relief for our consideration.

---

4 See, for example, his remarks on the "character of the ego" (1923, p. 36), secondary narcissism (1923, p. 38), "ego constructions" (1923, p. 82), and the ego taking itself as an object (1932, p. 84).

THE HOSTILE SUPEREGO

In this part of his theory, Freud saw the superego as a function of the ego concerned chiefly with the limitation of satisfactions (1921, p. 105; 1938, p. 19). The ego carries out defense largely at the behest of the superego (1914, p. 51; 1923, p. 75). In particular the superego limits those satisfactions which are close to the libidinal and aggressive oedipal impulses and their regressed, pregenital versions. In this respect, the superego is ever alert, uncompromising, and harshly critical and punitive. The rest of the ego lives in actual or potential dread of its wrath. Its opposition to the rest of the ego is felt as a sense of guilt and culminates behaviorally in the seeking of punishment.[5]

The superego is formed by intensifying already existing identifications with the parents (1932, p. 91), especially those representing the parents as prohibiting, commanding, and retaliatory. The child makes a one-sided choice of the harsh aspects of the parents and does not represent their loving care (1932, pp. 89-90). Though both parents are involved in so far as each is seen to be a rival, in the masculine and feminine components of the oedipal configuration, Freud emphasized the identification with the father in the development of the boy, and I shall adhere to this emphasis. Freud's rationale for this one-sided emphasis will become evident later. The introjected father is likely to be far more punitive than the real father, for it is not only his real aggressiveness that defines the internal image; it is also the strength of the child's oedipal wishes that must be repressed and of the aggression associated with them. It is reactive aggression against the father that is made over to the identification and that constitutes its initial source of restrictive power (1932, p. 150). The aggression arises in response to the frustrations the father imposes and in response to his retaliations as anticipated in fantasy (1930, p. 85).

Freud referred also to borrowing the father's strength in this

[5] In one place, Freud states that the superego even looks for opportunities in external reality through which it may inflict punishment (1930, p. 79). It seems more consistent, however, to limit the function of the superego in this respect to the testing of certain aspects of inner reality and to see that outward search as carried on by other ego functions in the service of the need for punishment induced by the superego.

process (1923, p. 45) and to a "continuation of the punitive energy belonging to external authority, preserved within the mind" (1930, p. 95). To be consistent with his closed-system economics of the mental apparatus, however, this statement can be understood to mean only that the punitive model is taken over in the mind as an organizing factor. That is to say, through identification a new structure with specific functions is established in the mind; this structure is organized around the image of the father, and in unconscious fantasy and in effect it is as if he had come into possession of the child's rage and turned it back on the child.

The superego stands apart from the rest of the ego and rules it (1923, p. 73). The superego observes the ego, criticizes it, and punishes it. To the superego, the wish is equivalent to the deed; hence, the ego, which is ever involved in ambivalence, is ever vulnerable to its reproaches. Before the final internalization of superego contents we should not speak of a sense of guilt and conscience; there is only dread of discovery (1930, p. 79).

By its very origin the superego is close to the id. It "knows" the id better than the ego does. With this in mind, Freud hypothesized that "a great part of the sense of guilt must normally remain unconscious because the origin of conscience is closely connected with the oedipus complex which belongs to the unconscious" (1923, p. 75). Because the identification with the parent continues to provide forbidden oedipal gratifications, even though some degree of desexualization of these gratifications must be assumed, the superego has additional reason to be hostile to the ego. Another reason for its hostility is that the ego is partly identified with the feared and hated parent and is attacked by the superego as a substitute for the parent himself. In this respect the superego secretly continues to express outwardly directed hostility (1923, p. 74).[6] Thus, ego and superego each represent parent *and* child in a continuing hostile interplay. This interplay may be accentuated by the development of moral masochism in which morality itself is intensely sexualized (1924a, p. 266). At the same time the male ego's response to superego criticism will be ambivalent, for, through its partial meaning of

6 This proposition has its roots in "Mourning and Melancholia" (1917, pp. 161-162) and *Group Psychology* (1921, p. 108), and is explicitly stated in *Civilization and Its Discontents* (1930, p. 84).

castration, this criticism signifies pleasurable as well as resented feminine relations with the father (1928b, p. 231).

The major motivation for this fateful identification is the boy's high narcissistic valuation of his penis and his anxiety over losing it (1924b, pp. 272-273; 1925, p. 196; 1926, p. 78). Dread of castration is transformed into dread of conscience, and castration anxiety continues to be expressed in fear of the superego (1923, p. 85). As described in *The Problem of Anxiety* (1926, pp. 75-79), castration and guilt are respectively the last two steps in a genetic series of danger situations. They are preceded by dread of loss of the love object and dread of loss of love, in that order, and all ultimately refer back to dread of the traumatic situations of helplessness in birth and infancy. Dangers preceding that of castration also figure prominently in the dynamics of the laying down of the superego, for establishing the superego expresses the wish to preserve as much as possible the tender and erotic ties to both parents (1923, p. 44). These ties are to be preserved at the price of renouncing direct instinctual aims and of living henceforth with a hostile authority within oneself. Once the superego is formed, the "torments caused by the reproaches of conscience correspond precisely to a child's dread of losing his parents' love" (1938, p. 122) as well as to that of castration.

Thus, superego criticism refers back to the antecedent danger situations. As all these danger situations have their origins in the prolonged helplessness and dependency of childhood, the superego is itself a monument to this state of affairs (1932, pp. 94-95). Also, once the superego is formed, the ego's fear of it and dependence on it may be elaborated in dread of the community, Fate or destiny, and death (1923, p. 86; 1926, pp. 64-67), and in religious experience and belief (1928c, 1930). Behind this genetic series, Freud envisaged the phylogenetic inheritance of the potentiality for superego formation stemming from the prehistoric murder of the primal father, repeated in many generations, and the psychological and social consequences of this murder (1930, p. 88).

Freud viewed the superego as a structure (1932, p. 92). It is an abiding pattern of inner behavior or set of functions with its own ends and its own energies (1932, p. 87). It binds the energy of the destructive instinct (1923, p. 77; 1937, pp. 345-346) and is an established, automatic channel for discharge of destructiveness in so far as the latter is not released onto the environment (1932, p. 150). As a consequence of the basic superego identification, a defusion of instincts occurs, destructive energy being bound in the superego and libidinal energy in the ego (1923, pp. 80, 83-84). From the standpoint of instinctual vicissitudes, it is an instance of turning round upon the self. Once this structure formation has been accomplished, all inhibited aggression flows into the superego and increases its severity (1923, pp. 79-80). A new, and in crucial respects preferred path has been cleared for the discharge of destructiveness; it leads to the ego instead of the outer world. Thus, apart from the founding of the superego, a vicious circle exists in which renunciation increases morality which then demands further renunciation (1930, pp. 83-85). Freud repeatedly stressed this point.[7]

The superego can regress to anal- and oral-sadistic modes and intensities, as evident in obsessional neurosis and melancholia respectively (1923, pp. 77, 80-81; 1926, pp. 46-48). These two conditions, along with paranoid disorders, appear to have taught Freud the most about the superego because in them there is such a high degree of tension between the superego and the rest of the ego. In normal functioning, the superego is not readily available for study; there it merges into the ego, meaning that the sense of guilt and the need for punishment are then imperceptible, and, by implication, that satisfactions close to the original oedipal impulses are neither vigorously sought nor obtained.

So much for the description of the hostile superego. I shall now discuss the reasons which, to my mind, compelled Freud to adhere to this systematic emphasis on a hostile superego.

1. It helped explain the negative therapeutic reaction, with which he was increasingly concerned (1923, pp. 33, 70-72; 1926, pp. 104-107; 1937, pp. 344-346). He came to consider it a major task of psychoanalysis to bring about the ego's increased independence from the superego (1932, pp. 111-112).

2. The crystallization of superego theory was inextricably in-

---

[7] In a related statement, which he termed "approximate," he said that in the case of repression of instincts, in so far as these combine destructive and erotic elements, the destructive ones are transformed into a sense of guilt and the libidinal ones into symptoms (1930, p. 97).

volved with the recently introduced theory of the death instinct (1920), which was itself formulated in part under the impact of therapeutic difficulties. With regard to the death instinct, the super-ego represents a high-level organization for binding and discharging its destructiveness, just as the ego manages the libidinal, unifying tendencies of Eros. Even apart from the pressure of the death-instinct theory, however, Freud's general theory required an account of the disposition of the aggression inevitably following on instinctual frustration and renunciation. It needed something comparable to the sublimation of libido and something that would give a place to the readily observed aggression in self-reproach and self-punishment.

3. Another reason favoring the conception of a hostile superego was the theory's need for something internal possessed of the fierce relentlessness required to contain the derivatives of the powerful erotic needs of the oedipus complex in so far as these are not smashed by castration anxiety (1924b, 1925). In this connection, Freud was ever impressed with the necessity, in civilized child rearing, to accomplish in only a few years an extremely high degree of instinctual renunciation and general socialization—a degree that had taken millenia to accomplish in the history of mankind (1932, p. 201). For this long view of human development, Freud had to keep the coercive and hostile elements of the parental function in the foreground and view their internalization as the basis of man's successful and lasting socialization.

4. A final reason for the emphasis on the hostile superego lies in Freud's method of theory building in this area. He drew heavily on observations of obsessional neurosis and melancholia (1923, pp. 73-74, 77-78) and paranoia (1914, pp. 52-54; 1921, pp. 69-70; 1932, p. 85). He used these three conditions as models because in them the clamor of guilt is the loudest and the need for punishment the most pronounced. Freud described superego function in these conditions as pathologically demanding, prohibitive, and primitive; he saw in the superego's cruelty something suggesting manifestations of "a pure culture of the death-instinct" (1923, p. 77) or of "the instinct of destruction . . . set free" (1923, p. 78). Further, after systematically formulating the crucial regression of the libido to anal sadism in compulsion neurosis, Freud went on to imply a corresponding superego regression in this condition: ". . . . the

superego, which derives from the id, is quite unable to evade the regression and instinct defusion which takes place there. It can hardly be surprising if the superego . . . should be . . . more sadistic than in normal development" (1926, p. 48). Yet, despite his recognition that these were pathologically intensified, regressive models, Freud tended to overemphasize them in his general conception of the superego. Consequently, he was uncomfortable when, in his paper on "Humour" (1928a), he recognized that the superego could also comfort the ego. He knew there was more to internalized parenthood than coercion and punishment on the one hand and the naïve emulation of primary identification on the other, but he was working within a new and difficult theoretical framework and apparently could not yet resolve all the difficulties or pursue all important lines of thought. Similarly, he did not synthesize his hostile superego conception with his generalization that one never encounters pure destructiveness but always some mixture of it with libido (1932, p. 152). And, although he did say that both instinctual tendencies are to be found in all parts of the mental apparatus (1937, p. 345; 1938, pp. 21-22), libido in the superego remained one of his theoretical embarrassments.

The Loving and Beloved Superego

The loving and beloved superego will be considered under five headings: The Superego as Representative of the Id; Protection and Comfort; Ideals and Pride; Punishment and Masochism; and Adaptation and the Parental Superego. These headings are selected for convenience of exposition only; in actuality, the development of each ramifies into the others.

The Superego as Representative of the Id

In the passage quoted from *The Ego and the Id*, Freud said of the superego that it "again appears as the representative of the id." He was referring to the superego identification as the internal, gratifying continuation of the oedipal relationships, though on a relatively desexualized basis. The ego deepens its relations with the id through making these identifications: it forces itself upon the id as a love object (1923, p. 37) and thereby forms the superego out of the id (1923, p. 52); it is a deposit left by the earliest object choices of the id (1923, p. 44). The superego is thus the "heir of the oedipus complex" (1923, pp. 47-48). That is to say, while identification is a means as well as an expression of aim inhibition and desexualization, it is so only in a relative sense; the child's relationship with the now internalized object is not thoroughly desexualized, and the potential always exists that it may become unmanageably resexualized. Anna Freud (1936) had this in mind when she described the adolescent's estrangement from his superego by virtue of its incestuous origin.

In the young child, the ego with its newly emphasized and organized superego contents is loved by the id as one has earlier loved the external parents, and it is loved by the superego as one has wished to be loved by these parents. While never stated as such, this position is implied in Freud's hypothesis that it is through the identifications leading to superego formation that the ego acquires energies from the id (1923, pp. 64-65), its so-called desexualized energies which are so important to the entire theory of the ego. Further, Freud stated that the superego also represents an "energetic reaction formation" against these preserved object choices of the id (1923, p. 44) and that the ego is punished by the superego for accomplishing these identifications. Reaction formation and punishment imply forbidden pleasure, which in turn speaks for the inference that Freud believed the two-way oedipal entanglements to be perpetuated in the formation of the superego. This erotic smuggling occurs within definite limits and with a noteworthy degree of aim inhibition in the normal case; on this basis the superego is in a position ultimately to attain relative impersonality—that is, a relatively great distance from the drives and drive objects in question (1924a, p. 265; 1926, p. 64; 1927, p. 125; 1931, pp. 256-257).

Part of this conception of the superego as representative of the id derives from the original argument in *Totem and Taboo* (1912) as to how conscience first came into existence (p. 879). There Freud emphasized that it is the ambivalence toward the murdered father that is crucial, the loving side of the ambivalence being the basis of remorse over the murder and the motivation for restoring paternal authority internally. In this hypothesis, love restores the murdered father to life in the form of conscience. Freud emphasized this view only in the context of his phylogenetic speculations. We may, however, safely apply to this proposition his other statements about the superego (e.g., 1930, pp. 88-89) and arrive at the following implication: fantasied murder of the father is part of each son's development; but, in the service of the positive side of his ambivalence, as well as for purposes of undoing, the son guarantees the continued existence or resurrection of his father in his inner world by establishing therein an enduring, authoritative paternal image. In this light we may account for an important part of the gain in the negative therapeutic reaction and in persistent self-reproach and self-punishment: it is the gain of a continued relationship with an involved, preserved, or restored father. This consideration brings us directly to the next section.

Protection and Comfort

To protect and comfort, in a nonrandom fashion, just as to love and punish, one must know at least a little of what is going on. Freud said in his *Group Psychology* that the superego tests reality (1921, p. 77) and then, in *The Ego and the Id*, he emphatically retracted this statement (1923, p. 34). He could have meant only external reality in this retraction for otherwise he repeatedly emphasized that the superego knows the id better than the ego does; and that it observes, watches over, judges, and censors the ego (1930, p. 93), guides it (1932, p. 89), corrects it (1938, p. 121), cares for it (1938, p. 122), and protects it (1926, p. 167; 1928a, pp. 220-221): ". . . nothing is hidden from the superego, not even thoughts" (1930, p. 79). All these attainments and activities imply a reality-testing function. We know that Freud ascribed observing and reality testing also to the ego; therefore, we must conclude that he meant to refer observation of the inner world for the sake of moral evaluation and regulation to the superego, and fact finding, organizing, and executive observation of the inner and outer worlds to the ego. Ultimately he would have maintained that observation of any sort is an ego function because he saw the superego itself as a structure within the ego.[8]

8 We may also note here that on several occasions Freud stressed that the superego represents external reality too. It repeats an external relation (1921, p. 103). Its first objects come from external reality, and these objects represent the traditions and the values of the surrounding community and culture (1924a, p. 264; 1938, pp. 122-124). See also the section, Adaptation and the Parental Superego, below.

Also, if nothing is hidden from the superego, then it is implied that superego function, like ego function, is never entirely suspended. The superego may be more or less antagonistic, and thereby more or less observable in its effects on the ego, but it is ever on duty. When it is not critical, its tacit approval may be assumed. Even in mania, contrary to the view Freud accepted in "Mourning and Melancholia" (1917) and in keeping with more recent investigations, the superego continues to function powerfully.

From the superego's observations arises the sense of guilt. In one place Freud said that guilt is a topographic variety of anxiety (1930, p. 92). This implies that the sense of guilt may function as a signal, as an indicator of defensive and adaptive tasks to be met in order to avoid situations of danger, and in the extreme, of traumatic helplessness. This is one way the superego may be said to be guiding and protecting the ego. The "signal" concept also implies that typically the superego does not strike full force all at once; that anticipatory feelings of discomfort and unrest related to the sense of guilt precede tormenting guilt, even though, as in the case of anxiety, the premonitory feelings may well be denied conscious recognition. Thus, while the superego treats the wish as equivalent to the deed, it apparently also can discriminate degrees of evil and react accordingly.

The idea of protection and comfort by the superego was introduced in three other connections—humor, traumatic neurosis, and religion. In the case of humor, Freud noted that the superego comforts the intimidated ego in the face of the stresses of reality; it reassures the ego by fostering the temporary illusion, " 'Look here! This is all that this seemingly dangerous world amounts to. Child's play—the very thing to jest about!' " (1928a, p. 220). Noting his deviation from his typical emphasis on the superego's hostility to the ego, Freud remarked that this showed "we have still very much to learn about the nature of [the superego]" and that in any case its protecting the ego from suffering "does not conflict with its derivation from the parental function" (1928a, pp. 220-221). Freud assumed that in this process a large-scale displacement of cathexis from the ego to the superego takes place. This displacement inflates the superego and enables it to view the ego as tiny and its interests as trivial (1928a, pp. 218-219). The full implication of this mobility of cathexis between the ego and superego has not, to my knowledge, been further described or analyzed, despite its great suggestiveness. It was implicitly used by Freud in this connection to account for the presence of tendencies in the superego of libidinal origin. Carrying this trend of thought further, we may infer that an abiding sense of humor, which is one of the hallmarks of optimal distance from inner conflicts, is based on a steady and free availability of libido in the superego.

Of the traumatic neuroses, Freud said that they occur in situations where one feels forsaken or deserted by the superego, in the form of its externalized representative, the powers of destiny; in such a situation there is an end to all security (1923, pp. 86-87; 1926, pp. 66-67). We may infer from this that normal courage, endurance, and ability to withstand intense stimulation or deprivation, all depend on the feeling of being recognized and attended to by the superego or destiny. This is another place where a major theoretical position is implied but not worked out. What we ordinarily call ego strength, for example, is seen in this connection as a matter of the mutual relations of ego and superego; the availability, and possibly the quantity, of energies in the ego to be used in adaptation seem to depend in large part on a faithful, benevolent superego.

In connection with religious belief Freud emphasized the need for "protection through love"—a need stemming from terrifying helplessness and its continuation into adult life (1928c, p. 51). The strongest childhood need is for the father's protection against superior powers of fate (1930, p. 11); and the dread of loss of love is the dread of losing this protection as well as of being punished (1930, p. 78). This explains man's clinging to a belief in the existence of a protective God-father, a figure more powerful than he discovered his real father to be (1932, pp. 223-224).

Why, we must ask, is it the father who is the first and only powerful protector? We come here to Freud's relatively one-sided treatment of bisexuality in the superego. Freud discovered and conceptualized bisexuality in the superego. In *The Ego and the Id*, for example, referring to identification with father and mother, he said, "The broad general outcome of the sexual phase governed by the oedipus complex may, therefore, be taken to be the forming of a precipitate in the ego, consisting of these two identifications in some way combined together" (1923, p. 44). Yet, in this monograph and elsewhere, he virtually restricted himself to the boy's identification with his father as a punitive rival and as a powerful protector. In *The Problem of Anxiety*, for example, he speaks of the superego as the impersonalized father (1926, p. 64).

Was this emphasis on the father just an expression of a paternalistic bias reflecting Freud's cultural background and personal values, including, as has sometimes been maintained, a low opinion of women? I believe this is not necessarily so. Freud has left us a number of discussions which, put together, clarify this feature of his theorizing. They show it to be rooted in his basic hypotheses and findings. I refer specifically to his observation that women do not typically develop as stable and unyielding a superego as men do. Their superego is "never so inexorable, so impersonal, so independent of its emotional origins as we require it to be in men" (1925, p. 196). He saw this as a consequence of the anatomical difference between the sexes and the fantasies and anxieties corresponding to it. The incentive for abandoning the oedipal position and for establishing the superego is weaker in women because they have already been deprived of the penis. Consequently they remain more on the developmental level of the wish to be loved and the fear of loss of love. Their internalizations are less stable, and they are more tied to the immediate give-and-take of real relations, especially in so far as these carry implications for the strongly persisting oedipal configuration.

Freud gave due recognition to individual variability among the members of each sex in this regard. He noted that the feminine component in men often limits the effectiveness of their superego formation. By the same token, we may add, the masculine component in women would contribute to their structuralizing their own definite superego. Thus, in the individual case, there would be no foregone conclusion about superego development based on a person's biological sex. Freud attributed differences in the strength of maternal and paternal identifications to constitutional differences in the strength of the two sexual currents in bisexuality (1923, pp. 42, 44). Today we would put at least as much emphasis on early object relations in this respect. We would also consider carefully how the difference between the sexes with respect to internalization is one of kind rather than, or as well as, one of degree; that is, we would ask on which levels of organization, with what admixture of gratification and renunciation, and how stably these internalizations take place in each sex.

The identifications that establish the superego are particularly with the parental superego rather than the parental ego or what Freud called the "real" parents (1932, p. 95). So far as Freud's conclusions about sexual differences in superego formation are valid, it follows that in normal identification with the mother the child would therefore be identifying with a less rigid and impersonal superego, and that the strictness of his superego would therefore owe less to her influence (1925, pp. 196-197). Here the problem of superego intertwines with that of sex differences in general, and for the present we must leave this extensive problem. Before doing so, however, we should recognize the mother as the original, undifferentiated, protective parental figure, as Freud did in the passage with which I opened this paper. There he referred to the early anxiety in response to "separation from the protecting mother." Elsewhere he spoke of the undifferentiated "parents" prior to the discovery of the difference between the sexes (1923, p. 39). Thus, the father as a separate entity is a later achievement in the child's conceptualization and object relations. He crystallizes as a figure of strength and self-sufficiency once the child begins to recognize the anatomical, social, and occupational differences between the sexes, and gains some notion of the father's role in procreation and providing for and safeguarding the entire family. I would add that the mother's own sense of inferiority with regard to the phallic male, her fear of losing his love and her fear of and pleasure in his aggression point the way for the child's recognition of the masculine father as the especially powerful protector. Yet, her own protective, comforting successes and failures also remain forever significant.

It is relevant in this regard that Freud spoke of a significant mental, "spiritual" advance in the historical change from matriarchal to patriarchal society (1939, p. 145). He regarded this change as a major conceptual attainment. In *Totem and Taboo* he had already assumed that the first theoretical accomplishment of man was the creation of spirits, an accomplishment that had the same source as the first moral restrictions (1912, p. 879). As Freud put it, this change meant rising above the level of the senses, which establishes

maternity, to a theoretical accomplishment which establishes pater-
nity; it is "a declaration in favour of the thought-process" (1939,
p. 146), of memory, reflection, and deduction (1939, p. 150), and
thus of the secondary process. This advance raised man's self-
confidence (1939, p. 148) and opened the way for his respect for
intellectual work (1939, p. 158), and it was defended by his ego
which took pride in it (1939, p. 151). I think we may apply this
consideration to Freud's psychology of the superego and see in
superego formation a shift from maternal to paternal authority and
protection, a shift which accomplishes a decisive advance in mental
organization and self-esteem for both sexes. The advance itself must,
however, be an outgrowth of some preceding ego development,
particularly of the capacity for hypothetical thought.

That in Freud's formulations the father as protector and identification figure in the superego overshadows the mother appears
therefore to be based on a number of more or less systematic
considerations. It is not a simple consequence of incomplete theoretical exposition, neglect of the psychology of women, or paternalistic bias. It is also strongly suggested by these considerations that
the father's importance in the female superego extends beyond
Freud's emphasis on consequences of the girl's masculinity (1923, p.
42). The subject obviously deserves considerable further study.

Ideals and Pride

Although originally synonymous with the superego, the ego
ideal was ultimately conceptualized by Freud in a narrower sense
as one of its functions (1932, pp. 92-93) along with self-observation,
conscience, censorship, and the instigation of defense. The ego ideal
comprises two related goals. One goal is to relinquish the oedipal
position through defense and sublimation. The other is to be like
the admired parents or father (1921, p. 60; 1923, p. 47). In fact, it
is admiration, along with hate, that motivates superego identification
(1928b, p. 229). "The superego is the advocate of the impulse towards
perfection" (1932, p. 95). Later in development, surrogate models
are used, though they do not alter the basic structure of the superego
(1932, p. 92). It is in failing to reach these goals that the ego feels
inferior. According to Freud, inferiority feelings are the erotic
complement to the sense of guilt (1932, p. 93). That is to say, they

correspond to feelings of loss of the superego's love, just as guilt corresponds to feelings of the superego's hatred. In this discussion in his *New Introductory Lectures*, Freud unequivocally assigned libidinal energies to the superego, yet he did not explore the implications there.

Later, in *Moses and Monotheism*, he went on to point out how the superego perpetuates the dependency of the ego (1939, pp. 149-150). The ego is forever concerned with retaining the conditional love of this new master, and it experiences the superego's appreciation with relief and satisfaction (1939, p. 149), if not triumph (1921, p. 106), and with increased self-respect and pride (1938, p. 122). In making a renunciation "it expects to be rewarded by being loved all the more. The consciousness of deserving this love is felt as pride. This good feeling could acquire the peculiar narcissistic character of pride only after the authority itself has become a part of the Ego" (1939, pp. 149-150). Freud viewed pride as a substitute satisfaction or pleasure gain for the ego.

Pride in the conceptual advance from maternal to paternal orientation has already been mentioned. In this advance beyond the world of the senses, or, in other terms, further from the tendency toward immediate gratification or discharge, the ego gains in ability to endure pain, privation, mistreatment, and abandonment. And it gains in intellectuality, so important in meeting its obligations. In achieving this independence and fortitude, the ego approaches its other ideal goal, that of being like the admired father. For in addition to being big and strong in all important physical respects, the father is what Freud called a "great man" to the young child. Freud described the great man as decisive in thought, strong of will, forceful in deed, self-reliant, and independent; he is capable of acting with the "divine conviction of doing the right thing, which may pass into ruthlessness" (1939, p. 140). And, he adds, such a man may be admired and trusted, though one cannot help also being afraid of him. Identification with this man begins prior to the oedipal situation (1921, p. 60) and is therefore called "primary" (1923, pp. 39-40). It may be considered an instance of ego identification, though once the process of superego identification reinforces it, it takes on an imperative moral quality; that is to say, it becomes so closely connected with instinctual renunciation that from then on failing to be a "great man" results in loss of the superego's love, felt as inferiority.

Much earlier, in his paper "On Narcissism," Freud had noted how primary narcissism is lost in reaction to parental criticism among other influences, and he described how it is regained through the formation of the ego ideal. One's self-love is directed to this ideal which is deemed perfect and deems itself perfect (1914, p. 51). The ideal may be loved and respected even when the ego falls short of it. And, if the ego measures up to its standards, it provides narcissistic gratification or love with resulting increase of self-regard (1914, p. 51).[9] Later he summarized this discussion by saying that the ego ideal is heir to infantile narcissism (1921, p. 69). This paper on narcissism is therefore a precursor of the conception of a beloved superego as well as a loving superego.

Freud was ambiguous in one important respect in this connection. He tended to say that the ego measures itself against the ego ideal (e.g., 1932, p. 93). Yet even in "On Narcissism" he also said that it is conscience that watches over the real ego and measures it by its ideal (1914, p. 52), and his later formulations consistently suggest that the superego does the measuring or at least observes and judges the results of this measuring, for only then could it be in a position to respond with love or withdrawal of love (e.g., 1932, p. 86). I believe the apparent inconsistency can be resolved: that it is an instance where Freud sometimes used "ego" in the comprehensive sense which includes conscience, and, later, superego, as a function of the ego.

In the superego's "measuring the ego" we encounter a repetition of the parents' estimations of the child. It follows that the parents' attitudes toward primary as well as secondary identifications will play a significant role in the definition of the superego. If the child's tendencies in this regard are not ignored, shamed, competed against, and suppressed, but rather recognized and, within appropriate limits and with appropriate exceptions, encouraged and rewarded, then these favorable evaluations will be taken up in the superego

---

[9] Freud also remarked in this paper that homosexual libido along with hostility is included in the ego ideal (1914, pp. 53, 59); presumably he had in mind his views that love of the brothers and father contributes to the origin of remorse and conscience (1912).

identifications, and the child, and later the adult, will be free to feel that it is good to try to meet the ego ideal, that one can love oneself for making the attempt. In this way the ego ideal does inherit and restore the wounded infantile narcissism.

Punishment and Masochism

Freud recognized or implied several benign or at least pleasurable aspects of the superego's punishing activities. One such aspect—perhaps the fundamental one—is that of sustained contact with parental care, or what one might call nonabandonment. In discussing the Jews and their religion, for example, Freud pointed out that they found it necessary to emphasize their guilt and their deserving punishment in order to account for their hard lot (1939, p. 173). That way they could still regard themselves as the Chosen People and retain the security of feeling under the protection of a higher authority. Rather than leading them to feel abandoned by the father, adversity only proved his watchful presence. Freud also believed that privation of erotic needs provoked aggression which, if inhibited, flowed into the superego and expressed itself in a sense of guilt (1930, p. 96). Thus, the correct formulation of this point would be that the emphasis on guilt in relation to God expresses ambivalence: need for His protection and hatred. We know that children sometimes follow the same pattern both in their fantasies and in their provocation and interpretation of parental criticism and punishment. In one respect, if the parent expresses anger or disapproval, it means to the child that he is bad and deserves to be censured and that he need not fear loss of contact with the parent. Also, in so far as superego reproaches serve as warnings of traumatic situations, they may, like parental reproaches, imply protective concern.

This aspect of gratification through superego criticism shades over into a second, that of sexualization of morality. Sexualization of morality is seen in extreme form in moral masochism (1924a, p. 266).[10] To some degree, however, it appears to have been regarded by Freud as a built-in feature of the superego (1930, p. 193). Earlier, under "Superego as Representative of the Id," I discussed the con-

[10] See also "A Child Is Being Beaten" (1919, pp. 183-184, 189-190).

tinued love relationships implied in the mutual relations between superego, ego, and id. In the present context, punishment may be seen to be part of this relationship. That is to say, sexual pleasure is obtained in the guise of criticism and punishment. As Freud put it, the ego brings part of the death instinct into itself in the service of its erotic attachment to the superego (1930, p. 93). Freud further pointed out how each punishment by the superego signifies feminine (castrated) pleasure in relation to the father (1928b, p. 231). The concept "borrowed sense of guilt" (1923, p. 73) is also relevant here, for, as Freud saw it, it is in identification with the father's guilt that the libidinal relation to him is preserved. These factors would provide at least part of the pleasure premium associated with being aggressed against, within limits, by the superego. As in the case of certain aspects of the superego's protective function, the pleasure referred to is not ordinarily conscious or immediate; there is no conscious sense of being "loved."

As a third aspect, Freud saw ambivalence, and therefore guilt, as inherent in human relations (1930, p. 188). A sense of guilt and need for punishment inevitably build up in the mind, though we know that the degree and tempo of this increasing tension vary from one individual to the next. A superego strong enough to balance the crime through the suffering, sacrifice, and reparation it enforces, like a justly punitive parent, will provide a basis for relief from guilt (1923, p. 76) and free the individual to resume adaptive functioning.

Finally, in this regard, Freud steadily emphasized the ego's aim of recreating actively what it has suffered or feared to suffer passively. His analysis of play and of traumatic neuroses are cases in point (1920). There can be no doubt that parental disapproval has its painful side. And so, in setting up an internal substitute for parental authority, the ego advances to a position of activity. It thereby fulfills its basic goal of protecting the mental apparatus from excessive—unexpected—quantities of stimulation.

The feeling of sustained contact, the sexual pleasure to be derived from morality, the relief from the inevitable sense of guilt, and the substitution of activity for passivity, all contribute to and derive from the experience of loving and being loved by the superego.

Adaptation and the Parental Superego

Freud clearly saw the laying down of the superego as a decisive factor in preparing the child to fit into and participate in the civilized community. When he spoke of society's accomplishing in a few years of childhood training what has taken many ages for civilization to achieve, he recognized the adaptive aspect of the superego and society's stake in it (1932, p. 201). The superego is as important a carrier and protector of cultural continuity as the ego; in fact, it is obviously the more conservative of the two in content and resistance to change. In *Group Psychology*, pursuing his discussions in *Totem and Taboo*, Freud pointed out how social conscience and the sense of duty grow out of the mastery of sibling rivalry (1921, p. 88), and in *The Ego and the Id* he clearly set forth how the establishment of the superego preserves object relations (1923, pp. 41, 42, 44). The advances of civilization, the binding of men together in social organizations are founded on the sense of guilt (1930, pp. 89, 90).

It is here that we should consider in some detail Freud's point that in rearing their children, parents are "glad to be able to identify fully at last with their own parents"; they then repeat their own parents' severe and exacting pattern with the result that the superego of the child is not built on the parents' egos, but on their superegos (1932, p. 95). From the adaptive point of view, the meaning seems to be this: the parent provides, in the form of his superego, a preestablished structure for his child to adopt so that the child will not have to accomplish anew all the cultural achievements in the history of his group. A considerable psychic saving is involved for the child. The child takes over or internalizes this "parental function" (1932, p. 91). He thereby becomes father to himself and acquires basic equipment for later becoming psychological father of his children. By introjecting the parental superego, he also establishes a motivational base for learning and perfecting a certain moral, protective, and comforting know-how. This know-how is part of being grown up.[11] In this process the child is additionally helped to meet his ego ideal, as described above, and subsequently to feel worthy of love. And in being prepared for life in the community he is put in the

---

11 We have already seen that, in Freud's eyes (1928a), humor is an adaptive process of self-comfort.

position of being able to find, engage, and use alternative or modified real models and object relations such as he needs to complete
his development. As Freud pointed out, the neurotic with his defective superego is, by contrast, asocial and cut off from the great institutions of society (1912, p. 864; 1921, pp. 124-125).[12]

Obviously, this line of thought indicates the necessity of examining the parent's superego in order to understand the child's. Much
will depend on how right or conflict-free the parent feels in his role
of moral guide, how much he can genuinely and realistically act
"in the divine conviction of doing the right thing." In so far as his
superego is immature, hostile, and distant from his ego, it will
produce disruptions in crucial parent-child interactions, in particular
those interactions concerning the child's budding instinctual and ego
expressions. It is under these conditions that we might expect the
child to develop an oedipus complex, both masculine and feminine,
that is especially difficult to relinquish, and consequently a severe
superego. I have in mind here Freud's view that it is the strength
of the oedipus complex and its incomplete resolution that underlie
the severity of the superego (1923, pp. 45, 52-53). In other words,
severity of superego function testifies to the inadequacy of superego
formation. It is therefore no great jump to recognize that disturbance
in the parental superego plays a double role in disturbing the child's
superego development: it exaggerates the oedipal conflict and provides a faulty model for dealing with it. In this way, superego
pathology is perpetuated.

To extrapolate further, when the parent has a healthy superego
and is relatively unambivalent in exercising parental superego functions, he furnishes the child with an adaptive model for the internal
as well as external disposition of love and aggression. If nothing else,
he expresses some of his inevitable aggressiveness toward his child in
the form of useful moral guidance and restriction. Both by imposing
meaningful limits on behavior and by administering real punishment, the parent corrects the terrifying archaic fantasies of punishment introduced by the child in his struggle with his own impulses.
As a result, the child will experience less alienation from real objects,

---

[12] Freud also emphasized that the ego ideal plays a key role in love. The love object
is chosen to appeal to the ego ideal (1914, p. 58) and the object takes the place of the
ego's ideal (1921, pp. 74-76).

less damming up of impulses, less devious discharge or sudden erup-
tion, and less sense of guilt and need for punishment.

Parental gentleness and leniency form no obstacle to the child's
forming a critical superego, as Freud well knew (1930, p. 85; 1931,
pp. 89-90). And while he did not say in so many words that the child
needs a parental superego of optimal strength in order to live and
develop, he did say that the ego needs the superego's love to live, and
by that he implied the child's vital need for a healthy parental superego to introject. Furthermore, by rigid permissiveness, as we well
know, a parent often attempts to deny the tension between his ego
and superego; in this he is bound to fail for his unconscious superego
will express itself in countless subtle though powerful ways and the
child will take over this ill-concealed superego. Unconflicted gentleness is likely to go hand in hand with unconflicted firmness.

Finally, this line of thought concerning the parental superego
leads a way out of the contradiction implied by Freud's proposition
that every time the ego gains energy by desexualization through
identification, a defusion of instincts results, free aggression accumu-
lates within the mind, and the severity of the superego increases
(1923, pp. 80, 83-84). Taken literally, this means that in developing
itself the ego is simultaneously and constantly undermining itself, a
proposition which, without further qualification, seems to lead to
confusion. The difficulty lies in the fact that Freud's formulations
were closely tied to the depressive, obsessive, and paranoid models he
used. But these are models of transmitted superego pathology as well
as of regression; they do not apply to higher levels of ego and superego development. When the family situation permits the phallic
level to be reached, fully experienced, and transcended, the destructive and erotic trends involved in psychic functioning are at a further
distance from the basic drives; they exist in forms, probably relatively securely fused, that contribute to adaptive superego functioning rather than to the archaic, exhibitionistic and instinct-loaded
manifestations of guilt such as are found in the obsessional neuroses
and melancholia. Precisely this integration and this distance from the
basic drives and oedipal objects make possible that desirable "im-
personalization" of the parental authority in later superego development which Freud so often emphasized (1924a, p. 265; 1926, p. 64;
1927, p. 125; 1931, pp. 256-257).

Thus it comes about that the normal superego is close to the ego and often indistinguishable from it. With the passing of the oedipus complex, a base is established for object relations in later life that are firm, not excessively ambivalent, and not prone to give way to identification; through its closeness to the superego identifications, the ego becomes resistive to a piling up of unmanageable later identifications (1923, p. 68). By implication, an inadequately formed superego hampers the ego's synthesizing efforts and the ego's definition of its boundaries. Although at the time he wrote *The Ego and the Id* Freud seemed to assume that the normal superego was open to significant influence after the passing of the oedipus complex, he was not decided on this point. Subsequently he seemed to conclude that while images of authoritative figures encountered during latency and later on may be linked to the parental images in the superego, especially as the parents lose prestige in the child's eyes, these new images need not be internalized, or, if they are internalized, they will be so in the ego (1924a, p. 265; 1926, p. 79; 1932, p. 92).

SUMMARY

Summarizing these observations, formulations, and implications concerning the loving and beloved superego in Freud's structural theory, we arrive at the following conclusions. There is a loving and beloved aspect of the superego. It represents the loved and admired oedipal and preoedipal parents who provide love, protection, comfort, and guidance, who embody and transmit certain ideals and moral structures more or less representative of their society, and who, even in their punishing activities, provide needed expressions of parental care, contact, and love. The maturing child will identify himself with these parental aspects. The identification will take place partly by way of imitative primary identification and partly by way of identification for purposes of mastering the oedipal crisis. The former comes under the heading of ego identification primarily, the latter under the heading of superego identification primarily. By means of this identification the child ultimately attains the position of being able to love, protect, comfort, and guide himself and his children after him, and of doing so according to relatively ego-syntonic, culture-syntonic, and impersonal sets of ideals and moral stand-

ards. In this development much importance is permanently transferred from the mother of the world of the senses and the primary
process to the great, Godlike father and the secondary process. The
ego values, depends on, and loves this inner, paternal source of
strength and organization. As with the id, the ego's relations with
the superego are not simply antagonistic and the therapeutic task
with regard to the superego is not simply to establish the ego's independence from it.

This developmental achievement establishes the superego as a
structure for the binding and discharge of libidinal as well as destructive energy. Variations in the disposition of libido in the superego
give rise to a range of feelings and actions, extending from the sense
of inferiority and abandonment by all protecting powers on the one
hand to pride, fortitude, humor, and effective transmission of cultural ideals on the other. The superego is not the reservoir and inner
channel of hatred alone, even though its structuralization appears to
be tied to the oedipal crisis and to a new deployment of the aggression originally directed toward the feared rival. It is not a static or
regressed product of instinctual defusion, except perhaps in pathological cases. Just as parental criticism itself need not imply defusion
in the parent, the establishment in the mind of the complex parental
image that is the core of the superego is not normally based on a
thoroughgoing and permanent defusion of libidinal and destructive
energies. We must assume that ego structure and superego structure
alike bind and discharge energy associated with both types of drives,
and that in the analysis of ego and superego it is always a question
of varying degrees of fusion and varying distances from both basic
instinctual drives. In the case of the superego, the degree of defusion
appears to depend on the related factors of regression, pathological
intensity of the oedipus complex, and transmitted superego pathology. Preoedipal factors, which have not been extensively discussed
here, also may exert a major influence in this regard.

In the hostile aspect of the superego, object hate is turned around
and transformed into self-hate; in the benign aspect of the superego
it is object love which is turned around and transformed into that
aspect of self-love or narcissism felt as pride and security in relation
to society and destiny as well as one's own conscience and ideals. The

superego builds and upholds as well as splits and tears down, just as the ego does.

In these conclusions the ego and superego remain, as Freud meant them to, the mind's two great structures for the disposition of love and hate. But it does not appear necessary or correct to assume compartmentalization of libidinal and destructive energies in the ego and superego respectively. Even though Freud sometimes assumed this compartmentalization, at other times he saw that his theory would have to be further revised, developed, and synthesized.

BIBLIOGRAPHY

Fenichel, O. (1945), *The Psychoanalytic Theory of Neurosis.* New York: Norton.

Freud, A. (1936), *The Ego and the Mechanisms of Defence.* New York: International Universities Press, 1946.

Freud, S. (1912), Totem and Taboo. *The Basic Writings of Sigmund Freud.* New York: Modern Library, 1938, pp. 807-930.

—— (1914), On Narcissism: An Introduction. *Collected Papers,* IV. London: Hogarth Press, 1946.

—— (1917), Mourning and Melancholia. *Collected Papers,* IV. London: Hogarth Press, 1946.

—— (1919), 'A Child Is Being Beaten.' *Collected Papers,* II. London: Hogarth Press, 1946.

—— (1920), *Beyond the Pleasure Principle.* New York: Liveright, 1950.

—— (1921), *Group Psychology and the Analysis of the Ego.* New York: Liveright, 1951.

—— (1923), *The Ego and the Id.* London: Hogarth Press, 1950.

—— (1924a), The Economic Problem of Masochism. *Collected Papers,* II. London: Hogarth Press, 1946.

—— (1924b), The Passing of the Oedipus-Complex. *Collected Papers,* II. London: Hogarth Press, 1946.

—— (1925), Some Psychological Consequences of the Anatomical Distinction between the Sexes. *Collected Papers,* V. London: Hogarth Press, 1950.

—— (1926), *The Problem of Anxiety.* New York: Norton, 1936.

—— (1927), *The Problem of Lay-Analyses.* New York: Brentano's, 1927.

—— (1928a), Humour. *Collected Papers,* V. London: Hogarth Press, 1950.

—— (1928b), Dostoevsky and Parricide. *Collected Papers,* V. London: Hogarth Press, 1950.

—— (1928c), *The Future of an Illusion.* Garden City, N.Y.: Doubleday, 1957.

—— (1930), *Civilization and Its Discontents.* Garden City, N.Y.: Doubleday, 1958.

—— (1931), *Female Sexuality. Collected Papers,* V. London: Hogarth Press, 1950.

—— (1932), *New Introductory Lectures on Psychoanalysis.* New York: Norton, 1933.

—— (1937), Analysis Terminable and Interminable. *Collected Papers,* V. London: Hogarth Press, 1950.

—— (1938), *An Outline of Psychoanalysis.* New York: Norton, 1949.

—— (1939), *Moses and Monotheism.* New York: Vintage Books, 1955.

Waelder, R. (1930), The Principle of Multiple Function. *Psa. Quart.,* V, 1936.

GENETIC ASPECTS OF SPECIFIC EGO
AND ID PATHOLOGY

FURTHER NOTES ON FETISHISM

PHYLLIS GREENACRE, M.D. (New York)[1]

Fetishism is traditionally regarded as a disorder of males, a perversion in which the ability to perform the sexual act is dependent on the concomitant awareness of an accessory and specific inanimate object. This object, the fetish, clearly represents the penis and is necessary to ward off the intense and incapacitating castration panic which the patient would otherwise suffer (Freud, 1927, 1938). To be sure, it has a bisexual meaning, too, but it is the phallic significance which is serviceable in permitting intercourse, or, in some instances, masturbation. According to my view of the situation, the fetishist not only endows his partner with the removable and adaptable penis, but in doing this he can incorporate the penis himself through vision, touch, and smell, and thereby bolster his uncertain genitality. The disorder is one which has at its base a faulty body-image and body-ego development, with consequent disturbances of the senses of reality and of identity, and of object relationship (Greenacre, 1953, 1955).

The fetish of the adult has something in common with the transitional object of infancy, which normally plays its part in the establishment of reality and of object relationship (Stevenson, 1954; Winnicott, 1953; Wulff, 1946). But the persistence of the fetish into adult life indicating the need for so prolonged a bridge bespeaks the chronic fault in the somatopsychic structure. The transitional object, on the other hand, is ordinarily given up with the rise of genitality, except in those cases where it merges into the adult fetish because of the severity of the underlying disturbance. The transitional object is not sex limited and seems to be derived more from the relationship to the mother's breast and soft body and is not especially focused on the genital.

[1] From the Department of Psychiatry of the New York Hospital and the Cornell University Medical College.

It is clear, however, that the perversion of fetishism is inherently a male disturbance. Nor is this fundamentally contraverted by von Hug-Hellmuth's case of a female fetishist published in 1915. There is not sufficient history (and the patient was not analyzed) to give us an adequate understanding of the real structure of the illness. But the rather florid clinical picture suggests a bisexual woman with a well-established phallic illusion, which in turn may have caused her to suffer masculine as well as feminine castration problems of considerable severity.

The persistent use of a fetish may occur in women, of a less deviate sexual make-up than von Hug-Hellmuth's case, and in the setting of a neurosis rather than a perversion. As Freud pointed out, patients generally do not initially complain of the need for a fetish and bring it into the analysis only incidentally. In the cases I have observed in women, this was especially marked. The use of a fetish was discovered only incidentally. Its apparent unimportance, however, might mask the tenacity with which its real significance in the whole neurotic picture was kept as a secret. The relation of the fetish to the sexual life in women is less apparent than in men, since the woman may more successfully conceal disturbances of sexual function, and frigidity can be covered up to a degree which is not possible with the disturbances of potency in the man. In less manifest cases of perversion in men, however, there may be partial impotence the crippling nature of which is denied by the man, very much as so many women deny frigidity. In this paper, the clinical reports will be focused on the relation of the fetish to pseudo addiction; to charm and amulet fetishism; and to the secret.

CLINICAL REPORTS

There is a small group of patients who take drugs over a period of years ostensibly for the help of insomnia, but continue this self-dosage even when the insomnia is not severe or has cleared up. They do not increase the amount of the drug, and do not always concern themselves with what drugs have been taken, commonly substituting less active drugs if the original one is not available. What seems important is the appearance of the drug, the size, shape, and color of the pellet or capsule. Even aspirin or soda mint may be substituted for the original sedative with the knowledge or even on the initiative of the patient without affecting his attitude toward its habitual usage. This may be continued over years seemingly almost ignored and yet strictly adhered to by the patient. Similarly while the solid form of the drug (as pill or capsule) with the use of two or sometimes three pellets, is most frequent, medicine in a fluid form is sometimes used. This group of patients includes both men and women, but the women have been in the majority in my cases. This pill fetishism first became clear to me in a man who was one of my early analytic patients.

Case I

He was in a severe homosexual panic accompanying an acute outbreak of pathological jealousy. In his early forties, married, and with half-grown children, he was frantic because he suspected his wife of being unfaithful with his younger brother, to whom he had been extremely attached. After his marriage, he had seen little of this brother although they had previously been intimately associated in business. He put a geographical barrier between them which had been maintained until recently. But now that the brother had surmounted this, and the triangular affair had quickly sprung up, his periodic rages were almost uncontrollable. It was apparent that he actually provoked and abetted this affair, constantly throwing his wife and brother together. But being completely unaware of this, he felt outraged and persecuted.

He was a large man, of splendid physique. But he frequently had the expression of an angry child, and his mouth was shaped in a chronic pout. Intelligent, personable, self-made, seemingly aggressive, he had made a rather unusual business and social success until this personal catastrophe overtook him. He was generally given to vivid self-dramatizing activity, and now, in critical situations, he brandished a revolver rather frighteningly. On the other hand he could be quite seductive and persuasive with both men and women, especially if he was in a tight spot, as the story of his business career indicated. He had in the past seemed to get himself into emergency situations partly for the sweet triumph of getting himself rescued again. Of all of this he was quite unaware, though it was obvious in his attitudes on coming for analysis.

He had previously been treated by another analyst who had originally been his wife's therapist. Naturally then the situation of three, which seemed to be pursuing him in life, began to be acted out in the analysis to an unmanageable extent. His business career indicated a continual search for a father, in a way which was probably the repetitive living out of a family-romance fantasy. He had first attached himself to his most successful maternal uncle, then to a rather conservative, able and well-established older man, and finally to a flamboyantly successful businessman of the promoter type. At last he had succeeded in making himself independent of this man, and at this point the affair between his wife and his favorite brother had developed and threatened his whole life.

He had always felt in some way unsubstantial, guilty, and even phony. Of German Jewish parentage, from a very simple background, he accepted the changed version of his name which had been adopted by his father's brother but not by his father. He never directly denied his Jewish parentage, but he associated almost entirely with Gentiles, and became a member, then president, of an exclusive country club. His wife was not Jewish. He allowed people to think he was a graduate of a college which he had attended only briefly. He was, however, meticulously honest in financial affairs and never told a deliberate and outright lie. His greatest feeling of phoniness arose from the fact that in spite of his handsome physique and his success among men, he could never rely on his potency. He had been a virgin at the time of his marriage in his late twenties, suffered severe castration anxiety (with fear of disease, etc.), and had never really courted a girl until he fell desperately in love with his wife and married her after a brief and tempestuous courtship. He was vaguely aware that he was saving himself from the threatening homosexual drives. He regarded his wife as a princess. He tended soon to worship her, put her on a pedestal, and keep a safe distance from her.

The first analyst rather bluntly gave him an interpretation that he felt phony because he really had wanted to steal his mother from his father. The verdict had struck home. He knew in a blind way that this was true and returned to it in a pondering but unusable fashion over and over again. It served as a very strong resistance.

This man was the oldest of six children. A puny baby, born seven months after the parents' marriage, he could not accept the explanation that it was a premature birth and felt disgraced and distinguished at the idea of having been conceived before marriage.[2] His first years were disturbed ones. A sister was born when he was only a year old. Toilet training was vigorous, and cleanliness was established early but at the expense of great anxiety and an erotization of urination which continued into later life. There was much analytic evidence of early and frequent exposure to the primal scene,

---

[2] Certain aspects of this case are reported under Case II in my article "Vision, Headache and the Halo" (1947).

and during his second year the development of great jealousy at the sight of the suckling baby sister. His jealousy of the breast as part of this situation later merged with the envy of the father's penis, and the rage at the baby sister was partly converted into an identification with her. As soon as she was old enough to toddle the two children were cared for much together, became inseparable, and were regarded as twins.

On entering school, he developed a severe fear of leaving his mother, finally going when he could be accompanied by his "twin sister" on whom he developed profound dependence. Another child, a boy, had been born, the brother who figured so strongly in the patient's later jealousy. This brother, born when the patient was five, was not only his oedipal child whom he adopted as his own, but was also later to become a second twin to him, since there was a remarkable resemblance between the two. By the time the patient was in his early twenties, they might really have been taken for twins. Toward this brother he had the profoundest ambivalent attachment.

Both parents were rather forceful, driving people, simple, superstitious, and ambitious. Punishments were vigorous and castration threats were open. The patient respected and intensely feared his father who had a violent temper and an equally strong conscience. He could conquer his father only by rising above him in the social scale, a circumstance about which he felt very guilty. The mother was a warm and hearty person, very much the housewife, toward whom he had a deep affection, but with whom he felt always a distance. Younger children seemed always to be in the way. He was undoubtedly caught in a strong unresolved oedipal attachment to both parents.

The use of the pills—two each night at bedtime—was a minor theme in the course of the analysis. It was rarely spoken of and then usually incidentally or in the course of free associations. The habit may have begun some years earlier. It was well established, however, at the time the patient first consulted me, and continued throughout with brief interruptions.

The probable significance and possible importance of this pseudo addiction became apparent in connection with the understanding of similar symptoms in other patients, and especially through the investigation of cases of fetishism. That the pills represented the breasts of the mother and the penis of the father was obvious from the context in which they were referred to. But they seemed to refer to the breasts, represented by the nipples, more as envied possessions which had been observed than to the actual experience of nursing (Greenacre, 1947); to have more to do with the envy of the little sister having the mother's breast and the mother. The wish was more to bite off and possess the nipples than to be comforted by nursing. Certainly it was jealous anger which excited the patient and kept him awake. This had been derived from the primal scene as well, which he constantly revived in his jealous fantasies of his wife and his brother. The fetishistic pills served to protect against the dangers of helplessness in sleep rather than directly to promote sleep itself.

The case of amulet or lucky-stone fetishism to be described next was published in some detail elsewhere (Greenacre, 1951). The carrying of the lucky stone was not greatly emphasized and was merely mentioned in the original clinical report.

The lucky stone or amulet is rather well accepted socially. As a charm for the man's watch chain, or a bangle for the girl's bracelet, it does decorative and sentimental service. Religious power or luck is more clearly admitted with the St. Christopher's medals and other such charms. The bridge here to the religious relics is close at hand. Latency children especially seem delighted with lucky pieces, "pocket pieces," stones, coins or other small objects, which generally, however, must have the distinction of being unusual. The deeper connections of this patient's lucky stone with her individual problems and the unique place it occupied in her development can be deciphered from her history, although as the fetish stone appeared in use it probably seemed one of the run-of-the-mill bits of childhood-play magic which is so characteristic of the prepuberty years.

Case II

This patient's use of a fetish became evident in certain behavior during the analytic hour: when very anxious, she would reach out and clutch strongly at a wooden moulding which was part of a panel design on the wall beside the analytic couch. She seemed really trying to get her hand around this, rather than merely to finger it lightly or casually in a doodling fashion. When I called her attention to this, she said only, "It makes me safer."

Some days later in the course of giving associations to a dream, she mentioned that as a child she had carried a stone in her pocket for a period of years and had not been willing to leave home without it. She thought this had begun around the time she started school, and it had continued until she was nine or so, about the time she was withdrawn from school, probably because of a panic induced when the teacher punished the whole class by making them sit on their hands. It was clear from the other material presented, but very difficult for the patient to understand, that she had reacted to this as though it had been a specific punishment for masturbation. At that time she was already preoccupied with ruminative obsessive fantasies about the genitals and their functioning, some of the fantasies having been so intense that they invaded her visual perceptions. The period during which the fetish lost its importance coincided with her absence from school which lasted for several years. It may have been that she no longer needed it so much as a protection against her separation anxiety. It was reinstated when she returned to school at puberty, but never was as constant as it had been earlier, and later drifted into such clutching mannerisms in anxious moments as she had demonstrated on the couch. There was a long history of an infantile blanket fetish as well. It was reported that she had insistently buried her face in one favorite blanket which she carried with her and had given this up sometime before the age of four.

The patient's life story resembled in many ways that of more conspicuously fetishistic patients. Her mother was aggressively conscientious and zealous, rather than having much direct warmth and affection. When the baby did not nurse well at three months, the mother plied her with a bottle, frequently and assiduously, so that by eight months she had become enormously fat. At the same time vigorous toilet training was being carried on, and the baby was reported as "clean" by one year. The bottle feeding and the fatness continued until eighteen months, with, for some unexplained reason, a complete deprivation of solid food. Following the birth of a boy when the patient was sixteen months, the mother allowed her somewhat more freedom to grow up. But by the time she was twenty-two months and the brother six months old, the two children were cared for together as much as possible, being bathed together, put to bed together, wheeled in the same perambulator, and often dressed alike. She had some fantasy that this actually made them alike—"one and the same in the same bath water." Her postpuberty masturbation consisted of dripping bath water on herself in such a way as to stimulate the clitoris. She developed a very strong, conscious, positive identification with this brother.

She had lost weight rapidly and become a slender child after the brother's birth. It is probable that this was due to the relative loss of the mother, who was of a marked appersonating type, as well as to a spurt of growth and activity, and that later she again satisfied some of this symbiotic need in her close bodily and emotional contact with her brother. Whatever envy and jealousy she had felt toward him, became gradually allocated to another brother who was five years older. This hostility had been amalgamated especially in her latency years when he teased her openly and exhibitionistically with his superior genital and urinary prowess.

The phallic-oedipal period was specially disturbed in a way which vitiated her relationship to all males, except the beloved younger brother. At about four and a half, she engaged in some mutual body investigation with a neighbor boy a little older. They were in the bushes, she disrobed and eager, when the boy's mother appeared, scolded her roundly, and rushed her nude across the street to her home. The eager excitement turned rapidly to hot shame and resentment. Only the cooling breeze felt good on her skin. This seemed to be the nucleus of a later shift of erotization to contact with the air. An intense oedipal attachment then turned largely to a fierce aversion to being touched by her father or older brother. There was an overly strong attempt at spiritualization, with an interest in the sun and the winds, the development of fantasies in which God played the part of the acceptable father, who, like the Sun, entered and influenced her spiritually, while her own father appeared as a dirty and ogrelike person. In latency there was a constant preoccupation with the genitals, with intercourse, pregnancy, and birth, both directly and in hidden ways, but the direct interests were quickly denied. The acting out of any direct sexual interest was limited to solitary experiments to test her own masculine possibilities and to investigate animals. But it was at this time that she carried the lucky fetishistic stone.

From the analysis it appeared that this represented a magic, but degraded fecal phallus, which like the fetishes of perverse patients gained value through being concrete, indestructible, and smelly. It is interesting, however, that it played no part that I could determine in her masturbation. It is possible that the dripping bathtub faucet played this role in postpuberty when the stone had mostly been given up; and that with the faucet, the penis was incorporated through vision, more than by touch. The water, however, made the direct contact, which she had felt in infancy with the younger brother in the tub with her. It appeared that the fetish stone was used also to counteract some of the feeling of body dispersion associated with the air erotism in movement. It was literally something to hold onto, and "made her safer."

The third case illustrates the relation of the secret to the fetish. It has already been noted that the fetish often *is* something of a secret. Freud (1927) noted that the existence of the fetish is frequently only incidentally revealed. It may seem to be treated as something of no great moment, yet further investigation shows that this is not true. Its importance may depend on its appreciation as something quite essential; yet there is sometimes an element of shame about it too.

One has only to ponder a bit to realize the powerful influence of the secret and of its close kin, the mystery. Alfred Gross's charming article on the secret (1936) describes its two parts: the significance of there being a secret and the meaning of its content. He compared them to a body sac and its secretion, emphasizing too the constant pressure to release the secret, but its loss of at least part of its value when it is told, a loss essentially of its capacity to endow its owner with narcissistic distinction. The contents may be either something highly prized or something shameful which must be hidden. But as long as *they* remain secreted they can be of no real use in themselves. The sense of the exclusion of others enhances the narcissistic value of the secret.[3] If it is shared, then its joint owners must be held together by some special and primitive ritual bond, or the secret is in danger of becoming only common property.

Mysteries and secrets lure men into intellectual activities to divine their meaning, first by magic, later by science. Still the opposing value of cherishing a secret is very great and not readily relinquished. Harry Houdini, the great technical magician, was so impressed with the evil power of the secret that he carefully showed how he performed his magnificent tricks. Yet it is doubtful whether this was the antidote he expected it to be. Like children not ready to give up Santa Claus, his audiences largely believed in his magic. The secret also becomes a powerful binding force in groups—its group possession binding the members together and tending to render individual allegiances secondary to the fidelity to the group.

The basic secrets are those of the origin and fate of life, implied in the riddle of the inscrutable sphinx, which Oedipus solved and so was permitted to live. This nature of the secret is further discussed by Freud in the article on the Three Caskets (1913). Indeed, literature, myths, and fairy tales are replete with illustrations of the enticement, danger, and meaning of the secret.

[3] A. A. Milne (1929) has a delightful story "The Secret" based on this theme.

According to Hesiod, Pandora was the first woman, the All Giving. She was made by Zeus to counteract the blessings bestowed on mortals by Prometheus when he stole fire from Heaven. Having made her beautiful and seductive, he gave her a jar full of all the evils and instructed her to keep it shut and its contents unknown. Thus equipped, she was sent to Epimetheus, the earth-bound brother of Prometheus, who, forgetting his brother's warning against accepting any gifts from Zeus, married her. Curiosity overcoming her, she opened the jar allowing all the evils to fly out into the world. When she succeeded in replacing the lid, only Hope was left within.

But Hesiod, the proverbial shepherd poet, of the eighth century B.C., was a bachelor of misogynic views. Other later writers had another version. The jar held benefits not evils which were intended to be preserved for mankind. They escaped and were lost to the world (rather than infesting it) when man's curiosity caused the violation of the pact of secrecy. In any case, Hope remained.

Certainly the symbolism of the Pandora story and of the Three Caskets is in accord with Gross's conclusion that the secret relates at its most primitive level to body organs and processes, but that it contains more fundamentally the struggle with the fear of death by the live relationships of life.

The case here presented is that of a patient who came to me for two different periods of analysis with a number of years in between (see Greenacre, 1947). Consequently there was the opportunity to see her development during nearly two decades. I shall give only a very schematic statement of the case, focusing chiefly on the details concerning her secret.

Case III

The first period of this patient's analysis had been relatively successful in that she had overcome many of her neurotic difficulties to the extent that she had been able to go ahead with her life in a definitely more effective way than had previously been true. She had been an overly gentle and even shadowy person, moving quietly through the periphery of life's situations, but participating in them with little real involvement. Some-relic of this quietness remained, though she became a real person with a life of her own.

In her childhood there had been a particularly strong and complex ambivalent attachment to her father. When she was born, after two older sisters, he was openly angry at not having a boy. And when a boy actually was born when she was five, she became the favorite daughter but never quite recovered from the sense of being a disappointment. This situation was further complicated by her having, in her third year, intruded on a miscarriage of her mother's and by her subsequent knowledge that the miscarried child had been a boy. This matter of the miscarriage was the central analytic secret of the first period of her analysis. It was strictly *her* secret, however— for it later became evident that it was by no means a secret from her (as she had intimated) having been openly enough discussed by her family many times in her hearing.

The shock and guilt aroused by this event had contributed much not only to its denial but also to the development of a major capacity for denial. Consequently she would and did avoid or delay dealing with many disturbing situations or thoughts by throwing them out of focus again. The passive aggression in this was superb and had a magic quality. In her childhood she had "killed" people by unfocusing her eyes or looking the other way. Later she could cut people dead by seeming not to see them. In the analysis she was seemingly too compliant, but the denial and undoing were consistently at work here too. At the end of an hour in which she would seem to have understood something quite well, just as she left she would make some gently obliterating remark with a sigh. This would be followed by a period of withdrawn interest in, or even lacking memory of, what we had been dealing with. This behavior repeatedly made me think of a person who takes some possession out of pocket or a box, looks at it furtively, and slips it back out of sight again.

Toward the end of the first period of analysis she mentioned incidentally that she sometimes had trouble having a bowel movement in the morning and could do so only if she was insured absolute privacy and unlimited time. She had earlier told me of a period of constipation and a spasmodic tightening of the anal sphincter which had occurred with her first sexual arousal from caressing with a man when she was still in her teens. It had in fact come on simultaneously with her awareness of the boy's erection. As this symptom was worked with in this period of her analysis, it seemed derived from her extreme penis envy and its special significance in connection with the traumatic experience of the mother's miscarriage, and her own feeling that she could never be really accepted by her father as a boy or as a girl unless she had a penis, i.e., that she must at least be a phallic girl. The experience of the miscarriage had involved her seeing the male foetus in the bathroom, her awareness of the mother's damaged genital, and the occurrence of this at the height of her own anal phase. The retained bowel movement appeared as a (visually) stolen and guilty object as well as something that intrinsically belonged to her and must not be taken away. She must hide it out of guilt and keep it, for its narcissistic body value. She had also from time to time suffered mildly persistent kleptomanic impulses. At the time of the termination of the first analysis this bowel symptom was reported as having improved.

She returned to me years later in a state of acute anxiety precipitated by a minor accident to her child, which signalized the rearousal of castration problems in anticipation of the menopause. It became apparent then that the bowel symptom had never really undergone a substantial resolution; that she had overemphasized a modest improvement and unfocused her attention to it. It had become her carefully guarded secret. During this second analysis the nature of the constipation as a bisexual masturbatory performance was revealed. The struggle to have the bowel movement and simultaneously to retain it was a masochistic gratification terminating usually in the use of a suppository. The performance was endowed with powerful sadistic fantasies, for the most part kept unconscious and defended against by compulsive reading while on the toilet.

I have had other cases of secrets firmly held by patients, as frequently by men as by women. But always there has been a strong bisexual identification. The rectum has been the great hiding place, the fortress of resistant power. Nor is this surprising in view of the deep connection of feces with ambivalence, power, sadism, and magic. My first encounter with this particular site of the secret as a symptom was in a Lesbian paranoid patient in a hospital. She took poison and secreted the container in her rectum, thus creating a mystery which was only solved by the post-mortem examination. One recalls too that Hermann Goering carried capsules of poison in this hiding place, using them in a final gesture of power in taking his own life before he could be executed.

Selma Fraiberg's article on "Discovery of the Secret Treasure" (1954) points out how universal is the theme of the secret treasure in the myths and fairy tales—and, one might add, in the great religions of the world. She points out that the complete story consists of the accidental discovery of a secret which permits the uncovering of the buried treasure, which then allows the finder great good fortune and ultimately the marriage to the Princess—in other words the completion of oedipal success. She quotes Marie Bonaparte's account of her conversation with Freud on the possibility that the secret treasure may conceivably represent an important event in the history of the race, in the accidental finding of an embryo or foetus in the abdomen of the victim. It is clear that the case from which material in this paper has been selected may very well support the idea of the fateful discovery of the dead foetus, with its re-embalming in the rectum as the foetus-penis-stool, which served then, in its condensation, to permit the hidden masturbation. In cases of imposture and allied conditions, I have thought that often the buried treasure was like the divining rod, the magic or Godlike phallus, which would lead to omnipotent and multiform power.[4]

The third of the Grimm's Fairy Tales, "Our Lady's Child," is particularly pertinent.

A poor woodcutter and his wife, having no food for their three-year-old girl, yielded to the enticements of the Virgin Mary to take the child as her own. Until fourteen the little one lived in heaven and played with the angels. Then the Virgin left on a trip, giving the child the keys to the thirteen doors of heaven, with instructions that she might open twelve but must keep the thirteenth inviolate. Behind each of the twelve doors she found one of the Apostles in the midst of great light, with magnificence and splendor. Finally unable to resist her urgent curiosity, in spite of the warnings of the angels, she opened the thirteenth door, just the slightest bit to get the merest peep within. But with the unlocking, the door sprang open, revealing the Trinity sitting in fire and splendor. When she touched the light with her finger, the finger turned quite golden, and no matter how much she rubbed or washed it, the gold could not be removed.

When the Virgin returned and saw the golden finger, she asked the child, not once but three times, about her unlocking of the thirteenth door. Each time the child firmly denied what she had done. As punishment, the child then fell into a deep sleep from which she awoke in the wilderness and stricken quite dumb. When her clothes had fallen away in rags, she covered herself with her long hair and sat year after year in front of a protecting tree, feeling the pain and the misery of the world. There she was discovered by the King, who fell in love with her and carried her to his castle, dumb though she was.

A year later when her first son was born, the Virgin appeared to

---

4 When Joseph Smith, the founder of Mormonism, found the buried golden plates, it was seemingly at first a conscious hoax but met such wide belief that he became converted by the success of his own trick (Brodie, 1945). Cagliostro was an alchemist dealing in transformation of baser metals into gold, before he became a practicing impostor. There are other such examples in the crew of the spectacular impostors of history (Greenacre, 1958).

her, offering to restore her speech if she confessed her misdeed, but threatening to remove the newborn child if she continued to deny her guilt. Still the stubborn girl persisted in her lie, and the young princeling disappeared in the night.

When another son was born in the second year and a daughter in the third year of her marriage, the same queenly stubbornness prevailed and the children disappeared. The people began to suspect she was a man-eater and rose up against her, condemning her to burn at the stake as a witch. Now, however, her pride melted with the fire, her voice returned with her decision to confess, and she cried out, "Yes, Mary, I did it." Rain fell and put out the fire, the children returned unharmed; the Virgin untied her tongue and forgave the repentant sinner.

The secret is closely related to the fetish. One sees a continuation of the two in secret magic rituals, both in certain severe neuroses and in the initiation rites of secret societies. Like the fetish, the secret is Janus-faced, and has the value of an illusion. Since it can frequently be sustained only through external subterfuge and internal denials, it may weaken rather than strengthen the individual's relationships with others.

DISCUSSION

These clinical reports have been brought to illustrate the relation of the secret (especially a tenaciously held one) and of pseudo addiction to the fetish. Other symptoms, such as compulsive rituals and certain tics, may also be related, as Glover (1939) pointed out.[5] In contrast to the situation in well-developed perversions, such fetishistic symptoms are not so intimately and clearly connected with sexual functioning, but serve more exclusively to support and reinforce phallic (or clitoral) value as part of a general body safety and so defend against bodily and separation anxiety. In many instances the symptomatic use of the fetishistic practice has appeared remarkably isolated from sexual activity. Deeper investigation in my own cases revealed that either a pseudo sexuality had been established at a performance level, but with impairment of pleasure; or that the

[5] Glover states that many fetishists pass through phases of drug addiction, and may carry the drug with them, not so much for its emergency use as to avoid the anxiety of separation from the symbolic love object (p. 247). He further relates some cases of compulsive stealing and of obsessional delinquency to the seeking of objects of fetishistic value (p. 275).

functioning itself was actually impaired, but not nearly so completely as in the perverse patient. It has been especially clear that in women neurotic fetishistic practices might retain still active elements of the intense masculinity complex which continued to interfere with adequate sexual responsiveness. It is probable that in both sexes, the fetishistic use of pills contains, and defends against, strong infantile dependence on the mother and wish for the breast, and similarly may interfere with adequate mature sexual functioning.

The structure of the basic disturbances underlying the neurotic symptom is different, however, from that of the ones in which the perversion arises. In both groups of cases there is some confusion regarding the genitals, sometimes arising in part (as in Cases I and II already described) from an early twinlike association with another child of the opposite sex or from prolonged body contact with the parent of the opposite sex, yet neither the deprivations nor the positive traumata were as great in the neurotic group as in that of the perversions. The father, especially, was not so devaluated or actually missing from a very early age in the patient's development, in neurotic patients as in the cases of perversion. Although the oedipal conflict was especially severe due to bisexual identifications, it was less narcissistically involved. Object relationship was not so grossly impaired.

The case of the fatherless boy reported by Meiss (1952) is of interest here. In this instance the child had had a good relationship with the father up to the time of the latter's death during the patient's fourth year. From the clinical report it would seem that the oedipal phase was already well begun at the time of the father's death, and that the dead father became in fantasy even more powerfully punishing than the living father might have been with his reassuring presence. Even so it was felt that the child would have been unable to solve his oedipal problem without the aid of the analysis which was begun when he was five, and involved unusually intense transference reactions with re-enactment of the early relationship with the father. This is in contrast to the early situations of the perverse patients in whom the father has died, or left his family, during the child's first or second year; or, remaining with the family, has suffered chronic devaluation by the mother. Under these circumstances the serious disturbance of the oedipal relationship from its very inception is reflected in the continued narcissistic quality of the later oedipal conflicts. The living father, consistently looked down upon by the mother, can neither be the model, nor the rival, nor the reassurance that he is in ordinary life.

"The Secret" has been discussed by Namnum (1960) with significant emphasis on its ego-strengthening quality. Certainly the ability to keep a secret for the sake of a deferred constructive aim is the indication of ego strength already established. In cases of fetishistic secrets, neurotically embedded, however, the effort of the individual is to attain *a sense of greater ego strength*. But this is achieved only through the use of the secret contents for extreme narcissistic power gains,[6] or by the emphasis on the illusion of power through withholding. In either case fundamental and progressive ego development is impaired since the very tenacity and passive aggression of the secret make consistent inroads on object relationship.

In summary, this paper has used clinical material in an effort to sketch in some outlines of early development in differentiating perverse from neurotic conditions, in which somewhat similar symptoms occur. It would further indicate the need for specific study of the impact of traumatic conditions and defective body-ego developments in influencing body identifications in the first two years to two and a half years of life, comparing them with the results of disturbed conditions of the phallic and oedipal period, in their respective influences on the form and the outcome of the oedipal conflict. This is of further importance in the later pressures on the formation of

---

[6] There are patients who have secret fantasy formulas with which they would control whatever happens by interpreting it in a way favorable to themselves. A patient, encountered in my preanalytic days, after the disruption of a love affair, pulled a blanket of fantasy around herself by turning each evidence of her lover's desertion into a secret sign of his devotion. This seemed an impregnable defensive system by which she maintained herself in a state of dreamy happiness. But twice in the middle of the night, the hunger for reality and actual contact broke through. With tears and real show of emotion she admitted to the nurses that she knew this was all make-believe but felt she could not get herself out of it. Indeed, the downward spiral of narcissistic fantasy control did ultimately engulf her. It seemed probable that this fantasy control was an old device of hers which came into this floridly self-destructive form in adult life. Such defensive systems may be more circumscribed in neurotic patients. Indeed it is not uncommon in the course of analysis to see an allied phenomenon in which the analysand uses the newly acquired tool of analysis, which still seems a mysterious and secret weapon, to analyze other people's behavior in regard to himself, thus giving him a sense of superiority when the need is to look inward. There are few analysands who do not adopt this defense at some time, but its habitual use vitiates any analytic work, and sometimes is an ominous sign.

the ego ideals; and the complications of the flow and fulfillment of libidinal development.

It is the belief of the writer that the disturbances of the body ego especially in the first two years of life are likely to be associated with inadequacies of parental relationship (from whatever source) and leave lasting effects in a tendency for a primary emphasis of the castration problems and the complementary sustaining of narcissistic defenses.

BIBLIOGRAPHY

Brodie, F. (1945), *No Man Knows My History*. New York: Knopf.
Fraiberg, S. (1954), Tales of the Discovery of the Secret Treasure. *This Annual*, IX.
Freud, S. (1913), The Theme of the Three Caskets. *Collected Papers*, IV. London: Hogarth Press, 1948.
—— (1927), Fetishism. *Collected Papers*, V. London: Hogarth Press, 1950.
—— (1938), Splitting of the Ego in the Defensive Process. *Collected Papers*, V. London: Hogarth Press, 1950.
Glover, E. (1939), *Psychoanalysis*. London: Staples Press, 2nd ed.
Greenacre, P. (1947), Vision, Headache and the Halo. *Psa. Quart.*, XVI.
—— (1951), Respiration, Incorporation and the Phallic Phase. *This Annual*, VI.
—— (1953), Certain Relationships between Fetishism and the Faulty Development of the Body Image. *This Annual*, VIII.
—— (1955), Further Considerations regarding Fetishism. *This Annual*, X.
—— (1958), The Impostor. *Psa. Quart.*, XXVII.
Gross, A. (1936), The Secret. *The Yearbook of Psychoanalysis*, VIII. New York: International Universities Press, 1952.
Meiss, M. E. (1952), The Oedipal Problem of a Fatherless Child. *This Annual*, VII.
Milne, A. A. (1929), *The Secret and Other Stories*. London: Methuen.
Namnum, A. (1960), On Secrets. Paper read at the Western New England Psychoanalytic Society.
Stevenson, O. (1954), The First Treasured Possession. *This Annual*, IX.
von Hug-Hellmuth, H. (1915), Ein Fall von weiblichem Fuss-, richtiger Stiefelfetischismus. *Int. Ztschr. Psa.*, III.
Winnicott, D. W. (1953), Transitional Objects and Transitional Phenomena. *Int. J. Psa.*, XXXIV.
Wulff, M. (1946), Fetishism and Object Choice in Early Childhood. *Psa. Quart.*, XV.

DISTORTIONS OF THE PHALLIC PHASE

ANNY KATAN, M.D. (Cleveland)[1]

As an introduction to my subject, let me begin with the following observation.

A naked thirteen-month-old baby boy was sitting on a rug in the sun. He had a cracker in his hand. With him was his rubber doll, to which he had given his own name, identifying with it. As usual, he offered his cracker first to the doll with a gesture of undangerous generosity; then with exactly the same gesture and expression he offered his cracker to his own penis, making the same encouraging sound; and finally he put it into his mouth.

There could be no doubt that the boy had identified his penis, as well as the doll, with himself. The boy was in the animistic stage of development, in which dead material or a part of his body can be regarded and experienced as a living being like himself. Children in this stage often also feel as if they were parts of other people's bodies.

This phase—a completely normal, transitory developmental stage —can, under the influence of certain traumata, assume special significance for later developments. Under such conditions this early developmental phase acquires more than its normal share of cathexes, thus leading to distortions of the phallic phase. These will later manifest themselves in adults in pathological fantasies.

CASE ILLUSTRATIONS

My first patient had a circumcision performed when he was eighteen months old. When during the analysis his amnesia partly lifted, he remembered his train ride with his mother to the town where the operation was performed. After the operation he was enuretic for many years. He felt extremely disgusted with his penis,

---

[1] Professor of Child Analysis, Western Reserve University, Cleveland, Ohio.

was convinced that it was mutilated and worthless, with the result that he later felt his body to be a compensation for his inferior penis. He was the only boy in his family, and the mother adored and admired his body, telling him how beautiful he was. The boy, who never could be proud of his penis, cathected his whole body as if it were a penis, under the influence of the mother's admiration. This identification of his penis with his body became later a disturbing factor in his relation to father figures.

In his analysis which he started as a young man, he once reported having had a strange reaction while attending a dancing class. He had taken a terrific dislike to the dancing teacher, who tried to impress his pupils with the necessity for practicing at home. He could not make himself practice, for, contrary to our expectations, performing well would have made him feel ashamed and wounded in his pride. By neglecting to put forth the effort and showing himself as a failure, he could make the teacher impotent and feel himself as the victorious rebel. If he performed well, the teacher would feel potent, but he himself would feel less than a person.

Clearly, in this relationship my patient had become the penis of the dancing teacher. The analysis soon revealed this relationship to be a repetition of the relationship to his father at a certain period in puberty. Against this father, who was a very violent man and made furious attacks upon his son at times, he never dared to rebel openly. He always felt keenly that his father loved him only narcissistically, wanting to show off a handsome, well-performing boy.

The boy's adolescent masturbation conflict reactivated and aggravated his disgust with his damaged, worthless penis. In his early adolescence, to use his own words, he looked and behaved "like a mess": he failed in school, was unable to do anything, looked dirty and sloppy. By this behavior he felt that he was making his father impotent. We see clearly demonstrated that this mechanism was used as a reaction against the father, who loved only the boy's performances if they were excellent, but not the boy himself. If the boy had functioned well, he would have given his father the satisfaction of showing off an ably performing good looking penis.

Another young man sought analysis because of his inability to study. His father was an authority in his profession, as well as at home. He was "like God Himself," my patient said. "Nobody would ever think of contradicting him." At the age of about six or seven, my patient once jokingly called his father a dummy. In a sudden outburst of rage, the father grabbed the boy, threw him onto a bed, and shook him so fiercely that the boy felt his father would kill him. The boy had previously experienced the same terror while witnessing parental intercourse, identifying himself with his mother. This sudden violence of the father was the more impressive because he had always appeared to be a man devoid of emotions whose entire life was controlled and mastered by intellect. To teach his young children the facts of life, he brought a male human foetus home from a laboratory and dissected it in the sink, splitting first the penis and then the body of the foetus, explaining the organs as he went along, and not noticing that his children were frozen with terror.

The father's hobby was carpentry, and his little son was expected to watch him but was never permitted to touch any of the tools or to do any work himself. At school the boy was expected to function in accordance with his superior intellect as a matter of course. He merely "got by" in school, however, picking up information but never really learning. His symptom became apparent toward the end of high school. In the beginning of his college course he became a failure.

His masturbation conflict was then at its peak. His penis had always seemed inferior and abnormally small to him. He had every occasion to compare himself with his father, as the latter was in the habit of showing himself naked to his two daughters and son alike. The sisters used to refer contemptuously to my patient's penis as "just a little tag." His inability to control either his masturbation or his first emissions convinced the boy even more of the worthlessness of his penis. He tried at times, in fact, to behave as if he had none, in order to save the small penis, which he felt he had, from the fate of the foetus.

My patient, when left to himself, was incapable of functioning well intellectually, but he could do so at times when he was in close contact with a man. Some man—a teacher, for example—had to become interested in him and give him a pep talk, which the patient called and experienced as "being pumped up." Then he felt "erected" and capable for a very short while, only to be deflated and incapable again soon afterwards. He could never function on his own unless he felt as if he were the erect penis of an interested teacher.

But even this achievement in relation to certain teachers never happened in relation to his father. To function on his own intellectually would have meant becoming his father's penis. Success in this area, therefore, would have meant submission and loss of personality. Failure to him signified rebellion. He feared his father so much and had seen so many examples of his sadistic attitude that an identification with him and his capabilities was impossible.

On occasion my patient would start suddenly to talk in a dictatorial, pompous voice, putting on an obvious act of authority which he never felt. At such times he felt as though he were slipping into the shell of his father. This was his only way of being like his father, i.e., playing a magical role. The alternative was to function as a penis attached to his father. This he felt compelled to resist, but, even so, he never felt as though he had a personality of his own.

A third patient needed treatment because of homosexual fantasies. These fantasies and masturbation comprised his whole sex life. He had never, as an adult, committed an overt homosexual act, nor had he ever had intercourse. Intellectually he had always functioned extremely well and later was recognized for his efficiency in his work.

His fantasies were always about very young boys who had to be blond with short haircuts. He would imagine such a boy tied up, his penis exposed, "sticking out." He would play with the penis up to the point when the boy was about to ejaculate, but would never let it happen.

These he called the "soft" fantasies. They were never vicious—merely enjoyable. The short haircuts and blond hair meant to him that these youngsters had no pubic hair and so had not yet reached puberty. They were at an age when masturbation happened without ejaculation and therefore seemed less dangerous.

He also had other fantasies, the "tough" ones, in which there was a victim with whom he would always identify. These fantasies were infrequent and not as enjoyable as the "soft" kind.

As already mentioned, in these fantasies he would masturbate the blond young boys but stop before ejaculation, which seemed a danger to be avoided, often referred to as an "explosion." He was afraid that if he went further, he would become too excited and rough and would finally destroy the boy.

There could be no doubt that this boy, in his fantasies, represented his own penis at a time when he could play with it without the danger of ejaculation. While masturbating with this fantasy, he would have an ejaculation. Clearly, this fantasy enabled him to masturbate, for it kept his anxiety from becoming conscious. Such anxiety would have made masturbation impossible or at least have disturbed it considerably.

The fear of dying under great excitement was a very extreme one, and he felt protected against this danger by a strong tie to his mother, feelings which he transferred to me in the analysis. He used to function beautifully, as his domineering mother wanted him to, and she never passed up an occasion to show him off. In the analysis the patient would produce beautiful associations, functioning in this situation as he expected that I wanted him to function. The analytic situation seemed to afford my patient the utmost satisfaction and protection. Needless to say, he made no progress until we understood that he was my penis attached to me, as he had been to his mother. Any thought of severing this strong and protecting unit would virtually drive the patient into a panic. Once, when it was necessary for me to interrupt the analysis for a few days, he implored me not to do this, with the words, "Don't cut me off from you like that! I am and feel just a part of you. I cannot exist on my own!"

In the aforementioned homosexual fantasies he was the mother; and the boy was his penis, sticking out nude, waiting for someone to handle it and make it function. As a very small child, he would be taken to the bathroom by his mother and she would hold his penis while he urinated.

His fear of ejaculations—the explosions—led back to anal material. The mother had given the patient innumerable enemas. The enema stick in his rectum excited him tremendously and he felt as if his mother and he had one penis together, inserted in his rectum and coming out in front. He was afraid of the anal explosion and retained the enema until he had to let go, holding on to his penis with both hands lest it, too, would go down the drain. When the patient's "unit" with me was recognized and analyzed as the defense it was, his fear of women became apparent. He could not think of the vagina without feeling terror and always imagined the opening as enormous with a lot of blood around it.

The analysis revealed that at the age of about four the patient had witnessed a miscarriage of his mother in the fifth or sixth month of pregnancy. According to his description, out of this terrifying opening, surrounded by blood, had come a long white thing. It had been called "mummified," he remembered. To him it had looked like a large penis and baby combined. My patient, who had witnessed intercourse long before that time, had the fantasy that what he saw was his father's penis, which his mother had detached and kept inside of herself, and finally was giving up.

To have intercourse seemed to him the greatest danger in a man's life. To be attached as a penis to the woman helped to deny the fact that the woman had a vagina and protected him from ever inserting a part of himself into a woman! When in puberty my patient by chance saw his mother's genitals again, he turned in his fantasies to the boys.

DISCUSSION

My first two patients had the fantasy of being functioning penises of their· fathers; they would lose their personalities and their self-respect if they acceded to their fathers' demands. Therefore, they had to be rebellious and at puberty became failures. Both, however, managed to have sex relations with women.

My third patient was never rebellious. He never fought against the fantasy of being attached to his mother and functioning as her penis—a fantasy which the mother herself might have had also and which she therefore reinforced in her son. He accepted fully and lived out his fantasy, for it served so well to protect him against the women he feared. Because he was so accepting of this fantasy, he became outstanding as a capably functioning person in every area except sex!

Identification of the penis with the self seems to be a normal developmental phenomenon occurring after the baby boy has discovered his genitals, as we have seen in the observation of the thirteen-month-old baby boy. This identification accompanies the child through the subsequent developmental phases. In the anal phase the child identifies the stool with himself. In the phallic phase the boy has reached a height of penis cathexis and proudly exposes his organ to his mother. If early traumatic events disturb these developments and cause the boy to feel that his penis is inferior, mutilated, disgusting, and practically nonexistent, as was true of the aforementioned patients, the prephallic and phallic phases cannot take their normal course. Instead of cathecting an organ that seems worthless, the boy cathects his whole body as if it were a penis. These pathological developments are often aided by the attitude of the mother, who may not appreciate the genital of her small son but instead may show admiration of his body and pride in his intellectual functioning.

In all three of my patients these defensive fantasies were a means of avoiding castration anxiety. The two patients who felt attached as penises to their fathers had to rebel against this function, for in this way they protected their active sexuality. Notwithstanding their high intelligence, they could not function in this area, but they kept open the way to women. The third patient, who related his body-penis fantasy to his mother, was highly capable of functioning intellectually but had to exclude heterosexuality.

BIBLIOGRAPHY

Fenichel, O. (1936), The Symbolic Equation: Girl = Phallus. *Collected Papers of Otto Fenichel*, II. New York: Norton, 1954.
Ferenczi, S. (1926), Gulliver Phantasies. *Int. J. Psa.*, IX, 1928.
Freud, S. (1918), From the History of an Infantile Neurosis. *Standard Edition*, XVIII. London: Hogarth Press, 1955, p. 102.
Hárnik, J. (1923), The Various Developments Undergone by Narcissism in Men and Women. *Int. J. Psa.*, V, 1924.
Lewin, B. D. (1933), The Body as Phallus. *Psa. Quart.*, II.
Sachs, H. (1933), The Delay of the Machine Age. *Psa. Quart.*, II.
Tausk, V. (1919), On the Origin of the "Influencing Machine" in Schizophrenia. *Psa. Quart.*, II, 1933.

PATHOLOGIC FORMS OF SELF-ESTEEM REGULATION[1]

ANNIE REICH, M.D. (New York)

"Self-esteem," in common usage, is defined by Webster as a high opinion of oneself, respect for oneself. This positive evaluation of the self obviously is a precondition for one's well-being.

There are many ways in which human beings attempt to keep up a positive evaluation of themselves. The methods they use may vary according to numerous factors, such as age, character and capacities of the ego, individual nature of conflicts, and so on. A comprehensive study of these various ways would exceed the frame of a lecture. My discussion will limit itself to certain abnormal modes of self-esteem regulation which are characteristically found in some types of "narcissistic disturbances."

Obviously, disturbances of self-esteem are a frequent symptom in schizophrenic as well as in manic-depressive states. However, I shall not deal with the psychoses but intend to concentrate on "narcissistic neurosis."

I am well aware that Freud used the term "narcissistic neurosis" to designate exclusively psychotic illness, delimiting it from transference neurosis. But it seems to me that narcissistic pathology cannot be viewed as restricted to psychosis. I would like to use this term in a much wider sense. In the course of the last decades, we have become less inclined to regard clinical entities as pertaining exclusively to certain phases of development. We know overlapping of phases to be ubiquitous. There is usually a partial regression to earlier ego and libidinal states mixed with later, more highly developed structures. Even a marked narcissistic orientation need not be completely so; i.e., it need not be characterized by a withdrawal of

[1] The Abraham A. Brill Lecture, presented to The New York Psychoanalytic Society and Institute, March 29, 1960.

the entire cathexis from objects. Indeed, we now even question the usefulness of a too narrowly circumscribed nosology. We are much concerned with so-called borderline conditions, and we tend to look upon the boundary between psychosis and neurosis as somewhat fluid.

Narcissism denotes a libidinal cathexis of the self, in contrast to object cathexis. Without repeating the well-known facts about the development from primary to secondary narcissism, I merely wish to stress that narcissism per se is a normal phenomenon. It becomes pathologic only under certain conditions: (1) in states of quantitative imbalance; e.g., when the balance between object cathexis and self-cathexis has become disturbed, and objects are cathected insufficiently or not at all; (2) in infantile forms of narcissism, which are frequently—but not always—present in the states of quantitative imbalance. Infantile narcissism consists in cathexis of the self at a time of incomplete ego differentiation and insufficient delimitation of self and object world. The absence of the ability, at this stage, to distinguish wish from reality manifests itself in the use of magic to achieve need satisfaction and mastery of reality; thus, the infantile narcissism has a megalomanic character.

Narcissistic pathology becomes especially noticeable in the methods used for self-esteem regulation.

Fenichel (1945), following the ideas of Ferenczi (1913), regards self-esteem as the expression of nearness to or distance from the infantile feeling of omnipotence. With advancing ego development, the values against which the self is measured change and become more realistic; equally, the methods that are used to keep self-esteem on a stable positive level. The longing for omnipotence, obviously, stems from fixation at a still undifferentiated ego level. By using it as a criterion, Fenichel thus framed a static definition leaving no room for the maturation of values. I prefer the more flexible one given by Edith Jacobson in her fundamental paper on "The Self and the Object World" (1954b), which has helped me to clarify many aspects of narcissistic disturbances. Her definition seems to cover the complexities of the problem more adequately. She considers self-esteem to be the expression of discrepancy or harmony between self-representation and the wishful concept of the self.

Or, to put it differently: in the course of growing up, we must learn to evaluate our potentialities and accept our limitations. Continued hope for the impossible represents an infantile wish, revealing a basic lack of ability to face inner and outer reality. Self-esteem thus depends on the nature of the inner image against which we measure our own self, as well as on the ways and means at our disposal to live up to it. That this inner image is influenced by many factors, especially by the particular form of the superego, is obvious. Living up sufficiently to the demands of one's superego is a mature form of self-esteem regulation.

What we loosely describe as "narcissists" are people whose libido is mainly concentrated on themselves at the expense of object love. I shall not speak here of those who without visible conflict entertain an exceedingly high opinion of themselves. Another type of narcissists frequently has exaggerated, unrealistic—i.e., infantile—inner yardsticks. The methods they use to deal with the resulting inner tension depend on the general state of their ego and often are infantile ones. This is the specific pathology I wish to discuss, concentrating at this time on the forms it takes in men. As a starting point, I may bring a few clinical data to illustrate some characteristic patterns of such pathologic self-esteem regulation.

Daniel K. was a very accomplished writer who wrote one book after another, with marked success. But he did not feel gratified by this. Nothing he did was as grandiose as he wanted it to be. He would feel reassured, for a time, when he looked at his book shelf and counted: "Here are seven books I wrote, six volumes I edited; there are twenty-three articles I brought out in other people's publications; I am quoted so and so many times:—*There are about two and a half feet of Mr. K. on the shelf.*" The phallic meaning of this little game was obvious. He had to reassure himself that his phallus was not only there, but of extraordinary size.

Daniel's life consisted to a large extent in behavior of this kind; he was constantly preoccupied with attempts to feel great and important. He was active in innumerable civic and cultural enterprises and had attained a leading position in his community. But neither this nor his prolific literary production nor his erotic successes sufficed to make him happy. He was a man of considerable talent, well informed, and rich in ideas. But frequently his writing was careless and superficial, not up to the level of his capacities, because he was driven to produce too fast. He could not *wait* for results, could not stand tension and unpleasure, although he *knew* better. He had an inner standard of quality for his work as well as the gift for it, but was unable to muster enough self-discipline to realize his potentialities. He had to have the immediate gratification of success. This need was so overwhelmingly strong that he had little control over it. He also was touchy, quick to take offense at the slightest provocation. He continually anticipated attack and danger, reacting with anger and fantasies of revenge when he felt frustrated in his need for constant admiration.

Obviously, Daniel was overconcentrated on himself; his object relationships were weak and apt to be relinquished under pressure. His main aim was to increase his self-esteem and to ward off the underlying danger of passivity by incessant masculine activity.

The narcissistic goal against which he measured himself was most clearly expressed by his fantasies in puberty: he would see himself successively as the Mayor of New York City, the President of the United States, and as the president of the world, until he had to stop with the painful question: "And then what?" Later, he wanted to be the outstanding genius of his time. Of course, no success in reality could measure up to such limitless inner demands, and his state of dissatisfaction was all the more intensified because he had to sacrifice more mature superego demands in reaching out for his illusory aims.

This bottomless need for grandiosity is clearly a compensatory striving. He has to be president of the world, he has to have a symbolic phallus two and a half feet long, because he is under the impact of unbearable castration fears.

Compensatory narcissistic self-inflation is among the most conspicuous forms of pathologic self-esteem regulation. Frequently, the attempt at compensation proves unsuccessful; instead of producing a feeling of "narcissistic bliss," it results in severe symptoms.

Thus Daniel continually felt not only slighted, unloved, unappreciated by others, but also awkward, embarrassed, and "self-conscious." Moreover, he harbored severe anxieties regarding his state of health. He was forever anticipating early death from cancer or heart attack, etc., and anxiously watched himself for signs of disease. "Self-consciousness" and hypochondriacal anxiety both are typical symptoms in persons with narcissistic pathology. They represent, so to speak, the reverse side of the narcissistic self-inflation. I shall have more to say about this later.

Two factors which are characteristic of the pathology in compensatory narcissistic self-inflation were implied in this material: (1) there is a large amount of unneutralized aggression which contributes to the hypochondriacal anxieties; (2) there is a superego disturbance that causes an overdependence on approval from outside, thus contributing to the symptom of "self-consciousness."

It should be stressed that in spite of his low tolerance of tension and unpleasure, Daniel's narcissistic orientation was not combined with a general regression to infantile narcissism. The pathology, in his case, rested predominantly on the megalomanic content of the ideals he had set up for himself. He tried to reach his goal of self-aggrandizement through achievement and did not indulge in regressive confusion between reality and fantasy.

However, owing to the regressive character of the narcissistic orientation, one often finds that the infantile-megalomanic ideal is accompanied by a barely disguised sexualization of originally non-sexual activities. Frequently the ambitious narcissistic fantasy is expressed in the form of sexualized and concrete images, thus revealing features of ego infantilism, deficient sublimation, and primitive thinking. In severer cases of this type the ego disturbance dominates the clinical picture and is not confined to an isolated area, as it was in the example given here.

Let us now examine the origin of the narcissistic imbalance which determines these compensatory efforts. The need for narcissistic inflation arises from a striving to overcome threats to one's bodily intactness. Obviously, such a threat is ubiquitous in all danger situations; but under favorable circumstances, defenses are mobilized that permit a permanent conflict solution. Anxiety is overcome via a modification or relinquishment of instinctual aims, while object cathexis can be retained. The development of reliable, solid defenses presupposes a considerable degree of ego integration. The ego must have the strength, while circumventing violent anxiety attacks and using small amounts of anxiety as a danger signal, to mobilize defenses and to influence the drives in the desired way. But if a traumatic situation occurs too early and is too overwhelming, at a time when the ego is still in a rather primitive state, the ego will

not succeed in binding the anxiety. The impact of such early traumata thus can seriously interfere not only with the formation of
defenses, but also with the integration and general development of
the ego. States of panic in themselves represent grave disturbances
in the balance of cathexis. That is to say, during intense anxiety
there often occurs a *passing* withdrawal of psychic interest from
objects to the self. Under the conditions of too frequently repeated
early traumatizations, the narcissistic withdrawal of libido from the
objects to the endangered self tends to remain permanent.

Such early traumatization at a time of ego immaturity creates a
predisposition to react in an infantile way to later danger situations.
The imagined danger is taken for reality: it is not something that
might occur in the future and might still be avoided, but something
that has already occurred. In the case of my patient, for instance,
the overwhelming castration anxiety stemmed from repeated early
observations of primal scenes experienced as. violence and total
destruction, which had led to a feminine identification; i.e., to a
latent homosexual orientation. The personality of the mother, a
severe hypochondriac who constantly indulged in dramatic performances of being on the brink of catastrophic death, made a later
re-evaluation of danger impossible. Femininity remained equated
with complete annihilation. It represented not a threat in the future,
but an accomplished fact. Hence the persistent orientation aiming at
repair of the damage.

This infantile equation of danger with a castastrophe that has
already occurred seems to be characteristic of such early disturbances.
The only possible defense, therefore, consists in methods which were
available to the infantile ego, particularly in *magical denial*: "It is
not so. I am not helpless, bleeding, destroyed. On the contrary, I am
bigger and better than anyone else. I am the greatest, the most
grandiose." Thus, to a large extent, the psychic interest must center
on a compensatory narcissistic fantasy whose grandiose character
affirms the denial.

Fantasies, to be sure, always have to do with easy ways of wish
fulfillment. But they obviously differ vastly in kind, and they range
from the most primitive to highly differentiated forms. Being rooted
in magical denial and characterized by primitive features of an early

ego state, the compensatory narcissistic fantasies often are poorly integrated into realistic, adult thinking.

The exclusive production of fantasies that aim at one's own aggrandizement reveals a serious disturbance of the narcissistic balance, particularly when these fantasies persist after puberty. For example, I remember a patient whose masturbation fantasies were consistently and exclusively concerned with self-adoration: "I am the greatest general in the world; I am the greatest all-round athlete; I am winning all Olympic ski races," etc. Grandiose fantasies of this type are not just a pleasant pastime whose wishful and unreal character is fully recognized, and which can be "turned off" at will. They have become an intrinsic part of the personality. Indeed, they have become life's main purpose, and the self is being measured against them.

I shall show later that such fantasies are based on primitive identifications with idealized infantile objects and thus represent primitive ego ideals.

The degree of pathology resulting from the persistence of these archaic ego ideals depends upon the structure of the ego. Ability to function adequately in reality, availability of sublimations, etc., determine whether any attempts can be made to transpose the fantasy at least partially into reality. Sometimes it may be tuned down to a pitch that is realizable in some degree, sufficiently to keep the self-esteem on a stable high level.

In the predominantly narcissistic personality, however, the withdrawal of interest from reality and object world frequently entails regressive trends. As a result, the wishful fantasy becomes or remains overcathected and the distinction between wish and reality will become blurred. Thus the fantasy is not only a yardstick, but is also experienced as magically fulfilled. The degree of pathology in a given case will depend on the degree of indulgence in such magic gratification and neglect of reality testing.

What is of interest for our special problem is the fact that such regressive abandonment of reality testing with respect to self-appreciation occurs frequently as an isolated lacuna in an otherwise well-coordinated personality. In other words, self-evaluation may remain infantile in certain restricted areas. For instance, the high sense of gratification which arose when the child was able to master certain difficulties may persist throughout later life, even though "objectively" such activity no longer represents any particular achievement. Rather minor activities and productions can thus be experienced as extremely important, sometimes, as though a hidden narcissistic fantasy had been realized. The resulting feeling of increased self-esteem, of exaggerated self-assurance, creates an impression of unwarranted conceit, since others cannot share the archaic value judgments which underlie it.

When an adult still finds magnificence, let us say, in being able to ride by himself in a train, he manifests an infantilism of inner standards. Usually the survival of such infantile values, too, is the end result of compensatory needs; but the intensity of inner conflict is less pronounced in these persons than in those with exaggerated standards. It is likely that their fixations took place on a somewhat higher level of development.

It would of course be artificial to delimit the compensatory narcissistic fantasy too sharply from the superego as the embodiment of "mature" values transmitted by education. Although the superego is the more complicated structure, both may exist simultaneously. They may overlap or may be fused and mixed with one another.

The differences between the two structures are self-evident. Narcissistic fantasies often stand in sharp contrast to superego demands, since they contain many elements of an unsublimated, instinct-fulfilling character. The primitive values comprised in them are expressions of body narcissism.

Overstrong body narcissism is rooted in traumatic experiences, pregenital as well as early genital, which had shattered primitive feelings of pleasure and unquestioned security. These traumata had thus destroyed the infantile feeling of power to subject the disobedient object world, including the own body, to the wishes of the infantile ego. Uncontrollable feelings of helplessness, anxiety, and rage ensued. These represent what we call "narcissistic injuries" that necessitate continuous reparative measures. The result is a turning away from love objects to an enormous overvaluation of the body or particular organs: of their intactness, size, strength, beauty, grandiosity. Most glaring here is the overvaluation of the phallus, in contrast to the concept of the female organs as being destroyed, bleeding, dirty, etc.

It should be stressed that castration threats, with ensuing over-valuation of the phallus, represent only the most conspicuous and the most tangible narcissistic traumata. However, any need for repair or restitution may be condensed into fantasies about phallic intactness and greatness. Castration thus is equated with object loss, emptiness, hunger, bowel loss and dirtiness, while phallic intactness also expresses the undoing of pregenital losses and injuries. Most important in this context is the equation of the whole body with a phallus, whose oral background was pointed out by Lewin (1933).

The megalomanic character of the body-phallus equation has to do with fantasies about incorporation of early objects (or of their organs) seen in an idealized way. Thus, to use Jacobson's formulation, fusion has taken place between self- and object images. The grandiosity originally attributed to the object belongs now to the self. Archaic object relationships of this kind, with fluid boundaries between self- and object image, represent the matrix of increased body narcissism.

The body-phallus equation usually reflects a narcissistic erotization of the whole body. This fantasy often has an out-and-out perverse quality and may lead to dire consequences.

To give an example: I once treated a professional actor, a handsome fellow, who was in a continual state of self-infatuation. That he really experienced his whole body as a penis was revealed by the fact that he liked to masturbate facing a mirror, with the fantasy that his neck was as thick as his head. This patient's constant preoccupation with his own body had disastrous effects. He became plagued by continuous, severe hypochondriacal anxieties. He was afraid of innumerable fatal diseases, worried that his nose would be disfigured by a chronic eczema, etc.

My other patient, Daniel K., showed the same pattern of self-adoration in a slight disguise when he admired his almost yard-long row of books. This transparent displacement from the body-phallus to his brain children did not avail him; he suffered from the same intolerable hypochondriacal fears as the actor.

Frequently, attempts are made to modify the sexual body narcissism and to transform it into something nonsexual and nonobjectionable; these attempts sometimes are on a rather primitive level. Certain tokens of masculinity are used in place of the real thing. I have repeatedly observed this in patients who attached a strong masculine connotation to particular garments or to the pipes they smoked, to the cars they drove, etc. This displacement represents a not very successful attempt at desexualization. The thinking remains symbolic, unrealistic, and incommunicable. (I never could establish, for instance, why one suit was regarded as more masculine than the other.)

Successful modification of body narcissism depends primarily upon the ego's capacity for sublimation and, as we shall see, deaggressivization.

Unsublimated, erotized, manic self-inflation easily shifts to a feeling of utter dejection, of worthlessness, and to hypochondriacal anxieties. *"Narcissists" of this type thus suffer regularly from repetitive, violent oscillations of self-esteem.*

It is as though the warded-off feeling of catastrophic annihilation, which had started off the whole process originally, were breaking through the elegant façade again each time. The brief rapture of elated self-infatuation is followed by a rude awakening. Usually the tiniest disappointment, the slightest physical indisposition, the most trifling experience of failure can throw the patient into extreme despair. He does not suffer from a cold: he has lung cancer. He did not meet with a minor setback because a contract fell through: his whole career is ruined; and so on. Thus, the grandiose body-phallus fantasy—for instance, "standing out high above everybody else, like an obelisk"—turns *suddenly* into one of total castration, often with a pregenital coloring: "I am falling apart at the seams," or "I am just a bagful of excrement," "I am full of poison that is going to kill me," etc. It is as though the original castration fear had extended from the penis to the whole body.

This infantile value system knows only absolute perfection and complete destruction; it belongs to the early time in life when only black and white existed, good and bad, pleasure and pain, but nothing in between. There are no shadings, no degrees, there are only extremes. Reality is judged exclusively from the standpoint of the pleasure principle; to evaluate it objectively is still impossible. Nor does a realistic evaluation of the self exist as yet. Like tolerance for others, tolerance for oneself is a late achievement.

The amount of aggression, both in the positive and in the negative phase, is conspicuous. The state of self-inflation is intensely competitive as a rule. My patient Daniel's grandiosity, for instance, could be measured in feet and inches, just as others measure theirs in dollars and cents. Such a concretization and oversimplification of values facilitates competition with others: "I am bigger than you— I am better—I am the best." The primitive correlation of value to size is of course a rather common phenomenon; this type of crude comparison easily lends itself to be used for purposes of aggressive competition. The very process of self-admiration involves contempt for others. Undisguised phallic-exhibitionistic impulses of this type generally are combined with unmitigated, primate aggression: the patient "blinds" others with his magnificence; he "rubs in' his successes, as though he were forcing his enormous penis on his audience.

But with the collapse of his phallic grandiosity, this vehement aggression instantly turns back upon his castrated self. Instead of admiring and loving himself the patient now hates himself. A drive diffusion has occurred, which the ego in its state of regression is unable to master. This explains, I believe, the intensity of the hypochondriacal anxieties regularly present in narcissistic disturbances.

In a number of these cases I have found the fantasy that only one grandiose phallus exists in the whole world. When the patient is in possession of it or is identified with it, everyone else is deprived of it and thus totally destroyed. In the negative phase, the tables are turned: the grandiose phallus belongs to somebody else—perhaps to its rightful, original owner—who, full of contempt, now destroys the patient. Either way, the acquisition of this glorified organ is accomplished through violent aggression.

This fantasy about the single glorified penis shows quite clearly that this and similar primitive forms of self-esteem regulation are based on a persistence of primitive types of object relationship; i.e., a fixation on infantile levels of libidinal and ego development.

At that early stage, the ability to perceive reality objectively is but *in statu nascendi*. Instinctual needs are so overwhelming that the sexual characteristics of the object flow together with the object as a person. Drives prevail toward oral—or anal—incorporation of the admired and envied objects; in this way, a feeling of *being* the object is temporarily achieved. But with growing ego differentiation, the child becomes increasingly aware of his own smallness as well as his separateness from objects. Hence the still completely sexualized and glorified object is set up as a primitive ego ideal, as something he longs to be. Under unfavorable conditions, however, the boundaries between this ideal and the self-image become blurred again, time after time.

Reverting to magical identification, the patient who has regressed to this infantile level may feel as though he *were* the magnificent phallus-father, as though he *were* his own ego ideal. Repair is achieved once more via magic fusion. But after a short time, as we have seen, this wishful identification turns into the opposite; it is doomed to break down, as the uncontrollably mounting aggression destroys the glorified object.

To relieve the ensuing intolerable feeling of annihilation, the aggression must be counteracted by a renewed elevation of the object; hence the grandiose phallus is restored to it and the entire process starts all over again. This state of affairs is reflected in the instability of moods, rapid oscillations of self-esteem, perpetual shifts from positive to negative feelings about the self, from megalomanic elation to hypochondriacal anxiety.

Let me illustrate this with a case characterized by a particular instability of self-esteem and body image. The origin of the primitive, still completely sexualized ego ideal in severe infantile traumatization can be clearly demonstrated here.

Robert L., a successful lawyer, suffers from repetitive mood swings. For a while he feels strong, victorious, much more creative and intelligent than his peers. He is proud of his slim figure; his whole body, to him, has definitely phallic characteristics. The analyst and everyone else during this period is seen as inferior, old, weak, defective. He feels that he is arousing envy in the analyst. He wishes to dazzle with his brilliance, to overpower by his masculinity. By exhibiting his own greatness he aggressively annihilates all others.

The slightest disappointment, however, or even the mere passage of time, transforms this state of phallic grandiosity into the opposite. Now he is afraid of the consequences of his aggressive wishes. He feels unsuccessful, hopeless, threatened by illness; he is affected by peculiar body sensations, as though he had a hang-over. The analyst and other objects appear changed; they have gained in stature. The analyst looks younger, stronger; she is brilliant, wonderful. Now he wishes to be "adopted" and helped by her. She should give to him of her wisdom and her riches which will help to restore him. During such periods, he cannot evaluate objects at all critically or realistically. He hangs on every word of the analyst as a revelation, and it is as though her mere physical presence could do wonders for him. Now he idealizes the object, clings to it, wishes to become one with it. By this fusion he can participate again in the greatness of the glorified object.

Here we see not only the rapid change from phallic grandiosity to hypochondriacal anxieties and depression, but also a rapid change in the appearance and value of the object. Again, there are only extremes: the object either is glorious or it is nothing. Besides, the object is not experienced fully as a person. Like the patient's own body, it is treated only as a phallus, as a wonderful and life-giving breast, or as a gaping, dirty wound.

This severe disturbance of object relationship was caused by a series of early traumatic events. When he was little more than six months old, Robert's obsessional mother started toilet training by means of regularly given enemas. For years to come, this interfered with his development of the sense of being a person separate from his mother: it was she who had power over his body. At the same time he experienced himself as an open bag full of excrement: things were put into him and came out of him. He could have no control over his body content. An operation early in his third year confirmed the feeling that the intactness of his body was constantly threatened. Then around the same time, his parents' marriage broke up. With the loss of his father he lost all security of permanent object relationships, particularly as the mother soon became involved with a series of lovers of whom Robert was intensely jealous.

Somewhat later, the little boy learned to retain his stools. He would sit for hours by himself, playing aggressive fantasy games in which he would kill and destroy tin soldiers, at the same time pushing and withholding a fecal column in his rectum. This gave him a feeling of mastery and of being completely solid and intact within his body, as though he had a powerful, aggressive anal phallus inside himself. In identification with his father, who was considered an aggressive monster by the mother, he became now "Freiherr von Richthofen," the German war pilot, seen as a murderous giant able to destroy the whole world. But this aggressive, anal-sadistic game led to a state of constipation which he could not overcome any more. It led to feelings of being sick and full of poison, to a new series of enemas, so that his sense of helpless annihilation broke through again.

These pregenital traumatic experiences were condensed with the child's envious admiration of his father's large penis and the simultaneous, terrifying awareness that the mother lacked this organ.

All this necessitated magical restitution. As we have seen, infantile states of elation persisted into adulthood in a slightly disguised form. They prevail for short periods, to be abruptly displaced by the sense of being worthless and destroyed. The peculiar "hangover" feeling, which assails the patient at the same time, can now be understood. By the destructive incorporation of everything that had caused his envy before, he destroyed the very power he acquired. He feels poisoned from within: he has incorporated something bad.

To repeat, the attempt at repair through primitive identification becomes intolerable due to the intensely aggressive feelings that may emerge at any moment. By destroying the object, the patient likewise destroys himself. Seeking to restitute himself, he again must endow the objects around him with ego-ideal qualities; and so the cycle is endlessly repeated.

This material throws into sharp relief that if the archaic character of the ego ideal has persisted, it invariably results in a complete failure of such attempts at self-esteem stabilization. Indeed, it is the primitive, crudely sexual quality of the ego ideals, conditioned by a fixation on the primitive levels where traumatization had occurred, that represents the quintessence of this pathology.

In the course of a more normal development, identifications with other than openly sexual aspects of the objects acquire importance. Hence the identifications lose their magical character. They bring about real changes in the structure of the ego, or they become more sublimated ideals to be incorporated in the superego. Primitive ego ideals may survive, nevertheless, while maturation of the personality progresses. In the "simpler" forms of self-esteem pathology I described before, their persistence expressed itself predominantly in a narcissistic orientation of the inner standards. The condition was not complicated by a reprojection of ego ideals onto the object world.

However, it should be stressed that a reprojection of ego ideals onto external objects need not by itself imply a greater degree of pathology. Ego ideals of a more sublimated nature may be so reprojected, and restitutive merging with real love objects may become a method of self-esteem stabilization. In my paper on "Narcissistic Object Choice in Women" (1953), I showed how the attempt to undo narcissistic injuries via identification with the partner's greatness may effect a rather stable solution if it is undertaken by a mature ego.

I should like now to come back briefly to another symptom which frequently occurs, as I mentioned before, in persons of the narcissistic structure here described, namely, "self-consciousness." This excellent term, as far as I know, exists only in the English language. Webster defines it as follows: "prone to regard oneself as the object of observation of others. Embarrassed or stagy on account of failure to forget oneself in society." *Self-consciousness* thus describes an accentuated state of awareness of the own self and also indicates the assumption that the same exaggerated amount of attention is paid to one's person by others.

The remarks which follow are somewhat tentative. The symptom of self-consciousness is not restricted solely to the compensatory narcissistic personality. Structure and dynamics may be different under different conditions.

To be the object of admiring attention is frequently sought for as a means to undo feelings of insufficiency. But the imagined fulfillment of this wish can be experienced as extremely unpleasant. The attention desired from others is contained in and replaced by the ego's concentration upon the own self. The ego thus plays a double role: it is the observer and simultaneously the object of observation. What is relevant in pathologic cases of this kind is that cathexis has been shifted to the self not only from objects, but also from normally neutralized ego activities, to a degree which is intolerable.

Here the hypercathexis of the self is accompanied by a disturbance of sublimation, i.e., by a (voyeuristic-exhibitionistic) sexualization of ego activities. This reflects itself in the fact that any activity —any thought or feeling—exists not for its own sake, but exclusively for the purpose of narcissistic exhibition. It is as though the person would say: "Look, I am walking, speaking, thinking. Look, I have such beautiful feelings, deep interests, important thoughts." Normally such activities áre invested not only with neutralized energy, but also with aim-inhibited "love" for some particular field, subject, etc. This type of "thing-love" or interest is precluded by the accentuated self-concentration we describe as "self-consciousness." The ensuing narcissistic imbalance generates disturbances of the sense of reality, ranging from feelings of emptiness or ungenuineness to severe depersonalization.

In addition, we must take into account the aggressive components of the narcissistic exhibitionistic strivings. Self-conscious people seek to undo feelings of inadequacy by forcing everyone's attention and admiration upon themselves, but they fail in this defensive attempt. They feel that attention is indeed focused on them in a *negative* way: as though others, instead of being dazzled, were discerning the warded-off "inferiority" behind the false front. The exhibitionistic drive contains contempt for those whose admiration is needed. Due to the re-emergence of inferiority feelings and to the concentration of cathexis on the self, the direction of the aggression changes; hence the contempt for others turns into self-contempt, which is experienced as shameful exposure.

The painfully increased self-awareness of the self-conscious persons thus results from a shifting back onto the self of resexualized and reaggressivized cathexis which can no longer be bound in a stable way by attachment to objects or ego activities.

Not rarely, the symptom of self-consciousness becomes further complicated by a deficiency of the self-evaluating functions. It is as though such persons were unable to form any independent moral judgment about themselves, but needed "public opinion" as a yardstick. Their superego is not fully internalized or, frequently, has become reprojected onto external objects. Here the impairment of ego functions, which is so often seen in narcissistically oriented persons, includes also a superego defect.

When the self-conscious person imagines himself being judged by an outside observer, who stands for an externalized superego, he makes an unsuccessful attempt to get rid of inner conflicts, of unacceptable strivings, by means of projection. This contributes to the feelings of unreality and estrangement. It is as if he were saying: "I am not the one who wants to exhibit himself aggressively, but other people aggressively observe and judge me." Self-consciousness thus is a first step in the direction of a paranoid pattern, and this feature is in keeping with the disturbance of object cathexis which I described before.

It is obvious that the oscillations of self-esteem in compensatory narcissism bear similarities to cyclothymic states, but there are considerable differences. These mood swings are of shorter duration than the true cyclothymic ones. Notwithstanding the severity of the disturbance, large areas of the personality usually remain intact and are not involved in the pathologic process. Most noticeable is the difference of the role played by the superego. The sadistic intolerance of the superego, so predominant in the depressive phase of cyclothymia, is absent in the cases here described. The phase of lowered self-esteem is characterized preponderantly by anxiety and feelings of annihilation, not by guilt feelings. Thus, it is not the dissolution of an overstrict superego that brings about the positive phase, but a compensatory narcissistic fantasy of restitution via fusion with an archaic ego ideal. And while object loss causes regression to narcissistic identification in melancholia, these patients react with permanent vacillations between libidinous and aggressive hypercathexis of the self to an infantile traumatic situation necessitating endless attempts at repair.

BIBLIOGRAPHY

Bibring, E. (1953), The Mechanism of Depression. In: *Affective Disorders*, ed. P. Greenacre. New York: International Universities Press.

Deutsch, H. (1927), Über Zufriedenheit, Glück und Ekstase. *Int. Ztschr. Psa.*, XIII.

—— (1942), Some Forms of Emotional Disturbance and Their Relationship to Schizophrenia. *Psa. Quart.*, XI.

Fenichel, O. (1937), Early Stages of Ego Development. *The Collected Papers of Otto Fenichel*, II. New York: Norton, 1954.

—— (1939), Trophy and Triumph. *The Collected Papers of Otto Fenichel*, II. New York: Norton, 1954.

—— (1945), *The Psychoanalytic Theory of Neurosis*. New York: Norton.

Ferenczi, S. (1913), Stages in the Development of the Sense of Reality. *Sex in Psychoanalysis*. New York: Basic Books, 1950.

Freud, A. (1936), *The Ego and the Mechanisms of Defence*. New York: International Universities Press, 1946.

Freud, S. (1914), On Narcissism: An Introduction. *Standard Edition*, XIV. London: Hogarth Press, 1957.

—— (1917), Mourning and Melancholia. *Standard Edition*, XIV. London: Hogarth Press, 1957.

—— (1921), Group Psychology and the Analysis of the Ego. *Standard Edition*, XVIII. London: Hogarth Press, 1955.

—— (1923), The Ego and the Id. *Standard Edition*, XVIII. London: Hogarth Press, 1955.

—— (1926), Inhibitions, Symptoms and Anxiety. *Standard Edition*, XX. London: Hogarth Press, 1959.

Greenacre, P. (1947), Vision, Headache and the Halo. *Psa. Quart.*, XVI.

—— (1952), *Trauma, Growth and Personality*. New York: Norton.

Hart, H. H. (1947), Narcissistic Equilibrium. *Int. J. Psa.*, XXVIII.

Hartmann, H. (1939), *Ego Psychology and the Problem of Adaptation*. New York: International Universities Press, 1958.

—— (1950), Comments on the Psychoanalytic Theory of the Ego. *This Annual*, V.

—— (1953), Contribution to the Metapsychology of Schizophrenia. *This Annual*, VIII.

—— (1960), *Psychoanalysis and Moral Values*. New York: International Universities Press.

—— Kris, E., & Loewenstein, R. M. (1949), Notes on the Theory of Aggression. *This Annual*, III/IV.

Jacobson, E. (1953), Contribution to the Metapsychology of Cyclothymic Depression. In: *Affective Disorders*, ed. P. Greenacre. New York: International Universities Press.

—— (1954a), Contribution to the Metapsychology of Psychotic Identifications. *J. Am. Psa. Assn.*, II.

—— (1954b), The Self and the Object World: Vicissitudes of Their Infantile Cathexes and Their Influences on Ideational and Affective Development. *This Annual*, IX.

Jones, E. (1913), The God-Complex. *Essays in Applied Psycho-Analysis*, II. London: Hogarth Press, 1951.

Lewin, B. D. (1933), The Body as Phallus. *Psa. Quart.*, II.

—— (1950), *The Psychoanalysis of Elation*. New York: Norton.

Reich, A. (1953), Narcissistic Object Choice in Women. *J. Am. Psa. Assn.*, I.

—— (1954), Early Identifications as Archaic Elements in the Superego. *J. Am. Psa. Assn.*, II.

CLINICAL PROBLEMS OF THE PRELATENCY AND LATENCY CHILD

FUNCTIONAL IMPAIRMENT OF THE SENSORIUM AS A RESULT OF NORMAL ADAPTIVE PROCESSES

HAROLD BALIKOV, M.D. (Chicago)

This paper is an attempt to present some observations of an unusual family of blind parents and three physiologically normal children. The interesting aspect is that the children of this family look and act as if they were blind. A search of the literature over the last ten years reveals no similar material, therefore I have attempted to offer some suggestions and explanations of the findings.

The family was studied in the Child Development Center of the Infant Welfare Society of Chicago over a period of several years, since each child entered the nursery school as he or she came of age. This paper contains a condensed version of the observations made by the staff at the Child Development Center during the children's everyday activity in the nursery school.[1] The paper concerns itself with Carl because he was the most verbal of the three and best illustrates and includes the factors common to all three children.

The father's blindness was due to illness and dates from the time he was two years old. The mother at a very early age had extremely poor vision which became progressively worse until at the age of sixteen she became totally blind from glaucoma. The parents met at a school for the blind and married after graduation. They then moved to Chicago. Their apartment was always kept dark, with all the shades drawn and lights off. Not a window shade was raised until the eldest child, Mary, was old enough to do so. The apartment, in addition, was barren and dirty. The two younger children spent the first two years of their lives almost entirely in the dark, dingy bed-

---

[1] The staff of the Center is composed of the director, social worker, nursery school teacher, public health nurses, dietician, psychologist, consultant pediatrician, and consultant psychiatrist.

235

room, limited to the confines of their crib and playpen, and with the bedroom door closed when they cried.

Carl was twenty months younger than his sister Mary. He weighed 8 pounds, 9 ounces at birth. He was bottle fed and gained well. At five and a half months he cut his first tooth, began sitting up at eight months, talking at eighteen months, and was walking at twenty-two months of age. His toilet training was completed at thirty months while he was in the nursery school. At one year of age the boy was described as a plump, flabby child who was relatively inactive. It was at this time that his mother became pregnant and developed a hypertension which severely limited her activity. The parents stated that Carl smiled readily during his first year and seemed responsive to both adults and children. His mother reported that during his infancy she had fed him by first feeling for his mouth with her fingers and then inserting the nipple or spoon. In his second year, the rate of his progress seemed to be diminishing. He was twenty months old when his brother was born, and at twenty-two months he began to feed himself.

Carl entered nursery school when he was two years and seven months old. At first he vigorously resisted leaving the home, but he could be persuaded to go if a staff member would take him by the hand. At the school he was described as a shy, clumsy child who seemed fearful of many things such as unusual noises, the wind, strange men and animals. He walked with the gait of a much younger child and spontaneously practiced walking about the nursery school in the manner of a nonseeing person, that is, by feeling his way with his hands and feet instead of using his eyes. He did speak well from the start. At first he did not help himself with dressing and undressing, and seemed anxious and uncomfortable as evidenced by frequently wetting himself and crying a good deal during the first hour of each day of school. He followed adults around constantly with the refrain, "Hold me close," or "Hold my hand." Unlike most of the children in the group, he was able to accept this holding care from any adult present. Carl seemed to feel safest when sitting in some sort of enclosure; he could play for a long time sitting in a small box. Before he was able to move about freely with the other children, his play was largely solitary, unimaginative, and repetitive. He could spend a whole play period, for example, putting a lid on and off a can, opening and shutting the small doors on trucks, or putting paper clips in and out of a small container.

Rest periods were very frightening to the boy, and he would sit on his rug only if an adult had an arm about him. Even then he would not lie down or close his eyes. He could not bear to be looked at and seemed particularly uncomfortable about people's eyes. The staff had, therefore, to hand things to him with their faces averted. He seemed to have unusual difficulties in using his own sight; for example, he could not find any objects through verbal direction, and could not follow the directions of a pointed finger. At the lunch table this seemed most dramatic. Here he felt for the table and for the food, and after drinking his milk he would feel for the table before placing his cup down. The staff reported that at times he seemed not to see the most obvious things. He would ask for milk, and when told that it was on the table by his plate, he would reply, "I don't see it." The father reported that it was impossible for him to go walking with Carl because the boy either wandered aimlessly about, or walked him into obstructions such as lampposts. One noon when his mother and sister came to call for him, he saw them crossing the street and said, "There's my mother." Someone replied, "And your sister is with her." He answered, "I don't see her." He refused to recognize his sister even when they joined the group. His mother once reported an interesting bit of play at home in which Carl asked his sister whether she was blind. She replied, "No, I'm not blind, and you're not blind, and neither are mommy, or daddy, or Martin."

With time, Carl moved from the solitary, repetitive play in a box to play with others. In his play he was much preoccupied with eyes and eyesight. When playing with clay he would poke his finger into the surface, saying, "I'm making eyes—I'm making lots of eyes." A little later he would put a piece of clay into the teacher's hand, saying, "I am giving you the broken eye." Following this act he would become restless and ask to have his hand held. On other occasions he would ask the play school assistant whether her eyes were broken. She once responded by opening them very wide and saying, "No, do they look broken?" Whereupon he answered, "Did you put them back in?" The assistant then asked him whether he knew anyone with a broken eye or with broken eyes. He denied that he did, and then wanted to be held in his usual fashion. After this exchange he did not mention broken eyes for the next few play periods, but spoke of whole objects as broken, for example "Look, I made a rabbit. The rabbit's broken. How does it get broken?" He persisted in a similar sort of preoccupation with a little hairy toy dog which had only one eye. Carl would always brush the hair back, look for the eye, and take the little dog to an adult in great concern about the eye that was missing. On a later occasion another child insisted that the teacher close her eyes and was very emphatic in saying, "And don't open them." Carl who was close by became quite frightened and asked the teacher to open her eyes and then to hold his hand. One day, upon being confronted with a blind child who had come to the nursery school he became panicky. On another occasion a visitor to the play school walked to the sandbox where the boy was playing, and, pointing to a rabbit painted on the sand pail, remarked on it. Carl said, "Can you see that?" About two months after he had entered the play school his mother reported that for the first time he was able to let her wash his face without crying. The problem up to this time had always been that he would not close his eyes, and consequently he got soap in them and thus resisted the whole process.

Considerable progress was noted in the short space of seven months when Carl was able to play outdoors and move about freely and was unusually friendly and happy. He greeted each child and adult by name and was accepted by the group as a peer. He often joined the direct play and learned to enjoy activities such as climbing the jungle gym, sitting on the teeter, walking on the balance board, and even started to ride a small tricycle. He continued to be interested in clay and also became absorbed in wooden puzzles, which he solved over and over again. In addition, he enjoyed playing in the doll corner where he was able to use his imagination. In this play he usually took the role of the father or husband and was gentle with the baby. His toilet habits became quite reliable, and he was now able to lie on the rug and relax during rest periods. At the lunch table, too, he now behaved like a seeing person, choosing and identifying his food. When after seven months he was finally tested by the psychologist—a woman whom he had not seen before—he asked, "Are you going to shut my eyes again?"

DISCUSSION

When Carl came to the play school it was clear that his behavior was not appropriate for making a good adaptive adjustment there. He walked in the manner of his blind parents, with eyes closed, feeling his way with his hands and feet. His manner of eating also resembled that of a blind person. At first, he seemed to feel safest and most comfortable when he could establish some sort of enclosure about himself, reminiscent of the two years he had spent in the crib and playpen. Certainly his fearfulness of strange noises and especially of moving things seemed in keeping with the usual cares of a nonseeing person. When Carl was with his father, his identification with him and imitation of him were so complete that the boy acted equally blind when they walked down the street together. His behavior at home can certainly be understood in terms of imitation of and identification with his blind parents and with his older sister who also acted as though she were blind. In this sense his behavior can be regarded as an appropriate adaptation to the life situation which confronted him; hence, as a stranger in the new land of the nursery school he behaved in his accustomed manner.

As Carl began to internalize his new experiences, he seemed to develop an intense conflict centering on the models of seeing versus nonseeing. We believe there is much material to support the presence of such a conflict. You recall that, although he was incredulous that another person could see or that he could see, he often walked about with his eyes closed, feeling his way with his hands and feet. He was unable to close his eyes during the rest period, and yet claimed not to be able to see the food in front of him at meals. At the same time he experienced greater anxiety about seeing the eyes of the nurse or other members of the staff and about being seen or looked at. The next development of his conflict was revealed when his attention was brought to the mother and sister approaching—he claimed to be able to see his mother, but not his sister. It would appear that seeing and not seeing appear together.

The incident in which he gave the nurse the "broken eyes" of clay offers several interpretive possibilities. He might be saying that he would prefer the nurse to be like his mother with broken eyes, so that he might feel familiar and secure. On the other hand, he might be offering his old, nonseeing self to the nurse in order to be (or "become") a seeing person like her. Later he asked the nurse to keep her eyes open when another child asked her to close them. This would appear to represent a further development in which his seeing self became the more highly valued self. When at about this time he was confronted with the blind child, he became quite disturbed, probably because of the threat to his new-found status.

As time went on the conflict persisted, but it was obvious that now there was much more preoccupation with the fear of losing the vision, in contrast to the earlier material which suggests conflict about using it. As an example of the fear, Carl asked the nurse assistant, "Are your eyes broken?" The nurse answered, "No." Carl then responded, "Did you put them back in?" This is much like the exchange with the nurse when she asked him whether he knew anyone with broken eyes, to which he said, "No." Even later when he had made an increasingly adequate adaptation as a seeing person, some of his fear still persisted—fear about the possibility of having to go back to the old pattern as exemplified by his first contact with the psychologist after he had been in the play school for seven months. On this occasion he asked, "Are you going to shut my eyes again?" By this time it was difficult to induce Carl to go home from nursery school.

The introduction of these children into the nursery school created great problems for them even though this was the healthy and appropriate thing to do, for in the play school they were exposed to a well lit environment with many gaily colored and interesting decorations and toys which offered much visual stimulation. This was all in great contrast to their own home. It is likely that the children obtained a sense of deep gratification from this visual stimulation. This feeling of gratification from seeing could not be denied after it had once been experienced because of its pleasurable aspects. The children's sense of security, on an environmental level, had been connected with their home in which there was darkness. The basis was thus laid for a conflict. On one side of the conflict were Carl's attempts to adapt to this new (seeing) environment, which resulted in feelings of anxiety and insecurity because the environment was unfamiliar. On the other side of the conflict were his attempts to give up the seeing in the interests of security, but these attempts resulted in anxiety due to a deep sense of loss of visual gratification.

Another problem precipitated by the entry into the play school arose from the fact that the child was surrounded by seeing people who offered him easy access to warm, active relationships and who were using their visual abilities and genuine friendship to increase the richness of his personal experiences with them and with the environment. This experience, too, so different from his experiences at home, gradually became a source of profound gratification, but then tended to threaten his security in the ways just mentioned. Carl was thus confronted with the difficult choice of having to give up the security of his earlier, nonseeing adaptations or of giving up his new identification with people who reacted to him and his environment in a seeing manner.

My attempts to understand this unusual material led me to the following speculations. I believe that Carl and his siblings perceived their environment correctly and adapted to it appropriately with those sensory functions which were stimulated by their environment and the people in it. Furthermore, a sensory organ must be stimulated by appropriate stimuli of adequate intensity in order to be brought into useful function. This dark home did not provide adequate visual stimuli although the stimuli in other areas such as touch and hearing were sufficiently adequate. Thus the working model of the physical character of the home, which the children internalized, and which became a source of security, was a model built on impressions received from the functioning of only those sensory modalities which were adequately stimulated. This did not include adequate visual impressions. Secondly, through the experience of being reared by blind parents, a model of the parental techniques for adaptation was internalized. These parents suffered from a sensory loss and were unable to provide for their children an experiential model in that modality which could be perceived, appreciated, and internalized. Thirdly, the function of seeing was not cathected, or given value, by these parents. Other modalities such as hearing and touch, which were used by the parents, were valued.

By the use of the normal adaptive processes of imitation and identification, these children acquired a model from the parents which was incomplete so far as their own physiological endowment was concerned. As a result the three children were left with an impairment of a particular sensory function by virtue of their adaptations to an environment which offered insufficient stimulation to this sensory function and to parents who offered no stimulation because it had no value representation or function for themselves. This adaptive pattern was later utilized as a defense. Correction of the functional lack or impairment occurred when the child was offered an experience with an environment which provided visual stimulation and in which the important persons placed a high value upon the function of the specific sensory system involved.

HAIR PULLING AND FETISHISM

EDITH BUXBAUM, Ph.D. (Seattle)

Hair pulling as a symptom occurs in both children and adults. Very little has been written about it in the psychoanalytic or psychiatric literature. May E. Romm's paper, "Some Dynamics in Fetishism" (1949), touches on this problem. In contrast, quite a number of psychoanalytic papers deal with the problem of fetishism; among them, following Freud, those by Phyllis Greenacre. Freud's theory (1927) that the fetishist reacts to seeing the mother's genitals and to observing her apparent castration at a time of masturbatory arousal is basic to psychoanalytic thinking on the subject. Phyllis Greenacre deals with the problem of fetishism in two papers, "Certain Relationships Between Fetishism and the Faulty Development of Body Image" (1953), and in "Further Considerations Regarding Fetishism" (1955). She described fetishism as a disturbance which appears

> clinically as an unusually severe castration fear [that] comes essentially from disturbances of pregenitality which render the child structurally unsound and insecure to meet genital-oedipal problems and especially to meet the normal castration threats of this period. In those cases which I saw these threats were already overwhelming, having appeared before the full oedipal development in unusually severe actual traumata of a specifically castrative type—threats not merely by seeing the mother's genital and observing her apparent castration at the time of special masturbatory arousal, as was first postulated by Freud (1927), but much more than this by witnessing or experiencing bloody mutilating attacks in the form of operations (on the self or others), childbirth, abortions, or accidents [1955, p. 187].

She thinks that the child is particularly vulnerable when he is exposed to such experiences between the first and second year. This conception of fetishism seems to me to be incomplete. It is common knowledge that all children go through a phase in which they are particularly attached to one or the other object—a stuffed animal, teddy bear, blanket or pillow, etc.—and I think that this kind of fetishism, like other disturbances, must go back to a fixation point in a certain phase of libidinal development as Greenacre describes, but also to the period when children have intense feelings about such objects.

Several authors have studied the significance of early possessions. M. Wulff (1946) wrote a paper on "Fetishism and Object Choice in Early Childhood," in which he in turn reports extensively on previous papers written by Freud, Sterba, and Friedjung. Olive Stevenson published a paper on the "First Treasured Possession," a study of the role played by especially loved objects and toys in the lives of children (1954). Her paper was of course based on Winnicott's study of "Transitional Objects and Transitional Phenomena" (1953) in which he significantly distinguishes between the pathological forms of fetishism and the early infantile love of things. He says,

> There is a wide variation to be found in a sequence of events which starts with the newborn infant's fist and mouth activities and that leads eventually on to an attachment to a teddy, a doll or soft toy, or to a hard toy. It is clear that something is important here other than oral excitement and satisfaction, although this may be the basis of everything else . . . I am here staking a claim for an intermediate state between a baby's inability and growing ability to recognize and accept reality.

Winnicott is dealing with the progress which the baby makes in handling truly "not me" objects. He says,

> To some extent these objects may stand for the breast but there are other things to consider, too. The first possession is used in conjunction with auto-erotic activities, such as thumb-sucking. [In some cases] there is no transitional object except the mother herself, [or in other cases,] an infant may be so disturbed in emotional development that the transition state cannot be enjoyed, or the sequence of objects used is broken. The sequence may, nevertheless, be maintained in hidden ways.

Winnicott, referring in a paragraph to Wulff's paper, protests about the use of the word "fetish" for these beloved objects of children, the first possessions, and says that Wulff "has taken back to infancy something that belongs in ordinary theory to the sexual perversions." Further on he says,

> But *I do* consider the transitional phenomena a healthy and universal one; moreover, if we extend the use of the word "fetish" to cover normal phenomena we shall perhaps be losing some of the value of the term. I would prefer to retain the word "fetish" to describe the object that is employed on account of the delusion of a maternal phallus.

This is in agreement with Freud's paper on "Fetishism" (1927).

CASE MATERIAL

During the past years I have treated two girls whose chief symptom was hair pulling. This symptom appeared to be related to the transitional object in Winnicott's definition and to a form of fetishism which bears out Freud's and Greenacre's formulation. Both children came into treatment quite young. Ann was three years old, and Beryl was six. They pulled their hair out in patches and used it to tickle the area around their mouths, lips, and noses, while they also sucked on one of their fingers. From time to time they swallowed the hair. Among the transitional objects which Winnicott enumerates is wool. He says, "In common experience one of the following activities occurs, complicating an auto-erotic experience such as thumb-sucking. [Point Three.] The baby starts from early months to pluck wool and to collect it, to use it for the caressing part of the activity; less commonly the wool is swallowed, even causing trouble." My patients used their own hair for exactly this activity.

Case 1

I saw Beryl, age six, for two years, three times a week in analysis, and the mother about once every two weeks. Beryl was the oldest daughter of three. The mother was Catholic, the father Jewish. He was financially and otherwise dependent on his father. Consciously, the mother had married him for his money and for the security which she hoped to get. She was a pretty woman, meticulously and expensively dressed, and vain to a ridiculous point. She wanted to be the belle of the ball, wanted to go to parties and to give parties, but she could never do it. She did not like her husband's Jewish friends and was ashamed to be with him in Gentile company. The parents were having severe difficulties in their marriage when Beryl was brought to treatment. The mother had been her own father's favorite and companion. Although there were sons in the family, he treated her like a boy, having her accompany him on hunting and fishing trips. She very much wished to present him with a grandson and was disappointed when the first child and the following ones were girls. However, Beryl seemed to have been well taken care of and was quite happy as a baby.

Her next younger sister, Mary, was born when Beryl was eighteen months old. According to the mother's report, Beryl was very jealous of the baby and attacked her by pulling her hair. She was slapped for it repeatedly, and finally she stopped doing this, but, according to the mother's report, started pulling her own hair.

When I met Beryl she was a whiney, painfully shy child, who was small for her age and who constantly had her thumb in her mouth. The mother admitted that she was so disgusted with Beryl's looks that she could hardly stand to wash her hair or to help her in any way to take care of herself. Beryl in turn was so ashamed of the way she looked that she would always appear with a stocking cap which would hide her head completely, and she refused to take it off either with me or in the schoolroom. Beryl represented herself and her problems with her family in her doll play. She brushed and combed a long-haired doll incessantly and was a loving mother, while she told me and showed me how her mother grimaced when the latter brushed Beryl's hair. Beryl was forever playing "going to parties" with her dolls. They competed with each other; yet taking the other one's boy friend away brought disaster and loss of beauty and life upon the culprit. Beryl mothered the youngest sister in a way similar to that in which she treated her dolls when she was friendly. She was jealous of her next-younger sister Mary, whose hair she had pulled when Mary had been a baby. Beryl's relationship to her mother was an unhappy love affair. She was in love with her, tried to kiss her and hug her—to the mother's annoyance and disgust. She particularly loved her mother's curly hair; this was what she wanted for herself. The mother felt guilty toward Beryl whom she compared to her husband; she was unable to set any limits for her; she tolerated her caresses without returning them, as she did with her husband.

After about six months of treatment, I gave Beryl a sleepy doll as a Christmas present. She immediately started to take it to bed with her and became inseparable from it. She pulled the doll's hair out instead of her own (which was fine). Still, when either the mother or I left her for a few days, she again pulled out her own hair.

In the second half of the first year of her treatment, Beryl behaved in an increasingly disgusting manner. She put her hand to her genitals, ostensively put her hand to her anus and again to her mouth. All this was done in an exhibitionist way. She would also eat candy in such a way that she put it either in her lap or sat on it before she put it to her mouth. The candy she chose was either red or black. When we played Old Maid, one of her favorite games, she hid the cards behind her, sat on them, took them out, kissed them, and then showed me her behind; obviously she was eating dirty stuff and whatever she was eating was supposed to have contact with the orifices of her body. The peak of this dirt orgy was reached one day when she made a mess of red paint powder which was slightly mixed with water, and squirted it through her fingers. I finally stopped that mess and started cleaning up. While doing so, I talked with her.

I knew that the children had access to the bathroom and bedroom at all times. I asked, "Did you ever see mommy's hair between her legs?" and her answer to it was, contemptuously, "Who didn't see that!" I continued: "Did you see daddy too, and his penis?" Again she replied, "Who wouldn't know that!" I proceeded, "Sometimes I wonder whether you pull your hair because you don't like hair down there." She answered, "That has nothing to do with it!" Such a distinct "no" can be a confirmation rather than a contradiction, but one cannot be sure. I continued, "Do you know what Kotex is?" She answered, "Yes." "Do you know what it is for?" the answer was, "You don't need to know." This answer was obviously a quotation. She did want to know and probably had asked about it, but apparently mother's frankness in showing herself had ended at this point and her mother had been unable to tell her about it. When I insisted, she said, grimacing and with great affect, "It was in the wastebasket all bloody." I talked about menstruation and wondered whether she had seen blood between her mother's legs in the bathtub or perhaps in the toilet. Again I received the answer, "You don't need to know." However, next day she came and showed me a very small cut in her finger and said, "It was a deep cut. It bled terribly."

Some time later the mother reported to me that she had overheard Beryl talking with some of her school friends who had been all aflutter and secretive about sexual secrets and discussions. Beryl had listened to them, then told them the straight facts, saying, "I know all about it. Dr. B. told me." So far the mother was cooperative, reported well and understood what was going on. The bathroom doors were closed from now on and everybody was granted the privilege of privacy and discretion of bathroom and bedroom. However, when we came to talk about Beryl's obvious masturbation, the mother was shocked at the idea, had completely repressed any observation of it, and was unable to accept it. I told her that if she could not accept Beryl, her genitals, her sexual feelings, and her masturbating, I did not see how Beryl would be able to give up her hair pulling. The mother admitted then that she preferred Beryl to pull her hair rather than to masturbate. At this point I suggested that she have analysis herself.

It took some time until she did; only then was the mother able to overcome her disgust of Beryl's appearance, i.e., of her being a girl. She could shampoo her hair without grimacing and Beryl in turn allowed the mother to take her to a skin doctor who would help her grow her hair. Mother and daughter treated this as a secret between the two of them. Mother's administrations, putting lotions on her head, brushing and combing her hair, were, from the dermatologist's point of view, psychotherapy rather than medical treatment. Beryl could now allow her hair to grow; feeling accepted by her mother, she could like herself and her appearance. Of course, this was not a straight up-hill development—there were many relapses, particularly when the family planned to leave the city, which meant leaving me. However, Beryl's conscious desire to have her hair grow continued. When she did pull again, she was afraid of losing her hair again and she cried bitterly, asking for help. Pulling her hair at this point was a sign of her conflict between going with her family and her desire to stay with me.

The father had always played an important role for Beryl. She was his favorite; he accepted her with or without hair. Beryl had for a long time seemingly paid no attention to him. That was when she had been afraid to compete with her mother for his attention, as she had shown in her doll play. She was even rather contemptuous of him in identification with her mother. In the course of her treatment, she became fiercely loyal to him, was belligerent about his or anybody else's Jewishness, and critical of her mother's attitude toward him. She changed from a shy, girlish demeanor to that of a tomboy. He played ball with her and enjoyed playing rough. When we talked about her wanting to be a boy, she said in her usual negative form of affirmation, "No, who'd want to have one of those silly things dangling between one's legs?" When she had overcome her fear of mother's jealousy and felt more accepted by her and accepting of her, she became quite flirtatious with her father, who was a little too pleased about it. However, eventually they both got on a more even keel and Beryl turned her attention to boys. She developed crushes on them, to her parents' amusement and delight.

When we terminated treatment, I gave her two things: one was a birthday present, the other a good-by present—a diary and a stuffed poodle dog. She had told me that she wanted a stuffed poodle dog as a replacement for a real dog which the family had had and which had been more the mother's pet than anybody else's. She explained to me that it would be too big and stiff to have it in bed with her, but "I could have it standing in front of my bed to watch me, if I should pull my hair."

A few weeks after she had left, she wrote to me: "Thank you for the diary and the dog. [Although she had thanked me before!] I have written in the diary ever since I got it. I sleep with my dog almost every night. I keep the key on my chain which you gave me." This is the chain which I gave her with a locket as a Christmas present the second year. Apparently the dog and diary became a substitute for me, or, as one might say, the intermediary objects. She finally replaced her hair with other objects and thus developed a relationship to a "transitional object." It is significant that all these objects were presents which I had given her. I heard from her a year later, she was doing all right and felt happy.

Case 2

Ann, my other little patient, was three years and two months old when she came into treatment. She was extremely shy and anxious and refused to stay alone with me. My contact with her went entirely through the mother who was present in the room. Once a week I saw Ann and the mother together, and saw the mother alone one time a week through eight weeks.

The pertinent points of the history as I got it before starting treatment were these: Ann was an only child who was very welcome, since the marriage had been childless for the first ten years. It was a peculiar marriage; the parents seemed to be very much in love with each other but unable to live together. The husband, who came from a wealthy family, refused to take any money from his family, and they always were on the brink of financial disaster. They moved innumerable times. The wife continuously tried to catch up with the husband. He would move first and let her wait until he called her to join him, but soon he would move on again. For a while he had a fishing boat, but he was so seasick that he could not fish, so they lost a lot of money on that. During the time of my contact with the family he was prospecting. Of course, wherever he did prospect was not the place for a family to live. His letters, some of which I read, were beautifully written, affectionate and to the point. I saw the man only once on one of the rare occasions when he was in Seattle. He was a highly intelligent, observing, and sensitive man. Yet he struck me as a lone wolf whom I could not imagine living in a settled-down family situation. The mother was a good-looking woman, not striking but pleasing, well dressed, with very little makeup. She was devoted to her daughter and in conflict with her husband because of her. For the first ten years of the marriage there had been no question about her following him around and she had gone along with whatever he had wanted to do. However, since she had the child she desperately wanted to have a home and stay there. Although she spoke of divorce, she did not want it. Her own parents had been divorced when she was a child. When her father who was a drunkard finally left the family, her mother said, "Good riddance." She expressed admiration for her mother, but I do not know what their relationship was like. In our weekly conferences this material was discussed, and she expressed a good deal of feeling in regard to her husband.

It was clear that Ann was disturbed when father and mother disagreed and quarreled. Ann, who was a bottle-baby, seemed to develop well until she was about eighteen or nineteen months old. According to the mother's statement, the baby stopped drinking from the bottle at nineteen months. "She gave up the bottle voluntarily." She started walking at twelve months. At around eighteen months when, according to the mother, she started to pull out her hair, she also woke up crying at night. This crying lasted for about six months. The mother said, "She started pulling her hair sometime after she was eighteen months old. I don't remember just when it started. At that time we had moved twice in four months, and my husband was in the hospital for minor surgery." As I learned later on, this surgery had been an operation for the removal of a tumor on a testicle and of hemorrhoids. During his convalescence and probably before he went to the hospital, the father locked the bathroom door, which was against the habit of the family. Ann had been used to going in with father or mother, but during this period he left her standing outside the door, wide-eyed, listening to his moaning and crying out in pain. It was at this time that she gave up the bottle, cried at night, and started pulling her hair. During the same period her grandfather, to whom she was very attached, lived in the house. He became sick and incontinent and finally died. Mother thought that Ann pulled her hair more when Ann's father was gone. She reported that at that time Ann was so upset about having her hair washed that she vomited; therefore, for the last few weeks the mother had desisted from washing her hair.

My first contact with Ann was around Eastertime in my office. We had a party for the three of us, including a few dolls. I had some Easter eggs as well as some feathery chickens. Ann took one of the chickens into her hands, quickly pulled out its feathers, and then fondled it, and would not let it go. I also had one of those whistles which blow out and have a little feather bush at the end. When I showed Ann how to blow it, she whispered, frightened, "Don't," and I apologized and threw it into the wastebasket. After a while she went to the wastebasket, took the whistle out, and learned how to use it. The things which we used during this hour were considered

presents, so she went home with Easter eggs, a chicken without
feathers, a whistle with feathers, and a doll baby-bottle which we
had used for feeding the babies. Through all this Ann spoke very
little to me. She wanted to write a letter to daddy, which she dictated
to me. We also made some Easter eggs out of paper, colored them,
and enclosed them in the letter to him. After this hour the mother
telephoned to let me know that Ann had talked all the time about
me and had wanted to play our games again; the mother had to play
my role or Ann's, while Ann played either me or herself. They
repeated the hour with me over and over again with reversed roles.
Ann also sucked on the baby bottle herself occasionally, but did not
show any wish to have a bottle herself although the mother offered
it to her. Her playing with the chicken without feathers and with
the whistle suggested to me again the idea to let her have something
with hair which she could pull out instead of her own hair.

The mother had made a habit of sleeping with Ann in the bed
when her husband was not at home. Upon my suggestion, mother
put Ann into her own bed and let her sleep there, but at the same
time allowed her to take some toy to bed with her. The mother
provided a woolly thing, I think it was a kitten. One time when Ann
was in my office we talked again about her father and where he was
and what he was doing. Ann had quite often said to her mother,
"Do you want me to go away?" which the mother interpreted, according to the books, as a sign of insecurity. While Ann was playing with
a small doll, she made the doll take a long walk all over the room,
all over the tables, finally getting to the mother and walking up and
down her body. For me it was a demonstration of the symbolism of
the mother's body as the world and the earth on which we walk.
When she asked, "Do you want me to go away?" she might have
added, "like my daddy." The wish to be like her father was promoted
by the mother's intensified attachment to Ann in the absence of the
husband and by letting Ann sleep with her. Ann's reaction to
unpleasant experiences was to do to herself what she did not want
to have done to her. For example, after having had a fight at nursery
school, she was quite aggressive at home and played out the whole
fight with her mother, showing her how that naughty girl had beaten
her up, but also how strong this girl was and how Ann admired her
and wanted to be like her. Her question to her mother, "Do you

want me to go away?" indicated that she preferred to do the going away rather than have father go away from her. The mother was able to understand this mechanism in Ann very well.

About four weeks after the beginning of my contact with Ann the mother wrote me the following note:

> I had a conversation with Ann that may or may not be important; I take a bath with her because she slips on the mat and is afraid to get into the tub by herself. I was washing my genitals and glanced at Ann who was looking at me with rather a frightened expression. I said, "Honey, does this hair on my body worry you?" She said, "Yes." I said, "It's nothing to worry about, dear. When people grow up they grow some hair on their bodies. Is that the reason you pull the hair on your head?" She said, "Yes." I said, "Because you don't want it to grow?" She said, "No, sometimes I just feel like pulling and sometimes when I'm hungry, it tastes good."

At my instigation, the mother repeated the conversation in front of Ann and we talked about it some more, wondering why Ann did not like hair and whether it was because she thought it was dirty. We talked about masturbation and about the difference between men and women. Obviously Ann differentiated between pulling her hair out in order to prevent it from growing so that she would look like mommy, and the other expression which she used, "just pulling her hair." I assumed that this interest in and horror at the genital region was connected with the observation of father's genital and his moaning and groaning behind the locked bathroom door when he was in pain. We also talked about this: that daddy had had something hurting on his penis but that mother knew, and Ann did too, that he still had his penis and he was all right now. Mother, however, as well as Ann and I, never did have a penis. A few days after this explanation Ann allowed her mother to wash her hair. Ann said to her mother, "Give me a shampoo." The mother was very happy but said to Ann, "I'll give you one if you give me one first." Ann was only too happy to do so and, as the mother said, "She was very careful not to get soap into my eyes, and did a good job." After that she allowed the mother to give her a shampoo for the first time in weeks without crying.

When Ann had overcome her anxiety in regard to having her hair washed, the father came home, praised her for her attempts to stop pulling her hair, told her how much he loved her, and suggested that she see a skin specialist who would help her to have her hair grow faster so that she could be as pretty as mommy. Ann went to the doctor very happily.

My contact with Ann was mainly a friendly one. We played whatever she wanted, we fed the ducks at the nearby lake, we fixed food and generally had a good time. While this was going on, my talks with her mother continued and contained whatever interpretations I wanted to give the mother and the child regarding her behavior at home. This is a technique which I find helpful in the treatment of young children (Buxbaum, 1946). Contrary to her previous behavior, Ann now was able to stay alone in nursery school.

The contact was interrupted after eight weeks when I went on a prolonged vacation. I had suggested to the mother to return after my vacation; however, she did not do so for a number of reasons, the most important one being that she again followed her husband. I received a letter from her in August in which she said:

> Ann stopped pulling her hair two months ago. She said to me, "Mommy, I don't want to pull my hair any more. I want it to grow"—and it is growing. She is taking great pride in it, doesn't mind her weekly shampoos, loves the water at the beach and turns the lawn sprinkler on her head when the children are playing with it. She is playing with four little girls on the block and is very popular with them. She is even minding pretty well, wets the bed occasionally at night when she has had too much liquids but never wets at nap time, seldom takes a toy to bed and she sleeps well. She is overcoming her shyness very well; she visits almost everybody on the block.

Comparison of Cases

The therapeutic process in these two cases shows some similarities and some differences. The similarities are: both girls resolved a conflict in regard to identification with mother when the misunderstood experience regarding the genitals was clarified. Such clarifications in children's cases have the same effect that interpretations have with adults. I discussed the importance of such clarifications in other papers (1946, 1954). Another similarity in both cases is the acceptance of an intermediary object (instead of their own hair) and its role in the transition to object relations.

The chief difference of the two cases lies in the children's relationship to their families, particularly to their mothers. Ann's relation to her mother was essentially a good one. Her neurosis was really a traumatic neurosis—a disturbance in development due to a trauma. Beryl's relation to her mother was a poor one; she established a relationship to me which became a corrective experience. It allowed the clarification and resolution of the traumatic experience. However, her response to the traumatic experience was only one part of Beryl's neurosis. In addition, the internalization of her conflicts had already led to a neurotic character disturbance, which was treatable only by psychoanalysis.

Discussion

Both girls had occasion to see their parents' genitals repeatedly at an early age. Ann saw her father's injured genitals, Beryl saw her mother's bleeding genitals which she misunderstood as being injured. In both children eighteen months was the crucial age. I assume that the hair-pulling syndrome was caused by these traumata, because in both cases the hair pulling stopped after this experience had been discussed and the misconception clarified. These traumata are very similar to those which Greenacre and Freud described as leading to fetishism. The children continued with their autoerotic activities, that is, sucking and stroking, and in addition used hair pulled from their own heads.

Beryl pulled her sister's hair before she pulled her own. She apparently turned this specific form of aggression against herself. The aspect of aggression turned against the self is present in Ann, too. She, as well as Beryl, accepted a gift with the explicit permission to pull its hair. Winnicott mentions, as one of the attitudes which children show toward the intermediate object, that they treat these objects very roughly, but as long as they are interested in them do not destroy them completely.

Ann's relationship to her mother was fundamentally a satisfactory one—she trusted her mother, she felt safe only when she was with her mother, and she wanted to be like her mother with the exception of having her genitals. She regarded mother's pubic hair as dirty, did not want mother to have any hair there; perhaps wanted to pull it out, but instead she pulled out her own hair on the only place where she had some, namely, her head. She refused to have her hair shampooed, and did not want mother to wash her own hair in the genital area. She did not want mother to touch this dirty part—as she had been forbidden to masturbate. Father's injured genitals supported the idea of punishment in the genital area. Pulling her hair was a form of self-castration, but also a way in which she tried to prevent her becoming like mother. She did not want to have the genitals of either mother or father. When the mother intuitively allowed Ann to wash mother's hair, she gave Ann permission to touch and wash her hair instead of pulling her hair; this meant to Ann that mother symbolically allowed her to touch the mother's genital region as well as her own. She also gave her a thing to pull which Ann accepted temporarily as a part of the mother as well as of herself. The kitten became her sleeping companion instead of the mother. She pulled its hair, sucked it, and masturbated by putting it between her legs.

This good mother allowed Ann to use *her* as an intermediate object (to use Winnicott's expression), alternately with an inanimate object—a true intermediary object—which Ann accepted from her and in her stead. With the help of this intermediary object furnished by the mother, Ann could finally give up her ambivalent relation to a part of her own body, namely, her hair, as a representative of her ambivalent relation to mother. Her attachment to the intermediate, inanimate object was only short-lived and led to true object relationships. She started to like other people and not just her mother.

Beryl's relationship to her mother was not a satisfactory one. Her mother was, to use Winnicott's term, a "not good enough mother." To call her "rejecting" would omit all the concern and sorrow which she suffered, and the efforts which she made on Beryl's behalf. But due to her own incapacity to form genuine relationships, she was not intuitive as Ann's mother was, and her attempts to help Beryl failed, although she made such attempts. Due to this lack of relationship in the mother Beryl felt hopeless ever to be able to win her mother over or to be like her. Beryl, like Ann, did not want to be like her mother in the genital area, that is, bleeding and maimed.

She was aware of mother's disgust at her genital area and of her disapproval of her masturbation. Mother's overcoming her disgust led to her washing Beryl's hair in a "good enough" way. As with Ann, this was received as a symbol of mother's accepting Beryl's genitals as good. Very soon during her treatment with me, Beryl accepted gifts from me as intermediary objects. She did not accept similar objects for this purpose from anybody else, including her mother. She slept with the sleepy doll whose hair she pulled, kept the locket around her neck, fondled it and never parted with it. The stuffed poodle and the diary became substitutes for me when she left treatment. These objects became important and were alternate recipients of her aggression. When her hair pulling stopped, her relation to the intermediary objects remained important. It seems that she could accept the intermediary object from me rather than from mother because I accepted her, whereas her mother did not sufficiently accept her. The diary and the poodle dog also became representatives of me; they stood for a benevolent superego figure, which "reminded her" not to pull her hair and allowed her to pet herself. Berta Bornstein (1936) has described the roles of these bedtime toys as representations of the child's id and superego. The intermediary object, the poodle dog, was further removed from the child's body and was at the same time invested with the qualities of the superego. Beryl apparently could not yet entirely dispense with a visible reminder of the superego. There might be other cases in which a photograph or a picture or symbol of an idol might take the same place. Beryl used the intermediary object as an aid in the formation of her superego.

Hair pulling cannot be described only in terms of aggression turned against the self. Ann pulled the chicken's feathers very gently; Beryl would sometimes slowly and carefully pull one hair. Beryl pulled her hair more when she felt deserted and unloved; Ann, too, pulled her hair when she was upset. We are reminded of the expression "to tear one's hair" as a sign of despair and mourning. In this respect, hair pulling resembles a form of masturbation to which the child resorts in periods of anxiety and loneliness, attempting to hold on to himself when people fail him; he reminds himself that he exists by making himself feel. These children were careful not to hurt themselves badly while pulling their hair; moreover, by using this hair to pet themselves, the slight pain was immediately connected with tenderness toward themselves. This amalgamation of painful and pleasant sensations is the point where masochism starts. The use of an intermediary object allowed the children to deflect these feelings from themselves. It may then be that in these cases the masochistic tendency was, at least for the time being, not pursued.

Apparently intermediary objects, as well as parts of the child's own body in this role, became carriers of the positive relationship of the mother to the child and recipients of the child's feelings for the mother, positive as well as negative. The children's positive feelings for the mother are expressed in their eating their hair.

Ann says, "I feel like pulling and it tastes good."

Beryl ate black and red candy with which she touched her genitals or her anus, kissed the Old Maid on which she sat—all of which indicates what hair means to her. It is good tasting, sweet—like mother's body, but also like her own excretions. She also ate mucus from her nose, saying, "It tastes good." It seems to me that eating serves both—to destroy and to preserve. What is dirty about the mother's body or their own should be destroyed by eating. What is sweet of the mother's body or their own should be preserved by eating. Hair is both dirty and sweet.

What these two children did with their hair, other children do by eating mucus, fecal matter, skin or nails.[1] This behavior is a normal phenomenon in all children before the barrier of disgust as a reaction formation has been established. It seems, however, that eating one's own sweet dirt is also a sign of the incomplete separation from the mother. It is a part of the child's body, symbolizing a part of the mother's body. These children use part of their own body as intermediary objects.

However, the edibility of hair as well as of other parts of the body is only one aspect of the satisfaction which the children derive from it. The other lies in the manipulation and the tactile and skin sensation. It is particularly this quality which becomes transferred onto the intermediary object. Stroking, petting, fondling of the hair is the satisfaction which the children seek. Beryl could give up her hair pulling when mother stroked her by shampooing and brushing

---

[1] It is usual for animals to clean themselves by eating their own dirt.

her hair. Ann, on the other hand, gave it up when she was allowed to stroke her mother's hair.

Apparently the mutual, active and passive skin contact is of as great importance as the oral contact. Escalona and Leitch (1952) as well as Spitz (1951) have called attention to this fact. Experiments with young monkeys removed from their mothers have shown that skin contacts are extremely important for their development and well-being. They develop adequately if they are given a terry-cloth figure, which is soft but without lactation, while they become disturbed if left with a wire figure which furnishes them milk (Harlow, 1959).

Mittelmann (1955) stated that children become aware of the distinction of what belongs to their body and what does not during the toddler stage, which he thinks is the crucial age for the development of fetishism. The crucial time in my patients was eighteen months—which would agree with Mittelmann's findings.

I think that inanimate objects are libidinally cathected as a reaction to the child's leaving his mother, i.e., putting distance between her and himself. An example is Linus in "Peanuts," who drags his blanket along like a string, holding, touching, sucking it, and reassuring himself that all is not lost. The toddler age is also the age in which cleanliness education takes place. The skin contact with the mother at times becomes unpleasant and occurs less frequently. In both my patients dirt and the genital area were associated. In their therapy both children became free to pet and stroke themselves in other areas of their body, but also, with the help of an intermediary object, to resume a friendly, physical contact with people.

The traumatic experience disturbed the children in a phase in which tactile and skin sensations are of great importance. Consequently their ability to adapt themselves became impaired, so that they remained fixed at the level of libidinal development and of object relations which they had reached at the time of the traumatic experience. When traumatic experience was brought into consciousness the children relinquished using their hair as the means with which to fulfill their need for tactile and skin sensations. They proceeded to accept "other than me" objects for this purpose. The intermediary object facilitated the transition from the undifferentiated (self and mother) to "other than self" objects. The mother became a separate entity for the child; the child moved in the direction of greater independence and formed relationships with other people besides the mother. Both children then were able to derive pleasure from touching themselves as well as from touching others; I would like to say that they were able to "feel themselves," because I think such "feelings" of one's body are precursors of feelings, i.e., emotions of his own which the child develops for himself as well as for others. They were able to continue in their libidinal development, to separate themselves from their mothers, and to reach out for other relationships; Beryl made a plunge into the oedipal relationship as if she had to catch up with a development which had been long overdue. As long as tactile contacts were disturbed, the ambivalent undifferentiated relationship to the mother's body and to the child's own body existed, and the genital feelings as well as object relations were disturbed.

BIBLIOGRAPHY

Bornstein, B. (1936), Leugnung in der Phantasie. *Ztschr. Psa. Päd.*, X.

Buxbaum, E. (1946), Psychotherapy and Psychoanalysis in the Treatment of Children. *Nerv. Child*, V.

—— (1954), Technique of Child Therapy: A Critical Evaluation. *Psa. Quart.*, IX.

Escalona, S. & Leitch, M., (1952), Emotional Development in the First Year of Life. *Problems of Infancy and Childhood*, ed. M. J. E. Senn. New York: Josiah Macy, Jr. Foundation.

Freud, A. (1958), Child Observation and Prediction of Development: A Memorial Lecture in Honor of Ernst Kris. *This Annual*, XIII.

Freud, S. (1927), Fetishism. *Collected Papers*, V. London: Hogarth Press, 1950.

Greenacre, P. (1953), Certain Relationships Between Fetishism and the Faulty Development of Body Image. *This Annual*, VIII.

—— (1955), *Swift and Carroll: Psychoanalytic Study of Two Lives*. New York: International Universities Press.

—— (1955), Further Considerations Regarding Fetishism. *This Annual*, X.

Harlow, M. F. (1959), Love in Infant Monkeys. *Sci. Amer.*, CCI.

Mittelmann, B. (1955), Motor Patterns and Genital Behavior: Fetishism. *This Annual*, X.

Romm, M. E. (1949), Some Dynamics in Fetishism. *Psa. Quart.*, XIII.

Spitz, R. A. (1951), Psychogenic Diseases in Infancy. *This Annual*, V.

Stevenson, O. (1954), The First Treasured Possession. *This Annual*, IX.

Winnicott, D. W. (1955), Transitional Objects and Transitional Phenomena. *Int. J. Psa.*, XXXVI.

Wulff, M. (1946), Fetishism and Object Choice in Early Childhood. *Psa. Quart.*, XV.

TREATMENT OF A THREE-YEAR-OLD GIRL'S SEVERE INFANTILE NEUROSIS

Stammering and Insect Phobia

HAROLD KOLANSKY, M.D. (Philadelphia)[1]

This paper will present in considerable detail the brief but intensive treatment of a three-year-old suffering with a very severe infantile neurosis. Freud (1938), in the seventh chapter of *An Outline of Psychoanalysis*, said of the infantile neurosis:

> It seems that neuroses are only acquired during early childhood (up to the age of six), even though their symptoms may not make their appearance until much later. The infantile neurosis may become manifest for a short time or may be overlooked. [Neuroses occur in this period because at this time in the child's development, the ego is] weak, immature and incapable of resistance . . . [and thus fails] in dealing with problems which it could later manage with the utmost ease . . . The helpless ego fends off these problems by attempts at flight (by *repressions*), which turn out later to be ineffective and which involve permanent hindrances to further development. The damage inflicted upon the ego by its first experiences may seem disproportionately great [pp. 83-84].

Although Freud indicates the universality of the infantile neurosis, he also implies that this neurosis can be severe and may hinder further development. Since Freud described the analysis of Little

[1] The author is indebted to Dr. Mitchell Dratman for the many helpful suggestions he made during the course of treatment and the preparation of this paper, and to the patient's parents for permission to publish this paper and for the interest they have shown in its publication. The author also wishes to thank Dr. Daniel Silverman, Mrs. Berta Bornstein, and Dr. Morris D. Galinsky for reading the initial drafts and making very useful comments.

Hans (1909), we have assumed the need for direct analytic intervention in the severe infantile neurosis.

Anna Freud (1945) stated:

> An infantile neurosis can be treated as a transitory disorder so
> long as the libido organization of the child remains fluid and
> shows progressive tendencies. Infantile neuroses disappear when-
> ever the normal forward movement of the libido is strong enough
> to undo neurotic regression and fixation. When the libido con-
> stellations become rigid, stabilized and monotonous in their
> expressions the neurosis is in danger of remaining permanently.
> This means that treatment is indicated.

CASE PRESENTATION

Ann, a bright, small, dark-haired, attractive youngster, was
brought to me for intensive treatment at three years and three weeks
of age. Her parents were very concerned about the fact that at twenty-nine months of age the child woke one morning and greeted
them with a deeply troubled facial expression as she said, "D-d-d—
daddy, M-m-m—mommy, I can't talk!" From that point on the child,
who had had no previous speech impairment, stammered almost
continuously, although there were brief periods—a day or two in
length—with relatively little speech difficulty. The speech impairment was later accompanied by vigorous slapping of her thigh, and
stamping of her foot, as she attempted to force through the difficult
first syllables.

During the next several months, the intellectually and physically
precocious little girl changed from an occasionally cranky child into
a withdrawn, continuously cranky child who began to stay in her
pajamas most of the day and demanded (and had) many naps each
day. Stickiness of her hands, which had been somewhat disturbing
to her prior to the onset of the stammer, now became quite intolerable. In fact, any dirtiness, and the mixing of one food with another
became equally unbearable. She could not eat vegetables or foods
of dark color. She became disgusted at the sight of raw eggs. Her
interests narrowed, her sulkiness increased, and she watched television much of the day. Meanwhile her speech became worse, and
she attempted to speak as little as possible. During this period,
although there was an occasional fit of temper, especially when her

father did not come home in the early evening, the child did not express anger directly.

Ann, a first child, was nineteen and a half months old when her mother became pregnant for a second time. Twin sisters were born seven months after the onset of the second pregnancy. The birth of twins was totally unexpected by both Ann and her parents. Ann's mother talked with her about the approaching birth, and noticed nothing unusual in the child's reaction to the new information. When Ann was twenty-seven months of age, the mother went to the hospital in the middle of the night, and the youngster woke the next morning to find her mother absent. Her grandmother had come to the house during the night to care for her. In the later course of treatment we learned that the child had not been told that her mother had gone to the hospital. Instead her grandmother had told her that her mother had gone shopping—a shopping trip that lasted three days!

During this brief period, the grandmother worked intensively at bowel training the child. Attempts at training had begun during the pregnancy and, according to the parents, had until that time been unhurried. Ann had done some self-training. By the time the twins were born, Ann had made great progress in bowel and bladder training, and within a few weeks was completely trained. The parents were concerned that Ann's grandmother had made the state of being untrained "dirty."

Because the twins were premature they remained in the hospital for three weeks. Meanwhile Ann had been moved to a smaller room, so that the unexpected, additional sister could be accommodated in Ann's original room, which was larger. When her new sisters, Betty and Ellen, were finally brought home, Ann began to play with her undershirt while sucking her thumb. Although some visitors came to the house and the phone kept ringing during the next month, there were no concentrated periods of visiting until a week end when the twins were two months old, at which time all the maternal and paternal relatives converged, primarily to see the twins. The parents later recalled that Ann stood in a corner, thumb in mouth, staring at the activities and not participating. It was on the morning following this visiting that the stammer began.

Two months later, Ellen, then four months old, became acutely ill and quite suddenly had to be taken to a hospital where she died of pneumonia a few days later. The parents were in the hospital during this period, and the grandmother again cared for Ann and Betty. During Ellen's hospitalization, Ann, in keeping with her general attitude of ignoring the twins, did not ask questions about Ellen. Four days after Ellen's death, Ann referred to *both* twins, and her parents told her for the first time that Ellen had been very sick, could not live, and had gone to heaven. Instantly, Ann's speech became markedly mutilated, and she could barely be understood. For weeks afterward she referred to her sisters as if both were still alive. Corrections were made again and again, and finally she expressed the wish that Betty join her dead sister. She stopped referring to Ellen only at the age of about three years, just before coming to treatment.

When Ann was thirty-two months old her grandmother again took care of her while the mother was confined to bed for more than a week because of illness. The child had originally been fond of her grandmother, but after the twins were born she reacted to the grandmother's presence with resentment. Ann's speech became worse during the period of her mother's illness.

Meanwhile the child began to attend a cooperative nursery group which met in the children's homes and was directed by the mothers of these children. When Ann was thirty-five months old, an event occurred that finally induced the parents to seek psychiatric help. One morning while the nursery group met at Ann's house, Ann wanted milk served in a green cup, but instead her mother served milk in this cup to another child. At once, Ann became very angry and threw her cup of milk at the other child. Ann's mother, feeling very angry and embarrassed, scolded Ann in tight-lipped fashion, ordered the child to the mother's room, and then spanked Ann in privacy. Immediately the stammer became more marked and continuous, and with this Ann became more withdrawn. There were no longer temporary remissions of her speech difficulty. At this time the mother became consciously guilty, and most anxious to have help for the child and herself.

A little before the child's third birthday, a pediatrician had advised the parents to adopt a permissive attitude toward the child's behavior and suggested that they encourage the child to use clay and finger paints (which she had never allowed herself to use before because of the "messiness" of these media). In the following three weeks there was a slight easing of the speech difficulty, and Ann became openly aggressive toward her baby sister and her mother, hitting, biting, and scratching them. Although she "shot" her sister Betty with a toy pistol, she could not do this to her mother "because I need her." Her mother reinstituted some prohibitions, because she found Ann's aggression difficult to bear. It was at this time that the parents sought psychiatric help.[2]

In my first contact with the parents I learned that the child had an insect phobia, and this was to prove as prominent a symptom as the stammer. Acompanying the insect fear was a fear of television's Zorro. The fear of insects (bees, "lightning bugs," flies) and the fear of Zorro both began at the age of about thirty-one months, immediately after Ellen's death, and soon became overwhelmingly intense. The child was terrified to leave the house, and constantly called the parents' attention to specks or cracks in the ceiling which she thought were insects. She previously had enjoyed Zorro, but could no longer watch him. When she saw an insect she would freeze in terror, with arms crossed in front of her, and would scream, "Mommy, come quick!" Before the beginning of her treatment she began a game of seeing an insect and saying, "Oh, look—a bee!" pretending fear, and then saying, "All gone." During this period she also had a nightmare about bees.

Before describing the treatment and trends in the case, several additional aspects of the child's early life must be mentioned. Ann was hypoactive in utero, and there was fetal distress with the heart rate dropping during labor. There were two other organic features:

2 Dr. Mitchell Dratman, who studied the child before referring her to me for treatment, made the following theoretical assumption: if there are known traumatic events prior to the onset of the neurosis in a child during the preoedipal phases of development, and if the mother with her intimate knowledge of the child has a personality flexible enough to allow her to participate with the analyst in the child's therapeutic sessions, a relatively brief but intensive analytic treatment may be attempted at the outset, and it may be presumed that the neurosis might be relieved despite its apparent severity. This assumes, further, that the defenses utilized by the child will not yet be firmly crystallized, and that the unconscious might be more easily accessible to the patient and the analyst in this age period.

The child and her mother appeared to meet these criteria. I agreed with these assumptions, and undertook the treatment. The treatment itself was based, to a large extent, on Bornstein's (1935) vivid description of the analysis of Little Lisa.

(1) a left metatarsus varus, requiring a Dennis-Brown splint day and night from age two months to age six or seven months; and (2) questionable seizures at three and five months of age. She was placed on an anticonvulsant drug and remained on a daily dose of this medication until she was eleven months old. She was described as being right-handed, and the parents stated that her coordination was good and that there were no apparent neurological sequelae. There was no recurrence of the seizures.

She was breast fed until the age of three and a half months at which time she was weaned to a bottle because for two weeks there had been an increasing irritability in the child as the mother's milk decreased. (The seizures started at three months.) Thumb sucking continued from early infancy. The mother paid considerable attention to Ann's eating, which had always been poor. She was gradually weaned by eighteen months of age. At about six to seven months, the splint was permanently removed. She sat at seven and a half months and walked precociously two days later, while holding on to furniture. At ten months, one week, she walked without support. She began finger feeding herself at eight months, and until she mastered this self-feeding two weeks later, she took very little food from her mother. At eight and a half months she refused to sleep at night. After the parents assured themselves that there were no physical problems, they let her cry for two hours one evening, and for twenty minutes the next night, after which she stopped crying.

At thirteen months, immediately after a move to a new house, a severe fear of a weekly air-raid siren began. This fear persisted until almost the end of her treatment. She would cling to her mother in terror while the siren sounded. By the age of thirteen months, the mother said Ann's vocabulary consisted of forty words, and at twenty months, she spoke in sentences.

The parents were unconcerned about leaving their bedroom and bathroom doors open until Ann was thirty months old. About that time she learned the word "penis" after seeing her father's penis, and she repeated the word all day long. After that, the father no longer permitted her to see his penis. During her bowel training the parents noticed some masturbation and did nothing to curtail it.

Between thirty and thirty-six months of age, the child was bitten by a dog, and subsequently developed a fear of biting animals.

A dog was acquired during the period of treatment, and gradually the child became very fond of, and unafraid of, this animal.

While she had little to do with the twins after their birth, she became interested in caring for dolls, but she did not participate with her mother in household duties. From the time of acquiring a bed at the age of three years, she wanted her covers pulled back so that she could get into bed and suck her thumb at any time. She preferred her father to her mother, and liked getting into bed with him, a practice which was stopped by the father when Ann was three years old.

When told she was coming in to see me, her first question was, "Does he have dirty toys like Dr. Dratman?" The answer was "Yes," and at once she began to stammer.

TREATMENT

Throughout the course of treatment, the mother gave me very detailed, pertinent, daily observations on the child. These notes were typed nightly. The treatment extended over a forty-day period during which time I saw the child thirty-six times.

Despite the seriousness of her symptoms, there was a twinkle in Ann's eye and she exhibited an engaging smile when I first saw her. In the first session she had no difficulty leaving her mother as she joined me in the playroom. She was delighted to find "play dough" which she used to make foods. She handled sand very gingerly, and as I put my hand in the sand she began to stammer so markedly that what had been clear and undistorted speech now became almost impossible to understand. As she tried to talk with me, she began to slap her thigh and stamp her foot with considerable force. Finally the words emerged. She did not stammer while handling the brightly colored and fairly dry "play dough," but when she saw the moist gray clay, her speech gave way to the same distortion. Later I encouraged her to make a sand-water combination to represent mustard. Very reluctantly she complied, saying that she was afraid she would dirty her dress. I told her that this would not be so bad; she did so and at once had to wash and dry her hands. Similar reactions were seen during the next two weeks.

She assembled all the play animals, knowing the names of each, and said, "Now we will feed them all breakfast." She picked up two cows, and when she noticed that their sides were torn, she became anxious and dropped them at once. I told her that it didn't matter that they were broken, whereupon she began to use them. (I later learned that both parents promptly discarded all badly damaged toys.) She picked up a toy crocodile and reassuringly said to herself, "He is just a baby; he doesn't have big teeth to bite. He won't bite." I said, "Even if he had big teeth, he wouldn't bite you." She repeated the reassuring words to herself.

In the ensuing sessions, play with sand, water and clay continued, followed each time by marked stammering and hand washing. I reassured her by saying that she need not be concerned about being dirty, and I told her that some children felt their parents would be angry and would yell at them if they were dirty. She said, "Mommy doesn't yell about that, but she yells because I nap." We had not yet formally brought her mother into the treatment sessions, but at this point we invited her to come into the playroom, and I told her what Ann had said. The mother told Ann that it had been wrong of her to do so, apologized to Ann, saying that she would not yell like this again. As the treatment progressed, the mother reversed previous positions toward Ann many times, after realizing that certain of her own attitudes and practices had led to difficulties in the child.

After several days Ann was able to allow clay, sand, and water to be mixed together. One day she discovered that the tail of a rubber dog was broken, and she saw a hole beneath the tail. She looked intently at it and said, "It's a hole now." I asked what she thought it could be used for, and she said, "For food." I asked, "Maybe also for B.M.?" to which she replied, "Then it's a 'tussy.'" Pointing to the space between the two hind legs of a dog I had drawn, she said, "It's a vagina," and then told me that she and her mother had vaginas, that her daddy had a penis, and that a penis was better than a vagina. When I asked why this was so, she could not say. Pointing to a toy cow, she said that the udder was a vagina. When I explained that this was not so, that the udder was for milk, she responded by saying that little babies had vaginas.

In the same session, and for the first time, she began to play with wet clay without encouragement, or verbal direction. She made a nonsense sound. I repeated it with some rhyming, and she giggled. Soon her mouth sounds had a distinct anal quality, and I said, "They sound like B.M. sounds." She was taken aback, and then laughed. There was no stammer.

The mother's note following this session sounded most encouraging. The mother had begun to spend more time with her children. While walking, a strange pup came over to Ann and was jumping around in a frisky fashion. Ann seemed to love this and kissed the dog on the head. She had previously reacted to such situations with fear. Her mother called Ann's attention to a branch lying on the sidewalk, and Ann picked it up and began to poke a patch of mud with it. Even more surprisingly, within a short time the child stepped into the puddle. The mother continued her note, saying: "Ordinarily my reaction would have been to say, 'No, your feet will be wet—you'll catch cold—you must not do it.' And, now it was as if she went back in time and did the wonderful exploring that she should have done a year ago and that we had so unwittingly squelched. She ate food that dropped to the floor. She mixed other foods together; she smelled cocoa and put her fingers into it. This was so unusual that both my husband and I stopped in our tracks."

In a subsequent session, a fly appeared fortuitously in my consultation room and gave me the unique opportunity to watch Ann's reactions. She became frightened immediately, and insisted that it was going to come down to hurt her. She trembled while telling me this. I told her the fly would not come down, or, if it did, it certainly would not hurt her. Then she told me to catch it, which I was able to do. Then, without fear, she touched the fly and said, "It wants to kiss me." As it began to crawl, she told me to get rid of it.

We went into the playroom and without difficulty she began to use moist clay, making food for a party. Much to our surprise, another fly appeared, and when I captured this one, she said to her mother, "Oh, it's so nice—I'll kiss it." Although this fly was by this time dead, Ann treated it gently and fed it "cakes." She decided to take it home. Her stammering was marked during these scenes.

At home that evening her spirits were high, she talked much about dead flies, played with the fly, and vigorously hit her grandmother, who was visiting Ann's family that evening. Also, on the same evening she began to eat soft, mushy foods, and for the first time her parents allowed her to spit out a food when she did not like it. Until then they had insisted that she keep it in her mouth.

After a little more than a week of treatment, the mother, who had begun to come into the playroom with us each day, actively began to tell the child that it was not necessary to wash her hands so much after she used sand—that sand was for fun, and there was nothing bad about handling it. I began to joke with Ann about her desire to wash her hands again, and before long she started to joke about this herself. Now when she stammered she paced up and down the room, stamping her foot. She began to pick up and name animals one day but did not know the name of the dinosaur. I told her what it was and that it had lived a long time ago, and that all the dinosaurs had then died. When she asked why they died, I said that she probably had ideas about this, and she said, "Yes, because they were very sick." I told her that was one way that animals died. Immediately after I said this, she went over to the paper-cup container and began to search for a green cup, which she soon found. She was about to fill it with water when I said, "I know about a green cup. There was trouble at your house the day you wanted one and Tommy got it . . . you got so angry." The child said, "Yes, I did." I told her that because she was so angry she threw the cup at Tommy and her mother then had made a mistake in getting angry at her for this. Her mother said, with a good bit of feeling, "You know, I made a terrible mistake getting so angry and spanking you. It will never happen again." The child looked disbelievingly at the mother, and I commented, "That wasn't the only punishment," at which time the child told me that she also went to her mother's room. Immediately after this exchange, and for the first time in these first eight sessions, Ann said to her mother, "I want to leave."

In the ninth session she greeted me and told me at once that she wanted to leave. Feeling that this was related to the fear she had regarding our discussion of her anger at her mother, I decided to take this issue up with her. She entered the playroom, and began to kiss and hug the animals that were covered with clay and said, as if to herself, "It's all right; I don't have to worry about playing in sand and water." After she played with these animals she said, with a laugh, "Now I'd better wash my hands." Finally I told her that she felt upset about the discussion of anger yesterday, and I added, "Often little girls are afraid to admit that they're angry." She became a little uncomfortable and asked to go into the consultation room.

On a table in this room there were two small, blue, porcelain Chinese dragon-dogs, with wide-open, fanged mouths. She ran to these figures and said, "Oh—I'm afraid," and then ran to the chair at the opposite end of the room. This was repeated many times and became a game. She told me she was afraid they would bite her, at which point I told her they were play dogs and that she need not fear to be bitten, and that in fact she could pretend to bite them. I added that many children like to bite. Ann denied having such a desire. Her mother repeated my statement. Ann increased the tempo and humor of the dog game, and in the midst of it, held her backside and informed her mother that she had to make a B.M. That day, as mother and child left the office, Ann tried to bite her mother in a playful way, and I overheard the mother say, "So, it's true—what Dr. Kolansky said—you see, you did want to bite me; it's okay to have these thoughts," and the child laughed.

The mother's nightly notes now described a gay child in very good spirits.

Clearly, at this point, the child's reaction formations against anal soiling and anal-sadistic activity, and some of her other defenses were beginning to loosen; she seemed to be freer in mood and behavior. Concurrently, we could observe signs of regression to oral sadism and the attempts at repression of these oral-sadistic impulses. The interpretation of her anger at the mother for the punishment following the milk-throwing incident, and the fortuitous fly in the session, seemed to bring these impulses and the fear associated with them actively into the treatment.

In the next session the child arranged a party and threw the contents of the green cup on the floor, looking at me expectantly. I said that this was exactly what happened to Tommy; she must have been so angry that she had wanted to throw things all over mother's carpet. With force, she agreed with me verbally and then proceeded to dump large quantities of sand on the playroom carpet. I then said that when she threw the milk at Tommy, she must have wanted to throw the milk at mother; moreover, I knew that on that very day her speech began to be more mixed up. Her mother told her again how wrong she had been to get so angry at Ann on that occasion. This was my first attempt to bring to Ann's attention the relationship between her anger and her stammering. Following the session the child was quite demanding toward her mother, and it was a trying day for the woman.

On another occasion when we discussed the milk-throwing incident, Ann began to make up and down mouth movements, saying that this was like spitting. As the hours progressed, and we talked some more about children's desires to bite others when angry, she said that she did not want me to talk about biting—that I must stop "that talk." I told her that she was very upset about her wishes to bite and the fear of being punished.

One day, while handling some moist clay, I told her that she now knew clay was not dirty, and even if it were, there was nothing bad about its being dirty. She then said, "Clay—B." I said, "There are two kinds of B's—the bee that flies and B.M." She responded with, "B.M.," and laughed. I continued: "No wonder you have so much trouble with things you call dirty—sand, clay, and some foods; all of them must look like B.M. to you. In fact, this clay does look like B.M." She went to the bathroom and had a bowel movement at this point. On returning, she began to make flatuslike sounds with her mouth, having me repeat these while she giggled and said, "They're like B.M. sounds." In the same hour she pretended to bite the dogs. So here, after having worked through some of her fear of the dirty activities, she herself related the dirtiness of play materials to feces and indicated the mechanism she had used, namely, displacement upward.

In the thirteenth session she told me she wanted to make B.M. noises with her mouth, and proceeded to do so. She continued to demonstrate the displacement upward of anal sounds to her mouth. She drew a house, commenting on those living in her house. Because I felt her dead sister figured prominently in the further development of her stammering, and probably in the insect phobia as well, I said, "And once Ellen lived there too, and we haven't heard much about her." At this point she wanted to go into the other room—a sign, as I had begun to learn, that she was anxious as a result of what we were talking about. It is possible that the desire to leave was equivalent to the excessive number of naps at home when she was anxious or frustrated. While she played at putting dolls to sleep in different rooms, I took the opportunity to tell her that I knew her room had been changed when the twins were born; I suspected that she had been very unhappy and angry when they were born. She must have felt very upset when she discovered that her mother was not home, when she awoke on the morning when the twins were born. I said, "Grandmother told you that Mommy was in the hospital." At this point the mother said, "Dr. Kolansky, Ann didn't know I went to the hospital. Grandmom told her that I went shopping." Ann looked puzzled and I said, "All the more reason for you to have been upset, and so angry and so hurt and so mixed up." I added, "Who could think that a mommy could go shopping in the middle of the night and stay away one, two, three, four days."

As I stressed her anger at her mother, she bent forward, as she often did in stammering, and slapped her knee and stamped her foot. I said that what she was doing now was part of being angry at Mommy and that there must have been times when she wanted to hit and kick and stamp on Mommy, but that she was not only frightened to do any of these things, but afraid even to tell Mommy that she was angry. I said that she must have had such feelings when her mother had to be away while Ellen was hospitalized later, and I talked of how children want to bite, hit, kick, stamp, spit, and punch when they are angry, but are very frightened to do so.

She was keenly interested in what I said, and abruptly and angrily told her mother how angry she had been. Then she asked to go into the other room, and there she found some candy. She asked for some and almost each day after that I had to have candy for her.

The next day I found her happily running through the corridor with her mother nearby. Her mother stepped into my office and a moment later we heard a terrified scream; the child evidently felt her mother had left her. Her joy had turned into intense apprehension, and she sobbed and trembled as her mother carried her into the playroom. She buried her head in her mother's breast and alternately cried and punched with force at her mother's breast. I interpreted her fear that mother had left her, and related it to the previous day's discussion of separation from the mother during the periods of the birth of the twins and the death of Ellen. She listened, then wanted candy, became quiet, and finally smiled.

I mentioned the occasions when the grandmother had cared for her in the past eight months, and I again referred to the episode with Tommy and how on each of these occasions Ann must have felt abandoned by her mother, frightened, and angry. I showed her how on each occasion her speech had gotten worse, and explained that this was a way of showing her anger—which she could not put into words. I said that with her crying and punching just now she had shown us how frightened and angry she was; that punching was what she wanted to do to her Mommy, but instead did to herself by slapping her knee. With this, she got off her mother's lap and with a grin said, "You mean like this," as she kicked the top of the metal playhouse. I said, "Yes, and you wanted to kick the twins, and the house, and everything." The kicking increased in violence. She agreed verbally, and I cannot describe the drama of the situation and the intensity of the child's emotions. She looked at her mother to see if her mother was watching, and, I suspect, to make sure her mother was not angry.

In a little while the mother was composed enough to tell the child that now she truly understood how Ann felt. Thereupon Ann was unable to talk, and instead stamped and banged her knee. I told her she could now tell me of the anger, that she need not stamp on the floor and bang herself. She did not have to be afraid to talk of anger. Ann then asked, in a clear voice, for real stamps for letters she was pretending to write. I said, "Let's use pretend stamps." At once her speech changed and I realized that I had made an error, and mentioned my mistake in not supplying the few stamps she wanted. I told her that here we could see how her speech changed when she got angry at me; as soon as I finished explaining this, the stammer dropped away.

In the same session Ann said, "Today I'm playing the bee game," and she began to run back and forth as if a bee were chasing her, and as if she were afraid. I said, "You're afraid the bee will bite you," to which her reply was: "No—sting me!" The mother clarified that they used the word "sting" for bee and "bite" for mosquitoes. Immediately after that, the child asked what television program she watched in July (the month of Ellen's death). "Maybe you had Zorro in mind. You were so frightened you stopped watching him," her mother said. Ann said that was so, and continued, "He had a stick in his hand." I told her she meant a sword. She shook her head affirmatively and made the sign of the Z in the air. I asked what a sword does, and she said that it "makes holes in people"; I commented, "Like a bee?" "Yes." I asked her whether she had wanted a bee to bite Ellen, and she told me she had. At this point, she also stated that she herself had wanted to bite Ellen. I said, "You put holes in people when you bite."

As she worked through more of the anger involved in the symptom of stammering, and its relationship to her feeling abandoned by her mother, especially in connection with the birth of the twins and the attention paid to them, the insect phobia and the Zorro fear came to the forefront in the sessions. It seemed probable that these phobias involved a displacement of her wish to bite and to destroy the twins—a displacement and projection that had to be made once the twin died, in order for her to disown her tendency. But we did not yet know the full story.

In the next session she made a peanut of clay and then was afraid to touch it, and repeated such things as "Bee-bo, mee-bo, bee, B.M." I said she was afraid of both B's, referring to the condensation of oral- and anal-sadistic impulses. At once she began to recite colors that were clearly fecal colors. The mother began to handle the clay peanut, and then the child did. Ann began to talk of preparing foods, and I said, "It's funny the way some foods look like B.M.," to which she replied, "Potatoes." Before long she actively began to play with words as if she were shaping them and rolling them around in her mouth. She seemed very happy, and I told her that I was very happy to see her become more and more jolly as she understood more about her fears, anger, and other feelings. She continued to giggle and to form new sounds.

Since I knew Ellen had died of an infectious disease, I asked the mother one day, in front of Ann, whether anyone had ever said that Ellen had a "bug" or "died of a bug." The mother was quite certain that this had been said. In the ensuing period of therapy there was a great deal of emphasis on naked hostility which had begun to take its toll on the mother, in the form of depression. Moreover, things were moving along so rapidly that little time was left for giving the mother adequate explanations of what went on. For these reasons I decided to see the child temporarily without the mother.

This separation was effected, and before long the child's resistance to coming to sessions, which had been in evidence for a few days, disappeared. Soon I had an opportunity to make use of the speculation regarding Ann's overhearing something about Ellen's dying of a "bug." I told her that I believed she thought a "bug" stung or bit Ellen. When she agreed, I added, "and caused her to die." Abruptly Ann said, "Pneumonia!" I said, "Yes, but maybe you also thought the 'bug' caused her to die." Her speech deteriorated at once. Perhaps she worried that she too might die, I said, and I knew that Dr. "X" came and gave her injections and maybe she worried about that as well. She took the information to her mother, who confirmed what I had said. I reassured her that she would not die, not even if a "bug" bit or stung her. Her mother agreed.

She pretended two dolls were Ellen and Betty and we re-enacted the scene of the week end when her stammering began—the week end when all the relatives had come to see the twins. I dramatized how Ann, sad, lonely, and angry, stood watching what went on, and that when Ann opened her mouth . . .—I was going to say, "to talk—and stammered instead," when Ann abruptly opened her mouth as if to bite and made a biting noise as she lunged toward me. My comment was, "Yes, and you wanted to bite them, of course, but instead of biting, out came the mixed-up talk, and the banging and kicking." The mother, who had now returned to the playroom, sat by, "wide-eyed" and stunned, and could barely speak as she saw this active demonstration of one of the components of the stammer.

After this session, the twentieth, the child's speech became much more lucid, according to the mother. Concurrently, Ann became even more spirited. During several subsequent hours she put the Chinese dragon-dogs in a drawer each day. While she continued to play games with the twin dolls, she told me, "We won't talk about Ellen dying today." Soon she provided further confirmation for the correctness of the following impression: that she had wanted to bite the twins, believed a "bug" bit Ellen and caused her death; then, after first identifying with the "bug," Ann displaced and projected all of her aggression onto the "bug" and began to fear that the "bug" would bite her and cause her death. Ann added a new element to the bee game in my office; she moved her arms up and down as if in flight, and went 'round and 'round in a circle. I said, "It looks as if you are the 'bug.' " She nodded affirmatively, and the game increased in vigor. I then added, "Now I can understand better. You wanted to bite Ellen. 'Bugs' bite and sting; you thought Ellen was bitten by a 'bug' and died. It was as if you were the biting 'bug'; then you were afraid that 'bugs' would bite you and you would get sick and die." Furthermore, I told her that the "mixed talk" was also connected with the biting; that it became worse when Ellen died, just as the "bug" fear began. She added, "I wanted them all to pay attention to me when they looked and looked and looked at Ellen and Betty." I told her that it was no longer necessary to continue to stammer, and that she now knew a lot about it and could try to talk clearly—and could tell me when she was angry.

In the next session her mother mentioned a "big surprise"—Ann had watched Zorro on television the previous evening. Ann smiled with pride and I congratulated her.

Ann had me repeat a demonstration of how older children would like to rage and cry when they have new baby sisters.

Ann then turned to her mother and felt her mother's breasts, and asked whether she, Ann, had breasts. I told her that she did, and her mother said they were now small but would some day be large. She wondered why they were not large now. I explained that they would be when Ann was a big lady, and that her mother would be pleased when eventually Ann would get married and have her own babies. Her mother warmly confirmed this. Ann next asked whether she could see and feel her mother's breasts, and I said she could not, but she knew they were there and her breasts would be like mother's some day.

Despite this discussion and although I knew the child was occasionally masturbating, no opportunity seemed to present itself in which I could discuss masturbation with Ann. Nor did she return to the early discussion of differences between the sexes.

At this time I suggested to the mother that she could begin to limit some of the child's demands, and the mother felt much relieved. Also, during this period there began to be days relatively free of speech impairment.

Another component of the Zorro fear emerged, namely, the fact that Zorro looked like a flying "bug" with a stinger, as he leaped, sword in hand, with cape flying, from a height to his horse.

Eight days before terminating treatment, I mentioned our ending date to the child, emphasizing her improvement. I said she could have her Mommy call me so that I could talk with her, and that she could see me even after the termination. She hit me playfully, and I said that she did not like what I was saying. By this time her speech had improved (perhaps 80 per cent), and the insect phobia was minimal. When her speech was troubled, there was no pounding or stamping.

In the next several days she attempted to bite me. After the first such session she feared being alone with me, perhaps because she feared I might punish her. The attempt at biting me increased, and I had actually to prevent this on several occasions. I made paper cut-outs to represent myself and told her she could bite these figures. The interpretation that her biting was a reaction to the termination was of no avail. When I made a transference interpretation, that she was reacting to the termination the way she wanted to react to her mother each time her mother left her or paid more attention to others, the biting attempt stopped.

Meanwhile, the parents reported that the child had been enumerating all the pleasant things associated with ending, including being home with her mother and playing with her toys. The child began to express the same ideas in the sessions. She appeared genuinely happy, high-spirited, and her vistas at home had increased considerably. She played at other children's homes, ate fairly well, and was no longer taking more than one or two naps daily. She was taking an active part in helping her mother at home, especially in the care of her sister Betty, and enjoyed talking with her mother. She watched television for much shorter periods of time each day, and could play with sticky media.

In the sessions she said, "Tell me the whole story from the beginning," and she listened intently to the story of her symptom development. Near the end of treatment, the mother brought a magazine into the consultation room, showing me a picture of a man who Ann said was dead. At first Ann could not tell us why she thought so. This was a photograph of a sad-looking man in an advertisement for a sinusitis medication. Several white, pointed markers circled his eyes, almost like two rows of canine teeth. Ann again said he was dead; when I asked her why she thought so, she said, "because of the

Band-aids" (the white pointers). I pressed for more associations. She said, "The holes make him dead," pointing to deep black indentations beneath his eyes, and then added, "And the pointed things." I said, "Like teeth, or stingers, or swords." She appeared very gay and started her "bug" game.

In the thirty-sixth and final session, she asked about Zorro's changes in costume, and I demonstrated these changes with dolls, and in the last moments of the hour she assembled all the biting animals, including the Chinese dragon-dogs, and began to caress them. She put them in a group, kissed each one tenderly, hugged them, and then pretended to feed them. I said she was telling me that she was happy now. For so long she thought of herself as being like a biting animal, and today she was telling me that she was not one, that there was no reason to fear these animals, and that now mouths were most important for eating instead of for biting.

Follow-up

During the year following the termination of treatment, I continued to receive reports from the parents and saw both parents and Ann at periodic intervals, and it appeared that the therapeutic gains were consolidated. The fear of insects and of Zorro did not return, and her speech became entirely free of stammer within weeks except for two occurrences mentioned below.

One of Ann's uncles died, and the child abruptly began to talk about her sister's death. Spontaneously she reviewed with her mother many of the things she learned during treatment. One week after the uncle's death, while her mother was driving her to visit the grandmother and Ann's widowed aunt, Ann was suddenly overcome with great anxiety, and said to her mother, "My speech is all mixed up!"— and it was! Her mother told her that this was because Ann had connected her uncle's death with Ellen's death, and that she was upset at the prospect of visiting her aunt. This relieved the difficulty within five minutes.

Several additional, transient, neurotic difficulties made their appearance during the six months after termination. The occurrence and handling of these difficulties is outlined here in summary:

1. She wanted to urinate while she was in a large store with her mother. This could not be arranged. That evening she had her first episode of enuresis. Her mother felt that Ann was angry at not being allowed to go to the bathroom. I told the mother to talk this over with Ann. This was done, and there has not been another episode of wetting.

2. Ann's difficulty of handling sticky foods recurred several hours after she saw her mother purchase a rubber pad for her bed after the enuretic episode. This difficulty disappeared within a short time after the mother removed the pad from Ann's bed.

3. On the evening following dental repair of a cavity, the child had trouble sleeping, and complained, "I see faces—I'm afraid!" She feared a "Boom" sound on the radio. The mother rocked and soothed her that night, and on the following day Ann asked when she would see me again, and was told that it would be in the next few days. She told her mother she wished she were two again (before the twins' birth). The fear of faces returned the next night, after which she told the following story to her mother: "A girl named Betty had a lot of troubles, and went to a doctor and he tried and tried and tried to help her. Then along came a bee, and he said to the girl, 'Good morning.' He was a friendly bee. He had broken his stinger." Later that day, Ann and her mother were cutting paper animals out of a book, and with anxiety, the child asked, "Are you going to cut their legs, ears or tail off?" Her mother reassured her. Her five-, six-, and seven-year-old dolls became babies again, and Ann's speech became mildly troubled.

I saw Ann twice in subsequent days, and she told me she feared only one face—a baby girl's face—and she thought it was like her sister Betty's face or Ellen's face. She drew a series of pictures of children with mouths open, having their teeth worked on. I drew a picture of a girl having a tooth worked on, and at once Ann said this girl was herself. I said she must have been very much afraid and maybe even angry at the dentist and at Mommy for the whole procedure, and I told her that I knew she went to the dentist just before the fear of the face began. I further told her that I knew she felt she was bad because she had eaten candy (her mother had told me that there had been previous discussions about candy not being good for teeth), and we also knew that she thought that biting had caused

Ellen's death, and that she had wanted to bite Ellen. I told her that the face might have been a punishment for these wishes. She listened very carefully. Her mother, who joined us after this discussion, mentioned the "boom" noise, at which point Ann spontaneously picked up a toy toilet, filled it with sand and water and pretended to be afraid of the flushing noise. The child said she thought she had blocked the toilet with too much toilet paper. Her mother told her that no paper was found when the toilet was repaired. Ann appeared to be relieved at what her mother said, and put a doll on the toilet several times. It was my impression that although she was showing us the component of phallic aggression, and the fear of her mother's castrating potential, the anal- and oral-sadistic components could more easily be accepted by the child.

Following these two sessions, neither the "boom" fear nor the stammering recurred. The fear of faces disappeared within a few days, but she now wanted a night light in the hall.

After the termination of treatment Ann masturbated somewhat more frequently than before, and other manifestations of the oedipus complex began to be prominent. These did not appear to be causing undue anxiety.

At the time of this writing, Ann appears to be free of her previous difficulties, and has been enjoying a regular nursery school. Her teacher's reports state: "She is very well poised, self-assured; plays well with other children, is always cooperative and well-behaved." On direct questioning, the teacher told Ann's mother that the child was cheerful and seemed genuinely happy. There is obvious ambivalence toward her sister Betty.

Discussion

The Nature of the Conflict

The analysis of this three-year-old child's neurosis disclosed that the stammering had at least two major components. One was a wish to continue anal soiling, which had to be sharply curtailed at the time of the birth of twin sisters. Later, the conflict over this wish led to the formation of defenses: the anal preoccupation was displaced upward (to the mouth), and concurrently marked reaction formations against soiling developed. The other component of her stammering was a regression to oral sadism, activated by the absence of her mother during hospital confinement when the twins were born, by the severity of the grandmother's final measures to establish bowel training, and especially by the attention paid to her twin sisters. The desire to bite had to be repressed and then gained access to the speech mechanisms, with consequent disguised return of the repressed. The child turned much of her aggression against herself, slapping her thighs while speaking, and becoming withdrawn and depressed. The stammering, as neurotic symptoms in general, were thus overdetermined and emphasized wish and punishment components. Her speech disturbance represented the wish to soil, bite, and to incorporate her mother, and at the same time it represented punishment through the fact that mutilation of speech embarrassed her and did not allow her to receive the approval and love she wanted.

The insect phobia (and a phobia of the television character Zorro) began after the death of the younger sister. Regression to oral sadism was prominent also in this phobia. The patient's desire to bite and destroy her sisters had to be repressed. There was an identification with a "bug" which Ann felt caused her sister's death by biting. A displacement and projection of her wish to bite occurred, and now she became fearful that she would be bitten by a "bug" (or stung by Zorro's sword), and that she would die—hence she had to avoid "bugs."

Freud (1909), Berta Bornstein (1935), Steff Bornstein (1935), Burlingham (1935), Schwarz (1950), Sperling (1952), and more recently Leonard (1959), all emphasize the importance of recognizing, interpreting, and working through the oral- and anal-sadistic impulses in young children. Often enough these component instincts have already undergone much inhibition, suppression, and repression by the age of three. Leonard (1959) described a two-and-a-half-year-old girl who was unable to walk after a tibial fracture healed; one function of this inhibition of walking was to prevent the child from getting to her baby brother and hurting him. In Ann's case, these component instincts played an important role in the production of her symptoms.

Berta Bornstein was among the first to describe the brief, intensive, analytic treatment of very young children. In her paper of 1935 she described the therapy of Lisa, who could sleep only in a tense sitting position before the analytic intervention. The conflict over the wish to soil and to be aggressive, and the fear of losing the mother's love if these wishes were acceded to, played a prominent part in Lisa's symptomatology, as it did in my patient, Ann. Steff Bornstein (1935), discussing the analysis of a three-year-old child, emphasized that early traumatic events interfere with later instinctual development. This was certainly true also in the case of Ann. In her it was quite apparent that the development of ego and libido, both of which had been impaired, could again proceed when the conflict caused by the traumatic events was resolved through analytic interpretations.

The Importance of Including the Mother

In the brief, intensive treatment of very young children it is extremely important to enlist the active participation of the mother. Berta Bornstein (1935), in the treatment of Lisa, included the child's mother. Steff Bornstein (1935), treating a three-year-old, also frequently drew the mother into the analytic sessions to clarify reality for the child. She stated, "This rare opportunity of turning to parents for explanation in questions of fact offered a therapeutic assistance that cannot be overestimated."

Burlingham (1935) stressed: "To maintain the sympathy and cooperation of the parents throughout the entire analysis of a child is a difficult and trying problem; and yet if one does not succeed in this, the analysis moves inevitably to an abrupt and premature interruption." In Ann's case, this cooperation was aided immeasurably by having the mother present during the sessions, and this in turn helped the parents to understand the child's problems.

Schwarz (1950) discussed the advantages of such a procedure in two of her cases, and said: "It is more difficult for the mother of the young child to decide to send her child to analysis than for the mother of the latency child . . . [Moreover,] the mother who follows the treatment of the child in the consulting room will be better able to cope with the neurotic child at home and will gradually adjust her own educational ways to our analytic efforts . . . For the child, the presence of the mother in the consulting room acts as a reassurance of her approval of the analyst and the analytic interpretations."

Many of the interpretations made to Ann were immediately reinforced by the mother, making Ann's acceptance of these more immediate.

Gero-Heymann (1955) discussed, in a brief presentation, how a mother of a two-and-a-half-year-old girl was able to understand and successfully aid her child in working through a traumatic episode which for the child had the meaning of castration.

Furman (1957) stressed that one of the basic premises of utilizing the parents for work with "under-fives" is "the unique relationship between the mother and her under-five, an interaction characterized by an unusual mutual unconscious closeness."

It seems to me that the mother's presence in the room had a doubly beneficial impact. On the one hand, as already stated, it gave full support to the treatment in the child's eyes. On the other hand, it had a direct impact on the mother who was visibly moved when she witnessed the emergence of the child's unconscious fears and wishes. Being faced with the child's unconscious motivations and conflicts caused her to become aware of some of her own conflicts, which she then attempted to handle differently. Therefore, her presence in the therapy room had a direct beneficial effect both on the child and on the mother.

Another brief technical point should be made. Among the thirty-five cases described by Levy (1939) in his paper on release therapy there were some children with phobias and stammering. The treatment of Ann differs essentially from Levy's therapy in going beyond the abreaction of traumatic events (the milk-throwing episode) and conflict-producing life situations (birth of twins, and death of Ellen), and the encouragement of play designed to give expression to inhibited instinctual wishes (the fecal representation through sand, clay, water play). The difference lies in the systematic analysis and interpretation of the symptom picture.

It is suggested that other children, in the preoedipal phases of development, who show incapacitating infantile neuroses, with known traumatic events and libidinal regression, can be considered as candidates for similar, brief, intensive analysis.

BIBLIOGRAPHY

Bornstein, B. (1935), Phobia in a Two-and-a-half-year-old Child. *Psa. Quart.*, IV.

Bornstein, S. (1935), A Child Analysis. *Psa. Quart.*, IV.

Burlingham, D. T. (1935), Child Analysis and the Mother. *Psa. Quart.*, IV.

Freud, A. (1945), Indications for Child Analysis. *This Annual*, I.

Freud, S. (1909), Analysis of a Phobia in a Five-year-old Boy. *Standard Edition*, X. London: Hogarth Press, 1955.

—— (1938), *An Outline of Psychoanalysis*. New York: Norton, 1949.

Furman, E. (1957), Treatment of Under-Fives by Way of Their Parents. *This Annual*, XII.

Gero-Heymann, E. (1955), A Short Communication on a Traumatic Episode in a Child of Two Years and Seven Months. *This Annual*, X.

Leonard, M. R. (1959), Fear of Walking in a Two-and-a-half-year-old Girl. *Psa. Quart.*, XXVIII.

Levy, D. M. (1939), Release Therapy. *Am. J. Orthopsychiat.*, IX.

Schwarz, H. (1950), The Mother in the Consulting Room: Notes on the Psychoanalytic Treatment of Two Young Children. *This Annual*, V.

Sperling, M. (1952), Animal Phobias in a Two-year-old Child. *This Annual*, VII.

THE ONE-PARENT CHILD AND HIS OEDIPAL DEVELOPMENT

PETER B. NEUBAUER, M.D. (New York)[1]

Over the years, we have been able to study children at the Child Development Center, who, throughout their early development, or for a prolonged part of it, have been deprived of either their mother or father. Their cases present a chance for the analytic study of "experiments provided by fate" (A. Freud and Dann, 1951).

We have had the opportunity to observe in four such children the effects which the absence of one parent had on the vicissitudes of oedipal development. These observations permit us to test the degree to which the physical and emotional presence of both parents is essential for the solution of the oedipal conflict. This, then, is a study of environmental deficiency coordinated to a specific developmental phase.

Reviewing the literature on children who grew up with only one parent, we find that attention has been paid mainly to the pre-oedipal period, and recently more to the first year of life, particularly to the absence of mothering in the need-satisfying phase and its effect on further development. These studies of maternal deprivation, as summarized by Bowlby (1951) and by Glaser and Eisenberg (1956), demonstrate the inexorability with which the infant requires need satisfaction through one consistent, empathetic mother; if the infant's needs are not fulfilled, e.g., through separation from the mother in the first year of life, his future may be threatened by vegetative dysfunction, and disturbance in object relations and ego structure. However, it is impressive to note the wide range of chil-

[1] Director, Child Development Center, New York, N.Y.

The Child Development Center is a research and treatment center for prelatency children and their families. The children attend a therapeutic nursery school daily, over a period of several years. The nursery school is an integral part of the Center's clinical program.

I am grateful to Sylvia Bauman for contributing much of the clinical material and to Rena Wallant who aided as a research assistant.

dren's reactions to maternal deprivation (Goldfarb, 1947; Beres and Obers, 1950). In some cases we see the possibilities of apparent recovery and reversibility of damage, either when the mother figure is restored (Spitz and Wolf, 1946) or when special therapeutic techniques intervene (Gelinier-Ortigues and Aubry, 1955; Alpert, 1957, 1959). We note also the provocative evidence from other cultures that children may develop stable personalities if they have *many* good (that is, constant) mothers (Mead, 1954a); that such children are able to "tolerate separation much more easily because they trust more people" (Mead, 1954b); and the suggestion from a study of Kibbutz children who, according to Kaffman (1956), have "a more balanced reaction to the trauma of a temporary or permanent separation from one of the parents." Yet, we cannot fail to consider the breakdown at puberty in the "concentration camp children" studied by Anna Freud (1954; A. Freud and Dann, 1951) of the "precarious normality" developed on the basis of object relations to group companions, in the absence of individual parental ties.

Bowlby (1951) summarized the number of variables on which the effect of early maternal deprivation depends: the age at which it occurs, the length and degree of deprivation, the quality of the previous mother-child relationship, and the availability of mother substitutes. Other yet barely measured variables, such as the varying cultural demands on individuals, and the constitutional "object-seeking" strength of the child himself, may play a part. Nevertheless, one may conclude that ego development will be jeopardized if the psychobiological unity of mother and child is seriously disturbed in the first year of life, because of the consequent interference with drive satisfaction.

As indicated, our own study deals with the effect of disturbances in the oedipal triangle, and the variety of oedipal solutions adopted by children under these conditions. We will attempt, then, to single out the effect of parental absence during the oedipal phase of development, a step which may permit a closer examination of processes of sexual identification and superego formation.

REVIEW OF THE LITERATURE

We found references to "oedipal deficiency" in several discussions of pathological sexual and social development. Freud, in his study of Leonardo da Vinci (1910)—whose "illegitimate birth deprived him of his father's influence until perhaps his fifth year, and left him open to the tender seductions of a mother whose only solace he was"—describes a type of male homosexuality in which etiological factors are the maternal seduction of a son because of the libidinal shift from husband to child, and the absence of paternal influence on oedipal development. In the 1915 edition of *Three Essays on the Theory of Sexuality* (1905), Freud continues this thought. Investigating patients with hysteria, he states that "the early loss of one of their parents, whether by death, divorce or separation, with the result that the remaining parent absorbs the whole of the child's love, determines the sex of the person who is later to be chosen as a sexual object and may thus open the way to permanent inversion."

Ferenczi (1914) refers to the absent-parent condition by emphasizing a fixation on the lost father in the early histories of male homosexuals, due to the absence of the otherwise "unavoidable conflicts between father and son." The same process is investigated by Aichhorn (1925) who is impressed by the inadequate ego ideal of the young, fatherless boy. Melanie Klein (as reported by Susan Isaacs, 1943) stresses that the inverted oedipus complex is reinforced in boys by the *fantasy image* of an absent father (both idealized and sadistic). In his paper, "Specific Forms of the Oedipus Complex" (1931), Fenichel adds other important factors: the guilt engendered by fantasy fulfillment of oedipal wishes when the same-sexed parent dies; and the fantastic idealization, based on unsatisfied oedipal longing, when the opposite-sexed parent dies.

The observations of fatherless children in the wartime Hampstead Nurseries made by Anna Freud and Burlingham (1943, 1944) are perhaps the best-known recent contributions to this topic. The intense and persistent attachments to a fantasied father which these children constructed out of even the most meager relationships to any man, or even in the absence of any father experience at all, state the case in reverse: they seem to indicate that children in the oedipal phase are compelled to create in fantasy what does not exist in fact. In an extension of this point, Nunberg (1955) views the idealized fantasy of missing fathers as a bridge to an attachment to a real man, through whom some children may achieve oedipal and superego development. He points out, though, that other children who grow up without fathers are full of resentment, behave ruthlessly, as if they had no guilt, and thus take revenge on the world for not having a father.

A search of the literature for clinical investigations of the oedipal irregularity of the one-parent relationship has yielded five male and five female cases, published between 1930 and 1954.[2] Two authors report the analyses of prelatency children (Isaacs, 1943; Meiss, 1952); one the treatment of a latency boy of poor ego endowment and barely average intelligence (who had also been studied intensively between the age of sixteen months and four years) (Bennett and Hellman, 1951); one the treatment of an adolescent girl (Keiser, 1953); the rest of the patients are all adults (Eisendorfer, 1943 [two cases]; Fenichel, 1930; Isaacs, 1945; Reich, 1954; Wulff, 1942). Of the five male cases four lost their fathers, one his mother; of the five women, the father was absent in every case. The ten patients were all without one parent throughout the oedipal phase; however, in all but two of the cases, the loss of the parent had occurred before the oedipal phase.

Despite the considerable variability of data, it is important to summarize these cases, in order to place our own material in its proper perspective.

The single parent's overcathexis and consequent seduction of the child described by Freud may be considered as the prototype. In several of the cases listed above, this process of overcathexis began at birth or before the second year. Some investigators have detailed the elaboration which the preoedipal pathology received in the phallic-oedipal phase. Thus, Eisendorfer (1943) describes the course of development in two women under the twin conditions of any early, abnormally intensified mother-child relationship and an absent father: an increased primary homosexual attachment to the mother occurred, with oral fixations, an immature ego structure, and repression of aggression against the mother which was then inevitably turned inward. With the onset of the phallic phase, the girl experienced her mother as a castrating, phallic figure, and withdrew to a secondary homosexual pattern in which she identified with a fan-

2 I have included only those cases in which the effect of parental absence on oedipal development is central to the author's investigation.

tasied image of the absent father in order to retain the love of the mother. "The unresolved conflicts of oral dependence, oral defiance, and oral aggression resulted in the development of an intensified oral annihilating superego structure." Eisendorfer concludes that "one of the important conditions for being loved in these single-parent situations is the identification with the absent parent: a homosexual bond is thus established between the patient and the remaining parent."

Similar early processes of maternal narcissistic seduction, oral fixation, retarded ego controls, and repressed pregenital aggression are described by Annie Reich (1954). The pathology of this young woman patient was dominated by a readiness for fantasy wish fulfill-ment: the young girl's early identification with a glorified fantasy of the father's phallus persisted in the ego ideal. She thereby hoped to fulfill the explicit familial demand that she replace her dead father (and an uncle who had died at the same time as well!).

> Any desexualization of the fantasy became impossible. No stable identification with nonsexual qualities of the objects could be attained, since the child was . . . trying to identify with objects that existed in her fantasy only. The normal impact of reality on this fantasy object, which would have helped to achieve some degree of desexualization and also to reduce to normal size the figure of the father that was seen in such supernatural dimensions was absent . . . hence the unsublimated phallic character of the ego ideal and its megalomanic scope. [Reich concludes:] When early identifications with unsublimated sexual behavior have taken place and sexual characteristics as such remain an ego ideal, a fixation on or regression to primitive, aggressive, pre-genital levels is frequent, which leads to a persistence of particu-lar, cruel superego forerunners. This combination of opposite factors—of megalomanic, sexualized ideals and of particular, sadistic superego elements—must lead to a type of superego which cannot possibly be lived up to in reality [pp. 236-237].

The idealization of a dead father, as a young boy's defense against early maternal seduction, contributed to the homosexuality of one of Isaacs' patients (1945). His secret hatred and resentment against a mother who had demanded not only his exclusive devotion, but that he share her hatred of his dead father as well, made it too dangerous for him to love another woman, lest this new love bring with it the same fear and hatred as the old. Never daring to withdraw love from his mother lest the hatred escape, he turned instead to idealized and sadistic love relationships with men, reflecting his secret, chronically disappointed search for his idealized absent father.

The difficulties in normal masculine development in the absence of the oedipal rival and an object for identification are stressed in Bennett and Hellman's (1951) study of an illegitimate boy. Intense fantasies of both an extremely idealized and extremely punitive father helped him avoid the anxieties of the near-fulfillment of his incestuous wishes through his mother's seduction. This mother was hostile to men, and also, her "excessive oral stimulation and physical contact . . . throughout and beyond the oedipal phase, had resulted in fantasies of her as a sadistic phallic mother"; therefore, the boy felt that "any heterosexual fantasies about her can only be fraught with danger for his masculinity." In flight from his "castrating" mother, the boy developed homosexual fantasies toward his father. The punitive, destructive father image expressed his oedipal jealousy and fears of punishment; the strong, benevolent protective fantasy father helped him deny castration danger at the hands of father and from mother as well.

The development of a young man's overt homosexuality is traced by Wulff (1942). This single example of an absent mother is significant because, unlike all other cases, there is no mention of a fantasy replacement of the absent parent. Wulff describes a peculiar oedipal constellation of an absent mother (she died when the child was four but was chronically hospitalized before that) and a seductive and punitive father, who became the boy's primary object. Later heterosexual strivings in this boy could not compete with his "subservience to the original homosexual love object."

Two other cases illustrate that the pattern of the remaining parent's seduction of the child is by no means universal. In another of Isaacs' patients (1943), an uncle, serving as father substitute, is the dominant object in a boy's early life. The boy's oedipal relationships were additionally complicated by the fact that his uncle had two women to look after—aunt and mother. The early loss of his father had enhanced the boy's frightening impulses about him; these, together with an intense longing for him, emphasized the boy's homosexual attachment to the uncle. His mother's restrictiveness and her hostility to the boy's maleness had a further inhibiting effect; and his uncle's "two wives," exemplifying that it is possible to rob the mother of the father's love, stimulated even more the inverted oedipus complex.

An example of Fenichel's (1930) illustrates the familiar distortion of development due to the persistence of a girl's preoedipal tie to her mother. In this case, an ambivalent, disappointing mother and a totally ungratified child present conditions opposite to those previously described, but with similar effects: the child's longing for love was frustrated on all levels; her aggression against the mother was repressed; she turned to an identification with the idealized fantasy of the father who had died the day she was born, only to be always disappointed since no man could be the right one. Her sadistic relationships to real men ultimately screened the primary unfulfilled wishes for her mother.

I have found only two examples in which the effect of the loss of oedipal objects can be compared with the influence of fantasy objects. These illustrate that the loss of a parent during the oedipal phase intensifies the fears and wishes of an already existing positive oedipus complex. Moreover, it leads to a readiness for the fixation of those conflicts which were uppermost in the parent-child relationship at the time of the parent's disappearance.

Keiser (1953) describes the manifest oedipus complex of an adolescent girl whose father left when she was four. Her superego defect had its genesis in the missing opportunity to desexualize the original oedipal attachment. The father "was neither a dead parent whom the child mourned and finally forgave, nor was he present for a real relationship with its frustrations, which lead to the ultimate resolution of the oedipus complex." He remained a sexualized image, perpetuated by his own partially seductive, partially disappointing behavior (tempting her from afar with the fantasy of his return but never keeping any promises) and kept alive also by the mother, to remove the girl as a rival for her lovers.

Meiss (1952) describes the development of a boy who lost his father during the oedipal period. The absence of continued real experiences with a father made it impossible for the boy to correct his image of an omniscient, angry father, an image formed at a time when he had already wanted to replace the father. This child's case was further complicated by an unusual symptom: a fear that his mother would die. His anxiety state thus had a twofold origin: his father's death had intensified and fixated his oedipal rivalry and castration fears; in contrast, his fears in relation to his mother derived, not from death wishes against her, but from the fantasy that her death would reunite her with father, thus leaving him totally alone.

This detailed survey of ten cases cannot fail to impress upon us the pathogenic potential which an absent parent may exert on sexual identification and superego formation. In this small sample, the antecedent factors of an early loss of one parent and a pathological preoedipal relationship to the other parent predominate. The data do not permit etiological differentiation between the effect of the parent's absence and the pathology of the remaining parent. Other significant variables in the oedipal development of children with only one parent are the timing of the loss, and the relationship of the child's sex to the sex of the missing parent. Fantasy objects, immensely idealized or endowed with terribly sadistic attributes, replacing an absent parent are nearly ubiquitous; their frequent occurrence in dynamically very different situations underlines their significance in the development of object relations.

The case I shall present belongs to the category of those children who grew up with only one parent.

CASE HISTORY

Rita M. was brought to us by her mother in July, 1955, at the age of three years six months. The mother's difficulties were expressed in the three problems which concerned her most: (1) how to deal with the disinterested, absent father, and Rita's questions about and wish for him; (2) the excessive eating, which Mrs. M. considered to be a forerunner to Rita's becoming a fat, ugly child, as she describes herself as having been. In this connection, Mrs. M. expressed guilt about the punitive way in which she handled the eating problem; and (3) Rita's sexual confusion and expressed wish to be a boy, which Mrs. M. felt at a complete loss to deal with.

The mother's stated purpose in turning to us was to find out how to be a better mother. It was felt from the very beginning that

Mrs. M. had some awareness that Rita's problems were her own as well, and there was little doubt that she was seeking treatment for herself.

Our attempts to include Mr. M. in the study failed. He was frank about his total lack of interest in Rita; he visited Rita at school once, but otherwise refused to cooperate with us in any planning or in any sustained relationship with the child.

I shall list only a few facts about the mother, although we have a wealth of data about her. Mrs. M.'s father had failed her in many respects. At the age of four, moreover, she had lost an uncle to whom she had transferred her oedipal attachment. Thus she longed for an acceptance she never received. Mrs. M. had had a lonely childhood, had felt herself unloved and unwanted.

When she married her husband, she saw him as a "strong, dynamic man," in contrast to her own weak father. With this fantasy she blinded herself to the many psychopathic manifestations which were abundantly clear to all who knew him. She had supported him by working as a bookkeeper, and after their divorce she continued to work because Mr. M. constantly failed in his very minimal legal financial obligations to Rita and her mother, frequently omitting his payments, issuing bad checks, and so on. The mother's inability to let go of her divorced husband was an important factor in Rita's development.

Mrs. M.'s two pregnancies prior to Rita's birth, both of which terminated in early miscarriage—as well as the successful one with Rita—were frankly initiated by her conscious wish to have Mr. M. assume the responsibilties of marriage and by the vain hope that the birth of a child would transform him into a reliable husband. He desired only a son, but her own preference was for a girl. Rita was born at the beginning of the ninth month. Though the mother had never considered breast feeding, Rita's premature birth made this an academic question. Mrs. M. expressed her sadness at not being able to feed or hold Rita or take her home from the hospital when she left. She was alone for the next few weeks, because the father had already left.

The growth history is marked by rather rapid physical strides.

Frequent and early separations, not merely from the father, were prominent in Rita's early life. At two months of age, she was taken to the home of a maternal aunt for a week while Mrs. M. went away to determine the future of her marriage, deciding to agree to a divorce. Again, when Rita was four months old, she was placed with the same aunt for the summer to permit Mrs. M. to keep her job in the city. On week ends, she joined the baby in her sister's household. Removing Rita from the aunt's care, Mrs. M. took her back to New York and a part-time housekeeper was engaged to help. This woman remained in the home until some time in Rita's second year, when Jean, the current housekeeper, took over. Jean, a woman in her fifties, is present during the day, but returns to her own household each evening. Rita has always been strongly attached to Jean, who appears to be overly permissive with her, in contrast to Mrs. M., who is the partial and unsuccessful disciplinarian. In June, 1955, the housekeeper became ill. Mrs. M. was unable to find a temporary substitute for her, and a hasty decision was made to place Rita in a day nursery from 8:20 A.M. to 6:00 P.M.

Rita's father, who had begun a clandestine affair during his wife's pregnancy, left one week after she was born, excusing his departure with, "This is a good time to leave, before I establish a relationship with the child." He had, as we have stated before, expressed preference for a boy, and his aversion to accepting a daughter has never diminished. He has visited her only twice, on her second and third birthdays, and then only upon the mother's insistence.

We find Rita, at the age of three and a half, approaching phallic development. Her previous longing for her absent father now changed to overidealized fantasies about him, accompanied by sexual confusion, expressed in her preference to be a boy. At this time, too, begin the bouts of excessive eating; the complaints of feeling itchy, of her clothes being too tight or too rough; and an intensified meticulousness. These are connected with earlier prephallic problems, such as difficulties in feeding, skin sensitivities, and concern that doors and drawers be closed, or rugs and blankets be smooth. While in the past she had accepted many important separations from her mother without showing overt signs of being disturbed, now she reacted with severe anxiety.[3]

[3] The emergence of Rita's separation anxiety as an expression of phallic conflicts may contribute to the understanding of this symptom in those children whose castration fear reinforces the fear of loss of the object. A similar constellation existed in Meiss's case (1952) previously cited.

The shift toward phallic conflicts with increasing symptomatology had been precipitated by traumatic events, almost in the sense Freud used the term originally. Her mother's inability to leave her job, when her housekeeper was suddenly hospitalized, required Rita's hasty and unprepared placement in a day nursery. After a week of apparent adjustment to the nursery (as to previous separations), Rita began to plead to be permitted to stay at home. We learned later that during this week she was exposed to other children's sexual exploration, to which she reacted by saying, "Last week I was a boy," and on several occasions, "I lost my penis." Mounting separation anxiety and increased masturbation accompanied these castration fantasies. When she was asked by other children in the school to dress up as a bride in a wedding game, she complained, "I don't want to get married," and continued to beg her mother to be permitted to stay at home. When this request was ignored, she had to be carried screaming into the school bus. Finally, the continued, forced separations culminated in a furious outburst. Upon her return home at the end of the second week of school, she would not talk, attacked mother physically, and refused to enter the apartment. Forced to do so, she exploded in a scene that took hours to run its course. She took off all her clothes, screamed, and sat down on the floor to urinate. Mother, who had been withholding the desperately sought protection from both castration and separation anxiety, each heightening the other, now began to panic when she was faced with this massive disorganization and regression. Supported by her pediatrician's advice, she turned for help to her divorced husband (an idealized expectation on her part in view of her past disappointment in him) and insisted that he visit the child.

The father, who a month before these events had remarried a woman with a nine-year-old son, responded to the urgency of mother's request and visited Rita twice in the following week. It is of interest, in view of Rita's further oedipal development, that as soon as the father joined them, she now banished her mother into another room with the same determination with which she had previously fought separation from mother. Alone with her father, she immediately acted on phallic impulses, nagging so insistently that he urinate in her presence, that he allowed her into the bathroom with him. Stimulated by Rita's phallic wishes and fears, he responded with his own sexual pathology: he played with her roughly, pulled her hair, and teased her with taunts of "Hey, boy!" She protested, "No, no, no, don't say that," clung to him when he left, and once again separation from him had to be forced.

Rita's wish for a penis was accompanied by increasing castration anxiety. We are not sure of the extent to which her identification with this mother prepared her for the fantasy of a phallic girl, or whether the penis envy was stimulated primarily by the exposure at school to the anatomical differences, as expressed in sexual games to which she, a fatherless, only child, may have come unprepared. The mother not only failed to permit the prephallic regression which might have protected Rita against the castration fear, but she also set the example of the powerless woman who has to be rescued by the man. Rita tried to turn away from her mother and seek help from her father. But then she had to face the specific condition for his acceptance—that she be a boy. The wish for a penis, therefore, was a defense against the castration anxiety, as well as the only means at her disposal to reunite with father; the wish was not only to be *like* father, but to be *with* father. In this case, the penis envy was in the service of the positive oedipal relationship.

The confluence of various factors—the traumatic separation from mother, the sudden appearance of father with his pathological behavior, and the child's developmental readiness—raised these questions: Would this have a fixating effect on the phallic level of development? Would it force regression, or would it exert a precipitous, premature push toward the unfolding of pathological oedipal processes? The case material of others suggests that this constellation of forces is a dynamic precondition of homosexuality. In our case, interestingly enough, the most telling influence in this direction stemmed, not from the remaining parent, but from the almost totally absent father. His absence was naturally only a physical one; in the emotional life of both mother and child he was very much a part of everyday wishful thinking.

One could speculate that it may have been fortunate for Rita that the father continued to visit only on very rare occasions; otherwise, he might have reinforced her phallic readiness, and brought about a fixation on that level. Since he remained absent, Rita was

kept uncomfortably poised between the wish to defend against both
the phallic overidealized longing for her father, and her reality
dependency on mother. She did not react to this with regression, nor
was she able to make a choice between accepting castration or insisting on the fantasy penis; therefore, the phallic ambivalence remained
suspended.

Before her father visited, Rita's initial reaction to her phallic
confusion was regression to a demanding, pregenital relationship
to mother. But meeting disappointment, she turned toward the
oedipal choice; indeed, in Freud's words (1932), "as though it were
a haven of refuge." The father's implicit demand, however, that
she would be acceptable to him only as a boy, imposed upon her a
narcissistic type of object choice (Freud, 1914):[4] to love, in effect,
what someone else wanted her to be. Thus, for the next two years,
Rita tried to live up to her one-sided bargain with father, to become
a boy in order to maintain his love. She preferred pants to dresses;
in the Child Development Center's nursery, she played the role of a
father or a cowboy; and she augmented the masculine fantasy with
belligerent, demanding, controlling behavior (though this was not
without prephallic determinants).

It is dynamically important to emphasize, though, that from the
beginning on, she was never fully at ease with the wish for a penis.
The uneasiness of her phallic identification was expressed in her
attempted retreat from facing issues of sexual identity ("I don't
want to get married!"); in her initial protest ("No, no, no, don't say
that!") when father proposed that she be a boy; and in the increased
symptoms of compulsive behavior and skin sensitivity, when she
finally "tried on" the phallic fantasy. Though her attempt at phallic
completion brought no acceptance from father, which increased her
anxiety, she continued to endow him, as the possessor of the penis,
with the omnipotent capacity to bring her happiness. This image
did not change with his disappointing, often cynically rejecting

---

4 Freud states: "We may conclude . . . with a short survey of the paths leading to
object-choice. A person may love:

    (1) According to the narcissistic type:
        (a) What he is himself (actually himself).
        (b) What he once was.
        (c) What he would like to be.
        (d) Someone who was once part of himself" (p. 47).

attitude; he remained in her fantasy a protective, all-loving, all-powerful figure. The idealization was so nearly complete that when he broke a promise to visit her in the Center's nursery, she claimed he had come, but at rest period or lunchtime, and therefore the teachers were not permitted to allow him in. (Characteristically, as I shall amplify later, this invasion of reality testing by idealization was balanced by her need to include rules and regulations to justify the fantasied behavior of the teachers.)

During this period, a cyclical pattern became evident. Any separation from mother (and later from the therapist), or any physical illness, brought an intensification of castration fear and an increase in symptoms: itching, temper tantrums, a shift to aggression, and a new attempt to reach the father (a repetition of the original traumatic sequence). Since she had tried to fulfill father's wishes, and he still had not satisfied hers, she then sought other solutions, which were expressed in her fantasies in treatment. For instance, she played that she herself was a man who had a baby boy, who "cried because he had no mother," and later, "because he had no father." As a man, she could "produce" a boy, but then she, as a girl, was still without a father. As a boy, she would have to make a choice to give up mother and stay with father; this forced her to change the child's sex back to a girl, and then back and forth again, interminably. We see, in her contradictory phallic wishes, her inability to find a solution; and ambivalence, in her need for both parents.

Aggression—the killing of a parent—was introduced into her play when all attempts at a peaceful solution had failed. In kidnaping fantasies, the "bad" father-cowboy came each night, killed mother, and stole her away. As further material came to the fore, it appeared that, in her view, to be aggressive meant to be like a man and to turn against mother. This phallic aggression became mixed with oral and anal conflicts, as expressed in temper tantrums, demandingness, enuresis, and itching. When she was good, mother would take care of her, but there was another alternative, namely, to be sick. In her play there was an itching baby, who could not be taken care of by mother; only a doctor, a cowboy, or some other father figure could cure it. Her emerging concepts of good and bad therefore stemmed from her relationship to mother. When she was aggressive-phallic, she became bad, in mother's eyes, and acceptable to father.

It is important to investigate these identifications in order to understand Rita's superego development. In comparison to Nunberg's formulation (1932), that the boy's ego ideal is formed by the love of the mother and then followed by the fear of the father which leads to superego formation, we find the following process in Rita: while the father was physically absent, he was very much a part of her emotional life and represented direct wish fulfillment; when the mother became the object of aggression, good or bad was connected with mother's acceptance or nonacceptance. Rita expected punishment for instinctual wishes to come from the mother, who thereby reinforced the already existing castration fear. In this way, mother counteracted Rita's phallic identification, and consequently also father's influence. Being a model of a woman who seeks and longs for a man, mother influenced Rita's ultimate heterosexual position.

There seems to be an additional source of superego formation. Suspended between dependency on mother and the wish for the phallic father, Rita could not shift toward the oedipal organization, and could not give her loyalty or allegiance to either mother or father. She saw the family as falling into groups of two; we have noted her dichotomous tie to boy and father, girl and mother; as a boy, father would stay with her, as a girl, she could stay only with mother. But needing both parents, she incorporated a sort of uneasily balanced double identity: she was at times a boy, and at times a girl. An early interest in and appreciation of numerical and arithmetical concepts expressed her concern with these problems of equalization and distribution[5]—a concern which she translated into a precociously developed sense of social equivalents, namely, prematurely strict ideals of correctness, justice, and equal status. We have to assume that originally anal difficulties have contributed to this morality, which no doubt now assumed phallic significance. We see, therefore, the beginning of a superego formation, based not on the oedipal conflict but on preoedipal ambivalence, on the sublimation of her phallic suspension. This resembles Nunberg's patient (1949) who felt "that his entire body is divided into two halves," "that it is dual" . . . man has two arms, two eyes, two ears, and so on! Nunberg, viewing this

[5] V. Rosen (1953) and E. and R. Plank (1954) have discussed mathematical interests of still other derivation.

material as a manifestation of the bisexuality of man, states that these hermaphroditic fantasies attempt to solve the problem of the origin of man and the difference between the sexes.

Her ambivalent, see-sawing identification did not permit her to rest with the fantasy that father stole the baby; she continued the play by reinstating mother who then, in turn, had to steal the baby back. Unresolved struggles between the parents for the child continued with wearisome repetitiveness, until the anxiety engendered by the continuous necessity to choose one parent and thereby separate from the other finally forced Rita to flight into fairy-tale-like fantasies of a complete, happy family. Characteristically, this had to be a family of four, in which, in addition to mother and father, there was almost always a brother, and then Rita could comfortably become the girl. Only then did she find magical peace; then there was calm and order, as if she had already reached the latency period. Now that there was a girl *and* a boy, everyone was happy; each had what he wanted. This had the trappings of an oedipal position; sexual roles became neatly and correctly differentiated: "Father will be Mr.; mother, Mrs.; and I shall be Miss." She added to these seemingly oedipal fantasies that she would grow up to become "a mommy with three little girls and three little boys, and five little girls and five little boys." It was as if her bisexual condition was resolved by the equal distribution of each sex. This need for regularity and order had surely been influenced by her obsessive and compulsive traits which she had carried into the phallic conflict. It was important to realize that the idealization of father had spread to the *idealization of this complete family*, in which oedipal rivalry, jealousy, and true identification have by avoidance led to premature pseudo solutions.

In this fantasy of a larger family, the boy would bring the father back. Her acceptance of a boy corresponded to an expansion of her relationships in the nursery group. She now could accept the attentions of a boy, a much-sought-after oedipal partner for the other girls, but their relationship was mainly nonsexualized in nature. If we view this as a parallel to the family fantasies, he was accepted only as a sibling to gain father. Confirmation that this maneuver resolved her ambivalence and permitted her to see herself again as a girl lies in the resultant decreased symptomatology: an easing of her need to control, a release of tension, and a marked relaxation in the nursery.

The mother's plan to remarry when Rita was six years old gave us an additional opportunity to study the development of this child. We had several questions in mind: Would she continue to cling to the fantasied image of her father, particularly since she had neither introduced substitute fathers into her play, nor had she in reality formed any attachment to another man; or would she shift her relationship to a stepfather and then continue with him where she had left off with father, namely, to seek phallic completion from him, and with it return to the original behavior of the banishment of her mother when her father first visited? Would she regress, or how far would she progress toward facing a true oedipal conflict in the continuous presence of a man?

For a short period after her prospective stepfather was introduced, oedipal conflicts flared up, with Rita vascillating between not wanting to lose mother to this man, and then wanting him for herself. (Perhaps the stepfather contributed to oedipal stimulation by wooing the mother through the daughter, as one frequently finds under these circumstances.) But the idealization of her complete family soon reasserted itself, supported perhaps by finding in her stepfather's own children the siblings she had prepared for so well in her play. Very much to the relief of mother and stepfather, Rita became a good girl, that is to say, obedient, happy, wishing for the marriage and thereby an early realization of her family dream. After the marriage, her general mood continued to be cheerful and affectionate; she found new friends and seemingly made a good adjustment to the new home and school. We see, then, that her fantasy family had become so cathected that reality was used to support the fantasy rather than to correct it. We had expected that the man who would take part in her real life, unable to live up to idealization, would have to disappoint her, and that this disappointment would be necessary to correct her fantasies and contribute to normal development. Instead, she transferred the idealization of her father to her stepfather; *he* then became the object of her fantasies, whereas it was her fantasy father who disappointed her. The disappointment, therefore, was experienced due to the shift of cathexis from one fantasy father to another but not due to reality testing. It seems that reality came too late to disengage this process. When the idealization was shifted, her own father became the stranger. This was strikingly demonstrated when she was actually confronted with him again at adoption proceedings. At first she did not know him, but when she recognized him finally, she commented critically, "I didn't remember that he had such an ugly nose!" With the shift of cathexis, her father then became devalued, as unreal in the negative sense as he had been before in the positive.

As to the question of oedipal progression, we had no indication that she was able to use her new family to work through her oedipal conflicts. Jealousy, rivalry, fears of castration, and the other oedipal concomitants remained absent.

At seven, Rita is without striking clinical symptomatology. Her sexual identification has proceeded from the initial phallic ambivalence to that of a pseudo-latency girl, without her ever having truly mastered the oedipal conflict. Her superego development is based on anal conflicts and emerged from phallic ambivalence. Her rivalry with mother was too short-lived; castration fear was insufficiently mastered to permit realistic integration through guilt with its anticipation of punishment.

DISCUSSION

We shall now compare our clinical material with similar studies in the literature. Though the cases described do not show a unique clustering of symptoms, there is characteristic pathology of phallic fixations, whether the parent of the same or opposite sex is absent, leading to homosexuality; and superego disturbances, expressed in either a too severe superego with sadistic features of a harsh, pre-oedipal quality, or a deficient superego which allows incestuous acting out. There seem to be a number of dynamic factors which have a decisive influence on the child's development. The most conspicuous one is the remaining parent who, in this sample, was seen to be the preoedipal seducer of the child. This factor is not significant when the child loses a parent after he has reached the oedipal position—a finding which emphasizes the significance of the timing of the loss. The patients of Meiss (1952) and Keiser (1953) each reacted to the loss of the father with the intensification of already existing oedipal conflicts. Meiss's boy endowed his dead father with magically omnipotent and punitive powers, in the service of superego demands; Keiser's girl idealized her absent father in the service of libidinal gratification. Each tried to fulfill his developmental requirement—one in relation to the same-sexed parent, the oedipal rival; the other in relation to the opposite-sexed parent, the oedipal object—thus confirming Fenichel's generalization (1931): "when the parent of the child's own sex dies, this is perceived a, a fulfillment of the oedipal wish with strong feelings of guilt. If the other parent dies, the oedipal longing which remains unsatisfied leads to the fantastic idealization of the dead parent, and to an increase of the longing. The rest depends upon when and how the parent's death becomes known to the child."

The development of fantasies about the missing parent, mentioned here by Fenichel, is a characteristic finding in the literature I have surveyed. While he delineates only the fantasy idealization of the oedipal object for libidinal gratification, the data already described indicate that fantasies of the missing parent have either an extremely idealized or extremely punitive character, or both, depending not simply on the relation of the child's sex to the sex of the missing parent but on the child's developmental demand in accordance with the timing of the loss. Idealization either of the same-sexed parent (Isaacs, 1945) or of the opposite-sexed parent (Fenichel, 1931) in the service of preoedipal needs may predominate when he is lost early in life.[6] We can add that "the rest depends" also on the particular relationship to the remaining parent and on other variables as well: whether the lost object has died, and if not, whether he is totally or only partially unavailable. Whatever the weight of any one factor in an individual case, the fantasy replacement of the missing parent, resulting in disturbed object relations, is one of the dynamics most specific to the oedipal development of a child in a one-parent family.

In comparing our case with others, I shall refrain from drawing general conclusions in view of the small sample and the fact that each author investigated different aspects of the problem. However, in evaluating our data, we found several features which differ from the findings in the literature. Disturbances such as severe fixation,

---

[6] See also Lewin's report (1937) of the idealization of the same-sexed absent parent (lost between the ages of five to ten) at puberty, as a protection against resurgent incestuous conflicts, intensified by the close relationship to the remaining parent.

homosexuality, and superego deviation to the degree found in other cases were not present. Despite the early absence of the father, his influence proved to be more pathological than that of the remaining parent; in addition to his pathology, the timing of his visits, rather than the timing of separation, intensified the already existing developmental conflicts. Yet our data also confirm that the remaining parent's influence is of great importance, but not as maternal seduction. In Rita's history, the mother's influence explains the relative *health* of the child. Mother, with her heterosexual orientation, and in spite of her oral disturbance which she had transmitted to the child, was able to counteract the father's pathology sufficiently to avoid fixation.

In many of the cases cited, the pathological preoedipal relationship to the remaining parent has been shown to affect the vicissitudes of aggression, thus precluding the development of an oedipal relationship to the primary object. In the case of the girls, what has been described is essentially the arrest of development at the primary homosexual level. Rita's case provides an interesting contrast: she too evades the oedipal conflict, though not through phallic fixation, but through a premature flight into latency as an escape from unendurable phallic ambivalence. Without underestimating the effect of the parent's pathology on the child (either the preoedipal mother, or the absent father in Rita's case), this specific factor should be separated from the more general difficulties in facing the oedipal conflict inherent in the absent-parent situation.

The lack of oedipal stimulation, normally found in the continuous day-to-day interplay between the child and each parent, and especially as evidenced by the relationship of the parents to each other, imposes a primary imbalance. *Synchronization* and dosing of oedipal experiences in a continuous reality context, within which phase-specific events can be absorbed, is not present. In the absence of the parental interplay—that is to say, in the absence of the primal scene with all its social equivalents—developmental forces crystallize too suddenly around events, rather than being slowly but continuously interwoven in experience, and hence have an extraordinarily traumatic effect. Thus, in the phallic phase, Rita reacted with exaggerated intensity to separation from the mother; made an attempt at an intense, precipitous oedipal solution following the discovery of her anatomical deficiency; and showed readiness to accept her father's suggested cure.

As we have seen, father's presence, fleeting though it was, threw Rita immediately into an oedipal relationship in which she turned her libidinal interests toward him, and her aggression against the mother. But after her father left, continued aggression against the only remaining object proved too dangerous to maintain; thus, we see phallic ambivalence rather than true oedipal choice. It is possible that under these circumstances even the most optimal mother-child relationship is burdened by a desperate *all-or-none quality*, so that the fear of the loss of the only object masks and dominates the reality of the relationship. Repression of aggression against the mother would therefore seem to be almost inevitable, even without the additional reinforcement of phasic fixations. This may explain why we so frequently find a history of so-called seduction of the child by the mother in the absence of a complete family. Freud points out that this seduction is due to the parent's shift of cathexis from the missing partner to the child. We may add here that the child represses the aggression against the remaining parent and thus reinforces the actual or apparent seduction.

In the continued absence of her father, Rita maintained a pre-oedipal relationship to both parents. The father's image was protected from any aggression on her part by the process of idealization. On the other hand, the aggression manifested itself by her using the father as a vehicle for expressing aggression against the mother (see the kidnaping fantasies). In the fantasies of their future which mother and daughter shared, Rita began to consider a new father, but never risked placing herself in a rivalrous position in relation to mother. She demanded a new father from mother as another pre-oedipal supply—"I love you, do you love me? If you loved me enough, you'd get me another daddy!" Significantly, she never had any opportunity to seek a substitute father. If this had been possible, would she have maintained the fantasy of her idealized father and her dependency on mother?

With the repression of aggression, the castration grievance and all the prephallic grievances which it includes remained unresolved; therefore, an oedipal identification with father or mother was impossible. The continued idealization of the absent father in the face of consistent disappointment finally spread to the image of the family. In her fantasies of a happy family, she established a make-believe world in which comfort and peace were found. Though there was token role-playing in which the sexes of the players were correctly identified, these fantasies never included a true oedipal girl's relationship to the father or an identification with the mother. The family lived happily ever after, but how, we do not know. Without evidence of rivalry with the mother or aggression against either parent with the concomitant guilt, the fantasy of a complete family, from the viewpoint of oedipal development, stops where it should start.

Thus the pseudo-latency solution evades oedipal commitments and betrays its preoedipal origins. Therefore, we can conclude only that the seemingly differentiated representations of self and parents merely cover rather than resolve the phallic ambivalence. When Rita finally found a complete family in reality, idealization of the true father did not lead to disappointment in the stepfather; it seems rather to have perpetuated the state of unrealistic wish fulfillment and contributed to the cathexis of the pseudo-latency imagery. While Rita does not seem to have gross superego deficiency, idealization appears to have impaired reality testing. Hoffer's (1949) differentiation between fantasy and idealization states the process aptly: Idealization, "in contrast to fantasy . . . impels the child to change reality according to his ideals. In his fantasy he turns disappointing parents into satisfactory ones, in idealization he denies what is disappointing without withdrawal from the objects." We are reminded here of the idealization of political leaders, with the same pathology of reality testing and absence of guilt. Greenacre (1959) maintains that the play of children is an attempt to master traumatic experiences under more favorable conditions and therefore is an attempt to establish the sense of reality. Rita's play helped her defenses against injury but did not serve reality testing.

While the absence of a parent in Rita's case has not led to serious pathology, she remains with a developmental deficiency which stems from the lack of having lived through and mastered the oedipal conflict. Jealousy and rivalry, punishment and guilt, instinctual renunciation with resulting ego expansion—these ingredients are missing to provide an adequate texture of the mature psyche, with its "categorical imperative," won only through oedipal participation and solution.

When a parent is absent, there is an absence of oedipal reality. The absent parent becomes endowed with magical power either to gratify or to punish; aggression against him, and the remaining parent as well, becomes repressed. The cases reported in the literature show that existing oedipal conflicts are intensified when a parent leaves during this period. In Rita's case, in which the father was almost totally absent from birth, we predict an oedipal disturbance, which, though only subclinical in degree, is specific in its textural deficiency. Rita is now in her late latency. Further study of her development is needed before the effects of her early experience can be judged with more assurance. A follow-up in her adolescence is essential to test our evaluation and prediction.

Though we have learned to know children who need little aid in development, whose innate strength can do much with little, there still remains an irreducible minimum. At times during the study of Rita, we stressed this innate factor to explain her strength: her capacity to follow the inner unfolding of the maturational and developmental processes. But, just as the autonomous ego is structured by need satisfaction through mothering, so does, as it seems to us, the oedipal Anlage, "the readiness for oedipal experience" described by Anna Freud (1951), require the stimulation of both parents for the unfolding of all the complexities of the oedipal organization.

BIBLIOGRAPHY

Aichhorn, A. (1925), *Wayward Youth*. New York: Viking Press, 1935.
Alpert, A. (1957), A Special Therapeutic Technique for Certain Developmental Disorders in Prelatency Children. *Am. J. Orthopsychiat.*, XXVII.
—— (1959), Reversibility of Pathological Fixations Associated with Maternal Deprivation in Infancy. *This Annual*, XIV.
Bennett, I. & Hellman, I. (1951), Psychoanalytic Material Related to Observations in Early Development. *This Annual*, VI.
Beres, D. & Obers, S. (1950), The Effects of Extreme Deprivation in Infancy on Psychic Structure in Adolescence: A Study in Ego Development. *This Annual*, V.
Bowlby, J. (1951), *Maternal Care and Mental Health*. Geneva: World Health Organization Monograph.
Eisendorfer, A. (1943), The Clinical Significance of the Single Parent Relationship in Women. *Psa. Quart.*, XII.
Fenichel, O. (1930), The Pregenital Antecedents of the Oedipus Complex. *The Collected Papers of Otto Fenichel*, I. New York: Norton, 1954.
—— (1931), Specific Forms of the Oedipus Complex. *The Collected Papers of Otto Fenichel*, I. New York: Norton, 1954.

Ferenczi, S. (1914), The Nosology of Male Homosexuality (Homoerotism). *Sex in Psychoanalysis*. New York: Basic Books, 1950.

Freud, A. (1951), Observations on Child Development. *This Annual*, VI.

—— (1954), In: Problems of Infantile Neurosis. *This Annual*, IX.

—— & Burlingham, D. T. (1943), *War and Children*. New York: International Universities Press.

—— ———————— (1944), *Infants Without Families*. New York: International Universities Press.

—— & Dann, S. (1951), An Experiment in Group Upbringing. *This Annual*, VI.

Freud, S. (1905), Three Essays on the Theory of Sexuality. *Standard Edition*, VII. London: Hogarth Press, 1953.

—— (1910), Leonardo da Vinci and a Memory of His Childhood. *Standard Edition*, XI. London: Hogarth Press, 1957.

—— (1914), On Narcissism: An Introduction. *Collected Papers*, IV. London: Hogarth Press, 1925.

—— (1932), The Psychology of Women. *New Introductory Lectures on Psychoanalysis*. New York: Norton, 1932.

Gelinier-Ortigues, M. & Aubry, J. (1955), Maternal Deprivation, Psychogenic Deafness and Pseudo-Retardation. In: *Emotional Problems of Early Childhood*, ed. G. Caplan. New York: Basic Books.

Glaser, K. & Eisenberg, L. (1956), Maternal Deprivation. *Pediatrics*, XVIII.

Goldfarb, W. (1947), Variations in Adolescent Adjustment of Institutionally Reared Children. *Am. J. Orthopsychiat.*, XVII.

Greenacre, P. (1959), Play in Relation to Creative Imagination. *This Annual*, XIV.

Hoffer, W. (1949), Deceiving the Deceiver. In: *Searchlights on Delinquency*, ed. K. R. Eissler. New York: International Universities Press.

Isaacs, S. (1943), An Acute Psychotic Anxiety Occurring in a Boy of Four Years. *Childhood and After*. New York: International Universities Press, 1949.

—— (1945), Fatherless Children. *Childhood and After*. New York: International Universities Press, 1949.

Kaffman, M. (1956), *Investigation of the Behavior of 403 Kibbutz Children*. Israel: Institute for Research in Collective Education.

Keiser, S. (1953), A Manifest Oedipus Complex in an Adolescent Girl. *This Annual*, VIII.

Lewin, B. D. (1937), A Type of Neurotic Hypomanic Reaction. *A.M.A. Arch. Neurol. Psychiat.*, XXXVII.

Mead, M. (1954a), Some Theoretical Considerations on the Problem of Mother-Child Separation. *Am. J. Orthopsychiat.*, XXIV.

—— (1954b), In: *Discussions on Child Development* (Proceedings of the World Health Organization Study Group on the Psychobiological Development of the Child), II, ed. J. M. Tanner & B. Inhelder. New York: International Universities Press.

Meiss, M. (1952), The Oedipal Problem of a Fatherless Child. *This Annual*, VII.

Nunberg, H. (1932), *Allgemeine Neurosenlehre*. Berne: Huber.

—— (1949), *Problems of Bisexuality as Reflected in Circumcision*. London: Imago Publ.

—— (1955), *Principles of Psychoanalysis*. New York: International Universities Press.

Plank, E. N. & Plank, R. (1954), Emotional Components in Arithmetical Learning as Seen Through Autobiographies. *This Annual*, IX.

Reich, A. (1954), Early Identifications as Archaic Elements in the Superego. *J. Am. Psa. Assn.*, II.

Rosen, V. (1953), On Mathematical Illumination and the Mathematical Thought Process: A Contribution to the Genetic Development and Metapsychology of Abstract Thinking. *This Annual*, VIII.

Spitz, R. & Wolf, K. M. (1946), Anaclitic Depression. *This Annual*, II.

Wulff, M. (1942), A Case of Male Homosexuality. *Int. J. Psa.*, XXIII.

FANTASIES OF A BORDERLINE PATIENT[1]

MARIE B. SINGER (London)

Systematic investigation of any patient's fantasies should ideally reveal not only the etiology of his own disturbances but also the nature of repressed instinctual activity in the normal person.

Such an investigation should be particularly rewarding with children of latency years, since here the normal child uses much ego and superego energy to establish fortifications against instinctual drives. His fantasies are often of a high social order, involving glorification of socially accepted heroes, but the break-through of occasional instinctual drives is no more prevalent or abnormal than the overzealous behavior of many adults; indeed it is this fact which establishes his fantasy life and activities as normal, and a preparation for community life. We seldom, however, come in close contact with the normal child's fantasy life, except to observe his exaggeration of the hero's importance, his almost overidentification with the hero.

With neurotic latency children, however, the cracks in the foundation of these similar fortifications are more evident, coming to light in the form of symptoms such as bed wetting, temper tantrums, stealing, etc., which represent a compromise between the ego and the defended instinctual impulses. Long and hard work is needed before the neurotic latency patient will admit glimpses into the fantasies that overlay the instinctual activity.

The barricades of a child on the borderline between neurosis

[1] This case was treated by the author at the Hampstead Child Therapy Clinic in London. Since it was begun as part of her training in the Hampstead Child Therapy Course, she would like to acknowledge the help received from Mrs. H. Abraham Schwarz in supervision.

The Hampstead Child Therapy Course and Clinic are maintained by grants given by the following Foundations: The Field Foundation, Inc., New York; The Ford Foundation, New York; The Foundations' Fund for Research in Psychiatry, New Haven, Connecticut; The Anna Freud Foundation, New York; The Grant Foundation Inc., New York; The Estate of Flora Haas, New York; The Old Dominian Foundation, U.S.A.; The Psychoanalytic Research and Development Fund, Inc., New York.

and psychosis, however, are more brittle. In spite of solid areas, they are ready in places to give way to the slightest pressure, so that great quantities of instinctual material seep through—sometimes, indeed, flood through and almost overwhelm the patient, not to mention the therapist, whose job is then not so much to manage the material as to patch up the holes. If this should happen during the early weeks, when the main effort would be used to acquaint the patient with therapeutic technique and to establish a firm relationship, it is even harder to maintain therapeutic poise.

This was one of the problems presented by Albert, a borderline patient of latency years. At the age of ten years, eight months, he brought fantasies to the first analytic hour, and in the weeks that followed, he dominated the treatment situation with a variety of fantasy activities. And although the form changed at various stages during the seven years of therapy, he continued to communicate with me mainly in terms of fantasy.

For the purpose of this discussion, I have organized the analytic material in six phases. These will be considered, from the standpoint of normal, neurotic, and borderline[2] manifestations, in the section headed "Consideration" at the end of each phase. However, it should be noted that in the treatment of borderline patients such as the present one, sheer volume of analytic material alone poses overwhelming technical questions. Whether it comes in profuse acting out in bodily forms or in a steady outpouring of fantasies and other associations, the atmosphere of the treatment hour is one of chaos. Often the therapist must act before she understands, in order to prevent the patient's becoming hopelessly overstimulated and caught up in his own excitement, which often rises to a rapid momentum during the session. Daily note taking following the hour may fill many more pages, and periodic review of these for staff reports is likely to involve hours of sorting.

In the preparation of a paper such as this, which covers almost eight years of therapy, the problem is greatly magnified. Volumes of notes must be reviewed (now in the light of new insights) and, in the case of this patient, dozens of his own notebooks containing fantasy

2 By "borderline" in the research at the Hampstead Clinic mentioned below, we mean the border between neurosis and psychosis; in the case discussed here, as became apparent, paranoia.

stories, drawings, and paintings. Once more, the therapist becomes engulfed in chaos and disequilibrium in her search for lines which she may follow to bring the material into focus. But this very process of organization is misleading, because it gives the impression that the material originally came in an orderly manner, that it was fully understood at the time it was dealt with. It becomes all too neat and systematic. An alternative method is to record the process of the material just as it came, and the fumbling insights as they developed. This method would be essential to a technical discussion. However, when the focus is on some particular aspect of the material itself, such as the subject I have chosen, process recording would seem to defeat the purpose of the work, since the reader could only be caught up in a whirlwind, where motion, speed, and confusion would blur the object.

For convenience, I give here a brief anamnesis of Albert's case up to the beginning of his analytic treatment; a full anamnesis would be very lengthy, including, for example, much significant parental material. The present one is confined to what is most relevant to this paper, including some incidents which on their recall during analysis were shown to have an especial, usually traumatic, significance.

Anamnesis

Albert was born in September, 1941, a first baby. The birth, and that of later babies, was by Caesarean section. His father was a regular soldier, and mostly away in the war. His mother was a working woman and, so far as the care of Albert and later children permitted, took jobs as cleaner, etc., to help support the family. During the war Albert traveled a good deal in trains with his mother, or went to railway stations, in connection with his father's military service. They spent some time evacuated with the maternal grandparents. His grandfather worked on the railway and, when Albert was three and a half years old, had an accident involving the loss of a finger.

When Albert was two and a half a brother was born. Hitherto Albert had been the chief person in his mother's world, with especially close contact in wartime circumstances (such as travels in blackouts and air raids and times in air-raid shelters), and had also had much attention from other relatives. All this naturally changed at this time, and his history of troubles began. The father returned home when Albert was three years old. It appears that at the time of Albert's birth, and in later years, the father accused the mother of unfaithfulness and declared that Albert was not his own child; this accusation was not made in respect of the later children.

The mother reported that up to two and a half years Albert was a well-behaved and clever child, "very normal." Her evidence for this, however, included such points as very early cleanliness, remarkable quietness, and other signs of what she called "forwardness," which make the picture of "normality" somewhat suspect. Her accounts in general, and those of the father, were difficult to evaluate, largely owing to their own difficult though close relationship. At any rate, it seems that at the age of three and a half Albert started to be violently destructive and disturbed. He swallowed a coin and was hospitalized, being strapped to the bed for his own safety (and that of hospital property); his mother was kept away. When he returned after eight days he started soiling, had uncontrollable tempers, and wandered about a lot. His behavior now and henceforward was generally regarded by all acquaintances, including doctors and teachers, as abnormal.

At the age of five Albert went to infant school, where his unusual behavior included drinking paint water, eating plasticine and chalk, and biting people. He was sent to a child guidance clinic because of his aggressive behavior and his inability to stand frustration. He had attacks resembling petit mal, but the medical report on this states that although "the E.E.G. showed a dominant frequency of 7 a second . . . no epileptic activity was recorded."

When Albert was seven years old another brother was born. During this pregnancy, which Albert knew of and violently resented, he spent eight weeks in an isolation hospital with scarlet fever. He was extremely aggressive with the new baby and could not be safely left with him. During the next year he developed his most alarming symptom—walking on the Underground, along the railway lines. Other abnormalities of behavior developed, which will be noted in the account of his analysis. His schoolfellows often called him, not unnaturally, "Mad Hansom."[3] Altogether he got on badly at school.

3 "Albert Hansom" is not his real name; there is an onomatopoetic reference to his real surname in connection with the familiar term "Mad Hatter."

At the age of seven years there were masturbatory incidents with a delinquent man.

At the age of ten Albert was referred by the child guidance clinic to the Hampstead Clinic, as more intensive therapy seemed the only hope of cure. The degree of abnormality in behavior, with extreme subjection to fantasies, suggested the borderline of psychosis; and the I.Q. was 80, although the tests suggested that emotional difficulties rather than mental inadequacy might be responsible for this low score (as later proved to be the case). The boy himself made a good physical appearance, and could show himself as alert, well spoken, and prepossessing. We hesitated to take him, but a preliminary period of two months was encouraging and it was decided to try. The case forms part of the project described by Anna Freud (1958) under the heading "An Inquiry into the Analysis of Borderline Cases." Albert's progress, with its limitations, is described in what follows. The material is presented as a contribution to the understanding of some kinds of fantasy (with, I think, qualitative as well as quantitative distinctions from normal and neurotic) rather than as an assessment of possible progress with a borderline case.

First Phase

During the early months, Albert brought fantasies chiefly in the form of *body language*, in which a part or the whole of his body was in more or less constant motion. His most persistent and intense form of motility was a rapid side-to-side wiggling of the right index finger, rhythmical though jerky, over maps and street directories, which were his main preoccupation during the analytic hour. This continued for several years before it stopped as a result of interpretation, and was revived afterwards during periods of stress. The finger waving was sometimes accompanied by a loud purring sound, as the patient turned the pages of the street directories, or came to the end of a railway line which he traced on a map, or distinguished the route between stations on the Underground maps. It would go like this: "WHOOEEEEOO . . . . EALING BROADWAY . . . WHOOEEEEOO . . . WEST ACTON . . . WHOOOEEEEEOOO . . . NORTH ACTON," etc. The same sounds were heard as he entered and left the treatment room and the Clinic building, and it was evident that they served as an unconscious means of securing a feeling of continuity between his outside life and the treatment.

Another form of body language involved the whole body. This was a short-stepped trotting in circles. During this activity, which was also accompanied by engine noises and announcement of stations, he paused and made movements which resembled the opening and shutting of train doors, and he marshaled imaginary passengers in and out of his fantasy train. Both finger-waving and trotting movements were performed precisely and with great intensity. He could not be distracted from them. While Albert made no direct verbal contact with me during these performances, he maintained contact through frequent, furtive glances. A move of the hand or a brief glance away from him might result in the patient's withdrawal into silent study of maps and street directories. In these moods, he sat in rigid immobile posture and completely ignored me.

Any attempt to participate in his map world might serve as seduction; he frequently tried to kiss, cuddle, and feel my body. Whenever I tried to divert such bodily contacts by offering substitutes, he responded with another form of body language: random types of movements such as kicking, crawling, jumping, flinging arms, laughing, and talking wildly to himself. On such occasions, the index finger was used to scratch in the area of the penis, to pull mucus from nose—which he ate; or to dig in the area of the anus up his trouser leg. The finger, with feces under nail, had to be examined, smelled, and sometimes licked. Similarly he smelled the pages of the Underground maps and on several occasions commented: "They smell like electricity."

Thus far, the patient's body language and sounds, with routine repetition of street names and stations, told us the following:

(a) that he is a train engine;
(b) an engineer, who plans and examines train routes;
(c) a conductor—in control of the entering and leaving of passengers;
(d) that he himself personifies the stations at which the train stops;
(e) and that he has a penchant for the Circle and Central Lines of the London Underground.

It was apparent that the patient's main defense against instinctual activity was denial in fantasy, and that the central fantasy was that of omnipotently controlling the railway system. In body language, as in words, he dwelt upon symbols that left no doubt that we were dealing with oedipal material. From this he regressed at times to pre-verbal stages, and these were signaled by feelings of rejection when I failed to respond to his sexual approaches, or to satisfy other demands immediately, or when I interrupted his fantasy of omni-potent control.

Why did the patient make such extensive and intensive use of his body to communicate, when he had a good vocabulary and used words in the right sense? We know that the analytic process stimu-lates a certain amount of regression, but Albert used body language at home and in the street as well as during treatment. For example, he sat on his mother's lap, embraced and felt her body. In his rela-tionship with her, he had always been physically demonstrative. When he was a small boy, wartime conditions contributed to this closeness; they had cuddled in air-raid shelters and slept together during the father's absence. Her world had revolved round him, and he had also received a lot of attention and gifts from a large family of aunts, uncles, and four grandparents. He had been the first grandchild.

Then, all this had changed after the birth of Albert's first brother and the return of his father soon afterwards. The small boy of two and a half years had wandered from home into the neighbors' houses and gardens. His behavior during the treatment hour when he tried to draw me into a symbiotic-type relationship through attempts to use my body as an extension of his own, that is, as a sexual object, by withdrawing from me when I failed to meet his sexual wishes—all appear to be a re-enactment of this earlier experience, when it was said his disturbances began.[4] On the other hand, the social history does not adequately account for the particular form in which

[4] Ekstein and Friedman (1957) have discussed this stage in terms of object relation-ships: "The preverbal period of personality development, in which motility and motor developments are dominant, takes place usually in a symbiotic relationship. The mother is used as the auxiliary ego, which not only gratifies and prohibits, but also thinks for the infant who, in a certain sense, is capable of a kind of 'thought' only as is expressed through impulsive action whenever need arises. As the psychic apparatus develops, modes of problem solution grow richer and impulsive action is supplemented by play action" (p. 582).

the motility appeared, e.g., acting like a train. Although Albert came into continuous contact with trains as a small boy—traveling about the country with his mother to visit his father at various army camps, or meeting his father at railway stations or even witnessing the arrival of his grandfather in an ambulance, following an accident in which he lost his finger, while working on the lines—neither the contacts nor the excitement associated with them appear originally to have gone beyond the limits of normality. There is no single traumatic experience in his infancy which would account for the tremendous cathexis he later put on trains. There is, however, evidence that this cathexis was focused at a very early age—between two and a half and three years—by which time he had memorized the "Little Red Engine" series of books, and would go into tantrums when his mother failed to read every word accurately. Other causes for tantrums at this age were more normally whenever his mother failed to read for a certain time every evening; and more abnormally whenever she failed to arrange his books in the order he thought appropriate on account of their color. However, the medical history offers some clues to his alternation between stupor and overactivity: at about the age of six years, Albert had attacks resembling petit mal, even of absolute rigidity, following hyperactive display of bodily movements.

Albert's comment that maps smelled like electricity was no casual fluke. It hinted at one of his most dangerous forms of fantasy acting. He had come to the Hampstead Clinic with a long history of truanting from home and school to walk on Underground railway lines, through tunnels, from one station to another. What exactly happened in the Underground was not known, but Albert had been brought home by policemen on several occasions, with his body covered with tar and dirt, having been discovered at various points between Underground stations. It had been evident to them that he put his life in serious jeopardy. One slip and he would have been electrocuted. Repeatedly he had been warned of this danger, yet this symptom, which began at the age of seven years, when a second brother was born, persisted. During the first months of the analysis a condition of the Clinic's continuing the treatment was that this activity should cease. Although the patient had been in analysis only a few weeks when this prohibition was made, already he had formed a strong enough relationship with me to meet this analytic demand. He was, we might say, able to take advantage of a borrowed ego. The symptom did not, to my knowledge, recur.

Consideration of the First Phase

The form and content of the ten-year-old Albert's fantasy are those appropriate to a normal three-year-old boy, whose play at being a train is an acceptable form of communication. We know that neurotic patients of Albert's age make elaborate use of motility to bring their analytic material, but Albert's motility seemed more intense and obsessional than that of either a neurotic of his age or a normal three-year-old boy. Moreover, he not only fantasied himself to be in control of the railway system, but actually walked on the railway lines, and in fact "became" a train. This act exceeded neurotic boundaries, and showed a basic fault in testing the land between fantasy and reality.[5] Yet we find that the elaborate train fantasy, which was the ego's main defense against instinctual drives, broke down at times, and we find the patient making advances of a sexual nature, cuddling, kissing, etc. It is against the emergence of such instinctual wishes that the normal latency child builds strong intellectual defensive barriers. In the case of the neurotic child, compromise between ego, superego, and id would undoubtedly take the form of a symptom comprising a restrictive influence of the superego, in the direction of flight from danger—such as a train phobia. This is in contrast to the id method of acting out as a train. In fact, during Albert's fifth year of therapy, he "moved on" to a train phobia, and eventually mastered the situation to the extent of being able to use trains normally.

SECOND PHASE

During the next few months, the scope of the forms of expressing fantasy broadened. While the patient continued to bring his fantasies largely in body language, sound, and routine recitation of

[5] Anna Freud (1936) discusses the limits to which such behavior is accepted as normal: "The indulgent attitude of [grownups] towards the child's mechanism of denial vanishes the moment that he ceases to make the transition from phantasy to reality readily, without delay or hitch, or tries to shape his actual behaviour according to his phantasies—to put it more exactly, the moment his phantasy-activity ceases to be a game and becomes an automatism or an obsession" (p. 92).

streets and stations, he occasionally digressed from these into other forms of communication:

(a) *Marginal Comments.* As he traced or acted the route of the Circle Line, he would say this was his "favorite line," because "you never come to the end of it"; or that he would like to be a conductor on a "Main Line train." On other occasions, while reading map instructions, he inserted the warning as to what happened when children do not have a ticket and go on the railway lines. He said, "Children must not go on the lines because of the struggle. It is very dangerous." When asked about the "struggle," he said it occurred where the lines "clanged together" or where they "clang and make sparks."

(b) *Writing Long Lists of Street Names.* What seemed to be an arbitrary selection of tube stations and streets was reduced to one of Albert's systematic frames of reference. For example, streets were selected on the basis of some common aspect such as railway bridges, tunnels, parks. Streets with tunnels were "better" than those without tunnels. The most "exciting bridges" were those connecting streets over railway lines. Streets were also selected on an alphabetical basis: those beginning with the same letter had to be recorded by the patient in large, sprawling letters, in different colored pencils. He had filled several notebooks with these before he invited me to take part. Now the scope of my role broadened from that of provider of large numbers of maps, street directories, pencils, and that of attentive onlooker, to recorder of street names. These had to be listed accurately according to his rapid dictation and in appropriate color pencil. It was noted that Albert had a particular attraction for streets beginning with the letter A—such as Abridge Road, Acacia Place. Each day, the recording had to "begin with the A's," so that more than half of the streets recorded in his notebooks (also of different color) began with the first letter of the alphabet. The meaning of this practice came some weeks after the writing began. When he came to a street called Avenue Road, he roared with laughter and explained: "Here's somebody with two surnames and no Christian name."

A tendency to repeat from memory a specific number of streets, which on the surface had none of the common factors mentioned earlier, was puzzling until Albert gave the following clues: when he came to Campion Street, which was his own, he became excited and commented on this fact. After a time, he began adding numbers before the streets and postal zones after them. This he called "a mystery," which he later revealed in this manner: "These streets are the children in my class." Then he added their names to the addresses. He had, in fact, memorized the exact address of all his fifty-one classmates.

(c) *Fantasy News Reports.* After the first treatment holiday Albert brought the following news with the conviction of a factual experience:

> I went for a walk, and there was a sign at Holders Hill Road which read: "Dangerous Road, Just be Careful at This Crossing!" There were no gates, it was most dangerous. I was standing at the "STOP." The cars waited until the train left, then they rushed on, but one car was a bit quick and rushed into the engine, hitting the head of the engine. It made me jump. Five children were killed. The policeman took no notice. The mother and father were killed too.

(d) *Short Dramatic Sketches.* Like the fantasy news, the sketch was suggested by a place on the map, from which he digressed, using toy animals and people as actors. For example, at Acton Station, the following tragedy occurred in one of his fantasied dramas:

> Just before going through the tunnel, a little boy got on the train with a horse. People gave a surprised look and were afraid as the horse stalked through the train. The conductor was very surprised; he said, "We must get this horse out of here." Later, a sheep got on at Cockfosters. At Hendon Rising, the conductor threw the little boy out because he brought the animals on the train. Threw him on the lines. The little boy's head was split, and he had to have *stitches* in hospital.

The sketch had to be elaborated and re-enacted many times. It became as intense a form of communication as the finger waving and writing of lists.

In the form of verbal communications, the patient has given important clues to his fantasy world of maps and trains:

(a) streets equal people—not people in general, but particular people, e.g., classmates, and Albert is proud to be listed among them;

(b) tunnels and bridges are of special importance;

(c) he prefers to be a conductor on a Main Line train;

(d) dangerous things happen to children and their parents at railway crossings or on trains; they may land in the hospital or be killed;

(e) children, especially, are warned of danger at points where railway lines "clang together and make sparks."

In Albert's use of form in which fantasies were communicated, we encounter one of the basic differences between the neurotic and the borderline patient. While the neurotic fights analytic efforts by delaying insights into his fantasy world, the borderline patient resists with the well-formulated system which he has already devised. Albert's method consisted in the use of increasingly elaborate forms of expression and complexities in detail. And his control of the treatment situation, as shown in his employment of the therapist in the service of fantasy form (writing down streets), indicated a denial of his need of analytic therapy. By using elaborate motility and dramatic form to deter therapeutic work, he could not only become both patient and therapist, just as his finger took over the function of penis in his anal hole, but he could also assume a multiplicity of other roles in a magical way. He could be omnipotent. And there is no doubt here that the patient was identifying with the pre-oedipal, fantasied, omnipotent mother of his early life, to whom he longed to return, as shown in the persistent return to streets beginning with the first letter of the alphabet—A for Albert. In fantasy, he could also identify with his classmates: by writing their names down, he could achieve the normal latency boy's goal of becoming one of the boys. Thus, fantasy enabled him to deny his insignificant place among them in the classroom.

A working through of interpretations based on these insights brought about a gradual widening of Albert's reality span: he began to participate in his schoolwork, he acquired his first friend, and it is not surprising that at this time he identified with a delinquent boy in his class. In his company, Albert acted out the fantasy of

stealing the father's big penis, by pilfering money from a bus conductor's "big bag" at the terminal station. He was brought before
the Children's Court and placed on probation. In spite of this antisocial act, Albert had become more social at school, where aggressive
attacks upon schoolmates had stopped, thus demonstrating his ability
to respond to interpretations of his oedipal jealousies and rivalries.

Consideration of the Second Phase

During this phase, Albert's fantasies have provided additional
glimpses into the structure of the superego: on the one hand, we
observe the superego functioning on the embryonic level in which
admonitions of the parents, e.g., "Children must not go on the lines,"
are repeated in parrotlike fashion by the young child who has not
introjected them. But Albert was well over eleven years of age, and
still functioning far beneath the normal latency boy in this respect.
How do we account for his retardation in superego development?
We will look to his fantasies for explanation: from the same fantasy
story, we learn that prohibitions had become sexualized. It was not
for reasons of bodily safety and preservation that the children were
cautioned not to walk on the lines, but rather to avoid seeing where
the lines "clanged together and made sparks." Thus, the danger was
imagined to be in the "struggle"—which symbolized sexual intercourse. Here we observe the id making inroads upon the superego,
and the conflict between the two institutions is observable in the
ego's weaknesses. I refer to the earlier malfunction of the instinct for
self-preservation, and now to the inability to test ego boundaries—
he had treated the bus conductor's possessions as if they were his own.

A step further in superego development is suggested in the
fantasy sketch of the little boy's being thrown off the train. Here the
patient gives evidence not of having introjected the critical parents
or the idealized ones, as the normal latency boy does, but of setting
up the cruel, punishing imago so characteristic of the superego of
the neurotic latency child. But it was not only the punishing father,
symbolized by the conductor, with whom the patient identifies in
fantasy, but the physically handicapped mother—the little boy had
to go to a hospital for stitches as she had done when each of her
children were delivered by Caesarean section. Identification with his
mother had been observed earlier in his concentration on female

symbols: bridges, tunnels, Circle Line, holes; this he acted out upon his own body openings—digging in nose, mouth, anus, thus treating his own body as if it were his mother's. This double identification is also characteristic of neurotic children. Nor does the acting out in the form of stealing exceed neurotic boundaries. Yet there was a quality in Albert's persistent and compulsory exposure of his four-year-old brother to the traffic on a very busy highway, in spite of repeated warnings from his parents, which, coupled with his earlier disregard of his own safety, indicates that the ego was too weak to arbitrate between the overpowering id impulses and an essentially retarded and punishing superego.

Another aspect of the fantasies adds to the diagnostic picture: the revelation that for him streets were people. Our earlier observation of his intense preoccupation with streets now gives evidence that for Albert, fantasy had to a large extent replaced and remodeled reality. Now the therapeutic aim was clearer: instead of leading the patient from a confused reality to the fantasies that accounted for the confusion, he must be led from a world of fantasy gradually into bits of reality. For it had been shown that the patient was unable to tolerate more than small bits of reality. Slowly it became evident that with the borderline patient the usual management of fantasy needed to be reversed. Whereas with the neurotic patient the therapist leads the patient to disclose fantastic bits of instinctual material which lead to the core of his conflicts and to the etiology of his disturbances, with the borderline patient one must go from fantasy into bits of reality, broadening the scope of reality with every successive phase of analytic work.

THIRD PHASE

While the function and content of the fantasies changed during successive phases of the analysis, the forms, embodying the fantasies, initiated during this phase (approximately the second year of treatment when Albert was about twelve), remained the same. There were eight prevalent forms:

(a) Essentially, the *serial story* was the specific form in which Albert brought his fantasies. They appeared no longer predominantly in a system of body movements, nor a chain of street names and stations, nor disconnected verbal fragments, isolated stories, and dramatic sketches—though he used all of these occasionally within the framework of his stories—but there were ever more complicated series of stories which depended for their unity upon common characters: Chief Baby, Jaguar, the Hedgehog, Jesus, Chief Detective Clark, and finally, in a massive autobiographical sequence, Albert himself. These characters usually dominated series of a dozen or more stories. When a new character had gone on for a time, Albert had to go back and pick up the main characters of the previous series and weave them into the present sequence in subsidiary roles. Thus, the main characters replaced the Central, Circle, and Main Lines of his maps; and the subsidiary ones, the various branch lines of the Underground network. In this continuous reorganization, no character ever got lost.

(b) Further insurance against being lost came through the patient's forcing me to *write down stories* accurately in various colored notebooks, of which some dozen were compiled during the analysis. These books, which clearly symbolized the earlier "Little Red Engine" series, were his most prized treatment possessions. His first move when he entered the treatment room was to collect all the books, and he could identify the stories contained in them by the color of the covers. He became upset whenever a book was out of place.

(c) Later on, he used the *books for reference* rather than for dictation.

(d) Still later, the rapid *reading of stories* from these notebooks and from fiction books (whose characters and incidents were woven into Albert's own series) became the principal form of communication.

(e) At times, he resorted to *acting out the stories in dramatic form*, as he had done in presenting the animals on the train.

(f) Among all this, he gradually included *items of actual events*: from home, school, the Scouts, his paper route, and his various full-time jobs. However, these real events had to be got at through the analysis of his fantasies.

(g) *Exaggerated versions of real events* were brought in all of the earlier forms: stories, dramatic sketches, acting out, both inside and outside the treatment room.

(h) *Drawing, painting and clay modeling.*

Up to this phase, the train had been the central character of Albert's fantasy activities. People and animals were merely incidental. During this third phase, as the result of analytic explanations, the strong train defense deteriorated, giving way to fantasies about animate objects: animals and people. At first, animals emerged as title characters in the various sequences: "The Sheep on the Moors," "The Jaguar," and "The Hedgehog in the Haystack." In these stories, we observe extensive ego defense operations: complexities of forms of expression, depersonalization, confusion of role, and other means of camouflage so characteristic of dream patterns. But in spite of these elaborate attempts to disguise and to ward off instinctual activity, the latter frequently emerged in the form of acting out.

As for the content of the fantasy stories, the analytic work brought us ever closer to the various ingredients of the patient's instinctual life. For example, in "The Sheep on the Moors" sequence, the patient returned to the station Cockfosters, where the little boy had brought the sheep onto the train. Now the mother sheep and her little "Ba Ba" went for a walk on the moors, where they ate grass happily together all day long. Later, they were joined by several additional "Ba Bas," and the activities of this family of sheep formed the theme of many stories: fights between "Ba Bas"; attacks by fiercer animals and farmers—all dramatically acted by the patient with toy ainmals and people. Sometimes he played the role of mother, at other times the several "Ba Bas," or the intruding father sheep, or the Jaguar, "fiercest of all animals," who herded the sheep into enclosures, attacked and killed them. At other times, in the role of the eldest "Ba Ba," he rescued the sheep family and carried them safely back to Cockfosters. Sometimes the same "Ba Ba" incited the Jaguar to destroy them, or he employed the farmer to shoot the Jaguar and the father. All of these were restored to life by Jesus. But the repetitive enactment of these fantasies could not cope with the patient's unconscious ambivalence toward the various members of his family. He digressed from animals to a family of dolls, which he named after his own parents and brothers in a complicated way, presenting the father doll as the young boy, etc. With these dolls, he acted a series of family meals which were intensely exciting occasions. Here we find a repetition of the sheep themes: mother and baby boy enjoying a peaceful tea party, interrupted by brothers. Fights over food began, and the peaceful family meal became the scene of a battle—dishes and tea were thrown about the room, aggressive attacks were made upon the brother dolls, whose "bottoms" were bit into. On such occasions, Albert would rush to the lavatory. The father doll, who appeared during tea time, was kidnaped by a robber, who burned his legs for wood. Having assigned the role of the father to me, the patient was able to give vent to aggression toward me under the disguise of acting. Attempts to cuddle and kiss were now replaced by rough attempts to feel my breasts or overturn my chair. His earlier embraces could now be explained as attempts to ward off his urge to be sadistic and to kill.

In these dramatic fantasies, Albert described the intense narcissistic injury suffered by the toddler whose omnipotent wishes were shattered. The Jaguar, which symbolized his destructive wishes, and Jesus, standing for his loving feelings, now compete in almost equal strength in one of the Jaguar stories in which a baby boy is auctioned on the High Road. The Jaguar carries the baby on his head and cries out: "Baby to be had. Baby to be had."

As an "Old Woman," I was instructed to bid for the baby, who was sold to me with the warning that the child would be reclaimed if I hurt him. Then Albert instructed me to kill the baby in the following manner: "Cut him with a knife, then ram a gun up his bottom, and put a bullet up his bottom. Leave him to bleed and die."

The Jaguar then asked: "What have you done to this baby?" The Jaguar took the baby and bound the Old Woman in ropes. Then Jesus came to heal the child:

"He put a small hole in the bottom and then the business came out and the baby was risen and well again. God put his hand over the Old Lady's head, undid the ropes with his sharp teeth and they all went happily down the road."

Here the patient used the dramatic form to bring an early memory: that of his hospital experience at the age of three and a half years, when he had swallowed a coin. Like the Old Lady, he had been tied to his bed; like Chief Baby, he had been given enemas to "let the business out"; like Jesus, the doctors had healed him. But Albert had been forced to take the passive role in these earlier experiences. Now, in fantasy, he could take the active role. But this particular defensive operation of the ego was not successful in dealing with instinctual material. In the "Fire of London" series which followed, Chief Baby, with the help of the Jaguar, set fire to the whole of London, beginning at Hungerford Bridge, and destroyed all the big buildings: St. Pauls, Big Ben, Westminster, etc. Only one inhabitant survived—Mr. Hansom, Albert's father. It was he who called Jesus down from heaven to restore life and property.

Much later, I learned that a baby boy had, in fact, been born in Albert's home. A young unmarried lodger, of whom he was particularly fond, had been moved to Albert's room during confinement. Albert had been sent to his brother's room, thus repeating earlier events around the birth of his younger brother. The ego's deficiencies in reality testing were indicated in Albert's spreading news in the neighborhood that the baby was, in fact, his father's, and he persisted in referring to the child as his brother. On the day the Jaguar stories began, Albert came to the Clinic in a terrified state, claiming there was a gang of boys threatening to kill him.

"The Fire of London," symbolic of coitus, and the wish to destroy the father's big penis, symbolized by the big buildings, also represented the small boy's fear of castration and annihilation upon the advent of the father who joined the family late in the boy's life, for it was here that the father's strength and heroism began. And we later find him the title character of a sequence of stories: "The Adventures of Police Sergeant Hansom," assisted by Detective Albert Hansom, his son.

But the fantasied identification with the heroic father broke down at various points, and we observe the instinctual material against which the ego attempted to defend itself. For example, in one of the fantasies, Albert became a detective of his parents' nightly sex activities. With his brothers, he roamed the countryside, following them under bridges, where they engaged in smearing "dog's business" on each other. They had "lied" to the children, claiming to be searching for "gold nuggets in rusty pipes." The following excerpts are taken from his notebooks:

Mother and Daddy wee weed on each other—he out of his winkle, she out of her hole. They aim at each other, making noises: Whoooooeeeeeoooooo, Whoooooeeeooo.

This same sound was made by the "Spook Train," a character in another sequence of stories. The father begins as detective and ends in "dirty" activities:

While sitting on the moor near Totteridge Lane, we [Albert's family] saw smoke come from a hole in the ground. [This part of the fantasy was suggested by a picture in one of Enid Blyton's books.] It looked like a volcano. Mr. Hansom traced the smoke to a derelict railway line which was no longer in use. An old man, called Wooden Leg Sam, warned us of the dangers of the Spook Train. Sam said the Spook Train would take away my winkle to punish me for playing with it. He threatened to put a hole in my bottom if I told anyone about the Spook Train, which had dangerous explosives inside. It was operated by escaped criminals . . .
[Now, the "Spook Train" merges with the parents' nightly activities:] Mother and Daddy wee wee over each other to make each other into Spook Trains. That's why I make noises like a train on the streets—to let them know I heard them. I've told Mother and Daddy to stop this business of turning each other into Spook Trains. They could not make a living for us, and the three children will die. I wonder if they were Spook Trains coming out of a tunnel, would they be happy?

The natural outcome of these anal activities is an anal baby. Now the patient, in the company of his brothers, identifies with the treacherous parents and begins a search for the rusty pipe with the gold nuggets. They wander over fields and find in a haystack, not the iron pipe, but a hedgehog. The farmer attacks them and takes the boys to the police for trespassing his property.

These are familiar anal fantasies in which the child, denying his wish to participate in the parents' secret relationship, degrades them to dirty, forbidden activities. What is unusual is the patient's attempts to act out these fantasies during the latency years. After school hours and during week ends, Albert's leisuretime was spent walking obsessionally through the same fields for a certain number of hours each day—three or four. In the analytic sessions, he reported the following reasons for these trips: to count bridges, or to look for haystacks (at times, in fact, trespassing on property, since he was attracted to signs which read: "Keep Off, No Trespassing"). At other times, he looked for iron pipes. Whatever the particular explanation was, his parents and the youngest brother, who sometimes accompanied him, attested to the fact that he roamed the fields in search of the various things Albert described to me. This symptom did not respond to interpretation. Even when, much later on, Albert began work and could no longer engage in daily walks, he devoted most of his week ends to these obsessional journeys. That they were connected with the fantasy of his parents' sexual activities was shown in some of his acting out: it was in the fields, at the age of seven years, that (as was later learned) he participated in masturbatory activities with a delinquent man who paid him; it was during walks with a friend of his own age that Albert provoked the friend to beat him, and the excitement with which this news was dramatically reported indicated the sexual gratification he derived from it; it was in the fields that they entered an uninhabited hut and set fire to it, thus acting out the coitus fantasy of the "Fire of London" sequence.

Transference manifestations threw some light on this acting out of sexual intercourse: Albert roved the Clinic building, into offices, cupboards, and basement rooms in search of "another man," whom he fantasied I was keeping for sexual intercourse after he left the Clinic. The appearance of a male staff member filled him with great excitement and speculation about this man's sexual relationship with me. In this way, he accused me of unfaithfulness. On the other hand, Albert sought out secretaries and receptionists and made overtures of an affectionate sort. In his fantasy accounts he preferred them because they were more permissive than his own therapist.

Owing to the highly unsatisfactory evidence from Albert's parents, specific links with childhood experiences were missing on this and many other aspects of the analytic material. There was the dramatic account given by his father of how he turned from a gay young man to a haggard old man overnight, after witnessing his young wife in the arms of a soldier, whom he attacked on a surprise visit home; of his suspicion that Albert was not his son; of the grandmother's reports that the mother "walked the streets" for hours late at night during the father's absence in the Service. There was the mother's melodramatic account of all-night questioning and accusations during the father's leaves and of her "sticking to the same story" during the years. Whether based on fantasy or fact, the father did treat Albert differently from the other sons and still resented his presence in the home and the claims he made upon the mother even during the eighth year of therapy; the mother continued to express guilt about "conceiving in sin," and to offer evidence that Albert had been conceived during the father's leave. Although the father declared there had been no evidence of "unfaithfulness" since that time, repeatedly he referred to the earlier period during interviews. These facts no doubt throw some light on Albert's failure to identify successfully with his father, who not only rejected him but gave evidence of being sadistic in his relationship with the mother.

While the working through of anal material during this phase brought about certain changes, such as termination of soiling, better control over aggressive wishes, fighting, etc., there was a basic difference between Albert's response to interpretation and that of a neurotic patient:

1. He continued to bring very little of his immediate experience into the treatment; and when this was done, it came in the form of fantasy stories, as in the case of the hedgehog, which represented the real baby at home.

2. Fantasies became more profuse, responding less to interpretation, and in fact were accelerated by interpretation.

Hence, I tried to focus on the *form in which the fantasies were brought* and *their function* in Albert's relationship; to concentrate on *the use he made of words*, instead of interpreting fantasy content.

For example, the demand to write down stories was shown to represent his fear of forming a relationship that would enable him to bring his thoughts, feelings, and memories in more direct forms; or, more basically, his distrust of the analytic process, as shown in the persistent use of his own methods to cope with reality—fantasying, lying, acting out. This technique resulted in the patient's bringing the important memory of his mother's nightly reading from "The Little Red Engine" series of twelve books. He described the boys' faces on the engines, and recalled that they bore the names of people—George, Henry, John, etc. When I referred to the series later in the analysis, I found the following lines in one of them ("The Little Red Engine Gets a Name"):

> I've been through a tunnel and over a bridge;
> I've been through a town with a castle in the middle,
> I've been through a town with a church in the middle
> I'm a Main Line Train and I'm carrying the King.

The fantasy of being a conductor on a Main Line train now led to deeper levels of the warded-off id material. By being a conductor on a Main Line train, Albert could in fantasy control the arrival of the King, who symbolized his father. He could change his role from that of passively awaiting his father's arrival on leaves, and finally permanently, which had caused so much anxiety, to the active one of bringing it about.

The excitement which accompanied the "Little Red Engine" associations, dating back to his third year, left no doubt that this preoedipal period constituted one of the fixation points to which the patient longed to return. And the fantasy story of the mother sheep and the little "Ba Ba" and the dramatic sketch of mother and baby boy at the tea table had pointed to it. It was regression to this period of narcissistic gratification that the ego used so extensively as a defense against id anxiety.

Improvement in the transference relationship which followed these explanations was reflected outside the treatment room in other relationships: he no longer ignored his father's presence in the home, nor hurled words of abuse at him, but was able to engage in competitive games and to copy his father, whom he made a point of sitting next to at family meals. At school, he acquired a new friend, Bob, who continued to be "the most treasured friend in the world" for several years. Aggression toward his brothers lessened, and he rose several places in his schoolwork.

The technique of concentrating on the use Albert made of words and of attempting to find the meaning he attached to them brought the memory of early traumatic experiences. When I called his attention to Totteridge Lane, a road which he had mentioned repeatedly in stories, I learned that it carried many associations. Albert began hopping on one leg, and recalled a little old man who had "tottered along" the streets. Associations revealed that this old man symbolized his grandfather, who had lost a leg in a street accident, and thereafter had to use a wooden leg. The accident had occurred when Albert was four years old, some months after the other grandfather had lost a finger. This memory threw light on the burning of the father's leg for wood, in the earlier dramatic sketch, and also on the significance of Wooden Leg Sam, of the "Spook Train" series. It coincided with an even more important event in the etiology of the patient's disturbances: the grandfather's hospital experience had led to that of the patient's at the age of three and a half years after he had swallowed the coin. He recalled in fantasy:

"The Doctor pushed a tube as big as a steam shovel up my bottom. It felt so good I decided afterwards to push my finger up my bottom, and I've done it ever since."

When asked what finger he used, Albert jumped up and down, clapped his hands and told me: "I have the answer to the greatest mystery of the treatment!" He had used the index finger, and he waved it as he had done so constantly during the map reading. When the finger waving was interpreted to him as a defense against anal masturbation, the symptom, which had not previously responded to interpretation, was brought to an end.

In the same way, mention of the Highgate station initiated the fantasy that as he walked through a long tunnel, he came to a high gate, through which he passed in order to enter a nursery school. He had wandered through the rooms, where there were "lots of babies." He climbed into a play pen and murdered one of the babies. Here Albert appeared to recall the rage he had experienced after the birth of his first brother. He had to be kept away to prevent his hurting the baby. Since, as we have seen, tunnels symbolize his mother's body, this fantasy can also be taken to mean that he wandered about inside his mother's body, killing the unborn baby.

Now it became evident that Albert's fantasies were linked with actual experiences and that the therapeutic task was to lead him from words and stories to the specific memories which they covered.

Consideration of the Third Phase

During this phase, Albert's identification with the train became more complicated: on the oedipal level, Albert's body is the father's penis which enters the mother's dark hole (the underground tunnel), or anus; but he also is the castrated penis (the finger injured on the lines, and loss of leg, by association). When the connection was made with these past events, he brought castration material more fully into the analysis.

We know that the normal course out of the oedipus complex is through identification with the father. And we observe in Albert's fantasies an attempt to identify with the ideal father in his heroism during the Fire of London. But this attempt was not sustained, and he regressed in fantasy to the anal period in his identification with the father who soiled the mother. It was only this "dirty father" with whom Albert could identify in reality, and this identification was acted out in his persistent soiling and dirtying his body as he crawled on railway lines through tunnels. This tendency to identify with that *part* of the object which aroused great anxiety, like other defenses, failed, and the ego resorted to further regression—to the narcissistic oral phase, where he became his own idealized object.

In the normal latency child, narcissism often gives way to worship of persons who represent ego ideals. Omnipotence is sacrificed to the good of the group—a merging of the ego with that of others. This may be observed in strict adherence to rules, exposure of narcissistic behavior in members of the group. And we may expect sublimation, "a way out . . . *without* involving repression," or, we may say, excessive repression (Freud, 1914, p. 95).

In the case of the neurotic child, the exaggerated, punishing aspect of the ego ideal produces anxiety and inhibits constructive identification with parental figures, thus obstructing the true road to sublimation.

Why had our patient's ego not resorted to sublimation? Had the ego's energies been depleted by the elaborate fantasy systems it created? He had, by using interpretations in the service of the id, rejected analytic efforts to strengthen the ego; in a similar manner, intellectual abilities, such as memory, had been exploited by the id to the extent that there was insufficient "nonsexualized libido" for the purpose of learning. And there was also the fact of the patient's limited intelligence—he had come to analysis with an I.Q. of 80. Further resistance to ego strengthening was shown in Albert's over-activity during the treatment hour, which indicated that he had equated educational influence with passivity. Let us now examine his fantasies for a clue as to why he was so afraid of passivity.

Fourth Phase

About this time, beginning toward the end of Albert's thirteenth year, just before his puberty, there was a startling change in the content of his fantasies. From fantasies in which he was the active, resurrecting Jesus, he went on to fantasy himself as the passive, suffering Christ. He even went so far as to transfer his desire to get rid of his brothers to the story of Joseph (Albert), who was sold into slavery by these same brothers. This phase was introduced by a transitional one in which Albert was both active and passive: when he told me with great pleasurable excitement about how his father had beaten him, he spanked himself as he spoke the words. But this ambiguous attitude was soon replaced by a glorification of passive suffering: elaborate stories of schoolmates who kicked him "in the tummy and the winkle" or "crashed chairs into Albert." He could not defend himself against them, being such a "weak fighter," because he could not use his hands.

But there was the triumphant day when he was rewarded for passive endurance. In the fantasy sequence called, "The Adventures of Bob and Albert," the headmaster called the whole school together in order to give a prize to "the most outstanding boy who had been treated badly." This boy had had to have a lot of operations and stitches as a result of falling in dangerous places and being involved in too many fights. Only one boy had not fought him, and Albert displayed much excitement as he fantasied the boys clamoring for this role of friend: "Is it me?" The headmaster was fantasied as saying: "The boy is normal, he knows in his heart he's normal. He can't fight, he had a bad time from birth. . . ."

It was true that Albert was becoming more normal. He had been promoted to a senior school, where the boys were bigger and rougher; and there were, in fact, many bullies. Undoubtedly in his acting out the role of passive, cringing sufferer—cringing against walls during breaks—he had provoked their attacks. And it was a fact that the headmaster had appealed to Albert's form, during his absence, to show greater sympathy for the boy.

Interpretative work now aimed at helping the patient, not so much to understand his unconscious motives (since he immediately wove these into further fantasies), but to be aware of the differences between his real and his unreal problems; the real problems being his physical and intellectual inability to meet the competition at school, and his use of his unreal problems to avoid having to cope with the real ones. If he could not be the best in fact, he had to be a special person along the lines we have been describing.

A sympathetic discussion of this dilemma brought from Albert fantasies depicting his mother as the most unfortunate creature among women. Other women could bear any number of babies at home, while his mother had to go to the hospital to have her babies "cut out." His mother was "abnormal" because she had a "circumcised hole and lots of stitches"; he was "mad" because he had a "stitched penis." There followed a profusion of drawings showing that the circumcised penis was a great deal smaller than the uncircumcised ones; drawings showing the normal physique of all the boys in his class and Scout Troop, except three of them (all labeled Albert)—one with an arm missing, another with a finger missing, and still another with a wooden leg and crutch. In still another respect he fantasied himself to be different from his contemporaries: "Once every four days, I have mauve business coming out of my bottom. Mom saw it on the bed, and said it was spum."

By changing the word from "spunk" (a slang expression for emissions) to "spum," and by shifting the activity from penis to anus, he was able to be both a man and a woman, and thus satisfy his bisexual fantasies.

These fantasies revealed not only that Albert had been circumcised, but that he used this fact to identify with his mother through his "fragile body" and "stitches"—which symbolized his fear of castration. Analytic work therefore focused on this identification with his mother and was designed to break it, thus leaving free space in his emotions into which his father could fit.

There followed a rather rapid shift from the role of passive sufferer to that of the attacking boy and superior male. This began with aggressive fantasies about my color—I became the "black psychologee"[6]—and in most of the sequences that followed, the woman was depicted as silly, stupid, or inefficient. But here we had a distinct

[6] The therapist is an American Negro.

split between a Mrs. Johnson, who was one of his nursery school teachers, and was cast in his story as a beautiful woman of twenty-nine, and would say: "Try and do it again," and a "puggish, muggish, flickety" elderly woman of sixty-seven who was fantasied as his own teacher and quite mad. She was attacked by two gangsters, Bob and Albert, so that she had to retire and was replaced by a new young lady. These two figures can obviously be equated with the young, beautiful, preoedipal mother and "the nasty old bitch" she became when she had intercourse with his father and conceived children other than Albert.

These fantasies were acted out in the Clinic by his escaping from me to a young male therapist whom he happened to see in the Clinic one day. His demands to be treated by this man became so insistent that he was finally allowed to see Mr. Lussier for several interviews. To have forbidden these contacts would have corroborated Albert's fantasy of my weakness and ignorance, which he expressed in a fantasy interview with the male therapist, who was supposed to have said:

> Albert, you mustn't play with your winkle. It will stop you from doing things with your hands. Mrs. Singer cannot help you. Ladies do not know about winkles. They think a winkle is a deadly creature that could make you dead like an Antipas (a huge creature with a tiny neck, who has more teeth than any animal in the entire world). He has great claws to tear your stomach in half and leave you dying.

It is important to note that when Albert arrived in Mr. Lussier's room, he did not request the sex enlightenment nor ask questions about "the winkle," which had been his excuse for seeing the male therapist, but he plunged Mr. Lussier into an overwhelming series of fantasies about his search for a baby. The fact that he was unable to form a good relationship with the male therapist was merely another indication of his inability to identify with the father. The same stories were continued without interruption when he returned to me several days later:

He walks along the rail and decides that gooseberry bushes cannot grow in a tunnel, because it is filthy, dirty, and dark, but he investigates anyway:

So I went in the mouth of the tunnel. When I heard the train coming, I got up on the edge and let the train go by. I went on all day until suddenly I saw daylight. It wasn't in the tunnel. I went back home to the coal cellar, where I saw a man prowling about . . . .

Undoubtedly it was this fantasy which Albert had acted out in walking through railway tunnels.

This regression to earlier fantasies about babies was precipitated by his mother's fourth pregnancy, when Albert was fourteen, and which meant yet another Caesarean for her. On this occasion, the mother entered the hospital comparatively early in her pregnancy, underwent an operation, and produced a daughter, who died shortly afterwards. None of these events, nor even her hysterectomy which followed shortly afterwards, had much overt effect upon Albert's current behavior. In fact, he was able to express himself in a more direct verbal way and to become an active ally in finding out the meaning of his various problems. However, upon his mother's return home, strong resistances to analytic work were renewed. He could not stop laughing at me. This laughter did not stop until we reached the following interpretation: that he was systematically belittling me for having told him all about the birth of a baby but nothing about its death; and that he was linking me as a silly female (since the female has no penis) with his fear and horror of castration, which he denied through laughter.

Consideration of the Fourth Phase

Albert's original fear of passivity was transformed during this phase into a longing for it. This longing emerged in the analysis in the form of fantasies about being beaten by his father, and was also noted outside the treatment in his provocations to his schoolmates to hit him. These symptoms in turn were caused by his need for, and his fear of, identifying with the woman who had stitches and must go to the hospital. Much of this defensive activity can be traced to the reinforcement of instinctual drives provided by the patient's entering puberty, as well as the upset of his mother's pregnancy and separation from him to enter hospital. The latter event, however, seems to have brought about a crisis in Albert's development: his narcissistic fears of mutilation[7] were greatly intensified before his mother's entry into the hospital. With it, though, he became more reasonable and communicative, thus proving that he could cope easily with the dangers of the outside world, like underground railway lines or his mother's absence, and that what really frightened him were the internal dangers which formed the core of his fantasy systems.

The various defenses used by the patient during this period, such as denial in laughter, running away, belittling of women, provocation to be punished, are all familiar in the analysis of neurotic adolescent boys, as is the rapid shift in the use of various defenses and the quantity of acting out. Moreover, the normal adolescent boy often presents a similar picture of behavior. The feature that distinguishes Albert from the neurotic patient during this phase was his psychotic *use* of words. I have mentioned the associations of Totteridge Lane and Highgate for him. Other examples here are his use of "spum" and "spunk," and his claim to special privileges because he suffered from "Malajustice," a derivative of maladjusted, which implies that justice had not been done to Albert. In the next section, we will discover in what this lack of justice lay. Important for present purposes is the way in which Albert felt he could reverse an actual situation by verbal play. This symptom alone would put him in the borderline category. For, as Freud pointed out, psychotics treat words as things and they are subjected to the primary process.

This question of language proved crucial for diagnostic and therapeutic purposes. When it became obvious that Albert used words in a very esoteric way, I was able to interpret this device as a way of warding off external reality and with it object relationships. This interpretation cracked one of his main defenses, and he was able to show me some of the ways in which he used words, which represented his world more truly than real things and events. But this, in turn, brought me too close to his world and aroused fear of merging with the object, and he began to belittle me and to run away from this danger, just as he had previously run away from his mother. Thus, the borderline patient tries to ward off later objects as a

---

[7] "Fear of mutilation of any kind is based upon the narcissistic love of our whole body. The dismembering motive is the expression of the castration complex on the level of narcissistic self-love" (Schilder, 1923, p. 191).

defense against the fear of merging with the object or losing it as he had done earlier. This warding off of the primary object is, as we know, also characteristic of both normal and neurotic adolescents: the normal, however, forms relationships with secondary objects— children of his own age and adults other than his parents. The neurotic does the same but with varying degrees of maldirection, while the borderline patient is so closely tied to the primary object that he is incapable of forming these secondary relationships. Thus the real-life Bob, "the greatest friend in the whole world," was used merely as a sounding board for Albert's fantasies and was woven into them in this role, as indeed was I.[8]

FIFTH PHASE

We are now entering the fifth and last year of daily analysis. Albert was fourteen and beginning his last year at school. My attempts at reconstruction of the patient's past were frustrated by Albert, who launched his most ambitious sequence of fantasy stories, called "The Life of Albert Hansom." The stories began with his birth, which was described in Biblical fashion and placed in a Biblical setting. It developed in a dozen or more "Episodes," connected by musical accompaniment, which took the place of the engine noises. He used such titles as the following: "A Baby Is Born Unto Mrs. Hansom," "Albert Goes to School," "Albert Gets into Trouble with the Police," "Albert Goes to Anna Freud's Clinic."

While the patient held rigidly to his chosen form, i.e., expressions in stories, there were many differences in his attitude toward the stories and in their content. He was less intent on his fantasies than he had been earlier. He could be persuaded to bring facts about his life for a part of the hour, and also to listen to interpretations in a different way. Former interpretations were included as an organic part of the chain of events involving old characters, who were now subsidiary, like Chief Baby and Jaguar. But the new interpretations were not, as before, used as a reinforcement of his

8 I realize that this division is oversimplified, since the normal child may at this stage use any of these devices to keep the primary object at bay. But they are simply part of the developmental process; whereas with the borderline patient (who resembles the psychotic in this respect) there is no development. At the age of eighteen, Albert was still using his objects in the same way.

fantasies; and the new stories contained a wider range of real events, e.g., the principal characters of the new series were all *real* people. In the content of his fantasy stories it was as though he were trying to tell me that he was as good a therapist as I was. For example, he accounted for his disturbance in a story about: "Mad Hansom from Coney Hatch Mental Asylum," in which Albert was tied to a tree and one of the boys hit him on the head with a stone. Some men found him and took him to the hospital, where the doctor told him: "The Teddy Boys have unfortunately wrecked one of your nerves—the pain nerve. This means you will have trouble in your childhood. You will not be able to fight back. You are going to have operations in two places and lots of stitches in the brain and in the mind."

Following the operation, the doctor warned him: "Never do anything to aggravate anyone who you mix up with. Because if they start to fight at school, you will think you're being picked on for the rest of your life. Then you will have to go to a psychiatrist."

He imagined himself to be held together with stitches, just as his stories were held together by the recurrence of characters.

Other aspects of the stories were noted: the patient's need to be the hero, and the great amount of masochism which accompanied the hero's activities. Invariably he was treated badly, pounced upon, deserted, snubbed, or isolated from the crowd. For example, the story just described was supplemented by a drawing in which he showed the insides of his body. There were stitches, not only in the head, but in the chest and where arm and leg joined the body. The picture also showed a uterus, Fallopian tubes, and ovaries, one of which was stitched. There was only a very tiny penis.

Yet at school, the penis was very much in evidence: Albert was now achieving a special place by exposing his penis to schoolmates in the lavatory and masturbating before the boys, who he claimed forced him to do it. This form of acting out was linked with the inconspicuous penis in the drawing, when I interpreted the need to reassure himself that he did in fact have a penis.

Explanations such as this stopped the acting out at school for a time, and brought much of the exhibitionism into the treatment room, which now became a circus: he turned somersaults on the couch, or used a pillow to symbolize the woman in intercourse, as he lay on his back and made rhythmical movements—thereby taking the feminine-active role; or he engaged in grotesque dances, loud off-key singing, and conducting an imaginary orchestra, using the index finger in the same manner as the earlier waving of it. I discussed the various defenses he used to cope with his passive wishes, for example, how he tried to seduce me, as he had his classmates, to play the active, aggressive role. This brought about changed behavior so far as exposing his body was concerned, but now the acting out took on a verbal form: he told dirty jokes to the boys, and on one occasion gave a lecture on "Sexual Intercourse" to some boys and girls on the playground during a break at school. On this occasion he held forth about the various ways to "wank it up," how to get rid of "white stuff," and how he had "fucked" a six-year-old girl in nursery school. She had returned on the next day with "something jumping up and down in her stomach—it was a baby." And he used analytic interpretations to link his "madness" with the witnessing of parental intercourse when he was a child. He was almost expelled from school when a part of it was heard by one of the school staff.

Albert was consciously using this form of seductive behavior to impress his classmates with his potency ("I've got better sex information than you have") and to achieve a special place among them, this time through clowning. It was therefore necessary to show him how this behavior defeated his wish to be accepted by his schoolmates and to be one of them; how he set himself apart by having organs, such as uterus and ovaries, which the other boys did not have, persisting in his denial of the facts of life and telling masturbation secrets; how he exploited his problems, and made it impossible for his schoolmates to take him seriously. By making a fool of himself, he would make a fool of anyone who took him seriously, that is, who tried to form a relationship with him; and all this placed him in an isolated position where he had always to fall back upon his own omnipotence to try to overcome the loneliness he felt.

Following these explanations, Albert brought fantasies which dealt with the instinctual material beneath the defensive acting out. I quote from "The Life of Albert Hansom, Episode 4. The Terror of Finchley." (In this story, Albert had run away from home because his mother had another baby.)

Albert went over the fields, lived on hardly anything at all . . .
he arrived home low and downcast, dead of starvation. "What's
happened," said Dad. "This is our poor little son which has
come home again. Let us bring forth the best robe. Let's bring
forth the fatted calf. . ." Then Dad fell upon Albert: "Did you
have a hard time, poor little Albert?"

Thus, the Prodigal son, hated by his brothers, exalted and loved
by the father, became Albert's means of expressing unconscious
wishes to be loved by the father in a sexual manner, and to play the
feminine role. Now the dread of having stitches—which also represented the wish to have them—could be seen as envy of the mother's
role in reproduction.

Albert responded well to these interpretations; the verbal as well
as the bodily clowning stopped. He made an attempt to participate
in activities with children of his own age by joining a recreation
center. Although he failed to mix with them, his regular attendance
several times weekly served the purpose of removing him from his
home, which stimulated so much of his adolescent acting out. His
general improvement was so marked that when he begged for time
off from analysis, with the claim that he needed time to make
friends, we felt justified in granting this request in what seemed to
be a forward movement in his becoming more social.

After a period of six weeks, he was brought back to the Clinic
because he pilfered money from a news agent, and lost his paper
round as the result of it. Both the stolen money and his regular
wage had been used to buy enormous quantities of polo mints, which
he sucked incessantly. This new symptom persisted until the analysis
disclosed fantasies in which he captured car loads of money and
sweets from escaped prisoners. In these fantasies, he assumed active,
heroic roles. In others, he was the passive victim of "bad men" who
bound him and beat him until he was unconscious or dead.

It was some time before he would listen to interpretations, but
when he could at last be persuaded to do so, I focused on the use of
fantasying and acting out to ward off object relationships following
separation. This enabled him to bring an important memory: that
of having been seduced by a man, who forced Albert, then seven
years old, to suck his penis. The fantasy of being forced to "swallow
the white stuff" became prominent in a later symptom in which he

suffered from the delusion that people who coughed, and swallowed the phlegm, were doing so to annoy him.

Later, he started bringing current reality problems: he could not stop lending money to Bob, he provoked Bob to beat him with sticks on the behind; then, with his little brother, he could not resist games of mutual masturbation, in which his brother sucked his penis.

Further evidences of regression to the oral phase came in the form of fantasies in which he was the center of attention. In the Episode called: "Albert Gets a Job," he fantasied a massive conference called by me to plan his future employment. Membership of the conference included all his teachers, from nursery school onward, probation officer, children's court judge, employment councilor, the staff of both Clinics, and prospective employers. Each member was called upon to give a detailed account of his or her experience with Albert. On the final day, Albert would speak for himself and would be awarded the job of his choice. In this way, he told me how anxious he was about finding work upon leaving school. And he had to act out this fantasy by insisting that I should visit his home to hold a conference with his parents. In his home, he assumed the role of master of ceremonies, and for a short period stuck to his original plan of discussing employment, but there was an abrupt digression into his fantasy world, in which he continued the stories of the analytic hour.

Similarly, he attempted to act out the Fire of London by accidentally setting fire to his classroom before finally leaving school. Thus, during the closing months of this phase, when Albert was fifteen, the patient's id anxiety was so great that I was unable to deal with it through interpretations of his feelings about separation, but I attempted a practical solution and offered to see him at regular intervals. At first he accepted this offer, but he later decided he wanted to come daily. Yet, once he began to work, he returned for only one interview to tell me of his exciting job, and to exact my promise to wait for him every evening at the same hour.

Consideration of the Fifth Phase

This phase has brought us squarely into the middle of the adolescent years, when the ego frantically mobilized every possible means of defense. It was as though a dyke had burst and one set of men busied themselves in cementing it, but even as they got the better of that particular crack, another would appear some miles to the left or right of them and another group of men would have to dash there with sand bags and pumps in order to stop the leak. I put it this way in order to emphasize the variety of ego defenses at this time, as well as the hasty, imperative summonses with which they were called upon to help in one emergency after another. The patient, who had all along given evidence of functioning on regressed levels, now showed signs of being hopelessly caught up in his regressions—a characteristic of adolescents. The regression was dramatically shown in reverting to earlier forms of bringing his fantasies: reading rapidly and monotonously, waving his finger, and in acting out his sexual wishes by attempts to seduce me with movements of his body on the couch. In these ways, the patient revealed the strength of his regressed wishes for his mother during the earlier childhood period. The castration anxiety aroused by these wishes now came to light in a variety of fantasies and in the acting out by which the ego tried to defend itself, e.g., through denial in the form of exhibitionism,[9] and denial of identification with the female—he could take nothing from the woman, so he became his own analyst.

But these methods of defense were continually being washed away, and we find more than glimpses of the wish to identify with the woman, as shown in the tale of the Prodigal Son. In addition, there was also evidence of the anxiety producing aspects of femininity (e.g., menstruation—he had mauve business; childbirth—he had stitches), so that the ego was forced to use other defenses against the same wish. The most important of these was denial through clowning.[10] This too proved ineffective, so that further defensive mechanisms were needed, and this time the ego used regression to

[9] "The sexual pleasure of the exhibitionist consists in using the spectator to satisfy his narcissistic needs . . . [He needs] this specific type of pleasure for the purpose of counteracting inner fears" (Fenichel, 1946, p. 351).

[10] Fenichel (1936) calls attention to the sadomasochistic element in clowning: "It would seem that slapstick belongs under the rubric of sadomasochism: beatings are constantly administered. In such sadism, concealed as it is by clowning, one must take cognizance of two things: first, the striving of the clown, whose original wish it was to exhibit "seriously," to revenge himself secretly for the ridicule to which he is exposed; . . . and second, one justifiably thinks of a regression engendered by the circumstance that an original piece of ridicule has disabused the hero with regard to his phallicism" (pp. 12-13).

preoedipal levels; first to the anal—the phase at which he had been least well defended against instinctual drives.[11]

It was, too, at this regressed level that we were now able to observe the greatest effects of the analytic work. The patient verbalized his extensive anal conflicts instead of acting them out by soiling or returning to railway tunnels. Nor did he make sadistic physical attacks upon his brothers and schoolmates, as many adolescent neurotic boys do. The ego shifted the outlet—instead of doing dirty things, he talked about dirty things.[12] But when these tales were overheard, they brought him up against an even greater fear than that occasioned by loss of a part of his body: he was threatened with expulsion from school and with separation from his home. Thus, social prohibition helped to confirm his deep-rooted fears of separation. But here the anxieties connected with the conflicts between love and hate were still tremendous, as shown in his defensive turning passive experience into an active one by fleeing bodily from the treatment. Then, when he returned, it was an additional symptom, that of sucking sweets, which pointed to regression to the oral level. In this phase, he became self-sufficient, being both the breast and the sucking baby, the analyst and the analysand. In what follows I will attempt to show that this comprised the fixation level.

The break in the analysis afforded insights into the patient's inability to cathect objects other than those of the past. The libido, once separated from the oedipal object—now seen as flight from frustration rather than a flight to substitutes—did not make its attachment to other objects, but the ego regressed to narcissism, where Albert became his own loved object. This tendency may be observed in both normal and neurotic children during this phase of

[11] The Rorschach report, when Albert was eleven years old, shows "a child with a strongly psychotic type of character with a very loose, inadequate defense against anal phantasy."

[12] Freud observed the use of smutty speech in courtship: "If the woman's readiness emerges quickly the obscene speech has a short life; it yields at once to a sexual action. It is otherwise if quick readiness on the woman's part is not to be counted on, and if in place of it defensive reactions appear. In that case the sexually exciting speech becomes an aim in itself in the shape of smut. Since the sexual aggressiveness is held up in its advance towards the act, it pauses at the evocation of the excitement and derives pleasure from the signs of it in the woman. In so doing, the aggressiveness is no doubt altering its character as well, just as any libidinal impulse will if it is met by an obstacle. It becomes positively hostile and cruel, and it thus summons to its help against the obstacle the sadistic components of the sexual instinct" (Freud, 1905, p. 99).

development, but they do not get stuck there. Albert, at a stage in the analysis when neurotic patients are likely to make a final break from the therapist, for relationships with other objects, still regarded his own analysis as the center of experience.

As we noted, separation from the loved one induced in Albert an uncommonly strong degree of self-love. But separation did not end there. He felt that the self he loved would also be separated from him, i.e., that he would disintegrate. His fantasies tell us that disintegration begins with passivity; this allows him to be pounced upon and to be injured, so that he requires stitches to hold him together. But in order to be given stitches, he must remain in the passive role and allow himself to be stitched. This in turn leads to renewed passivity in the outside world, because the doctor tells him that he should not annoy anyone while the stitches are still in. And so the cycle continues.

We are now in a position to examine more fully the implications of these stitches: on the one hand, we have the fear of stitches, which are equated with passivity and madness; on the other, the wish for stitches, which will enable him to satisfy his passive wishes and also to hold himself together. And here we come to Albert's highly unusual and very concentrated use of language: in the single word *stitches*, he sums up a whole chain of events, from the father's coming home and having intercourse with his mother (the observation of which traditionally represents parents' madness to young children), and the passivity of the mother, to the birth of babies, with all its associations of separation and disintegration. At the same time, it is by virtue of the stitches that his mother is allowed to return intact to him—and so mend the results of her madness. Therefore, Albert too needs stitches, as he said, both in his "head and in the mind" if he is to be rescued from his madness.

The overpowering strength of this central fantasy is indicated by the fact that most of the patient's life had been spent in acting out some aspect of it. At the age of three and a half years, he brought on hospitalization by swallowing a coin, which, as we have seen, was in identification with the pregnant mother. Then again, he ran away from home, thus denying his separation anxiety. He walked in Underground tunnels, and this has been seen as identification with the father's penis. The fantasy of operating the railway system may be regarded as a denial of his helplessness to prevent his father's arrival, which represented the onset of his mother's madness.

We now understand the unconscious use he made of his various integrating systems: strings of streets, enclosures of railway systems, complicated networks of never-ending stories, where the characters go on in an endless relationship to one another and to the main character (inevitably Albert himself), all as a means of stitching himself to the primary object, his mother. And later, stitches were to prevent separation from himself, or total disintegration. Stitches were the clay, the plaster that held together the crumbling foundation of defense against instinctual material, and formed a network that bridged the wide volcanic gap. And the succession of treatment hours and days became enveloped in this system of patches. Hence, at what would have been the end of five years of analysis, the patient begged for an unlimited number of regular sessions. Without them, he felt he would fall apart.

Now we are in a position to understand one of the most obvious borderline symptoms of this patient: his pride in illness. If he could hold himself together by his own system of therapy-strings of fantasies, without the help of other objects—in other words, if he could achieve omnipotence, then he could use the object in a very limited way. All he needed from the object was physical presence, for his separation from it had started the whole chain of events which ended with madness, stitches, and eventually disintegration.[13] We will now look to the remaining years of the therapy to test this hypothesis further.

SIXTH PHASE

Albert left school to go to work at the age of fifteen and a half years. This phase covered the two-and-a-half-year period of weekly therapy, which brought him to his present age of eighteen.

He returned to treatment on his own accord, after an absence of

---

[13] According to Nunberg (1931), this phenomenon is due to a peculiar relationship between the ego and the symptom: "The ego . . . redirects libido towards the symptom, which it unites with itself and incorporates anew in its own organization. The symptom becomes once more an integral part of the ego, which derives pleasure from the union. In the struggle over the symptom it becomes impoverished in libido. Through symbiosis with the symptom it obtains narcissistic gratification or else escapes a narcissistic wound, and thus the deficit in the libidinal economy of the ego is made up" (p. 131).

five weeks. A typewriter, which had been lent to him for use in his typing class, was brought back with its ribbon tangled and its keys broken. He complained it was "skipping letters." This was the way in which he told me of his anxieties about himself. His parents told me how he had troubled them with his constant recital of the fantasy stories he had earlier brought to me. This gave me a clue as to how to treat him. It appeared that it was necessary for Albert to have some kind of audience to drain off his fantasies, thus leaving him freer to cathect reality. I, therefore, agreed to see him once a week, and these visits have continued uninterrupted, except for the usual holidays, ever since.

His first job promised to be a highly satisfactory one, since it offered opportunities for sublimating his interest in streets. He was hired as a delivery boy for a large department store in the middle of London, a section which had always attracted many of his fantasies. During the early months in this job, the patient used his therapeutic hours in reciting the addresses of persons to whom he had to deliver parcels. From these routine recitals, he sometimes digressed to tell stories, and it was learned that many of these were clustered round a core of reality. Thus, when he was crossing the street against the lights on a busy highway, a policeman had shouted: "Watch out, are you trying to commit suicide." Around this incident, he wove fantasy stories of a fatal accident with all the accompanying excitement of ambulances, sirens, crowds of people, and distressed fellow workers who craved to know about the missing employee. In a similar fashion, any slight incident might stimulate a whole sequence of fantasy reports, as when he overheard a fellow worker call another "daft." This developed into a fantasy spreading through all departments that Albert was suffering from "maladjustice" and attending the Clinic in Maresfield Gardens. Finally, this job, which he had held for eight months, ended. Albert claimed that some girls in the cafeteria were talking about him, and that some of them had called him a "male prostitute."

Although he was given assurance that the girls had teased him merely because he was so particular about his appearance—he was the best dressed and neatest worker in the department, always with crisp white shirts—he drew his pay and left. Thus began a long chain of jobs, which Albert listed as follows: packer ("I left because I had weak hands and could not lift heavy objects"); tool fitter ("I could not use my hands for fitting tool parts"); assistant to the driver of a laundry lorry (he flatly refused to obey orders; when told to hurry, for example, he walked more slowly, and there was always the excuse that he was too weak to lift heavy bundles).

With ease he found jobs through the Youth Employment Councillor, and with ease he lost them, showing no regret except that he had no money for sweets and nightly visits to the films.

At this point, he refused any job that required the use of hands in any capacity other than delivering messages or small parcels. When he finally found employment with a weekly journal that met all his specifications, he seemed to be very happy. Each day on his return home, he would tell his parents: "I've had another glorious day of work." But soon there were fantasies of his being kicked out bodily by the manager because he took too much time making deliveries. And finally, when he was asked at the end of his lunch hour to run a special errand, he flatly refused and was fired. This happened during the summer holidays, as had many of his other sackings.

Through his fantasies, I was able to learn that the reason for his delays in making deliveries was connected with travel. He told stories of exciting events on tube trains, where people crowded him into small corners and smothered him, so that he grew sick in the stomach and vomited. To remedy this, he had taken to prescribing for himself a variety of pills to cure "travel sickness." And much of his treatment sessions would be used to read the directions from the labels on these medicines. They, it was believed, would prevent vomiting, fainting, and pimples, from which he was suffering acutely, partly because he continually squeezed them to "get the white stuff out." I sent him to a physician who knew of his problems and could reassure him about his hypochondriacal fears. This, however, could not solve the traffic problem. He now demanded a job which would be easily accessible by bus, i.e., he had developed a train phobia. First, he excused this fear by saying that men were looking at him; later, because they coughed at him. The fear of being coughed at had become a prominent symptom in the Clinic, at home, on the job, and in the street. The person who coughed was doing so to annoy Albert, whether this person was known to him or not. The etiology of this symptom was described by the patient in a fantasy story called: "Why People Cough at Albert."

> All the time, right from when I was born until December, 1956, I had not heard a single person cough or sniff. But on the 1st January 1957 on the morning of the day I went to work, on the news, the announcer read something that made Albert's heart go thump: "There had been this plague come from the country of Asia over across the Atlantic. Many Asians have been bringing the disease to this country with them. It is a special kind of flu, named after them. People who get it will sound like this" [the patient made a dramatic display of exaggerated coughing]. The announcer continued: "about one-half of the people in England will have caught it before the 30th June of this year. There will be so much calamity, you will get pushed and shoved."

Here, the patient's fantasies reveal the instinctual drives, which were greatly stimulated and increased by riding on tube trains: there was first of all the conflict over his aggression, itself stimulated by separation from the analysis, against which the ego attempted to defend itself through projection onto other people, whom he accused of doing damage to his body. But this defense could not adequately cope with the mass of instinctual material, which also included conflicts between passive and actual sexual wishes. To cope with these, the ego now resorted to bodily restriction in the train phobia—thus showing a compromise between the defense and the break-through of instinctual urges. But again the defense failed, and we find the ego resorting to acting out: leaving jobs where he was forced to use hands, squeezing "white stuff" from pimples, etc.

Interpretative work along these lines was not sufficient to cope with the various emergencies that resulted from the acting out; it was necessary to supplement these with environmental measures. One of the means used was to have the realities of his unsatisfactory work adjustment brought home to him by the Employment Councillor, who explained to Albert the effect it would have upon new assignments in an employment market that was becoming narrower for boys his age. Also, it was necessary to have some further assessment of Albert's ability to work in the community. To this end, he was referred for a series of tests at an Industrial Psychology Bureau. There, it was interesting to note that in spite of the ego's impoverishment in keeping up abundant fantasies, he achieved an I.Q. of 101, which was 21 points higher than the results of the test given him during the early months of the analysis. The vocational tests noted that he had "a soft spot for maps," and this fact influenced their recommendation that he should be referred to jobs in which this ability could be expressed, e.g., "roundsman's work, preferably as a meter reader, postman, installment collector," etc.

But first the delusions and the irrational fears that hampered Albert in sublimation had to be coped with. And for this reason, I took him again into daily analysis for a short period.

He returned in a rebellious and defiant mood, making excessive demands upon my time—he came late for his sessions, refused to leave on time, and constantly demanded changes in schedule. Again he took over the analytic hour with an outpouring of fantasies in a new sequence called "Albert Loses His Jobs." The prominent feature of these fantasies was that he was always at the mercy of a gang of "bad men" who attacked him, beat him up, dropped him from planes or deserted him in mines where rats tore his body to pieces, or he died of suffocation. It was through the analysis of such fantasies that I learned of the loss of his "most prized friend" Bob. It is possible that the friendship ended for the simple reason that Bob was still at school while Albert had left to go to work; but in the patient's fantasies, Bob left, "deserted," because Albert had not lent him sufficient money, given him sweets, or allowed more sexual privileges. Whatever the reason, Albert still mourned the loss of this friend, and spent a part of his hour weaving fantasies about the loss. In this way, he expressed his anxiety about separation, which was used to avoid cathecting other objects.

Albert's latest job, as a delivery boy for an office in Soho, a mid-town section noted for street prostitutes, enabled him to bring many of his sexual fantasies. Stories poured in about his experiences with "streetwalkers." With them in fantasy he either engaged in mutual masturbation in open lots, where there was a lot of "dog business," or he "fucked their tits," or they invited him to sumptuous meals with wine in cellars, and overcharged him. There was no hint of a genital sexual relationship. Apart from the prostitutes, there has been only one fantasy, and no facts, relating to girls. In this story, he met a girl alone in the park on a foggy night. She asked for directions to Southgate, and Albert had given such detailed and complicated directions—a full recital of his old street names—she could not help but get lost.

The people on his new job never come to life, in his associations, except in some connection directly related to Albert, and these are usually embellished in fantasies, where the relationship is often one of viciousness and cruelty. There have been a few exceptions to this: on one occasion, the doorman had said to him: "Is this Albert Hansom? That same one? I notice a few silly grins, the same suit, but not the same face. He looks more masculine. If you are Albert, you've changed completely from what we've known in the past weeks . . . not with the look of someone who looks like a fool."

Albert had replied: "I am the real Albert, I'm not playing to be. Something happened to change my whole personality—adolescence has come off."

The occasion which provided the core of this fantasy was a rare instance of mature behavior which Albert showed at home when his brother tried to provoke him.

On another occasion, a fellow worker is said to have advised him how to effect a sudden change: "If you stop parting your hair on the side and using that slick stuff, and grow a crew hair cut, you will stop looking like a girl."

Albert immediately took his advice and proudly exhibited the results upon his next visit to the Clinic. He greeted me with: "Now I've changed from a girlish boy to a man. Perhaps I will get Bob back now."

The cycle of losing jobs during holiday periods was ended during the summer of 1959 when I was able to continue seeing him throughout the holidays. Thus, Albert has been able to remain on the same job for almost a year. On this job, he delivers small parcels containing belts and samples of material to various parts of London.

At home, he continues to make excessive demands on his mother, and makes a great display of trying to push his father out of the home. At first, this symptom took the form of refusing to enter while his father, who often works at odd hours, was present. Later, he had to be fed separately by his mother during—never before or after—the family meal. He resented any special thing his mother did for his father and made a scene of it. He demanded exclusive right to use the TV set and would abuse his father until the poor man finally left the room to keep the peace.

I was unable to deal with this behavior in terms of his revived oedipal envy of his parents' relationship, and so I sought the mother's help. Her reaction to my suggestion that she should herself take a firm stand against Albert's persecution of his father gave some insight into the triangular relationships in this home. She maintained that she did not want to risk "upsetting" Albert, that it would be easier for her to persuade his father to "ignore" or "make allowances" for his "queerness." She did not follow my advice. Some months later, when the situation deteriorated and Albert attempted physical violence against his father, she asked my advice about the feasibility of moving into a flat with Albert and leaving the father with the other boys. Yet, the father confirms her claim that they seldom have a "cross word."

Consideration of the Sixth Phase

During this phase, the patient's fantasies and his acting out of them tell us that he is dealing primarily with homosexual and masturbatory guilt. This is illustrated by his complaints of inability to use his hands and of other bodily handicaps. I purposely refrained from using the term "castration anxiety" because Albert's fear was not that of the normal or neurotic adolescent boy—that his penis would fall off or be otherwise damaged—so much as a fear of the total disintegration of his entire body. This fear was revealed in his fantasy of being trampled upon and smothered and of his body being torn apart by rats. In his customary way, Albert refused this passive role by taking on the active one and actually tearing his body, i.e., squeezing innumerable sores so that he left behind red splotches to show that he had been damaged; or by emptying his stomach out in compulsive vomiting. Also characteristically, he provided his own therapy through a succession of pills, which now took the place of the earlier stitches in holding his body together. This fear of disintegration severely restricted his body activities, e.g., he could not use his hands, he was unable to ride on trains, he could not sit by his father, he could not remain on certain jobs, and he could not go out to meet people. Any one of these activities confronted him with the danger of passivity which started the whole sequence that would end in disintegration. Thus, at the age when the normal adolescent resorts to complex defenses like identification with other adolescents in pursuing ego ideals, displacement and sublimations of all sorts, we find Albert still relying upon the most primitive defenses of all: denial in fantasy, projection, and identification with the "bad" parts of objects.

Yet, on the anal level, he was able to form strong reaction formations to dirtiness—he had become excessively clean and tidy in his physical appearance. He had been able to sublimate some of his obsessional tendencies, as shown in punctuality and having to do the same chores in a certain sequence. These have served him well in his jobs. But most of all, his preoccupation with maps, streets, and tube stations has been turned to some sublimatory account in his delivery jobs. Although there have been frequent breakdowns in this way of dealing with instinctual activity, it has been more reliable than the more primitive defenses. That none have been entirely successful is shown by the continual break-through of the instinctual wishes, against which the ego tried to defend itself. Thus, we find him, at the age of eighteen, becoming more involved than ever in his parents' sexual life. That they did not discourage this interest but actively promoted it—by using him as a broom handle with which to beat one another—did not help matters. Thus, his mother continually found excuses for his surly and contemptuous attitude toward his father, while the father used him as evidence of what he considered his wife's guilty past.

The signs indicative of a rebellion were misleading. There was, in fact, no renunciation of the mother, no attempt to identify with the father or substitutes of the father, but merely attempts to bring about discord between his parents, always with elaborate use of identification with his mother. There had been no attempt to shift to identifications with others as in the normal adolescent boy. This was most dramatically expressed in the fantasy of being changed from woman to man, in the fantasy story about "Adolescence Dropping Off." This story was a denial of his identification with the mother and an effort, through magical thinking, to bring about the desired goals of masculinity. But even this fantasy is misleading. Albert's focus was clearly on the possibility of becoming *changed*. He was saying, "If I can change from feminine to masculine overnight, then I can change the other way round." This may be seen, next to disintegration, as his basic fear. But the conflicts between passivity and activity were so strong at this level, we find him retreating again to the narcissistic phase in his wish to possess his mother— not as an oedipal object this time, but in the manner of the infant who regards his mother as a part of his own body. To lose her at this level does not represent castration in the sense of losing a part of his body, but fear of being left alone at the mercy of his own aggression, which he projects so freely upon his environment.

This gives us a clue to his need of the therapist, as in the case of other objects: she must not leave him, for separation from her starts a whole sequence of separations (which resemble the sequences of his fantasy stories). Left alone, he can resort only to the primitive defenses to which he adheres so rigidly—mainly turning passivity into activity; thus, he continues to fear that he would separate from himself, that both mind and body would fall to pieces. The therapist can remedy this, not so much by helping him to understand or anticipate the sources of his anxiety, but by providing a never-ending supply of thread (symbolized by a succession of treatment hours, days, months) to hold him together. There is no question of termination in the usual sense, since reassurance can be provided only in the form of physical presence, however limited the use the patient might make of it.

THE BORDER OF PARANOIA

Albert's fantasies, as we have seen, give abundant evidence of the depth of his defenses against passivity, which can be equated with homosexuality for present purposes. Sometimes, as in the Asian flu episode, or the occasion when he believed he was being talked about as a male prostitute, these defenses gave way to genuine delusions of a paranoid nature. It is noticeable that in both these cases, the defenses broke down following real or imagined social slights, i.e., in one case he was being talked about, in the other, coughed at. Freud (1911) noted that paranoia, especially in males, has often been triggered off by such real or imagined social slights, and he related this to the unconscious homosexual element in the affective life of his patients (p. 445). In Albert's case, this is startlingly clear. In his relationship with Bob, for example, his homosexual inclinations became fully conscious. But Bob was never an individual in his own right, but considered merely as an adjunct of Albert's own body. And, as we have seen in the earlier phases, Albert's own body and the products of his imagination represented for him almost the whole of reality. This allows us to go a step further and to realize that homosexuality itself was no more than a defense against primary narcissism—the level at which he was fixated.

Analytic treatment, as we have seen, broadened the scope of his reality and enabled him to achieve a precarious foothold in normality. But it cannot be emphasized too strongly that this foothold is on the border where normality meets paranoia.

BIBLIOGRAPHY

Ekstein, R. & Friedman, S. (1957), The Function of Acting Out, Play Action and Play Acting in the Psychotherapeutic Process. *J. Am. Psa. Assn.*, V.

Fenichel, O. (1936), The Symbolic Equation: Girl=Phallus. *The Collected Papers of Otto Fenichel*, II. New York: Norton, 1954.

—— (1946), On Acting. *The Collected Papers of Otto Fenichel*, II. New York: Norton, 1954.

Freud, A. (1936), *The Ego and the Mechanisms of Defence*. New York: International Universities Press, 1946.

—— (1958), Clinical Studies in Psychoanalysis: Research Project of the Hampstead Child-Therapy Clinic. *This Annual*, XIV, 1959.

Freud, S. (1905), Jokes and Their Relation to the Unconscious. *Standard Edition*, VIII. London: Hogarth Press, 1960.

—— (1911), Psycho-analytic Notes upon an Autobiographical Account of a Case of Paranoia (Dementia Paranoides). *Collected Papers*, III. London: Hogarth Press, 1949.

—— (1914), On Narcissism: An Introduction. *Standard Edition*, XIV. London: Hogarth Press, 1957.

Nunberg, H. (1931), The Synthetic Function of the Ego. *Practice and Theory of Psychoanalysis*. New York: International Universities Press, 1955.

Schilder, P. (1923), *The Image and Appearance of the Human Body*. New York: International Universities Press, 1950.

SIMULTANEOUS ANALYSIS OF MOTHER AND CHILD

SIMULTANEOUS ANALYSIS OF MOTHER AND CHILD[1]

ILSE HELLMAN (London)

in cooperation with

OSCAR FRIEDMANN and ELIZABETH SHEPHEARD

The persistence of an intimate bond between certain children and their mothers well beyond the usual intensity and age has arrested the attention of child analysts long ago. Problems concerning the nature of such an exceptional tie, its effect on the growing child, and the means of communication between mother and child have led to the wish to study mother-and-child couples by means of simultaneous analyses. This wish has grown from clinical experience with cases in which the mother's participation in the child's disturbance forms an obstacle to his recovery, and in which it is felt that lasting, favorable results can be achieved and maintained only if the existing conditions within the mother can be altered too.

Nearly twenty-five years ago, based on observations made in the course of children's analytic treatment, Dorothy Burlingham (1932) described the manifold ways in which a mother can experience the analyst's intrusion into her intimate bond with her child and how, for both child and mother, such intrusion into certain areas of their lives can be experienced as a serious threat. A great deal of research has been done in recent years concerning the problem of the mother's pathogenic effect on the child, especially with regard to psychosis and psychosomatic illnesses in children. Recently the mother's par-

[1] This paper forms part of a Research Project entitled "Simultaneous Analysis of Mother and Child," which is conducted at the Hampstead Child Therapy Clinic, London. This particular study has been financed by the Psychoanalytic Research and Development Fund, Inc., New York.

Paper read at the Scientific Meeting of the Dutch Psycho-Analytical Society, Amsterdam, on October 23, 1959, and at the British Psycho-Analytical Society, London, on December 2, 1959.

ticipation in the child's inability to separate from her, as in the condition known as "school refusal" (or "school phobia"), has been given much attention in England. Augusta Bonnard already in 1949 has emphasized this aspect, and Adelaide Johnson has been concerned with the same problems in the United States.

The child's awareness of and response to the mother's unconscious fantasies and the relation of the child's symptomatology to the mother's unconscious wishes have been studied by Melitta Sperling (1950, 1951, 1954) by means of simultaneous analysis. In her publications she has not dealt with the transference aspect of her cases and especially not with the complicating factor of analyzing both mother and child herself, but other analysts have referred to them in discussions.

In her study entitled "Simultaneous Analysis of Mother and Child" (1955), Dorothy Burlingham has avoided the pitfalls of the double transference by adopting a different method. Child and mother were analyzed by different analysts who reported the material separately in weekly interviews to her. These written records and verbal reports formed the basis for her research study.

The opportunity to work along similar lines, studying the material of two mothers and their children from their concurrent analyses, was given to me three years ago in the framework of the research project on Simultaneous Analyses at the Hampstead Child Therapy Clinic. Five mother-child couples and a mother and her twin boys are at present in analysis under this scheme.

The case material I have chosen comes from the treatment of a boy, Eric, aged eleven years at the beginning of his treatment, and of his mother, Mrs. A. The mother's analyst was Mr. Oscar Friedmann. With his sudden death in December, 1958, the mother's treatment was abruptly terminated after nearly two years. The boy is now in his fourth year of treatment with Mrs. Elizabeth Shepheard, a student of the Hampstead Child Therapy course. The fact that the concurrent treatments have lasted for less than two years deprives us of a great deal of insight which we would have needed for a full evaluation. Nevertheless, the observations made in this period are worth discussing. My work was based on written weekly reports, and regular meetings with the mother's analyst and the boy's therapist separately, to discuss and amplify points which appeared to me relevant. Moreover, in these conferences the therapists conveyed to me the subtle shades of feelings experienced in the transference and countertransference, which cannot be conveyed in writing.

Background Data

When Mrs. A. and Eric first came to the Hampstead Clinic, the staff members recognized in them many of the well-known traits of mother-and-son couples who consult pediatric outpatient clinics before they finally reach child guidance. Winnicott (1948) has described such couples in his paper, "Reparation in Respect of the Mother's Organised Defense." He speaks of the narrow demarcation line that exists between a mother's normal hypochondriacal fears for her child and her pathological hypochondriasis which extends to the child's body. He mentions a boy who came to his outpatient clinic alone, saying: "Please Doctor, my Mum complains of pains in my tummy."

In Eric's case there was little doubt about the demarcation line. One was struck at once by the intensity of the mother's hypochondriacal fears concerning her boy; and the boy was already beyond bringing his mother's complaint of his fears and pains. It was clear that his fears of illness were already his own, as well as his mother's. He seemed aware of the internalization that had taken place, when early in his treatment he said to his therapist, referring to his digestion: "Once, only Mum used to worry, now it's me."

The concurrent analyses brought simultaneous experiences of anxiety about their health and bodily pains to light. This was one of the main areas of interaction. The other, closely related to it, concerned the interplay of the unconscious meaning which feeding and eating had in the relation of mother and son. Both of these led to the boy's inability to separate from his mother and consequently to his refusal to go to school. He had never left her before he went to the hospital for tonsillectomy at the age of three years. His panic at the separation was such that he was returned to his mother after one day. The operation was finally carried out at the age of five when he submitted to it passively.

If Eric had developed only somatic symptoms, they would probably not have come for child guidance but continued to make the rounds of pediatric outpatient departments of famous hospitals. But suddenly, at the age of eleven, Eric became unable to attend school. He had been a successful pupil, had recently won a grammar school place without difficulty; he had an I.Q. of 132 and an uninhibited learning capacity.

Eric's refusal to go to school began in the last weeks of the summer term in his junior school. It coincided with his mother's decision to go out to work, which meant that he would have to eat at school. After she had been out to work for three days, Eric came home from school during the morning and rang her at work in a state of anxiety, asking her to return home at once. He said he felt sick and was afraid of vomiting. Everything was tried to convince him to return, but without success. The mother gave up her work. After the summer holidays, when Eric was due to enter grammar school, he went there only once, and was unable to return. For the greater part of the following year he could not leave his mother, even within the house. He said that two things had upset him most on the first day at the new school: all the new boys were shown the sickroom, and from his classroom he could see the cemetery.

Eric was pale and thin; at moments of anxiety—and there were many—he looked ill. His mother was a small talkative woman; her appearance varied strikingly with her changing moods: she could look gay, carefully dressed in bright colors, or look miserable and uncared for, in either event attracting attention to her state of mind.

She was the daughter of a second-hand clothes merchant in the East End, who contracted Parkinsonism when Mrs. A. was five years old, became progressively incapacitated, and died when she was twenty years old. During all these years, Mrs. A.'s mother nursed him with great devotion, though she was said to have dominated him. From the description it appeared that Mrs. A.'s mother too had had intense hypochondriacal fears concerning herself and her children. She committed suicide when Eric's mother was in her late twenties. Mrs. A. had a brother, three years younger, who died in infancy, and another brother five years younger, with whom she has always had an exceptionally close relationship.

Eric's inability to separate from his mother and the concern that mother and son shared about his state of health were obvious at once to whoever saw them at the Clinic. The other striking feature was the undisguised hostility which broke through in their dealings with each other, and which the mother did not conceal in giving his history.

She was able to say that she had not wanted him, had tried to abort him, had been desperate about her failure to do so. She gave a vivid description of the hostility she had felt against him from the start, and of her attempts to suppress his early signs of aggression and unruliness. Her growing failure to do so had led to mutual physical attacks, in which he gained the upper hand from the age of four when he was able to hurt her so much that she stopped hitting him. Open hostility, anger about his stubborn refusal to comply with her wishes, alternating with anxiety about his health, were the dominant feelings she conveyed to the Clinic staff in her first contacts.

With regard to her husband, two statements characterized her feelings: that he was below her socially, a workman (while her father had been a salesman); and that he had a thumb missing. This need to denigrate him, to deny his masculinity, and to treat him as a powerless, useless being was intense. In fact, he was a skilled workman, earned well, but submitted to her ruling in silence. He expressed disappointment about the boy and felt helpless about Eric's and his mother's troubles.

Her need to keep control over her boy's developing powers of independent action and over his masculinity will be shown in detail.

The boy's overt behavior to his mother, for much of the time, can best be characterized by the word "ruthless"; and ruthless he was in the treatment of his therapist whenever she stood for the dangerous aspect of the mother. He demanded, threatened, and attempted to hurt her physically. He also showed the total lack of concern which is characteristic of ruthlessness, and never attempted to make good the damage he had done. He was unable to experience guilt. When his demandingness, destructive and sadistic fantasies reached an intolerable degree, he collapsed into physical exhaustion, bodily pain, and hypochondriacal fears. In the sessions he lay on the couch or floor, looking ill, overwhelmed by his fear of illness and death. His fears centered on the dread of having eaten harmful food, having been infected by germs, especially polio. After outbursts of sadistic fantasies in the session in the form of games or actions, he was at times pursued by ghosts which made him run at great speed down the Clinic road to escape them—or rather his therapist's fantasied vengeance. For a long time, he brought his sane, active, and creative part into the treatment only when he transferred to the therapist the quiet, constructive aspects of his father. The need to keep this island of safety made him tenaciously maintain a one-sided positive image of the father; he denied that there existed a frightening aspect of the father as well as his own aggressive impulses against him, though his nightmares showed them clearly from the start.

The decision to offer the mother treatment came three months after Eric had started. Work with him over these three months had added to the initial observations of the mother gained in superficial contacts with her. There were now clear indications of the areas in which her own disturbance seemed to be deeply linked with his. They centered around his food intake and digestion, the dangers threatening his health and life, and her role in his oedipal situation.

Mrs. A. accepted the offer of treatment reluctantly, making it clear that she had no need for help, but was prepared to do anything for the boy's good. Later she thought of it as a possible cure for her migraine. As could be expected, she proved to be an exceptionally difficult patient who fought her analyst tenaciously, in all ways available to a patient in the analytic setting, especially in regard to coming to appointments regularly and on time. Her analyst's unfailing empathy, his understanding of her deep anxieties and of her depression—which made her turn in panic to attack the external world —slowly led her in the transference to experience good feelings in herself and to see the good aspects of her present and past love objects. First experiences of sadness and guilt relating to her dead parents emerged. It was tragic that at this point, when the first tentative loving feelings appeared, she had to experience the loss of her analyst. She did not want to continue with another analyst.

The Meaning of Food in the Analyses of Mother and Child

Eric's unceasing demands for time, his insistence on more and more materials to work with, his impatience and despair when his demands were not fulfilled, gave his therapist a vivid experience of his greed and anxiety. At the same time, the absence of belief in mother's safety and goodness, and in the therapist's capacity or wish to satisfy him, gave evidence of a child in whom anticipation of good, satisfying experiences was lacking. Each good experience remained separate from the preceding one; the next one had to be fought for and forced out of her. Any delay made his anxiety overwhelmingly strong, led to rage, and was followed by passivity and sadness.

Food itself formed the center of his present battles with his mother; demands for special luxury foods which he knew she could ill afford were forced on her. His awareness of her own unconscious conflicts relating to food became clearly visible, and his knowledge of her fear for his survival gave him control over her.

In the mother's own treatment, the analyst experienced her demandingness and aggression and the absence of good expectations. She had dealt with her oral aggression and consequent fear of starvation and emptiness by omnipotently gaining control over food and becoming the person whose power over her objects lay in the food she was giving them or withholding from them. Concurrently, she was haunted by the fear that the food she provided might be harmful and cause a person's death. Her death wishes against a baby brother, born when she was three, who had died soon after birth, had reinforced her belief in her destructive omnipotence. At present, Eric represented the object she fed abundantly, whereas her husband was kept alive on a bare minimum. She could never refuse Eric's extravagant demands which he repeatedly put in terms of: "She's got to buy me salmon at sixteen shillings per pound." The thought that he might eat nothing if she did not fulfill his wishes implied, in her mind, a suicidal threat on his part which filled her with panic. Her own mother had committed suicide. She felt that she had been totally unaware of her mother's state of mind preceding this event. She was equally unaware of Eric's and other people's sadness, depression, and need of support. She was unconsciously expecting a repetition of the suicide experience through Eric. The meaning of suicide and her death wishes against him, especially the attempted abortion, became clear and could be linked with her omnipotent fantasies of her power over life and death through food. Through food she kept him linked to herself and alive; but in break-throughs of her death wishes, she had in fact given him food which she knew was bad.

Eric's fantasies about his mother's food showed that he shared her own omnipotent belief in its power; only her food could keep him alive; and, through it, he remained joined to her. He was unable to eat food she had not prepared; but we found that at the same time he was suspicious of food, feared to be poisoned by her, and had to investigate every mouthful. Projection of his oral aggression in his paranoid fears relating to her food clearly played an important part. Later his fantasies led to impregnation fears and passive wishes relating to the father. He identified himself with the suffering woman, and identification with the pregnant woman led to a vivid experience of labor, with pains and exhaustion in the session.

Were we confined to the material from Eric's analysis only, we should have regarded the projection of his oral aggression as the decisive factor in his fear of being poisoned. Our insight into the mother's material, however, has shown us that her unconscious wish to poison him was real and broke through repeatedly. Eric experienced these break-throughs, the anxiety that followed them, and the subsequent intensified defenses as an ever-renewed proof that his fear of being poisoned was justified. In this sphere, the problem of communication is not difficult to solve. After meals, when she had given him food which was in fact not fresh or otherwise harmful, her anxieties became intense. She then questioned him repeatedly regarding his digestion, inquired about possible pains, watched him anxiously, and, whenever her anxiety became too great to tolerate the uncertainty any longer, she gave him one of her many tablets to counteract the fantasied harm she had done. Eric unfailingly took these tablets. He shared all her magic beliefs, wore articles of her clothing for extra safety, and they took the same tablets to prevent what they anticipated would be the same illness. He even took tablets which were given to her for menstrual pains. She in turn experienced his anxiety and pain as a proof that her fantasy of having harmed him was real, and the anxiety he perceived in her confirmed the reality of his own fears.

Both Eric and his mother showed intense anxiety about anything over which they had no power. He expressed this mainly in regard to the weather, the digestive process, and germs. An attempt to know details of bodily functioning and illnesses induced in both passing feelings of mastery, but more knowledge brought more threats as well. The magic belief 'in tablets and their taking of tablets in the wake of fantasied or momentary sensations were a constant feature. Their fantasies of bodily unity became clearest in the simultaneous experience of pain. They both anticipated and felt it, aggressively projected it onto each other, and identified with each other's pain in turn. Only in recent analytic work with Eric does separateness of his bodily sensations begin to appear in relation to his therapist, after a phase of fantasied common experience with her. This gradually brought to an end the magic belief that his and his mother's experiences were one.

In the mother's treatment, similar attempts to extend her pain to the analyst and her wish to have the analyst share her pain with her were observed. The most instructive session in this respect was one in which she desired the analyst to share her menstrual pains, thereby relieving her through the feeling that he too suffered, that there no longer was a difference between male and female, and that they became joined in this way.

The Sexual Tie between Mother and Son

The intensity of Eric's hostility which appeared undefended in the transference, and the unrestricted indulgence in sadistic fantasies were striking. In these he was for a long time a surgeon who deceived his patients in the hospital, promising them cure, but in fact making them suffer the most horrible pain by severing their limbs, skinning them, etc., so that they could never recover. He thereby expressed his suspicion of his therapist and the treatment, projecting his own sadism onto her. He attempted to master his anxiety by himself becoming the sadistic surgeon. Analytic work in this area led to his sadistic intercourse fantasies and to his castration anxiety, which was experienced in these sessions as sudden abdominal pains and anxiety about a possible appendectomy.

His aggressive impulses in rivalry with the father and his fear of the father were strongly defended and remained inaccessible for a long time. Whenever an interpretation had dealt with the sexual aspect of the sadistic fantasies he stayed away from sessions. This resistance showed that he could talk with comparative ease about killing and torturing, but that the libidinal, sexual aspect of his fantasies was closely guarded. This eventually led to the therapist's conviction that he was guarding a secret.

We later learned about the nature of this secret from the mother's analysis. She gradually became able to admit that her only sexual gratification lay in intensive love play with Eric. She was frigid with her husband and fought against his attempts to have intercourse with her, either by feigning illness or by having the boy in their room. However, she could reach an orgasm by tightly holding and stimulating Eric into complete helplessness. Such scenes began with fights with the excited, struggling boy until he finally was overwhelmed by his excitement and by her physical superiority. At times she pushed her tongue into his mouth.

The origin of this practice can be traced to her primal-scene memories in which fellatio observations or fantasies played an essential part. During or after these early intercourse observations, she had discharged her excitation and rage through masturbation and later by using her younger brother as a partner. In her masturbation fantasies and her sexual games with her brother, she had played the father's role, using her tongue to penetrate. Her horror of being penetrated and of feeling a man on top of her prevented her at times from attending her sessions. When she did come, she attempted to shut out the analyst's words, reversing the roles by attacking him, as she attempted to do in the fight against her husband. The full physical experience of the reversal of roles and of her power to overwhelm her partner were reached with Eric, who now assumed the role Mrs. A.'s brother had played in her childhood. The sex practices with her brother had continued until he reached puberty. When they finally stopped, she became depressed. Later at the time of his marriage, a prolonged illness, brought on by neglect of an ear infection, kept her immobilized in the hospital for two years, soon after her father's death. Through this she regained her mother's full attention, who now nursed her with the same devotion that her mother had shown her father.

Fantasies of robbing the analyst of his possessions and a number of acted-out delinquencies against male shopkeepers and ticket collectors revealed the fantasy of robbing her father's penis. These were linked with the father's illness and his gradual deterioration, for which she now felt responsible.

For Mrs. A., Eric stood for the brother of her childhood, who had also represented part of herself. The knowledge of this part of the mother's pathology, her sexual practice with Eric, and the absence of this material in his treatment made it clear that Eric's overt hostility against the mother had to be understood also in terms of his need to fight her seduction, which doubly threatened him in that he was simultaneously overwhelmed by his impulses and by her body. His fear of being poisoned and of choking can now also be understood in terms of the penetration by her tongue. No differentiated and specific details of these sexual experiences appeared in the transference, but his dread of being overwhelmed by uncontrollable powers was often experienced in the session. He would then resort to megalomanic mechanisms by which he attempted in fantasy to get control over the powers he feared. The elements, and especially the weather, represented his impulses projected onto the external world, which he sought to control by fantasies of a weather machine.

The reality of his physical experiences with his mother was known to us only from the mother's analysis. In regard to his fear of being poisoned, we found that the understanding and interpretation of his fear of being overwhelmed remained incomplete as long as it was seen only in terms of projection of his own impulses. Being stimulated into helplessness by his mother and feeling her large body holding him down were real experiences which continued to reinforce his anxiety and counteracted the analytic work in this sphere.

As the analytic work on Eric's dread of his own aggression progressed and he recognized his magic belief in the power of his death wishes, Eric became able to make his first attempts to move away from his mother. He returned to school after one year's analysis, made first contact with other boys, came alone to his sessions, but could not yet sleep in his room. Gradually we understood the sequence of fantasies which made it impossible for him to sustain the feeling that he was an independent masculine being. Feeling strong was equal to overwhelming his mother and meant being able to harm her through sadistic intercourse; it also meant being able to attack and kill the father. While working on these feelings in his analysis, he developed a temporary claustrophobic symptom, relating to the headmaster whose sudden death he feared. During the same phase, related problems were worked through: nightmares in which he was facing a bleeding woman with her head cut off; direct attacks on his therapist in which he hurt her "accidentally" with a knife; and many sadistic fantasies which were followed by regression and withdrawal into illness.

To grow up and become separate meant losing the unity with the omnipotent mother and either being powerless like the father, or powerful and able to harm her. The mother's own omnipotent fantasies were transmitted to him in words and actions. In the oedipal triangle she had far-reaching control over the father. This was an important factor in the boy's inability to separate from her and in his inability to identify himself with the father's masculinity. The sexual secret between mother and son, from which he had to exclude the father and the therapist, had to be guarded because giving it away would bring danger from both mother and father.

So far we have traced the incapacity of mother and son to separate from each other to their sexual tie, the mutual death wishes and their projection. Although the shortness of the mother's analysis did not make extensive work possible, the role of depression—their mutual awareness of it and anxiety about it—was a further important factor in their need to cling to each other. Eric's growing wish for separateness and his turning to the father and teachers had serious repercussions on the mother's state. She experienced Eric's pubertal physical changes and his consequent withdrawal from bodily contact with her as a threat. The realization that she could no longer control his mind and body increased her anxiety, which led to intensification of rages and the need for sexual experiences with him. Both served as a defense against her depression and the feeling of "nothingness," which she had without him. She could no longer resort to her defense of exhibiting gaiety and excitement, and began to feel devalued and unloved. After seeing a film in which a headmaster's wife seduced a schoolboy in order to save him from homosexuality, she felt intensely guilty and for the first time saw Eric as a child she had damaged. Her fight against continuing her sexual play with him led to masturbation with fantasies of an ideal, loving man whom she could love in return, and her first loving feelings in the transference. Early in her analysis she recalled feelings of love for her father, but now she experienced her first feelings of mourning for him and guilt about her total lack of concern for him during his long illness and after his death.

After her analyst's death and until the present, there were clear signs of her struggle to let Eric become free from her. She attempted to get satisfaction away from him in line with an earlier fantasy in which she was selling clothes in a large store, thereby outdoing her father who sold secondhand clothes. The crowds and life in the store counteracted her empty and dead inner feelings. At other times, she fell back into illness, had minor operations, and greatly enjoyed the regressed state of being in bed and cared for by nurses. There were definite signs of pride in some of Eric's excellent school achievements, and evident relief about his good physical health. Detailed insight into her fantasies was no longer possible in occasional contacts.

The Mother's Pathogenic Effect

From the material bearing on selected points of interaction in this mother-child couple, certain conclusions regarding the problem of the pathogenic effect of the mother's disturbance on the child can be drawn. Approaching the question from the developmental angle, the following picture emerges.

At birth, Eric met a mother who had no wish to meet him. The available material showed that pregnancy itself was experienced at first as "the proof that she had lost the battle," as she put it. Her husband had won, had pushed something into her against her will, and she felt compelled to try to do away with it. The baby inside her was felt as an enemy. She projected her own hostility against her pregnant mother onto the baby who in this way stood for the attacking part of herself as well as for her baby brother who died soon after birth. She remembered having reacted with anger to the baby's first movements inside her: she could not control his movements while she carried him.

Immediately after his birth, her fantasies led him to a state of deprivation of basic need fulfillment. When she felt him at the breast, the fantasies of being sucked dry and emptied out by him were uppermost; she experienced feeding as a fight for survival and her flow of milk remained inadequate. At moments when the sensation of being sucked became pleasurable, the content of what she projected onto the baby changed and her active fellatio fantasies made her abruptly withdraw the nipple. Through these fantasies, Eric was from the start deprived of good satisfying experiences at the breast, and felt actual hunger for the first weeks, while the nurses tried to establish breast feeding without the mother's capacity to cooperate. He remained deprived not only of the actual experience of good feeding, but also of bodily contact in general. While he was quite small, the mother's fear of crushing him made her avoid handling him as far as possible. Nor could she allow the father or other people to substitute for her, because she either projected her own impulses onto them or was overcome by sudden feelings of jealousy when she saw the father happily holding Eric, a sight which compelled her to interfere.

A post-partum depression led to withdrawal, inability to eat, and consequent loss of weight; her thoughts centered for the first time on her dead mother. She had to watch the baby constantly, never let him out of sight, lest she might suddenly find him dead. This acute fear had an immediate effect also on the early development of his motility. He was kept strapped far more often and much longer than is normal and was given little opportunity to move about freely when he did get on his feet. Thus Eric missed the important elements making for normal development in the early phase: he lacked the experience of good and loving handling and the anticipation of his needs by the mother. These could have led to establishing loving feelings in him, strong enough to mitigate his aggressive impulses and fuse with them, and to the picture of a safe, loving mother in him.

In contrast to the damage done by lack of need fulfillment in the bodily and emotional aspects of his development, there was continued overstimulation of his whole body throughout latency into early puberty. The ultimate damage of such intense sexual stimulation without adequate discharge cannot be estimated from this material, but it is clear that the passive physical experiences with his mother prevented his attempt at establishing his active masculine genitality. Moreover, the anxiety over loss of control was heightened by the fact that the only way open for discharge was through rages. The role of bodily stimulation throughout childhood, and its further impact on problems of identity have been discussed by Phyllis Green-acre (1958).

The part played by the mother's oral aggression and narcissism, and the role of the mother's penis envy and its harmful consequences on Eric will have become clear from the material.

Apart from the content of her fantasies, the damaging effect of the mother's defense mechanisms is of particular importance.

This mother, as has been shown, made of her son an object of projection. Mrs. A. did not react to the child's needs and impulses on the basis of her perception of his internal situation, but in line with her projections. The overt behavior and changing needs of the child revived a succession of different infantile conflicts in her. As these became preconscious, they brought forth manifestations of her own early anxieties, fantasies, and defenses. The child stood successively for aspects of herself and for the different objects of her past in relation to whom she had originally experienced these conflicts.

Moreover, she resorted to omnipotent thoughts whenever she had to admit that she could not know or control people's thoughts and feelings. In relation to her analyst, she denied her wish to know what he felt and thought about her as well as her curiosity about his private life. Instead, she triumphantly told him "facts" that she professed to know about him, laying great stress on her "unfailing intuition." The facts she knew "by intuition" were entirely the result of her own wishes and projections. It was particularly striking that she was obviously unable to make use of those perceptions which could have led to a correct knowledge. What she perceived was either not taken in, or subsequently distorted when the correct perception would have provoked too great anxiety; for example, she knew "by intuition" that the analyst was a bachelor. The thought that he might have a wife aroused her intense jealousy and the wish to separate them and attack her. Consequently she did not see facts clearly demonstrating that he was married.

On the basis of this "intuition" she bypassed the child's needs and forced her own needs in their place. The ensuing inconsistency of the mother's responses to Eric induced in him a constant watchfulness based on the need to anticipate her feelings and actions. In the last phase of his analysis, this watchfulness and his attempt to differentiate his feelings and perceptions from the therapist's became prominent features in the transference. He watched, perceived, and persistently tested his perceptions and their reliability. He had to make sure again and again that she would not suddenly confront him with behavior for which he was unprepared, that she had feelings which were separate from his. He gradually learned to accept his feelings and perceptions as true, and through this experience found his own identity.

The mother's distortion of external reality to which she subjected the child led to faulty reality testing in Eric. We find that the mother's magic thinking, the omnipotent denial she used in order to avoid intolerable facts of external reality, were introjected by Eric who then operated with her mechanisms in the service of his own defenses. Mother and child experienced his own attempts at reality testing as danger, though for different reasons. For the mother, the danger arose from the fear that the child would force her to face unacceptable facts and attempt to loosen the unity with her. For the child, reality testing and the acceptance of facts which were not in accordance with mother's distorted picture threatened to bring about the loss of unity with her and thus to bear the full brunt of her hostility.

In Eric's case, the distortion pertained particularly to the reality of the father, the image of him as a whole person whose potent and masculine aspects the mother denied. In line with her denial and for the purpose of defense against his anxiety concerning the father, he too denied the father's real role. His denial of the real facts in this respect was in turn constantly reinforced by his mother who thus increased his confusion. For instance, when confronted with Eric's beginning masculinity and his bodily changes, she reacted to his question about his first emission by saying: "This is nothing special. All men and women have this."

THE MOTHER'S BENEFICENT EFFECT

Although this paper is concerned with the pathogenic effect of certain aspects of the close bond between mother and child, I want to bring one example showing a link between an important aspect of the mother's relationship to her own mother, which—in its repetition with Eric—has led to an area in which Eric functions well and can be successful and in which his mother can share his success through identification.

In the early part of his treatment, Eric's capacity to verbalize was severely restricted; words themselves were dangerous. Most of his material was brought in nonverbal ways and through acting. With the progress of his treatment and the gradual disappearance of his persecuting projections, his use of words and the capacity to verbalize increased and a growing pleasure in beautiful language became apparent. He began to write poetry and this creative effort led to first experiences of pleasure about his good capacities and to success through appreciation by his teacher.

From the mother's analysis we know that poetry and the wish to speak beautifully had from early childhood formed a strong bond between herself and her mother. This wish had had a defensive quality and had been aimed at warding off their oral aggression. It had signified "a secret union" against the father, whose crude language had been distasteful to Mrs. A.'s mother. Moreover, "mother reading poetry to her" had been an actual experience of a peaceful time together which symbolically stood for good food—food which was given exclusively to her and in which her father and brother had no part.

While Mrs. A. was unable to give Eric good satisfying feedings, she had repeated with him her own experience of being read to. By reading to Eric, she made him feel her enjoyment of beautiful language. These were, as far as we have seen, the only moments when he could have felt that she was peaceful and when she was able in relation to him to concern herself with something other than his body. Through her double identification—with her own mother who said the beautiful words, and with the child who received them from her—she was able to share Eric's enjoyment and progress in this sphere. In other spheres in which his gifts and activities were derived from his identification with his father, she experienced them as rivalry and her envy compelled her to interfere with his progress and ruin his enjoyment.

In "Dreams and the Occult" (1932) Freud mentioned the problem of communication of thoughts between mother and child and cited an observation made by Burlingham (1932) in which an explanation other than direct thought transference between mother and child could be found for the child's apparent awareness of the content of his mother's thoughts at a given moment. In the concurrent analyses of Eric and his mother I have found no evidence of this, though the fact that I had no direct contact with either patient may be responsible for this. Eric's knowledge of the mother's fantasies, as far as I was able to trace it, could always be related to perceptions of her manifest behavior in relation to him and the people and objects in the external world around them.

Other investigators have made similar observations. Children whose tie to their mother is characterized by anxiety and distrust, as it was in Eric's case, and whose physical bond to her is abnormally prolonged, have also been found to become alert to and remain observant of minute nonverbal clues given unconsciously by their mothers.

Heightened awareness of external perceptions and their interpretation in relation to himself are characteristic of the paranoid patient. When the child's paranoid ideas resulting from his projections meet an external reality which confirms these ideas, when the mother's own destructive or seductive wishes make her not only a fantasied but a real danger, the child clings tenaciously to this watchfulness in relation to her, even after his projections have been understood as such. Only a change within the mother can ultimately free him from this aspect of the abnormal bond, and from the real need to protect himself from her.

BIBLIOGRAPHY

Bonnard, A. (1949), School Phobia—Is It a Syndrome? Paper read at the International Congress of Psychiatry, Paris, 1949. Published in *Archives*, V, 1949.
Burlingham, D. (1932), Child Analysis and the Mother. *Psa. Quart.*, IV, 1935.
—— & Goldberger, A., Lussier, A. (1955), Simultaneous Analysis of Mother and Child. *This Annual*, X.
Freud, S. (1932), *New Introductory Lectures on Psycho-Analysis.* London: Hogarth Press, 1933.
Greenacre, P. (1958), Early Physical Determinants in the Development of the Sense of Reality, *J. Am. Psa. Assn.*, VI.
Johnson, A. (1953), Factors in the Etiology of Fixations and Symptom Choice. *Psa. Quart.*, XXII.
—— & Szurek, S. (1942), Collaborative Psychiatric Therapy of Parent-Child Problems. *Am. J. Orthopsychiat.*, XII.

Levy, K. (1960), Simultaneous Analysis of Mother and Child. *This Volume.*

Sperling, M. (1950), Children's Interpretation of Their Mother's Unconscious. *Int. J. Psa.*, XXXI.

—— (1951), The Neurotic Child and His Mother. *Am. J. Orthopsychiat.*, XXI.

—— (1954), Reactive Schizophrenia. *Am. J. Orthopsychiat.*, XXIV.

Winnicott, D. W. (1948), Reparation in Respect of the Mother's Organised Defense. *Collected Papers.* London: Tavistock Press, 1958.

SIMULTANEOUS ANALYSIS OF A MOTHER AND HER ADOLESCENT DAUGHTER[1]

The Mother's Contribution to the Loosening of the Infantile Object Tie

KATA LEVY (London)

With an Introduction by

ANNA FREUD, LL.D. (London)

Introduction

Up to the present date, nine mother-child couples have been in simultaneous analysis in our Hampstead Child-Therapy Clinic, or are in such analyses at present. The material gained from these studies is useful for a number of purposes.

Above all, it is invaluable for highlighting the points of interaction between the abnormalities of mother and child, as Dorothy Burlingham has shown in an earlier publication (1955). In this paper which deals with the treatments of a highly disturbed woman and her young child (who entered analysis before the age of four), the author maintains that "the influence of the mother's actions, her manifest attitude, her conscious and above all her unconscious fantasies, is neither straightforward nor uniform." Ilse Hellman, in a recent study of the treatments of a mother and her schoolboy son, has confirmed this assertion in all respects.[2] The detailed clinical demonstrations of both authors represent a welcome step forward from the indications

---

[1] This paper forms part of two research projects, entitled "Simultaneous Analysis of Mother and Child" and "Enquiry into the Analysis of Adolescents" respectively. The analyses of Debby and her mother, and the coordinating work attached to it, have been financed by the Ford Foundation, New York.

[2] See Ilse Hellman, "Simultaneous Analysis of Mother and Child." *This Volume.*

derived from child-guidance work to the effect that "most mental disturbances of children can be traced back to the disturbances of their parents;" that a particular mother does "not want" her child to grow up, to become clean, to lose his symptoms, etc., precise information backed by analytic findings taking the place in this manner of the former rather vague generalizations.

Secondarily, our material suggests that not all the children studied in this project show direct reactions to their mothers' symptoms but that some of them are affected indirectly only, so far as their mothers' illness interferes, or has interfered, with the latter's capacity for effective mothering. In these cases the resultant disturbances of the children can be of a completely different nature from those of their mothers and show none of the characteristic consequences of identification, of the overlapping of fantasy activity, and of the *folie-à-deux* phenomena described by the two authors mentioned above.

Thirdly, our study throws light on some important facts which govern the therapeutic possibilities in child analysis and limit them in certain cases. Where the neurotic symptom, the conflict, or the regression of a child is anchored not only in the young patient's own personality but held in place further by powerful emotional forces in the parent to whom the child, in his turn, is tied, the therapeutic action of analysis may well be slowed up or, in extreme cases, made impossible. Our material shows instances in which the interpretations to the child have become effective, or regressive libidinal positions have been given up in direct relation to the mother's relinquishing either a fixed pathological position of her own or, in other cases, relinquishing her pathological hold on the child.

Finally, I should like to maintain that the tool of simultaneous analysis can be used profitably also to throw light on other developmental problems. To understand the interaction between parents and their children is of the highest importance not only where the first foundations of the personality or the roots of mental illness are concerned. As a child moves forward on the developmental scale, each step demands the giving up of former positions and gains, not only from the child himself but also from the parent. It is only in the most healthy and normal cases that both sides—parents and child—wholly welcome the progressive move and enjoy the child's increasing maturity and gradually increasing libidinal and moral independence. More often it is one or the other partner who lags behind, the child being unable to free himself from fixations, or the parent clinging to attitudes of protectiveness and mothering which have become unjustified. In the worst cases, mother and child may join forces in a regressive move. Such interlocking then becomes particularly fateful with the onset of puberty. In a research project on "Adolescence," undertaken in the Hampstead Child-Therapy Clinic (and directed by Dr. L. Frankl and Dr. Ilse Hellman), the analytic study of the various manners in which individual adolescents strive to free themselves from the infantile object ties to their parents plays a prominent part. Here, again, the simultaneous analyses of mothers and their children have proved helpful. Whereas we receive no more than a dim impression of the parent's responses in those cases where the adolescent alone is in treatment, simultaneous analysis enables us to trace the contributions made by both sides to the success or failure of this particular developmental task.

I have mentioned this fourth use of simultaneous analysis in detail to introduce the paper by Kata Levy on the "Simultaneous Analysis of a Mother and Her Adolescent Daughter" which follows here. I hope that it may serve to illustrate the points made above. It is true that this particular mother-child couple entered treatment for the usual therapeutic reasons and for the elucidation of the links between their respective disturbances. But in the course of the work, their analyses became significant for the exploration of the struggle of a neurotic adolescent to free herself from her preoedipal and oedipal attachments, and of her mother's part in this. The attached paper describes the story from the mother's side only, and shows her own battle. The story of the daughter's analysis, with all its implications for the mother-child as well as for the adolescent problem will be given independently at a later date.

Simultaneous Analysis of a Mother
and Her Adolescent Daughter

Though Debby's mother consciously wished to loosen the ties by which her daughter was attached to her, she had unconsciously prolonged her infantile attachment and built up a relationship in which both mother and child were caught. It was impossible to loosen or change this relationship by treating only one partner. Therefore, after Debby had been in treatment for two years, the decision to offer analysis to the mother was made.

What Does the Child Represent in the Psychopathology of the Mother?

There were difficulties in Mrs. G.'s personality, conflicting feelings about being a mother, which made her unable to find instinctively the way how to be "the ordinary devoted mother," though she very much wanted to be a good mother to the only child she could have. She had previously lost prematurely born twins and had been told, after a miscarriage in Debby's infancy, not to have any more children. These factors contributed to making her especially anxious in her care for Debby. She relied heavily on Truby King's widely used manual for the instruction of mothers, which is based on the idea of regular and consistent handling of babies, very much in contrast to viewpoints stressing feeding on demand. Debby was for her an object of duty, guilt, anxiety, and annoyance, of frustrated ambition and of competitiveness, and, on rare occasions, of pride.

Characteristics of the Mother's Love for Her Daughter

Before coming to us Mrs. G. had made earlier attempts to seek psychiatric help. On these occasions she had been told that she was overprotective, which she understood to mean that she loved Debby too much. The main characteristics of this "love" were its guilty origin and its body relatedness.

Body care with overemphasized oral and anal features were prolonged far beyond infancy into childhood. Mrs. G. continued in latency to assist Debby in washing and dressing, and in getting her ready for school. Otherwise Debby would not have been punctual because of her obsessional habits.

In addition to the prolonged physical care, Mrs. G. had many *worries* about body functions, particularly about feeding and the slightest dysfunction mainly of a digestive nature. Mrs. G. worried when her baby cried, and she worried whether Debby was still alive when she ceased crying. When Debby went to school, Mrs. G. worried about her going out in bad weather and about all the dangers of the road, etc. Later she worried about Debby's neurotic symptoms and behavior difficulties. At present Debby's future development causes her—not unfounded—worries.

Mrs. G.'s *interests* were essentially body-centered. She was always interested in her child's appearance, as indeed in her own. But she never had the patience or interest to sit down and play with the little girl. No common activities or interests were taken up which would have opened sublimatory possibilities.

Mother's Object Relationship to Child, and Its Influence on the Future Loosening of Object Ties

This relationship was rooted in a conflict over death wishes and the defenses against them, primarily by reversal into the opposite. This conflict—now repeated with Debby—arose in childhood and adolescent situations, when Mrs. G. had been tied down to duties too burdensome for her age, which had robbed her of her justified wish for freedom. Out of her guilt feelings, by turning her aggression against herself, developed a moral masochism in adult life, which made her suffer her motherhood like a punishment. Debby strongly sensed her mother's unconscious drives, anxieties, and guilt feelings. She became extremely possessive and willful and developed a wish for power. In their sadomasochistic relationship she dominated her mother, who felt compelled to worry constantly about her child and to be "her prisoner" as she expressed it. Her fear of insanity in her child was the basis of it.

The whole family used the mechanism of conversion: in expressing their inner stress in body complaints, or in using "flight into illness." Until her analysis Mrs. G. (whose family had an epileptic background) suffered from long-lasting migraine attacks, during which she was nauseous, did not eat, and had to lie in a darkened room for many hours. These headaches became rarer and milder after Mrs. G. had gained insight into their psychic origin.

Mr. G. too suffered from headaches and fatigue, particularly when he had professional worries. In addition, he kept to some special—quite neurotic—food restrictions.

Debby made the most of her overprotected upbringing and of this family feature. She used digestive troubles as a means of intruding into her parents' bedroom, asking her mother's assistance in forced or pretended sicknesses, in administering her "Andrews" at night, or wanting to be comforted and taken into her bed. Debby's jealousy could not bear her mother giving attention to anyone except herself. The worst scenes occurred when her father happened to be sick and was looked after by the mother. On such occasions Debby often "fell ill" too, wanting her mother to serve her meals in bed.

Normal educational means or pressure were unsuccessful with Debby because she always found ways of getting the upper hand. In verbal fights and reproaches, Debby played on and met her mother's guilt feelings. Screaming and shouting were successful weapons, as she knew her mother's concern with their neighbors' opinion. So Mrs. G. gave in quickly, or even avoided interfering with Debby's whims out of fear of scenes for which she felt responsible and from which she also wanted to protect her husband. But even during the periods when Debby had no outbreaks of open aggression she ruled the home by her obsessional habits. To any attempt at influencing her, a cross "You don't understand" was the answer. Her anal character made her oppose any suggestions her mother made, and her mother was well aware of it and deeply discouraged by it.

Mother's Interference with Daughter's Relationship to Father

Unlike other mothers who use the father's authority when they feel too weak to handle difficulties with their children, there was a tendency in Mrs. G. to isolate and separate father and daughter as if protecting one from the other. This tendency had been apparent quite early when Mrs. G. had put the child to bed before her father came home in the evening in order to be undisturbed by the always overexcited little girl. Mrs. G.'s wish to have one person's company undisturbed for herself originated in the crowded home in which she grew up as one of six sisters. She felt inferior to two of her sisters, being unable to compete with their glib speech and better formal education.

Debby was separated from her father during her first three years of life by wartime conditions. She reacted always with great excitement to his occasional visits. The very demanding little girl made it difficult for Mr. G. to assume his role of a proper father.

Mrs. G. on the other hand felt compelled to protect Debby from her father's interfering with her whimsical moods which she treated as an illness. This seemed to be a repetition of situations in which her own mother protected her daughters from all the restrictions imposed by religion, with which the father would have burdened the girls. Mrs. G.'s mother helped to cover and hide the girls' little sins with the excuse, "You must not excite father." The application of this warning *displaced* onto Debby's father led us to recognize the *displacement* of Mrs. G.'s possessive tendencies out of her own oedipal conflict. We shall refer to that later on in greater detail.

Debby's School Phobia

Debby's school phobia that brought her into treatment at the age of twelve and a half years was partly based on her fear of sickness in connection with sexual excitement at school, mainly of a homosexual nature, partly on her inability to separate from her mother, who unconsciously had paved the way for this.

Debby was a highly intelligent girl with an I.Q. of 156 on the Stanford Binet scale. Her school phobia already showed during her nursery school days, but stopped her regular schooling only after she had entered high school with a scholarship.

Her analysis disclosed that her whole digestive tract was highly libidinized, her oedipal conflict belated and unsolved, and that the root of all her troubles lay in her castration problem, i.e., an overt and overwhelming penis envy. This caused her regression to earlier instinctual levels, to which she was fixated by the oral and anal indulgence her body care had secured for her. Fear, clinging to her mother, aggressive outbreaks, and obsessional habits were the surface manifestations. After two years of Debby's treatment her anxieties lessened as she got insight into their unconscious background. There was some slight progress in her ego development. She had given up her interest in horses and riding with which she was preoccupied when she had entered her treatment. She accepted private tuition which was to enable her to re-enter school with her own age group. She even undertook some tentative steps to return to school, but was not able to carry on. It became clear that she was faced with the task of mastering her own instinctual drives as well as the tendencies inherent in her mother's unconscious which had a seductive effect on her. Her ego could not cope with this double task.

Mother's Analysis

This was the situation when Mrs. G.'s analysis began, which lasted for nearly three years.

Some of Mrs. G.'s dreams clearly disclosed her ambivalence in regard to relinquishing her hold on the child. In a dream occurring in the sixth month of her analysis, her protectiveness bordering on seduction was overtly displayed. She repeated in the dream what she constantly did in reality: watching Debby, who went out to school in the pouring rain, but protected by a mackintosh, umbrella, etc., to see if she really would go or turn back. Seeing her still waiting in front of the entrance, she slightly opened the door, sure that Debby *would* turn back. But Debby told her in a cross voice to shut the door and not to watch her. This dream occurred at the time when the mother tried to master her compulsive watching of Debby, when, at last, Debby left the house to go to school, where she always arrived late. Mrs. G. "secretly" used to watch Debby from the window going down the street, as if she wanted to pull the girl back with invisible ties.

The change Mrs. G.'s analysis brought about in her could not undo the harm done to her child up to adolescence. It could give her more insight into her ambivalence, more control over her own anxiety and guilt which had caused her preoccupation and holding on to the child.

Debby's Reaction to Her Mother's Analysis

It was not until Mrs. G. had started psychoanalysis that Debby's definite return to school occurred. The way to alleviating her school avoidance had partly been paved by her own analysis which had to some extent solved her own separation anxiety. But in addition Debby had to be exposed to the new experience that her mother could separate: that her mother could go out even when Debby stayed at home; that her mother could stand firm and resist Debby's ever renewed attempts to keep mother at home (by developing sore throats, etc.). This was the main contribution which Mrs. G.'s analysis made to Debby's returning to school.

Debby had to be weaned, as it were, in preadolescence from all her body relationships with her mother. But as she had experienced her mother's love only in the described body-bound way, the lessening of physical care caused her to feel deprived and unloved. She reproached her mother repeatedly throughout the years: "You don't care for me, you have no sympathy, no interest in me." She tried again and again to provoke sympathy with illnesses, even by deliberately catching a cold. She tried to re-establish the old feeding interest of her mother by linking it to her so-called slimming diet, in which she alternated between periods of starving herself and greedy overeating. She tried to arouse her mother's body interest by changing over from one cardigan to another, sometimes five times in one morning; by constantly asking her mother how she liked her hair style, and by pestering her, showing her ballet steps and body movements, following her mother into the kitchen and making incessant demands for attention. She could not accept being deprived of body care, worry, and interest by her mother's changed attitude.

Mother's Reaction to Debby's Change

When Debby was around fifteen years of age, she made some tentative steps to find other object relationships. Flirtations with boys in and outside her school were noticed by her mother, with an inner joy, who saw in them signs of normality. But in addition, Mrs. G. saw in these developments the future possibility of ridding herself of her burdensome daughter. She encouraged a holiday invitation to a friend's country house for ten days and also for a fortnight at a summer school. The following Christmas Debby kept invitations to the country or to Paris in suspense, until it was too late. Mrs. G. became conscious of her wanting so much to get rid of Debby that she would have felt guilty if she had tried to persuade Debby to go. Her rationalization for it was that her trying to influence Debby could only have the opposite effect.

Mrs. G. had many dreams dramatizing the dangers Debby would be exposed to when left to her own resources. One of them in the last months of her treatment showed that her ambivalence still persisted, but also that she had gained insight into it.

I went out taking my bird with me. I had it dressed in a nice little frock like a little girl. I was afraid of losing her and squashed her in my hand when I feared that I would lose her. Then I pressed her into my handbag and shut it. Someone warned me that I would suffocate it. Finally it ran away into a narrow bypath but I quickly grabbed it again.

She interpreted that her two-mindedness toward Debby—wanting to let her go and yet keeping her anxiously back—was the way of harming her.

Debby's social relationships seemed to develop quite normally since she had overcome her initial inhibitions. She was found attractive, received and enjoyed invitations and outings with boys. But parallel with this development, she renewed her former interest in intruding into her parents' bedroom at late hours. It was difficult to understand why Mrs. G. was never able to lock her door. There was nothing to confirm the suspicion that this could be the case of a frigid woman wanting to use her child as a barrier between herself and her husband. Debby's parents seemed to be very devoted to each other and anxious not to allow any discord between them. Mrs. G. was a good housewife, full of regard for her hard-working husband's comfort and peace. He on his part tried to do his best to provide for his family. She took his most neurotic dietary demands for granted and respected them. They seemed to be justified in their view that except for Debby they could live the peaceful life they both longed for. So one had to accept Mrs. G.'s explanation that it was her anxiety at leaving Debby alone when she could not lock her bedroom door. When Debby was a small child the mother had the feeling that to lock Debby out of the bedroom was tantamount to leaving her alone in the flat. That she never dared to do until her analysis, for fear that Debby "would do something," based on her distrust of Debby's normality. Toward the end of her treatment she was once firm enough to turn out the perplexed girl from her bedroom, as she intruded with an unfounded body complaint, and turned the key to secure herself peace. In the dream that followed extreme guilt feelings were expressed for having used the key for the first time. This happened following many comments about it in her analysis.

Mother's Infantile and Adult Relations and Their Influence on Her Own Child and the Loosening of Their Ties

Mrs. G. was greatly tied to her own family. She was the second of six daughters of a very strict orthodox Jewish father and a hystero-epileptic mother. She had been compelled from early adolescence to sit watching her mother in day-long half-unconscious states, through her feeling of duty and her love for her father. She had been very much a mother to her youngest sister. The way in which she constantly anxiously watched her own healthy baby reminded her of her endless watching of her mother's, as well as of her youngest sister's epileptic fits. She had had to observe the onset of these attacks and take precautions against them. She did not finish school, partly on account of these duties, which often kept her at home to the detriment of her achievements and position in school. Her ambition could hardly bear this. Partly it was a challenge to work like an adult in father's shop, and to be able to earn money for personal adornment. There was and still is much competitiveness and jealousy among the sisters, mainly with Pen, the second youngest. Pen, as a child, acquired by her excessively bad behavior the privileged position of accompanying her mother wherever she went. Toward this sister Mrs. G. still has a partly guilty and subdued, partly competitive attitude with the half-suppressed wish of showing off.

She had displaced her oedipal rivalry onto Pen, indulging in the knowledge that her father preferred her to Pen, while Pen had her special attachment to the mother. In identifying Debby with Pen, quite consciously and obviously, she repeated the same situation in her own present family. Thus her own unsolved oedipal conflict became entangled with that of Debby's. Identifying her own father with Debby's father she isolated the child from him, wanting to keep him to herself as in the past she had wanted to keep her father for herself alone. With that she created the unhealthy attachment of the girl to herself, which grew to be an unbearable burden for her.

In her treatment Debby complained that her mother showed herself so very sure in her possession of father and excluded her from their relationship. These complaints seemed at first to be a welcome manifestation of her normal oedipal rivalry. But they could be given more realistic value when the intricacies of Mrs. G.'s own oedipal conflict, in combination with her married life, were understood.

Debby was justified in sensing feelings of jealousy, rivalry, and competitiveness in her mother. But she could not know that she, as the object of these feelings, was not really Debby but Pen. Mrs. G.'s endless social competition with Pen was still going on, at present about "important people" and persons of high standing whom they wanted to meet or see at their house. Though Mrs. G. herself regarded this social competition as very childish, she could not help continuing it. Eventually it became understandable as a repetition of their childhood competition for the important figures of their own family.

Beside these unconscious motives of envy and rivalry, conscious ones went on changing at different periods of life. Clothes became an expression of this competition at one time and this particular interest has lasted until the present. Later she envied her sister's easy attitude to life. Pen with a less burdensome conscience managed to have an easier life with her five children than her sister with her one difficult one, as Mrs. G. repeatedly stated. In the course of the years their children became objects of competition. Debby denied her mother the satisfaction of outdoing Pen's less gifted daughter at school. Growing up she quite consciously prevented any possibility of her mother being proud of her in social life, even if this meant denying herself some pleasure. Mrs. G. had to pay with feelings of guilt and with migraines for every "bad thought" she felt toward Pen. She tried to suppress and control this as well as she was able to control her behavior.

From early adolescence onward Mrs. G. had suffered from fears, anxieties, lack of self-confidence, and feelings of insecurity. Her lack of schooling in contrast to that of her sisters' promoted her inferiority feelings and overshadowed throughout adolescence all the enjoyments of social life which a country town could amply provide. Many of these feelings—the fear of being "left on the shelf," not asked to dance, not asked for in marriage—were introduced into her analysis by a series of Cinderella dreams. In these the stereotyped complaint was expressed that everybody else could have their share of enjoyment, only she was not permitted to have it.

The masochistic character of her relationship with Debby was striking in the way it followed and repeated the same Cinderella pattern. Early in analysis she sat crying at the window one sunny Sunday morning, complaining that everybody was outside in the streets, only she was indoors, like a prisoner. She could not get out with Debby, who constantly made scenes, and dared not leave her at home either.

Leaving her family's home was a great problem for Mrs. G. when she married. She could not cope with her feeling of loneliness when they had moved to the next town, half an hour's distance from her family. She was not so very young at that time, having married at twenty-five years of age and having had Debby when she was over thirty. At last she succeeded in persuading her husband to settle in her parents' home town. During her husband's absence in the war, she lived with her evacuated family. Thus, moving away from her own family was not accomplished for many years until they finally settled in London, with Debby nearly three years old.

While Debby suffered no separation from her mother, there were repeated moves and changes of surroundings during her first three years. During Debby's first two years, Mrs. G. tried repeatedly to establish a home for herself and the child, wanting to be within easy reach of her husband in his wartime occupation. But she could not cope with the first difficulty of her crying baby and the neighbors' reaction to it. She took refuge in her parents' house when the baby had digestive troubles. Here the shared responsibility permitted her to relax, and the baby stopped crying. "I was settled, she was settled," Mrs. G. put it. Once, coming home from a week end she spent with relatives, the child greeted Mrs. G. with excessive joy. She wanted to sit only on her mummy's knees and stroke her face lovingly. Mrs. G. was surprised and astonished to be loved so much by her child.

It seems to throw some light on her own lack of genuine motherly feeling.

Summary

Anna Freud in her paper on "Adolescence" (1958) distinguished between children who, in an adolescent upset, aim at freeing themselves from their early objects and family ties, and those others without an adolescent upheaval who remain "good" children "wrapped up in their family relationships." She found the determining factor in the latter's ego and superego formation and in excessive defenses.

In Debby we found an adolescent with all the upheavals characteristic of her age group and with—strangely—*no* urge to detach herself from her parents and her home.

We wanted to find out what part her mother had played in forming and keeping up this relationship. We could understand Debby's peculiarities better by viewing the mother's difficulties: her anxious uncertainty in rearing a child; her making the relationship to Debby an exclusively body-related and sadomasochistic one; her excessive guilt feelings which inhibited her capacity to stand firm against her daughter's unreasonable demands and which prevented her from loosening her own tie to her daughter. In how far Debby's need for protection against inherent driving forces of a constitutional nature play a part in her clinging to her calm and controlled mother, cannot be clarified with certainty.

A true understanding of the main difficulties could be reached only by coordinating the vicissitudes of the oedipal conflicts of both mother and child, and their effect on each other.

BIBLIOGRAPHY

Burlingham, D. (1955), Simultaneous Analysis of Mother and Child. *This Annual*, X.
Freud, A. (1958), Adolescence. *This Annual*, XIII.

PROBLEMS OF PSYCHOPATHOLOGY IN ORGANICALLY IMPAIRED CHILDREN

COMMENTS ON THE PSYCHOLOGICAL CONSEQUENCES OF CRYPTORCHISM

A Clinical Study

PETER BLOS, Ph.D. (New York)[1]

I. Introductory Remarks

The psychoanalytic literature contains only scant references to the testicles and their role in the mental life of the male child. This fact alone invites a report on cases with undescended testicles in which these body parts due to their abnormal state assumed a role of specific psychological import. There is no doubt that the male child concentrates almost exclusively on one part of his genitals, namely, the penis, while the other parts (scrotum, testes) are but peripherally and transiently acknowledged. With reference to this fact Freud (1923) commented: "It is remarkable, by the way, what a small degree of interest the other part of the male genitals, the little sac with its contents, arouses in the child. From all one hears in analyses one could not guess that the male genitals consist of anything more than the penis" (p. 246). However, the male child is not totally unaware of the scrotal region and possesses tactile as well as visual knowledge of it. This is exemplified by the self-observation of a two-and-a-half-year-old boy who had noticed that an undescended testicle had come down into the scrotal sac. He had noticed the change and was perturbed by it. The father, a pediatrician, had paid no special attention to the previous condition and was surprised at the child's self-observation and negative reaction. The little boy wanted it changed back to the way it had been; he "didn't like" two testicles. The change and newness of this body part was initially disturbing to the child but was assimilated within a short time.

[1] Madeleine Borg Child Guidance Institute, Jewish Board of Guardians, New York City.

Analytic experience with male patients, children and adults, bears out the fact that the penis as a pleasure-giving organ is more highly cathected with libido and aggressive energy than the other parts of the male genital. However, under the abnormal condition of an undescended testicle the genitals assume a special role. It is not my contention to infer that in the deviate condition of an undescended testicle, there appears in magnified dimension a primary cathexis of the testicle. Quite to the contrary, I consider the dominant role of the testicle apparent in the following cases to be of a secondary order, namely, determined by environmental influences. I do not consider cryptorchism in itself as pathogenic. Only secondarily, within the matrix of a disturbed parent-child relationship, does this condition acquire a profoundly detrimental influence on the mental development of the child. The anxious (aggressive) preoccupation of the environment with the genital defectiveness of the child eventually designates the testicle as the focal genital part in relation to which the formation of the body image and psychosexual development in general becomes specifically distorted. The genital defect, then, serves in the mental life of the child as the "organizing experience" (Greenacre, 1956) and results in ego deformations of a rather typical pattern. Fantasy life, restitutive acts, ego functions and defensive operations, self- and body image, sexual identification were studied in a number of cases of cryptorchism; three of them are reported here in detail. It must be borne in mind that the usual body-damage anxiety of the male child is in these boys associated with a missing testicle, i.e., with an already accomplished fact over which they have no control. The body-part loss is no longer a threat because it is palpably verifiable. On the other hand, a restitution of the loss is always kept within the realm of possibility as attested by the frequent medical check-ups and interventions. Napoleon's famous dictum, which Freud (1912) paraphrased into saying that "anatomy is destiny," assumes in these cases a special meaning, because here anatomy remains alterable—at least, that is the promise which the environment never ceases to impute. Consequently, anatomical uncertainty is destiny.

It became apparent in the cases presented how the body image is shaped by sensory perception in conjunction with environmental responses to the body and its defect. In this connection it was particularly striking to see that the body change, such as spontaneous descent (case of Larry) or successful operative correction (cases of Steven and Joe) resulted in a rapid shift of behavior, attitudes, interests, and skills. This change cannot be credited to the resolution of endopsychic conflicts alone. The clinical observation of cathectic shifts which were brought about by the restoration of body intactness has theoretical and therapeutic implications which shall be discussed after the case material has been presented.

In all three cases there occurred a mysterious exclusion of the physical condition of unilateral cryptorchism from the rest of the case histories. In two cases the fact of undescended testicles had to be surmised through symptomatic acts of the child. The parents did not mention the child's condition initially, nor did the boy himself ever refer to it. Symbolic representation of the genital defect was abundant in the play material and behavior. In all cases a medical clarification of the genital status was attained. Therapy always came to an impass whenever the medical planning for restorative intervention (injection or operation) was indefinitely postponed. The therapist had hoped against hope that the child after having worked through his fantasies would in due time disclose spontaneously his genital condition. Only under the pressure of medical intervention became such fantasies available in therapy, i.e., could serve as a vehicle to interpret distortions and defenses. Anatomical as well as sexual enlightenment was given in great detail, especially in the cases where the child had to be prepared for an impending operation.

The three boys studied were in the prepubertal age. The orchidopexy on Steven was performed at the age of ten years three months; on Joe at the age of twelve years ten months; spontaneous descent was confirmed in the case of Larry at the age of ten years eleven months. This paper is in no way a report on the therapy of the three boys. Their respective diagnostic categories had little in common; however, their symptom pictures showed significant similarities which were due to the identical genital defect which they shared. The presence of this physical factor indeed blurred the diagnostic and prognostic assessment of the cases to a considerable extent.

Where the maldescent was corrected spontaneously there was far more doubt about and distrust in the permanency of the restoration than in the operative cases. In the latter the action was accepted as final, and more faith was lent to the surgeon's knife than was given to an act of nature. This difference we can attribute to the masochistic and the castrative wishes which contrary to all expectations turned the defective boy into an intact man. He who entered the lion's den had come out alive. Besides the assurance of body intactness, the operation also demonstrated that the body had not been permanently injured by masturbation. Of course, we can detect behind the masculine euphoria which followed the operation an overcompensation of persistent feminine strivings.

The mere condition of an undescended testicle certainly does not lead to similar diagnostic entities, because cryptorchism cannot be considered as pathogenic in itself. However, it lends different conditions some points of similarity since the genital defect assumes in these cases an influence of dominant importance. Whatever the diagnostic category, the "organizing experience," namely, cryptorchism, was the same for all of them. The existence of identical symptoms in our cases became apparent, such as motility disturbances (hyperactivity), learning difficulties, and accident proneness in the form of a compulsive toying with physical danger. To this triad must be added a state of social inadequacy and chronic indecision; furthermore, a tendency to exaggerate, to lie, and to fantasy. Most striking was the disappearance or drastic diminution of these symptoms once the intactness of the genital organ either spontaneously or operatively was established. The clinical material suggests that cryptorchism influences symptom choice, regardless of the nosological designation of the case. It seems that the different disorders represented in the case material found in the genital defect a palpable and visible reality around which the respective pathology of each case was articulated.

II. Clinical Material[2]

The Case of Steven

Steven, a slender, friendly boy of eight, was brought to treatment by his mother upon the recommendation of the school: in the third

[2] The three boys whose cases are reported here were treated at the Madeleine Borg Child Guidance Institute, Jewish Board of Guardians. The treatment was supervised by the author.

grade, he was still practically a nonreader. He gave the impression of an atypical (borderline) child, with poor motor coordination (clumsy gait, "like a drunkard," inept in games, illegible handwriting); infantile behavior (does not feed, bathe, dress himself; chews on his clothes; messy child: drops ink, flour, food on the floor, spills soil from flowerpots in his room and on his bed); intense preoccupation with death and time; anxious and worried.

Steven was born with the left testis undescended. A tumor on the scrotum was removed at five months. The mother felt that she had caused the tumor "by poking around these parts so much." At seven Steven had a tonsillectomy with subsequent hemorrhages which necessitated his return to the hospital. In the same year he received eight hormone injections which were not followed by a descent of the testis but increased the size of the penis and stimulated the growth of pubic hair. Numerous doctors were consulted. Finally, the source of all of Steven's troubles was thought by the mother to be located in a weak muscle of the left eye, but the ophthalmologist did not confirm this.

The mother was of the opinion that the boy was oblivious of his testicular condition and did not know why so many doctors had examined him. She believed that her show of pseudo confidence and unconcern had protected him from all doubts about his bodily intactness. This defensive attitude on her part was due to her narcissistic involvement with the child: having been disappointed in her own career, in her husband, and in her first son, she had made Steven the center of her emotional life and wanted him to be the genius who would fulfill her wildest ambitions. Steven's father was a passive and withdrawn man who, according to the boy, "did not know what goes on at home." Five years before Steven's birth he had suffered and recovered from a psychotic episode with paranoid delusions. He never showed any interest in Steven's therapy.

During the first interview Steven questioned the therapist as to why he was visiting a doctor again. His guidance teacher had wanted him to go to the eye clinic, but he had been told by the doctor that there was nothing wrong with his eye. In the second interview, he stated that he had kissed a girl and got two sores on his mouth from it; at least, that is what his mother had said, while he himself was not sure: he thought his lips were chapped before.

After this introduction he became involved in dramatic play in which he was the doctor taking care of dolls suffering from a polio condition, having been born with a knife which made them stiff; identifying with the aggressor, he was the surgeon and could be trusted having a sure hand. But at other times his anxiety came through: Steven's grandfather had died after an operation, the nature of which he ignored (actually a prostate operation); but he was sure "it was not in the leg system, it might have been bleeding ulcers." At such times of blatant denial he did not want the dolls to be operated on.

Later in the treatment the boy's play shifted to aggressive themes of shooting and killing; he and his therapist were the two best gunmen in the world. Dynamite (clay) had to be hidden from the outlaws, for it could easily have blown up the world. Over and over he was kneading clay without ever shaping anything; he always wanted the clay he had been kneading to be saved for the next session.

The mother still maintained that the child had no knowledge of his condition. But when the doctor decided to perform an operation, Steven had to be told of it. This the mother did gingerly, only to be interrupted by the boy who told her that he was not stupid and had known all along why people had been poking around there. In his treatment he now openly revealed his anxiety which was so intense that he was unable to comprehend an anatomical sketch his therapist drew for him. His play during these sessions had become very infantile.

Steven made a last effort to dispense with the operation. He wanted to sit in the therapist's chair: "I like to be you and you to be me." Could "hes" be made into "shes"? He was completely ignorant of the origin of babies and the function of the testes: the growing testis "in the stomach" was confused with the foetus. Soon after the boy had admitted that he had always "felt himself" (masturbated) he could listen to the details of the operation. He was then also able to recapitulate his long history of medical interventions. Several months after a successful operation, Steven described the sensation in his testes: he knew what he felt, he no longer was confused.

His play now consisted in building a Stevensville Museum: two marbles of special stone were on exhibit. He soon lost interest in this kind of play and became more oriented toward schoolwork, the boy scouts, friends, chess play, piano lessons, etc. His active interest in the environment reflected the appearance of a belated latency period. Peer relations and organized physical activities began to play an important part in his life. His clumsiness improved noticeably. Near the end of therapy, one year after the operation, he had advanced to his grade level in reading. His critical judgment about himself and others had increased; there was less need to ingratiate himself by being charming and cute; he had made striking gains in the realm of social effectiveness. But in times of stress he reverted to infantile and disorganized reactions. The separation from his mother, which he now aggressively enforced, was laden with guilt and anxiety. The simple comfort found in dependency was no longer available to him. As to the mother, she had been helped to refrain from involving the boy in her own fantasy life; her need to deny his imperfections had significantly lessened. The growing adequacy of the child was recognized by the father who became progressively more interested in his son.

The Case of Larry

When Larry was referred to the clinic at the age of nine years ten months, he presented such a variety of symptoms that it was feared that the neurotic manifestations in conjunction with conduct and habit disorders might mask a more malignant pathology. The major complaints were: soiling, nocturnal enuresis, psychogenic headaches, accident proneness; he fought with other children, refused to do his homework, could not concentrate in school; he had fright reactions to the dentist, to blood, and to monsters which appeared in his fantasies and nightmares; he had difficulty in falling asleep, refused to be covered up or held down. The mother was vague and contradictory in her description of the child: she appeared on the one hand to be indulgent when the child was "nice," but on the other hand she beat him with a strap for misbehaving; she was full of angry contempt for the weak males of her family, her husband and three sons. Larry had two brothers, one two years older and the other four years younger. The father, when he was finally seen, presented himself as a withdrawn man, afraid of his wife's criticism, and carrying out her orders obediently. Actually he had genuine and warm feelings for Larry, and much sympathetic understanding of him.

Larry had been a healthy infant. At two and a half years he was noted to have a hernia and a hydrocele, referred to by the mother as a "skin tumor on the left testicle." The conditions were corrected at a hospital where the child stayed for ten days. During this period he was frightened, depressed, or uncontrollably wild. The hyperactivity accompanied by many accidents had been part of his behavior pattern since that time: the most tragic mishap—it happened while he played in the park soon after he had started treatment at the clinic—resulted in the loss of his left eye. The child expressed to his therapist great rage at his mother who had not told him after the operation that his eyeball had been removed: he had noticed it on the doctor's chart while still wearing his bandage. This irreparable, self-induced injury was subsequently linked to the physical restraint imposed on him during the operation on the genital and to the mother's demand for passivity. A circuitous process had become established: the motoric rage had become turned against the self, bringing about actively what he feared of suffering at the hands of the "monsters."

A ritual accompanying the headaches was soon revealed: they were always due to a "strong light" hitting his eyes. He then had to lie down in the dark with his face covered and he would fall asleep. The headaches always followed an arousal of anger and hostility; they seemed to have started at the time of the operation on the genital. This ritual enabled us to understand the sadomasochistic conflict in Larry.

Ever since the loss of the eye, Larry complained of "bellyaches." A dynamic link seemed probable: the suspicion arose that the boy had an undescended testicle. The mother was questioned, and the assumption proved to be correct. Larry, however, was supposed to ignore this fact. His confusion about operations, needles, hernia contained a tacit accusation against his parents for never having told him the truth about his physical problems. The question arose whether the sacrifice of the eyeball was a substitute body-part relinquishment in order to salvage the more precious ball buried in his belly; or was the self-castrating act a masochistic surrender of his masculinity which brought temporary relief from an intolerable state of panic and terror, namely, to be attacked by a castrating monster-woman? Soiling ceased soon after his fear of going to the toilet was understood as a fear of losing his undescended testicle with his feces.

Finally, the boy's fear of "another operation" came to the fore. He had overheard his father speak of this possibility in case "the testicle does not stay down." This prospect made the child anxious, which in turn aroused in him aggressive feelings toward his parents and resulted in a bicycle accident. He became panicky about an infection of his good eye (which was in perfect condition) and feared going blind; he requested that a night light be kept on in his room so he could see whenever he woke up during the night. This assured him that his eyesight was intact and that his good eye was still there. He dreamed of getting pieces of glass into his good eye and losing it. He dreamed of an "eye bank" where new eyes could be gotten.

Treatment had progressively become the boy's refuge. He used the therapist's name at home to restrain the mother from undue interference. In his sessions he turned tables by playing the role of the teacher, who for so long had been a phobic object, and asking the therapist to be the pupil. At home, he was steadily gaining in independence; he bathed and dressed himself. At school he became more attentive and interested in his work. By the same token he had become more compulsive, and was worrying about his home-work, etc. When the boy urged his therapist to see his father, this facilitated a discussion of the boy's undescended testicle, and the father arranged for a medical examination to determine whether an operation was indicated. The examination ascertained the fact that the left testis had descended, was permanently located in the scrotum but was somewhat smaller than the right one. Larry, of course, knew this.

Constructive self-assertion and compulsive cautiousness gradually replaced the alternating bursts of destructive rages (such as "to blow up the whole family" with his chemistry set) and of the self-damaging activities which once threatened to make an invalid of him. His realistic interest in science had grown steadily; he had set up his own chemical laboratory at home. He no longer threw himself head-long into new experiences but interposed judgment before he em-barked on a new course of action. He now played with boys of his own age instead of with younger children. In his daily tasks he took initiative and was no longer a pawn in the hands of terrifying monsters. His aggressive drive had found sublimated expression in his activities: at school he became captain of the safety squad. At home he defended himself against his mother's influence with stubborn determination; nobody else found Larry any longer unreasonably difficult to manage or to get along with.

The Case of Joe

Joe, a tall, heavy, light-skinned Negro with pubescence already manifest, was nine years old when he was referred to the clinic by his school because of his restlessness, excessive boasting, daydreaming, and learning difficulties. He was found to be a lonely and fearful child whose history revealed that his activities had been restricted until the age of six because of a congenital heart murmur and that his urge for activity had then broken through and asserted itself in uncontrollable hypermotility.

The mother, who wanted her boy to be gentle and mild mannered, was doing her utmost to suppress in him all upsurges of male self-assertion. The child's two older sisters had been taught to baby the little "invalid." The father was disappointed in the lack of boyish behavior and interests in Joe, and although a good provider, he was spending little time in the home and did not share in the life of the family.

Joe had been in treatment for three years before his undescended testicles were inadvertently mentioned by the mother. His petty stealing, his tall tales, his constant references to secrets, the compulsive chair balancing which led to his falling, became intelligible when related to the genital defect. It was decided to concentrate on two areas: the ego dysfunction, i.e., his inability to read and the anxiety attached to the genital defectiveness. It was also decided to try and enlist the father's cooperation in spite of Joe's strenuous attempts to leave his father out of his treatment.

The interviews which the therapist had with the father resulted in his taking Joe to the doctor: the course of treatment was explained to the child. The period of injections which followed was one of anxiety for the boy. The fact that "nothing happened" after the injections opened up the frightening possibility of an operation. Joe refused to discuss this, insisting that he had talked to his sisters about it and that there was nothing more to say. His behavior became quite mischievous, almost delinquent, and he was full of complaints about the tutor who, he said, was unable to help him.

The now impending operation was linked by Joe with his tonsillectomy. The doctor might find that the testis was no good, cut it out, and throw it away. His fear of sterility, should he be left with only one good testicle, was talked over with the therapist. Joe could now ask questions about it, and while he felt free to do so, he was at the same time making progress in reading. His tutor also noticed an increased ability to learn and a longer concentration span. Joe at this time introduced a new topic in his treatment, namely, his girl friends. A sudden wave of interest had swept him into the realm of early adolescent emotions. With bravado he told the therapist that he knew everything about sex.

The father's distrust of doctors and the mother's helplessness in planning for the operation ("I only know how to take care of girls") forced the therapist to assume the main responsibility for making all arrangements with surgeon and hospital. Joe was appreciative of this help. Yet for the first time, as soon as the operation was planned, the boy's aggression against his mother came to the fore: she was not helping him, she was trying to make a girl out of him, he was not going to tolerate being treated in this way. He considered it an insult to his masculinity to have a woman doctor examine him at the hospital. At the same time, his fear of castration was being expressed: he often referred to his tonsillectomy when "the knife had slipped and cut a hole in his throat."

As the time for the operation approached, a flood of interest in sexual information burst forth. The rising competition with his father combined with his usual attempt to submit to his mother precipitated an acute struggle in sexual identification which became intensified by the impending operation.

After the operation was performed successfully, it was the healing process in conjunction with the imposed restriction of activity which made the boy anxious and angry. He oscillated between his passive-submissive and his aggressive-masculine trends. The doctor's opinion served during this time as a yardstick for the realistic evaluation of his condition. Joe now desired to learn to swim, to play ball and fight. He expressed the wish to improve himself generally. An itch in the genital area, which he located in his testes, opened up a discussion about masturbation and nocturnal emissions. It was essential now for the therapist, a woman, gradually to transfer the discussion of sexual enlightenment to the father because the excitement relating to such interchange promoted too intense an erotic attraction. The father, in the meantime, had become more accepting of his now "complete" son.

Learning, which had taken a leap since the operation, continued to progress. Joe could do his homework, he went to the library, he asked his father for help and opinion on such topics as elections and strikes. The struggle for his masculinity now dominated his life; therapy entered a drawn-out period of "working through" in which the liberated affects had to be guided into the phase-adequate conflicts of adolescence, preventing the extremes of a surrender to submissiveness or a blind thrust into frantic self-assertion and rebellion.

III. Discussion

Cryptorchism and Family Interaction

The pre-eminence which the genital defect plays in the mental life of the three boys appears to be of a secondary order. The three boys had mothers who promoted feminine tendencies either by rejecting the maleness in the boy who was afflicted with a genital imperfection (Steven, Larry) or by showing a strong preference for a female child and holding out a love premium for passive, submissive behavior (Joe). All three boys were dependent on their mothers in terms of her narcissistic needs. These needs became manifest in the mothers' extraordinary ambitions which had to be realized by her male offspring (Steven, Larry), or the mother's contempt of male sexuality which she considered destructive and undesirable; this led to her total acceptance of the genital defect in her son (Joe). In the latter case the genital defect represented for the mother an asset rather than a calamity. Whether the mother concentrated on this imperfection because of her own unrealized ambitions and hopes (overcompensatory expectations), or whether she welcomed the defective state of the son, in either case the attitude of the mother had to be considered as the pathogenic factor of primary order: it had a castrating impact.

This effect became further elaborated by the fathers' remoteness in the lives of all three boys. All concern and initiative had been delegated to their wives. The genital defectiveness of the child engendered in each father a sense of disappointment and dissatisfaction which deepened with the boy's fearful and "unboyish" behavior. The three fathers tried to disengage themselves from the difficulties their sons encountered and it was necessary in each case firmly to request the father's visit to the clinic. The fact that the father was subsequently made a partner and supporter of the son's therapy proved to constitute an essential dynamic configuration for treatment: it represented to the boy the paternal approbation of his male strivings and consequently facilitated masculine identification. As long as the boy was exposed to the mother's belittling attitude of the father, he felt that his own masculinity was acceptable only on his mother's terms.

The fathers responded to an earnest appeal by the therapist with cooperation and active interest. It goes without saying that their own precarious marital position had made them eager sympathizers with their sons' plight, and we gained the impression that the fathers had secretly waited for a cue to speak up and be heard. Forrer (1959) in a report on the mother of a defective child made the same observation, namely, that the belittled and excluded father turned out to be the child's respected and loved parent. The mothers' descriptions of their husbands all sounded alike: "A dull, uncommunicative and unreasonable man" (Forrer, 1959); on closer inspection this man turned out to be an intimidated, shy, but quite capable and loving father.

The emotional distance which the fathers maintained in the marriage extended to their sons who felt deserted by them and left to the controlling (castrating) influence of their mothers. A typical rescue maneuver which two of the boys employed in this dilemma consisted in the idealization of the father, or rather in a summary denial of the negative and depreciatory feelings he extended toward his son. An illusory father image, unshakable by reality, served as an anchor in the masculine position of the oedipus complex and could be upheld only by a scotomatized view of the father's role in family interaction. Joe, emotionally deserted by his father and pressed by his mother into feminine tasks, exclaimed with desperate insistence:

"My mind is my dad." The mother of Larry actually entered into a conspiracy with her son and allowed him to swim in unsafe waters in spite of the father's explicit disapproval. Consequently, he and mother shared a "secret" which aroused oedipal guilt and made itself felt as resistance in treatment.

While the genital defect occupied all the mothers either actively ("poking around," examining, going from doctor to doctor, etc.) or negatively (ignoring it, postponing examination, not following or forgetting medical advice, hoping naïvely for a spontaneous descent "because the sac is there to receive it," etc.), it was striking to notice how they either had managed to conceal the genital condition at intake or had sidetracked it in some fashion to forestall any definitive clarification. The insignificant role which the mothers tried to attribute to the genital condition was further obscured by their stubborn emphasis on other issues, such as the child's learning difficulty or his lack of friends. The referral was usually made by the school because only under duress could the mother be mobilized to take a step which would publicly demonstrate her own defectiveness and expose her inability in modeling the child according to her wishes. The mother's ambition for the child to be a genius, or to excel academically, or be perfect and well behaved, reflected her own insufficiency feelings, forcefully denied in the child by displacement of the genital defectiveness to areas of intellectual achievement and exemplary behavior. These three boys disappointed their mothers' ambitions; the school had to impress on the family that their sons had failed. The mothers maintained an illusory image of their sons in order to ward off a narcissistic defeat. They maintained the fantasy that their concentration and determination would succeed in changing the child (Forrer, 1959). They had a tendency toward depressive reactions in which their aggressive, retaliatory, and castrating wishes toward the male constituted an essential part.

The mothers' suppressed sadism became apparent in the unreasonable delays concerning medical intervention such as injection or operation. Their fear of a disaster (e.g., hemorrhaging in Steven's case) deterred them from an objective appraisal of a medical recommendation. Their impaired judgment appears throughout in relation to the child, especially in matters of health: this is exemplified by Steven's mother telling the boy that he got two sores on his mouth from kissing a girl; or Larry's mother telling him that he gets headaches from not eating properly. In this connection, of course, the devious and deceptive treatment of the genital condition deserves mentioning; in order not to arouse the child's self-consciousness or suspicion the mother might examine the boy without explanation or by giving an irrelevant reason; the deception appeared also in the falsification of facts as in Larry's case when he was told that he needed injections for a hernia which, the boy knew, had been corrected at the age of two and a half. Such parental opinions are expressed with a single-mindedness of conviction which leaves the boy in uncertainty as to the validity of his own observation, thinking, and experience.

The particular way in which the genital defect is perceived and experienced by the parents, particularly the mother, accounts for the child's preoccupation with the testes. The perpetrator of the body damage is in the child's mind identified with the mother. Her castrating possessiveness and the father's passive aloofness both constitute a matrix of family interaction in which cryptorchism gives rise to a typical symptom picture. The parents' attitude in conjunction with the child's own observation of his anatomical abnormality combine into a body schema, or body image, around which any existing psychological impairment is elaborated. The defective body image itself was found to be responsible for specific aspects of the pathology in each case.

The Prototypical Experience (Trauma)

An operation trauma had occurred in the lives of all three boys. This trauma became subsequently linked to the genital defect and to any medical intervention which might occur sooner or later. Fantasies and drive propensities which had rendered the first operation, such as hernioplasty or tonsillectomy, a traumatic event attached themselves by a process of direct substitution to the genital actuality.

In Steven's case we can recognize in the testicle complex an aggregate of experiences which date from various periods of his life. Their accrued effect appeared in condensed form in his play productions. The first operation (hydrocele) involved the scrotum. The mother's guilt and conviction that she had caused the "tumor" had made her particularly attentive to her son's genital region and to the clumsy gait presumably associated with it. This gait continued to persist up to the time of his orchidopexy. Another body-damage anxiety (castration fear) attached itself to the genital defect and found expression in the doctor play when Steven announced that his doll patients had to have an operation on account of their "stiffness." Steven, the doctor postponed the operation several times; when it was finally performed several of his patients died.

In this connection the consequence of hormone injections at the age of seven should not be overlooked or minimized. The sudden rise of sexual stimulation caused a flooding of the ego by instinctual pressures and became manifest in genital sensations (erections) and erotic feelings (kissing of women). At this very time of increased sexual pressures, a tonsillectomy was performed. This operation made a lasting and terrifying impression on the child due to two hemorrhages which followed the operation and required rehospitalization. Fear of doctors and operations, and fear of death remained with Steven from then on; all three fears found an eloquent expression in his doctor play. Furthermore, he ascribed the death of his grandfather either to the surgeon's clumsiness ("the knife had slipped") or to an uncontrollable bleeding, to a hemorrhage, to "bleeding ulcers." His fear of castration became affirmed by his negation expressed in the statement that his grandfather's operation (prostatectomy) had "certainly not been in the leg system." It is interesting to note that Steven attached the blame for the death of his doll patients to the nurse who was clumsy. He voiced in this accusation what I have already alluded to, namely, that the archaic mother is held responsible for the "genital death" (castration).

In Joe's case the tonsillectomy at four years of age left an indelible impression; the memory of it with the typical infantile distortions offered itself as a model of the impending orchidopexy. The testicle will be excised as the tonsils had been and thrown away if found to be no good. Joe was still convinced that the doctor had "cut a hole in his throat"; this "castration wish" phantom organ he expected to become real by the orchidopexy; i.e., he fantasied that the operation would make him into a girl.

In Larry's case the hernioplasty at the age of two and a half years served as the prototypical experience in which the attack on his eyes (bright light) became linked to body-image anxiety as a retaliation for his uncontrollable rages against the mother. His headache ritual preserved this trauma which he attempted to master by repetition, until it finally yielded to the combined effects of insight into his aggressive urges on the one hand and of the attainment of genital intactness on the other.

A twelve-year-old boy might be mentioned here who had a long history of medical examinations in connection with "one testicle being smaller than the other." Psychotherapy had been at a standstill for an alarmingly long time due to the parents' persistent plea not to have the testicle condition discussed with the boy since this only would make him "self-conscious" and add insult to injury. The boy's symptomatic behavior, such as walking around "blind" (i.e., with his eyes shut) in order to test whether he would hurt himself, pointed clearly to the "testicle syndrome" as described here. This made it mandatory to have the physical condition moved into the focus of awareness through medical evaluation. After the medical examination requested and arranged by the clinic had taken place, it was established that one testicle was atrophied. When the therapist discussed the examination and its findings with the boy he answered that the doctor could not find anything wrong with him. Confronted with the fact he admitted his knowledge of the testicle condition which he had rendered vague and unreal by "not having touched [investigated] himself for quite a number of years." Then he changed the subject, significantly, to a discussion of his tonsillectomy. Soon it became apparent that his knowledge of the male and female genitals was contained in a bisexual, distorted imagery. Only after the body had attained by medical dictum a state of definitive structure— in this case one of permanent genital defectiveness—was it possible to cope in treatment with the psychological implications of the body reality.

The various focal apprehensions as outlined above represented a fusion of the early operation trauma with subsequent drive organizations. Every threat to the body integrity revived the original trauma in a phase-specific modality. By reprojection the child experienced the current danger in terms of the past traumatic event. This might be paraphrased by saying: "What I thought happened to me then will certainly be repeated now." This reasoning is exemplified by Joe's equating tonsils and testicles, and by his belief that the testicle will be thrown away as the tonsils were, and last but not least, by the fact that the early operation was experienced as a castration. These connotations of childhood operations are well known and have been described by Anna Freud (1952), Jessner et al. (1952), and others.

In all three cases it became clear that the genital defect served as the "organizing experience" which subordinated early trauma as well as all subsequent phase-specific anxieties about body damage to the persistent genital defectiveness. How this condition affected the formation of the body image will be discussed later. The facts that the genital incompleteness had existed as far as memory extends and had at the same time remained uncertain as to its ultimate outcome; and furthermore, that operative correction remained for years a whispered prospect, necessarily kept the early operation trauma alive in terms of specific, primitive misconceptions and distortions. Body-damage anxiety became a chronic affect, the mastery of which was attempted by various means. Obviously an early operation trauma is not an obligatory experience in cases of cryptorchism in order to produce disturbances similar to those that are described here. Nevertheless, we shall find that traumatic body-damage anxiety (such as related to body-part loss in, e.g., bowel training or castration fantasies), which under normal circumstances is gradually mastered, remains in an unbound state due to the continuance of the physical defect to which it is attached. The concreteness of the defect in conjunction with the uncertainty of its correction does not allow any definitive settlement of the issue—indeed, not of any issue. It is therefore characteristic of cryptorchism that by its very nature it precludes the definite psychic integration of the defect and instead favors fluid defenses. These were found to yield rather easily under the impact of a definitive physical repair and were then replaced by more stable defenses and adaptive behavior.

Body Image and Ego Impairment

We are well acquainted with the fact that clarity and stability of the body image exerts an essential influence on the development and structure of the secondary autonomy of the ego. Any serious distortion of the body image will become manifest in some specific ego impairment. Experience tells us that some component functions of the ego possess greater resistivity to impairment than others.

In cases of body defect the choice of defensive measures as well as restitutive fantasy elaborations are influenced by the nature of the defect and by its physical location. The distinction of inside and outside of the body does not apply clearly to cryptorchism. The defect is palpable and observable but not exposed to the public eye; yet it is not definitive but reparable. These factors determine to a large extent the concept of genital defectiveness which the child evolves. The physical condition, due to its undecided and unpredictable nature, lends itself to the absorption of the specific emotional conflicts and body-damage anxieties which play a more or less transient role in the development of every male child.

The genital defectiveness has played a prominent role in the lives of the three boys from an early age on. Later it became the focus of comparison with and likeness to other boys, affecting the sense of identity and resulting in social incompatibility and maladjustment. Having no friends and not knowing how to make friends was equally evident in all three cases. Steven turned to little girls, Larry to a younger immature boy, and Joe to semidelinquents in order to gratify their social hunger. The emergence of more adequate social relations became evident in all three cases at the end of treatment.

The ego impairments most marked in these three cases appeared as disturbances in learning, memory, thinking, and time-space perception; they could be linked to the mother's inconsistent attitude by which she tacitly forbade the child to recognize his physical defect clearly or to think rationally about it. Furthermore, these impairments were due to a defective body image which had remained undeveloped by having retained primitive qualities of vagueness, of indefiniteness, and incompleteness; in some way, it had never been fully assembled. Peto's remarks (1959) are relevant to this point: "Symbolism in dreams and folk-lore indicates that finding and evaluating external reality is to a great extent determined by refinding one's own body in the environment. Thus the body image is of decisive importance in grasping the world around us. Peculiarities of one's body image may then cause to be conceived as a world which is different from that visualized by the average human being."

The concept of time played a particular role in these cases because only "time will tell" which form the body, namely, the genital, will finally assume. The close connection between spatial perception, spatial conceptualization, and the experience of the body needs no lengthy elaboration. Whenever the body-image formation is impeded a primitive spatial concept analogous to the body form continues to persist despite the fact that other ego functions have progressed normally. Werner (1940) in discussing spatial concept formation comments as follows: "Primitive terms for spatial relations suggest that the body itself with its 'personal dimensions' (Stern) of above-below, before-behind, and right-left is the source of a psychophysical system of coordinates. Therefore it may be inferred that objective space has gradually evolved from this primitive orientation."

The massive influence of body-image diffusion was well summed up in Steven's statement: "They [his doll patients] cannot see, hear or think until the operation is over." We might paraphrase his words by saying that the reliability of the distance perceptors and their usefulness for cognitive processes can be achieved only after the body has attained its complete and definitive form. The consequences of this state of affairs for reality testing and for the sense of reality is self-evident. For the time being then, Steven, as well as the other boys, took refuge in illusory accomplishments, in aggrandizement, in bragging and in fantasies of magic powers. These defenses permitted continuous narcissistic replenishment. I shall later elaborate on how ego impairments were rapidly surmounted after the genital intactness was established once and for all.

Steven, who was easily insulted by criticism, made use of all the aforementioned defenses in order to ward off a narcissistic injury. He considered himself a "magical person" who could make everybody smile at him by smiling at them. Thus he robbed everybody of their aggressive, i.e., dangerous, potential. Consequently, Steven had a poor grasp of social situations and was completely unable to recognize the correct motives in other children for their respective actions. Here we see the influence of the mother who maintained a distorted, idealized concept of her child and easily falsified reality in order to protect him. The mother, in denying Steven's physical defectiveness, devoted all her life's energies to its correction by magic. She gave up work and devoted herself totally to the child's care. The mother's denial became the child's erroneous self-image.

We notice that Steven, despite his "smiling disposition," was preoccupied with time and death. In these fears we recognize the tantalizing waiting time until genital certainty would be attained, as well as a "genital death" fear rooted in the still uncertain state of castratedness. In his earlier figure drawings, Steven gave the girl and the mother figure five fingers on each hand, while he drew a boy with no fingers at all. The boy, he said, is holding on to his parents' hand. Thus, his body deficit was undone by making himself part of a complete and powerful person.

Both Larry and Joe presented learning disturbances which were seriously aggravated in Joe's case by a stubborn reading disability. Again, illusory achievements and lies about school grades appeared as disclaimers of their academic deficiencies. Forgetting, i.e., memory disturbances, presented serious obstacles to a tutorial approach in remedial reading. A decisive turn for the better became noticeable when medical as well as psychotherapeutic attention was focused on the physical condition, its correction, and on body-damage anxiety generally.

The restoration and maturation of ego functions as well as their clinical evidence will be discussed later. Changes in the body image became indirectly observable through psychological tests. Steven's male figure in the second, postoperational test was large, compact, and had five fingers. Larry's "tree," which had first a hole in the center of the trunk, showed later a clear and simple outline without any aberrant features. Examples could be multiplied from the test material. Suffice it to say that the second test gave abundant evidence of a changed body image (self-concept) to allow the conclusion that the distorted, vague, and incomplete body image exerted a pathological influence on ego development. The ego impairments were erroneously treated for some time as if they were the result of endopsychic conflicts only. When the ego impairments were approached via the body image, its correction and completion—that is to say, when the physical (genital) reality was given a definitive structure—then a desirable change in ego functions was finally brought about. The clinical material illustrates the close relationship between body experience, body percept, body image, and ego functions.

Accident Proneness: The Masochistic Surrender

In the three boys hypermotility was conspicuously present. Its relatedness to physical self-damage was constantly demonstrated inside and outside the treatment room. Hypermotility in these cases constituted a complex form of behavior in which the pressure of instinctual drives, anxiety, and defensive operations were tightly organized. Hyperactive, aimless, and erratic moving about had a frantic, searching, anxious quality which at times invited danger and resulted in accidents. The tendency to self-damage, called accident proneness, revealed the child's concept of the genital defect as the result of an act of aggression, of a destructive attack on his body (castration). The identification with the aggressor, namely, the mother, prompted a feminine identification and turned passive submission into active execution. Thus the child made himself the victim of his own aggression.

It is difficult to say to which extent accident proneness or the compulsive toying with physical danger was linked either to passive masochistic castration wishes, or to the avoidance of narcissistic mortification. This avoidance can be paraphrased by saying that it is better not to be a boy at all than to be half a boy. We shall later see how the anatomical condition was unconsciously identified with femaleness. The masochistic yielding to female identity found expression in the many castrative actions of more or less serious consequences. The sense of incompleteness and castratedness was visibly, palpably, and permanently linked to a bodily condition; moreover, the idea of an operation had attached itself intimately to it. Both these factors contributed to the striking concreteness by which body-damage fear and wishes were represented and executed.

The body-damage complex was kept alive by its undecided fate of the testicle, a condition which fostered ambivalent relationships, worked against the establishment of stable identifications, and resulted in a fluid self-representation, particularly relative to aspects of sexual identity, namely phallic versus castrated. The ambivalence of drive propensities in conjunction with defensive maneuvers seemed to move along a circular path with the nodal stations labeled as follows: (conscious) Nothing can happen to me—I am in control of everybody—I know everything; (unconscious) I am not a boy—

I will never be a boy—I shall make myself into a girl—I deserve castration—I shall attack others—Surrendering of a body part is relief, is pleasure—I want castration.

Accident proneness as observed in these cases illustrates the substitution of the genital organ, more particularly, the testicle, by the whole body. This *totum pro parte* principle or the body-phallus equation is well expressed in Steven's play in which the patients have to undergo an operation for their "stiffness." The *totum pro parte* principle receives a massive support from the mother's attitude who customarily used the "total child" as a representation of his defective organ and concentrated her efforts at rectification of the genital defect in terms of substitutive perfections, such as academic excellence. Displacement from below to above is also apparent. In this connection the role of the eyeball as a substitutive organ for the testicle is noteworthy. This substitution is known from mythology and analysis. A blinking tic of an eleven-year-old boy reported by Fraiberg (1960) was traceable to the fear of damage to his testicles. In mythology, King Oedipus gouged out his eyes in symbolic emasculation to atone for his incestuous crime. An eye involvement appeared in all three cases, most prominently in the case of Larry with a self-induced eye loss.

I am inclined to attribute the accident in Larry's case to a compromise formation, consisting in the sacrifice of a body part, the eye, in order to rescue the missing testicle and, furthermore, to bring about the sought-after injury by his active submission rather than by waiting for the expected attack from the "monster woman." The boy's description of the accident clearly reveals the motoric paralysis of a masochistic excitement at the very moment when the stick came flying at his eye. The fear for his "good eye" repeated the original fear for his "good testicle." Both fears subsided with the correction of the genital defect. Larry was the one boy who most vigorously fought against a masochistic surrender, who, it is true, most damagingly victimized himself but nevertheless showed the most striking recovery.

Accident proneness is closely linked to the vicissitudes of the aggressive drive, to the erotization of injury, and to the need for physical punishment as a relief from feelings of guilt. The defective genital became almost automatically associated with sexual guilt since all three boys had progressed to a more or less firm foothold on the oedipal level. The aggressive-drive discharge was restricted to hyperactivity, counterphobic manifestations, and self-damage. In the course of therapy the intensity and primitivity of the aggression became apparent. Quite naturally, the seat of the explosive, destructive, and vengeful energy was to be located in the testicle. This we recognize in the hidden bomb of Steven's play, or in Larry's chemical experiments which were designed to blow up the house. Such expressions of unbridled aggressive fantasies eventually gave way to alloplastic adaptations when neutralized energy became available. Larry, for example, overcame his accident proneness successfully by making it his job to protect others from dangers: he became captain of the safety squad at his school. The other boys showed no signs of compulsive toying with physical dangers after the genital defect was corrected. The repetition compulsion was short-circuited by an anatomical change which facilitated ego alterations of a more complex kind. They became recognizable in characterological modifications and in the development of special, realistic interests and inclinations.

Symptomatic Acts and Organ Symbols

The anatomical defect of an undescended testicle favors expression of the condition through substitutive behavior or through symbolic objects in an effort to master anxiety. The concrete, direct, and symbolic nature of play and behavior are both strikingly demonstrated in the case material. The primitivity of thought implicit in this form of mastery leaves no doubt that the inferred, vaguely conscious temporariness of the defect foreclosed an integration by more complex psychic processes of which the three boys unquestionably were capable.

Werner (1940) remarks that "The structure of primitive thought is concretely determined insofar as it has a tendency to configurate pictorially, and it is emotionally determined insofar as it unites that which is affectively related." The case material indicates that aspects of "quantity" and "size" were definitely equated with power, potency, and masculinity. As another boy expressed it: "If I have two testicles I can have twice as many children." The frequent accidents represented symptomatic acts, explained by each boy circumstantially, but they obviously constituted reassurance actions by reaffirming repeatedly that no fatal damage was done.

The testicle as the seat of aggressive and destructive forces has been mentioned earlier. We can recognize this idea, furthermore, in the defensive belittling of the testicles the bearers of which are fear-provoking men. This attempt to attenuate castration anxiety is well expressed in the marching song of the British soldiers imprisoned during World War II by the Japanese in the Burma jungle: "Hitler has only one big ball—Goering has two but they are small—Himmler has something similar—But little Goebbels has no balls at all."[3]

Joe's insatiable interest in the contents of drawers, his running through the corridors of the clinic in order to see if anybody could stop him; Steven's curiosity about secrets and his use of the number three (male genital) in aggressive play—these incidents illustrate in displaced form the nature of their common concern.

The concrete representation of the testicle by objects is noteworthy inasmuch as it is somewhat out of keeping with the age and intelligence of the three boys. The directness of symbolic representation which we notice in Joe when he stole a ball from the treatment room only to return it after he had undergone a successful operation is almost ludicrous in its simplicity. The same is true for Steven's museum in which he exhibited a special precious marble for everybody to see after a successful operation had brought his testicle into a position where it finally became visible to the world. He also used to roll two small clay balls during the session following the operation; he remarked that he would make two more balls every week and he wanted the therapist to keep them for him. One is reminded of Larry's "eye (ball) bank."

By displacement the testicle is, furthermore, identified with other organs. Consequently, they assume attributes and meanings which render them fitting substitutes for the testicles. In this connection we can speak of organ symbols. The most outstanding substitute organs for the testicles are the following: eye, tonsils, breast, and foetus. (Their relatedness to bisexuality is discussed below.) It is partly the symmetric location, partly the operative history, partly the relatedness to component instincts which are responsible for the fit-

---

[3] While the melody of this song echoes through the sound track of the movie *The Bridge on the River Kwai*, the words of the song have, of course, been changed.

ness of these body parts to serve as organ symbols for the testicles.

One gains the impression that the genital defectiveness lends itself to direct, concrete, symbolic (substitutive) expression by objects in the outer world and, furthermore, to the use of the whole body or body parts for the mastery of the anxiety which the anatomical defect engenders.

The Bisexual Identity

The defective genital condition is perceived by the three boys as castratedness, i.e., femaleness. In these cases of cryptorchism we did not observe a genuine feminine identification but rather recognized in the self-image the compliance of passive, feminine tendencies to a physical genital reality. The passive tendencies received a powerful recourse from the operation trauma and a ceaseless stimulation from the physical condition of cryptorchism itself. In this connection the following remarks by Anna Freud (1952) are relevant: "When studying the aftereffects of childhood operations in the analysis of adult patients we find that it is not the castration fear but the feminine castration wish in a male child which is most frequently responsible for serious postoperative breakdowns or permanent postoperative character changes." To this we might add the finding that in the case of cryptorchism by the very fact of a defective genital the feminine castration wish did not advance to the state of an integrated self-representation but stayed attached to the genital organ in its physical reality. Feminine tendencies became, therefore, organized around this organ defect and remained in a state of unsettledness due to the implicit reversibility of the condition. The resultant bisexual identity was apparent in play productions, fantasies, transference behavior, and projective tests.

The confusion of sexual identity prevented any clear concept of the male and female genital to develop. An egomorphic image of a hermaphroditic nature became the universal body schema. Joe expressed this confusion in saying: "Does it mean that I have something other boys don't have, or don't I have something other boys have?"

Having one testicle was found to be identical with being half a man and half a woman, with sterility or with femaleness in general. Steven showed his doll patients to the therapist with these words:

"Look at them, they look like nothing." This better than anything else expresses the sense of self Steven had to contend with. In such a dilemma an operation was wanted and feared: in order to retrieve the lost treasure, the testicle, another organ, namely, the penis, might have to be sacrificed. In the overvaluation of the missing body part, we recognize an overflow of cathexis from the penis to the testicle.

Operation anxiety was warded off by identification, by assuming the active role vis-à-vis the therapist. Larry asked his male therapist to be his pupil while he himself was the teacher. The same reversal of roles we noticed in Steven who was the surgeon while the therapist became his nurse. When the operation was imminent, he seated himself in the woman therapist's chair and said: "I like to be you and you to be me." While it is not possible that "hes" can be made into "shes," Steven argued, why not have only "hes"? Then, we might add, castration would be eliminated once and for all. In his logical way, Steven concluded that in that case the "hes" had to get the babies in order to keep the world going. There was, after all, no way out of having two sexes.

This brings us to the equation of the deliverance of the testicle (orchidopexy) and giving birth. The testicle in the abdomen was equated with the foetus. Steven thought that it takes twenty-one days for a baby to grow in the mother, a span of time which represented the exact number of days he had to wait for his operation. Joe's figure drawing of a woman showed two balls in the abdominal region; when this drawing was repeatedly traced as the examiner suggested, the balls moved up in each consecutive figure tracing until they had reached the exact location of the breasts. The association of the absent testicle with the female organ of the breast only serves to emphasize once more the bisexual identity which we have found characteristic for cases of cryptorchism.

It was no surprise then to discover that the orchidopexy evoked a state of dual expectancy, namely, either to achieve masculinity or to meet with final castration. Partly, indeed, a confusion existed as to the simultaneous accomplishment of both. This is apparent, for instance, in Steven's idea that the testicle will be pushed from the "stomach" into the penis; this state of having obtained two external testicles would have canceled out the use of the penis for urination and necessitated another body orifice for this function. Such disturbing admissions were quickly extinguished by aggrandizing fantasies until a recourse to castratedness gained once more the upper hand. These shifts resulted in a chronic state of indecision and of fluctuating sexual identity. Fineman (1959) reported similar observations on a boy, aged five and a half, with a congenital genitourinary defect: "The first attempt to present his actual condition [extrophy of the bladder] to him, although softened by the additional statement that he could do everything else that boys could do, was met by him with considerable anxiety which he spontaneously brought under control by playing at being mother and cooking meals." The acceptance of being a boy took first the form of exaggeration, namely, "fantasies of being a powerful hunter who killed lions and tigers with his father's or grandfather's gun."

The bisexual sense of identity which we observed in the three cases poses some theoretical problems as to identification and instinctual fixation. None of the boys behaved in a, strictly speaking, effeminate or "girlish" way. However, they lacked in boyish assertiveness, in active pursuits, and definitely shrank away from competition within their male peer group. They all responded positively to a changed attitude of the father when he took a more active interest in their lives and acknowledged his own importance and influence in helping his son toward a more masculine orientation. After the father had rescued the son from the castrating mother, after he had shown pride in his son's masculine strivings, a competitive oedipal upsurge became manifest which soon was resolved by an identification with the father. None of the boys offered himself as the passive love object as might have been expected from the prevailing emotional trends. The flight into a feminine position, namely, castratedness, was not anchored in an instinctual fixation nor in a stable feminine identification. No doubt, these tendencies existed as they do in the young male generally, but they never progressed to a passive homosexual orientation. The defense of castratedness is akin to denial in so far as the child denies the genital defect be a radical removal of the last vestiges of maleness which gave rise to anxiety and upset his narcissistic balance. "Being a girl" was never sufficiently supported by a pregenital drive nor ego fixation to prevent a forward movement of the libido; however, the intolerable genital condition in conjunction with the dependency on a castrating mother provided feminine propensities with a ceaseless updrift. The perseverance of the female body image and the defense of castratedness (body-part surrender) was directly related to a body reality rather than to a psychologically integrated drive and ego organization. The bisexual identity reflected a physical reality; consequently, a change of the physical reality brought the provisional state of pseudo bisexuality to an end. The restoration of genital intactness gave masculine sexuality a decisive push. The overbearing quality of this newly acquired and unequivocal masculinity invited, however, doubts as to a completely victorious outcome. We shall return to this question later on.

The Positioning of the Testis in the Scrotum: Its Influence on Integrative Processes

The effects of the newly acquired genital completeness were followed by us with interest and surprise. First of all, it was the rapidity and the scope of ego maturation accompanying the new body reality which called our attention to the fact that the anatomical change itself must account for a specific impetus for ego change. The influence of the new body reality was so massive and immediate that the question arose as to the respective psychological processes initiated by therapy on the one hand and by the anatomical transformation on the other. While it is no doubt true that psychotherapy had, so to say, prepared the mental ground for the genital intactness to take roots or to effect a changed sense of reality, the physical change itself must be credited with an equally important contribution toward the improvement of mental functioning. The most striking changes occurred in the areas of learning, cognitive processes, elaboration of age-adequate interests, social adaptation, and masculine identity formation. The ego impairments affecting all these areas have been described earlier.

Let us first recall that a tacit parental prohibition existed, in all three cases regarding recognition and thinking about the genital condition. In Steven's case the mother's unconcern, her denial, was projected onto the child ("He does not worry, he knows nothing") and impeded his ego development, especially the faculty of reality testing. The child, consequently, lived in a state of confusion, not knowing what was real; he was at a loss to say whether what he perceived was real or what his mother wanted him to know. This global perceptual confusion was counteracted in treatment when the "veil of twilight vision" was lifted and a sense of reality restored. In the psychological test this change appeared as a "differentiated view of the world." Steven had predicted in his play already that after the operation, if successful, his "patients will be their own self again; everything depends on this operation."

It is interesting to note that he as well as the other boys expected a return to a genital state which once must have existed, so to say, in prehistory. They expected to receive what had always been theirs. Steven eagerly investigated his newly acquired testicle and described clearly his physical sensations related to the positioning of the testicle in the scrotum. Before the operation, Steven said he always felt confused. With finality an interim state had come to an end: "Once the operation was over, it was over." After the physical restoration, Steven's emotional and intellectual maturation took a remarkable leap. The infantile self-absorbed child became more and more oriented toward schoolwork, reading, the Boy Scouts, friends, chess playing, piano lessons, etc. Taking into account all the psychotherapeutic endeavors, the rapid consolidation of psychological gains derived a unique recourse from the bodily change itself. Before that change nothing was final or complete.

Larry and Joe were both retarded in reading and consequently seriously handicapped in school. In all cases a reading disability existed (e.g., Steven was almost a nonreader when he started treatment) which was strikingly ameliorated soon after the genital restoration or even shortly before the operation. In Larry an improvement in his spatial perception was also noticeable. The aimless wandering of his mind through horror movies and the destructive use of chemistry gave way to a genuine interest in science. Larry's accident-seeking turned into accident prevention. His second psychological testing showed startling changes: the serious ego impairment which raised the suspicion of borderline functioning was no longer in evidence. His body image had changed radically: the male figure, drawn earlier with fuzzy strokes and vague forms, was now set down with firm outlines and precise shapes. Passive submission had given way to active mastery of the environment. The higher level of integrative processes stands out as the most remarkable finding in his second test series.

Joe showed many of the same features of change described in relation to the other boys. The spurt in ego maturation in his case also was remarkable: learning capacity and handwriting improved, an interest in factual knowledge appeared, concentration span lengthened; moreover, he could for the first time think of the future in terms of a vocation, namely, in terms of being a man when he would be grown up.

All three boys appeared much more alert mentally, and capable of more complex psychic processes after body intactness was established. A higher level of differentiation and integration appeared in their second test series. On the behavioral level this became manifest in the delay of action and the interposition of thought between stimulus and motor discharge. Along with this came a decline in hypermotility, which had been characteristic for the three boys. It is assumed that the anatomical change affected the body image in terms of a definitive masculine identity. The influence of the anatomical reality on the ego via the body image resulted in a firmer sense of reality, consequently in greater clarity of thought and the establishment of more effective, namely, adaptive, defenses.

In spite of these gains we shall not overlook the fact that genital intactness was initially seized upon as the savior who would keep feminine strivings at bay. Efforts at repression or characterological absorption of these still powerful strivings were preceded by an overbearing show of masculinity directly following the physical changes.[4] The thrust into assertiveness following body intactness had two phases. The first was characterized by an upsurge of masculine sexuality and an exaggerated display of forcefulness and cocksureness. An almost euphoric sense of power became noticeable which can be paraphrased by saying: "Now that I am a real boy the sky is the limit to what I can do." Heterosexual excitement (e.g., Joe's pictures of nude women) became—perhaps too soon and too completely—repressed and a tendency to compulsivity and affective constriction took over. No material on the boys' masturbation was forthcoming

4 The positioning of the testicle into the scrotum does not affect—that is to say, does not increase—the hormonal activity of this organ. The suddenness of change in behavior is therefore a purely psychological phenomenon.

which left an unfortunate lacuna in the understanding of their sexual development.[5] There is no doubt that the display of phallic masculinity had a defensive quality. However, its ultimate effect on character synthesis cannot be assessed with certainty before late adolescence.

For the time being, treatment in conjunction with genital restoration had made psychic functioning on a higher level possible. Thus it facilitated adaptive processes and the use of stable defenses less damaging and debilitating than the ones originally employed. One might say that Joe was prevented from entering a delinquent career; Steven was saved from an infantile, autistic state; and Larry was rescued from physical self-destruction. Due to the fact that the defective ego development was firmly attached to a physical condition, the pathological retardations and distortions were, so to say, prevented from inundating the psychic life of the child and from causing irreversible ego alterations. The thought occurred to me that these boys might have been more seriously affected by their environment, especially the mother, if they had not been afflicted by a genital, reparable defect. The concreteness of body-damage fear had not been totally internalized and welded to instinctual and conflictual anxiety. This fact might explain the reversibility of symptoms which in children generally would have indicated a most serious disturbance. Much that seemed at first in diagnostic evaluation as ominous pathology changed radically under the impact of the genital restoration. Psychotherapy alone can hardly be credited with the massive improvements. The idea forced itself on the observer that the physical condition itself represented a reality according to which the ego became modeled and remodeled; furthermore, that which appeared initially as an endopsychic conflict represented in fact a body-reality confusion aggravated by reality fear. As far as the body reality was internalized, psychotherapy was the proper helper; as far as the body reality could be corrected, namely, made definitive,

---

[5] I am indebted to Dr. Mary O'Neil Hawkins for the idea that continued examination of the scrotal sac might sensitize, so to say, accidentally, this genital area which thus becomes the seat of erotic feelings. The manual investigation by the child of his bodily defect consequently could turn into a masturbatory activity with the focus of sensation in the scrotal region. Castration anxiety, on the other hand, might lead to a complete desensitization of the genital. Our clinical material is inconclusive as to the particular masturbatory practices in cases of cryptorchism; here further analytic investigation is needed.

the surgeon was called upon to help. Both specialists have to syncho-
nize their contributions in order to discharge their respective functions in a coordinated approach. The cases of Steven and Joe have
illustrated this point.

SUMMARY

Three prepubertal cases of cryptorchism were presented. The
complementary effects of psychotherapy, physical correction of the
genital defect (two operative, one spontaneous), and treatment of the
parents, especially the mother, were explored. On the basis of the
clinical data the following conclusions were reached:

1. Cryptorchism is not a primary pathogenic factor. The particular way in which the genital defect is experienced by the parents,
particularly the mother, accounts for the child's preoccupation with
the testes. The perpetrator of the body damage is in the child's mind
identified with the mother. Her castrating possessiveness and the
passive aloofness of the father both constitute a matrix of family
interaction in which cryptorchism gives rise to typical symptoms
despite the fact that the three cases belong to heterogeneous nosological categories.

2. In all three cases an early operation trauma had occurred,
and served as the prototypical model for body-damage (castration)
fear. The genital defect (cryptorchism) served as the "organizing
experience" (Greenacre) which subordinated early trauma as well as
all subsequent phase-specific anxieties about body damage to the
persistent genital incompleteness. An operation trauma per se is not
considered an obligatory experience.

3. A distorted, vague, and incomplete body image exerted a
pathological influence on ego development. Resultant ego impairments were manifest in defective functioning relative to learning,
memory, thinking, time-space orientation, and motility. These impairments could furthermore be linked to the mother's inconsistent
attitude by which she tacitly forbade the child to recognize his
physical defect clearly, or to think rationally about it.

4. The tendency to self-damage (accident proneness) present in
the cases was understood as the child's idea that the genital defect
was the result of an act of aggression (castration). Through identifica-

tion with the aggressor the child turned passive submission into active execution and made himself the victim of his own aggression. Castrative wishes were clearly in evidence.

5. Cryptorchism favors direct, concrete, symbolic (substitutive) expressions by objects in the outer world, the use of the whole body or body parts for the mastery of the anxiety which the anatomical defect engenders. Substitutive organs (organ symbols) for the testicle were found to be: eye, tonsils, breast, and foetus.

6. A bisexual sense of identity reflected the physical reality of anatomical indecision. The perseverance of the female body image and the defense of castratedness (body-part surrender) was directly related to a body reality rather than to a psychologically integrated drive and ego organization. This became evident through the reversibility of the body-image confusion once genital intactness was established.

7. Coordinated efforts of surgeon and therapist resulted in a striking amelioration of ego impairment. The changed body image exerted an immediate and direct influence on ego functions. What appeared initially as an endopsychic conflict represented in fact a body-reality confusion, aggravated by reality fear. Considering the influence of the anatomical correction on differentiative and integrative psychic processes, the conclusion was reached that the concreteness of body-damage fear prevented total internalization of the body reality and its amalgamation with conflictual anxiety. The delay of internalization was maintained by the reparable genital defect and the undying expectation of a changed body reality. This particular state of affairs in the presence of a bodily defect might explain the reversibility of an emotional condition with severe ego impairments, which in children generally would indicate an ominous pathology.

The findings in this paper are restricted to cryptorchism. It seems that the particular survival value, the interference with perception, with the physical grasp of objects, with phase-specific gratifications, and many more factors related to a defective body part, introduce elements which are absent in cryptorchism per se. The sifting of similarities and differences in cases with other bodily defects lies outside the scope of this presentation. The clinical study of three cases of cryptorchism aimed at an investigation of the mutual influence of body reality, body image, ego development, and internalization within the matrix of a specific pattern of family interaction.

BIBLIOGRAPHY

Fineman, A. D. (1959), Preliminary Observations on Ego Development in Children with Congenital Defects of the Genito-urinary System. *Am. J. Orthopsychiat.*, XXIX.

Forrer, G. R. (1959), The Mother of a Defective Child. *Psa. Quart.*, XXVIII.

Fraiberg, S. H. (1960), Observations on the Homosexual Conflicts of Adolescence. In: *Adolescence: Psychoanalytic Approaches to Clinical Problems and Therapy*, ed. S. Lorand. New York: Hoeber.

Freud, A. (1952), The Role of Bodily Illness in the Mental Life of Children. *This Annual*, VII.

Freud, S. (1912), Contributions to the Psychology of Love. *Collected Papers*, IV. London: Hogarth Press, 1949.

—— (1923), The Infantile Genital Organization of the Libido. *Collected Papers*, II. London: Hogarth Press, 1949.

Greenacre, P. (1956), Re-evaluation of the Process of Working Through. *Int. J. Psa.*, XXXVII.

Jessner, L., Blom, G. E., & Waldfogel, S. (1952), Emotional Implications of Tonsillectomy and Adenoidectomy on Children. *This Annual*, VII.

Peto, A. (1959), Body Image and Archaic Thinking. *Int. J. Psa.*, XL.

Werner, H. (1940), *Comparative Psychology of Mental Development*. New York: International Universities Press, 1957.

THE ANALYSIS OF A BOY WITH A
CONGENITAL DEFORMITY

ANDRÉ LUSSIER

(London, England—Montreal, Canada)[1]

This paper is based on the analysis of Peter, a thirteen-year-old boy born with malformed shoulders and abnormally short arms terminating in hands having only three fingers and no thumbs. When Peter entered analysis, the over-all measurement from his shoulders to fingertips was scarcely eight inches. As far as is known, the psychodynamic implications at the unconscious level of so severe a congenital deformity have not previously been described in psychoanalytic literature. The positive results presented here are to be attributed to the inspiration and close collaboration of the staff of the Hampstead Child-Therapy Clinic under the direction of Anna Freud.

A special objective of the analysis was to compare the castration anxiety associated with such a gross bodily handicap with that of a neurotic youngster having no physical abnormality.

A finding of unusual interest in this analysis was the specific constructive function assumed by the fantasy life in the development of a number of permanent skills—ego abilities.

BACKGROUND INFORMATION

Much of the information about Peter's family background came from the reports of social workers and Hampstead Clinic personnel

[1] This case was treated by the author in the Hampstead Child-Therapy Clinic under the individual supervision of Dr. Ilse Hellman which is gratefully acknowledged.

The Hampstead Child-Therapy Clinic is maintained by grants given by the following Foundations: The Field Foundation, Inc., New York; The Ford Foundation, New York; The Foundations' Fund for Research in Psychiatry, New Haven, Connecticut; The Anna Freud Foundation, New York; The Grant Foundation, Inc., New York; The Estate of Flora Haas, New York; The Old Dominion Foundation, U.S.A.; The Psychoanalytic Research and Development Fund, Inc., New York.

who had interviewed Peter's mother at various times prior to and during his analysis.[2]

The whole subject of Peter's birth and early childhood was fraught with anxiety for his mother. She said she had never got over the shock of seeing him for the first time . . . it was terrible! Never before had she spoken of this to anyone.

She was certain that Peter's deformity had been caused by her mother-in-law with whom she had not got along at all well. The mother-in-law, she said, used to "row" her during the pregnancy. This quarreling she knew to be bad, and one day to avoid a scene on the street she tried to pass the mother-in-law "without taking any notice of her." The ruse failed and the incensed mother-in-law seized her *by the shoulders* to bring her to a halt. While she was not injured, she was greatly upset by the encounter and her feelings were hurt. She was three months' pregnant at the time and was sure that Peter's deformity was a direct consequence.

Peter's birth was an easy one, his mother reported. She was not told of the child's deformity at the time of the delivery and discovered it only when the baby was first brought to her. The sight was a terrible blow. "His arms were so tiny," she recalled.

The Parents

Peter's mother said she had had a happy childhood and had been devoted to her own mother. She described herself, however, as having always been highstrung, and according to a medical report had suffered from neurasthenia when she was thirteen years old.

Her husband was the first boy ever to take any notice of her. Their marriage followed a five-year courtship. In 1940, when Peter was a year and a half old, the father was called up for army service, and the mother took Peter back to her native town to live with her parents. Except for leaves, the father was away until 1946.

A second child, a daughter, was born in 1941 when Peter was three.

When Peter was five, his maternal grandmother took ill and Peter's mother had then to keep house for four men—her own father and her mother's three brothers.

[2] Mrs. Bianca Gordon, psychotherapist with the Hampstead Clinic, saw Peter's mother at regular intervals.

The maternal grandmother died three years later. Peter's mother said she thought at the time she would never get over her mother's death. In fact, she said, it had kept coming back into her mind ever since, accompanied by what she described as horrible thoughts.

Peter's mother was a Roman Catholic but did not attend church. Her husband, she reported, did not believe in religion. Actually, the mother had little to say about the father. He was an engineer's mate, and while not regarded as an impressive figure for his son, was nonetheless looked upon as the authority in the family. Following his return from the war, he got along well with Peter, then seven, and often played with him.

After the war, the family lived in a poor district and the parents were far from satisfied with their housing. The mother said she would have liked to have had a house with a garden where Peter could have played without being seen by the passers-by. Moreover, the fact that Peter had to sleep in the same room as his sister disturbed his mother, especially in view of Peter's handicap.

Peter as Baby and Boy

Peter's mother breast fed him until he was two months old when she had to wean him because of cracked and festered nipples caused, she felt, by her own worrying. She had found it difficult to handle Peter because he could not put his arms around her. In the bath she would support him with one hand under his neck, and was constantly fearful he might slip out of her grasp and drown.

During the first six months Peter cried almost nightly. To comfort him his mother would carry him about and give him "gripe water" but would not feed him because she "kept to a schedule." Apart from this, he was a healthy baby and no trouble. His mother started training him to use a pot when he was two months old and said she had persevered in this training to have him clean and dry by about seven months.

During his first year Peter was twice separated from his mother for periods of about six weeks each while he was in the hospital for surgical interventions to separate the webbed fingers of his right hand and to provide greater mobility in shoulders and arms, one of which, the left, had no elbow.

From early infancy, Peter was clever with his feet and could pick up things with his toes. While learning to walk, he would fall down frequently because he seemed top-heavy.

The mother told the social workers that she had taken Peter to doctor after doctor, always in the hope that he could be "cured" although she had been repeatedly told that his condition was beyond remedy. When the doctors explained that Peter's left arm had no elbow she at first accepted the fact but soon began to believe she could see one and even that Peter was beginning to bend his arm a little.

When he was three, the sister was born. Physically normal, Mary was the second and last child. During this pregnancy the mother had imagined she was going to have another boy whom she was already calling "Stephen." She told Peter about "Stephen" and when Peter was naughty she would threaten him by saying that "Stephen" would not come to life because of his bad behavior. She claimed she had never been afraid that this second child would be deformed.

The mother reported that Peter and Mary got along well together, that Peter was fond of his sister, and that Mary, in turn, would "stick up" for Peter. Sometimes, however, Peter would torment Mary and his mother had to "smack him." During the analysis, very little emerged about the sister. Clearly, Peter compensated for his insecurity by regarding the little girl with her normal arms as no more than a baby, and consequently no threat to him.

When Peter's mother took him out as a baby and young child, she would cover him up to hide his arms. She said she felt very ashamed of him. She was especially embarrassed when people stared, and this uneasiness continued right up to the beginning of the boy's analysis. On his part, Peter would react to stares by turning to his mother for reassurance, but she would "just feel ashamed" and could not comfort her son. She realized she was failing Peter, causing him suffering and making him more insecure. Even so, she did not believe in spoiling him, although, she said, it was hard at times not to do so.

By the time Peter was about ten years old, he had acquired the hard-earned skill of feeding himself, even being able to use a knife and fork, although still needing help to cut meat. He was described as a very clean eater. He could partially dress himself. He could put on his socks and shoes but could not do up his laces and needed help with some garments. He also needed help in the toilet right up to the beginning of his analysis. Shortly thereafter, however, the slight growth of arms and shoulders associated with puberty made it possible for him to take care of himself in the toilet.

Peter started going to school at the age of three. He was enrolled at a regular neighborhood school and did well there. At seven, he was transferred to a special school for the physically handicapped. Here he gradually lost interest in schoolwork, becoming more and more preoccupied with his daydreams. His studies suffered to the degree that he was regarded as a backward pupil. His backwardness was, in fact, one of the motivating factors in the later decision to give him analytic treatment.

When he was about eight and a half, Peter began arriving home from school with his pants soiled. This continued for about four months. His mother blamed the school, explaining that Peter was too shy to ask for help when going to the toilet. The soiling never occurred at home.

Only two months after this problem had been overcome, Peter began wetting the bed. This happened right after another hospitalization for surgical intervention preparatory to the fitting of artificial arms.[3] He continued wetting the bed nightly for about five months until medication prescribed by his physician gradually cleared up the symptom. Enuresis, however, recurred a year later. His mother blamed herself for these troubles as she was still upset by the comparatively recent death of her own mother.

At the age of nine, when Peter was still able to read only a few words, mostly two-letter or three-letter words at that, he was given a Revised Stanford-Binet intelligence test which rated him as a low normal (I.Q. 85-90). Subsequent observations suggest the rating did not do justice to his intelligence.

The Problem

Manifest behavioral difficulties already referred to were instrumental in bringing Peter into analysis at the age of thirteen. The nocturnal enuresis appearing at the age of nine following the surgical intervention, and recurring at ten, was one of these. The backward-

[3] Before his physical growth stopped, surgical work had to be done to the inner articulations of the shoulder as a preparation for the future fitting of better artificial arms.

ness at school was another. But, as soon became clear during the analysis, the fundamental problem was an emotional disturbance expressed in a continuous and inventive evasion of factual truth and in the creating of a fantasy life of remarkable complexity and color. There were, too, some depressive tendencies.

For a boy with Peter's handicap and experiences, such difficulties were to be expected. But unexpected was the way in which Peter failed to exhibit either masochistic satisfaction, passivity, or self-pity —three characteristics only too readily associated in our mind with the psychology of many disabled people.[4]

Peter did not like to be handled, nor did he want to be regarded as an object of pity. He did not seem to derive or want to derive gain or gratification from his disability. Dominant in his behavior was the active striving toward the achievement of his goals.

THE ANALYSIS

The analysis proper, consisting of intensive work in daily sessions five days a week, lasted for about twenty months. Contact was maintained for a further sixteen months, but during the last year Peter's visits were irregular, varying from about once a week to once a month toward the end.

Compensatory Mechanisms

The early stages of the analysis produced many illustrations of the psychological mechanisms Peter was using to cope with his deformity. Three were dominant. He sought to push his handicap out of existence by intensive denial of its reality; he built a fantasy world from which he excluded his physical handicap; and he developed certain reaction formations as defenses against insecurity and inferiority. His aim, both consciously and unconsciously, was always to prove to the world that whatever anybody else could do with normal arms he could do as well or better with short arms and without artificial aids.

Early in the treatment, the sessions were filled with talk of his splendid exploits and great hopes. He would see himself excelling in all kinds of competitions and activities in none of which he would make even the slightest allowance for his handicap. In his fantasy

4 Conclusion drawn by Anna Freud following her diagnostic interview with Peter.

he was a remarkable tree climber, for example, and also something of a champion at cutting down trees, both obvious impossibilities. He boasted how skillfully he could ride a bicycle. He liked to imagine himself, too, as the youngest trumpet player in the world. "I want to be the best, alone on top, no one better than me." His greatest wish at this time was to own a trumpet.

The need to show off was continuously apparent in his behavior and his fantasies. He wanted his analyst to know that he was physically the strongest of his gang. He did, in fact, carry a large dagger at his side which he would brandish as a symbol of his prowess. Heroic in its denial of the deficiency of his arms was his boast that he could "slap the other boys in the face so hard!"

Again and again he would tell how he planned to organize special shows in London at which he would be the featured attraction, diving headlong from the Tower Bridge to the astonishment of the skeptical crowd.

Peter especially liked to acquire things that other boys did not have, so he could provoke their envy. "Look, you haven't got what I've got." "See my big dagger, mine is bigger." He expressed this kind of feeling more vehemently and more frequently than would the average boy.

His deep-seated insecurity due to his deformity constantly impelled Peter to essay exceptional feats of daring or skill. The day he started taking swimming lessons he commented: "I am looking forward to swimming with my girl friend; I want to show her that I can swim; perhaps she does not think I can do it well.... If I have enough pride, I will get my swimming certificate." Then he recalled an earlier incident at the pool when, feeling unsure of being accepted by the poolside gang of young swimmers, he had climbed to the upper springboard to display how fearless he was. When the other boys saw him up there, he said, they became frightened for him, and when he realized they were frightened, he jumped into the water. The boys were impressed. They applauded him and accepted him. This story shows how desperately hard Peter was working to prove he was in no way inferior to his peers in achievement.

During the first months of the analysis, it could be said that the intensity of Peter's fantasy life was so great as to verge at times on pseudologia phantastica and to carry him close to borderline capacity in reality testing. One day, full of excitement, he reported: "I have just won a bike by answering questions." The fact was he had entered a daily newspaper contest by answering questions and sending in the contest entry. At the time, this action was all the foundation he needed on which to build the belief that he had already won the bicycle. Moreover, he had moved on from this belief in ownership to the planning in minute detail of a 400-mile trip.

At this stage his fantasies were so intense that their realization in actuality seemed to him to be at most no more than a matter of time. This conviction led him into a number of dangerous situations such as that resulting from his bravado on the high-diving board.

Castration Anxiety

Peter's castration anxiety soon assumed a paramount place in the analysis. Paradoxically, his anxiety was in no way different in type from that of any physically normal neurotic boy except in that he had a permanent unconscious need to compensate for the lack of normal arms.

Peter's castration anxiety was related to masturbation fantasies and activities, to oedipal strivings, and to the resulting guilt and fear of punishment. In his case, the arm defect was unconsciously feeding the castration complex. The defective arms were, in a sense, equated with "defective" genitals and thus were unconsciously taken as evidence of actual castration.

Peter had all the classic masturbation fantasies but with unusually strong exhibitionistic components. In these, his symbolic exhibitionistic masturbating was always followed by symbolic castration.

The exhibitionism was shown in the fantasies in which he performed as a trumpet player and was cheered by huge, delirious crowds. Similarly in other fantasies, he performed notable exploits on a bicycle for which his photograph would appear in the daily papers.

The sense of guilt arising out of his strong sexual feelings for his mother and the consequent fear of punishment were shown through such actual dreams as this: He was riding his bicycle at great speed . . . he became more and more excited, then started going down a steep hill . . . his mother was there watching his performance . . . she laughed and was quite "thrilled" . . . a crowd of bystanders was equally thrilled . . . at the peak of his excitement he found he could not control the speed at which he was racing downhill. "I am going so fast it isn't possible to put the brakes on. I can't stop. I have an accident and break my leg."

It is interesting that Peter had a variety of fantasies revealing oedipal strivings in which he had to go to the hospital for a broken leg, not an arm.

In some fantasies so much emotional significance was attached to cycling that Peter's legs symbolically became his genitals. Cycling was sexualized and consequently injury to legs represented punishment by castration. The same process was also apparent in those trumpet fantasies in which the trumpet was broken.

This sexualization was so intense that Peter said he had to avoid thinking about *his* bicycle or trumpet at night. "It makes me feel too hot and too excited, and then it is hard to fall asleep."

Still another instance of phallic displacement was Peter's frightening dream of lying in bed, face down, and finding a big snake under his tummy. Peter used to masturbate at night lying on his "stomach."

During the period in the analysis in which Peter was longing for a bicycle or a trumpet, there were a few episodes of homosexual anxiety. He had indeed to miss some sessions to avoid becoming "too excited" while talking to his analyst.

The Significance of Enuresis

From the material provided by the analysis it became evident that the enuresis associated with Peter's intense oedipal fantasies had two meanings for him, as it does for most enuretics. It meant prohibited sexual activity accompanied by castration as punishment. And simultaneously, it had the reassuring meaning of an undamaged, well-functioning penis. For Peter, castration anxiety was intensified because unconsciously he equated his arm defect with castration. This unconscious equating of a real with a symbolic handicap intensified both his denial of his deformity and his great need to overcompensate for it. The arm defect, in itself a visible handicap, also greatly increased his need for displaced phallic exhibitionism.

Most of Peter's dreams show that this phallic exhibitionism was a basic factor in his bed wetting. For example, he had many dreams involving aeroplanes. In front of an amazed crowd including either his mother or the Queen, he would pilot a plane at a terrific speed. Then he would crash in water and break his leg. The dream sequence was obviously one of masturbation-erection, enuresis, castration-punishment. After Peter had been in analysis for about a year, the enuresis disappeared.

THE CONSTRUCTIVE ROLE OF FANTASY

The extent to which Peter was able to make constructive use of fantasy in the formation of ego abilities was the most unexpected development of the analysis.

As mentioned earlier, the boy entertained, for a time, a number of unrealizable fantasies such as climbing and cutting down trees. These soon dropped out of the analysis completely. But other fantasies and hopes, which my colleagues and I admittedly felt to be equally unattainable, remained for some time as central points of interest until these too were dropped one by one from the analysis but for quite a different reason. They moved out of the realm of fantasy into actual accomplishment. During the analysis, Peter learned to play the trumpet well enough to plan a career as a performer. He learned to swim and dive well enough to earn a life-saving certificate. In this he measured up to the standards required of all applicants; no special allowances were made for his deformity. And he learned to ride a bicycle in the face of the opposition of his apprehensive parents. These accomplishments showed that Peter had a more generous and, at the same time, more realistic assessment of his capabilities than did his parents, his analyst, or the other professional consultants. Moreover, he seemed to have at his disposal an almost inexhaustible fund of energy.

That Peter should talk about his hopes and fantasies just so long as they remained in the realm of unreality was an unusual and fascinating aspect of the analysis. He presented a succession of foci of intense interest—the trumpet, the swimming, the bicycle, and others. Each of these was talked about with great excitement, elaborated in imaginative detail, then dropped abruptly the moment Peter took action to make it a reality. For example, the entire subject of trumpet and music dropped out of the analysis when Peter was finally given a cornet. The analyst would therefore have been unaware of the details of the boy's real achievements but for the reports of the therapist who interviewed the mother.

It could be said, then, that the analysis dealt at any one time only with the residue of Peter's fantasy world, and the work of the analysis could be described as the continuing transformation of fantasies into ego abilities executed in reality. Peter was using fantasy to conquer reality. And through this process he was seeking a secure ego identity.

It was significant also that Peter's most highly charged fantasies all revealed strivings toward a masculine identity. This was particularly apparent in the way the trumpet and the analyst served alternately as means of achieving masculinity. When Peter felt he was gaining enough satisfaction from his trumpet, he felt he could dispense with the analyst by missing sessions.

Multiple Mechanisms

At this point it might be well to note that any one of Peter's activities must be recognized as having been brought about as the result of the interplay of more than one mechanism. Phallic displacement, overcompensation, and reaction formation were involved in the trumpet playing before large audiences, in the display of badges won in swimming, diving and lifesaving, and in the wearing of a dagger at his side. One striking instance betraying the extent to which Peter's short arm threatened his masculine pride was the determined attempt at fourteen years of age to win membership in a fishing club whose minimum age requirement was sixteen. He set his heart on this goal because he was convinced that, should he succeed on grounds of actual performance as a fisherman, the world would cease to entertain doubts about his potentialities. He would then belong to the category of men. Moreover, membership would entitle him to wear "a big badge" on his coat which he could show to all his friends. Here again, drawing upon his tremendous reserves of energy, Peter did win the coveted membership on merit despite his age.

From Fantasy to Reality

Some considerable time after Peter's fantasies relating to the trumpet had moved out of the field of the analysis, he brought the subject back in again in an unforeseen way. One day he brought his cornet (trumpet) to the analytic session. Secure now in his real achievements and repeated successes as a musician, he somehow felt able to bring this once highly cathected subject again to the attention of his analyst.

"You want me to play?" he asked, his eyes radiant. Hesitation and shyness were brushed aside by the determination to demonstrate his skill. He communicated the feeling that nothing in the world could have prevented him from playing.

On this occasion, Peter was wearing his new artificial left arm. He said this would be his first time to play for anybody while wearing the artificial arm, and that playing would be much more than normally difficult. The wonder was he could play at all. As the artificial left hand could not grasp the cornet properly, he perforce had to use his undersized, thumbless right hand with its three slender fingers to help hold the instrument while simultaneously fingering the valves. For extra support, he put one foot up on a chair so he could rest the cornet against his knee. In this awkward and little-practiced position, he played relatively well.

After playing several selections, one of which he had composed himself, he commented that "the next time" he would play twelve tunes in a much better way without his artificial arm. After a moment's reflection, however, he said it would probably be better for him to try to learn wearing his artificial arm because the arm would give him a better appearance on the stage. The comment indicated how far removed Peter was from seeking a masochistic advantage from his handicap, or, to express it in other terms, to exhibit with his defect.

Comparisons of Peter's fantasy life with that of more physically normal adolescents revealed one fundamental difference in the relationship between sexual (masturbatory) fantasies and symbolic activity. When a physically normal youth abandons a sexual fantasy, he almost invariably jettisons all related symbolic activity and interest. Peter, in contrast, was able to transfer the interest associated with symbolic activity to constructive activity. For him, fantasy was the precursor of, not the substitute for, real striving. His early intense preoccupation with his trumpet fantasy, for example, later became the driving power that carried him over the arduous road to competence as a musician.

Observations made by Anna Freud concerning the fantasy life of the physically normal boy indicate how unusual was Peter in this respect. Anna Freud (1936) writes:

> We must not suppose that an adolescent ponders on the various situations in love or on the choice of a profession in order to think out the right line of behaviour, as an adult might do or as a boy in the latency-period studies a piece of machinery in order to be able to take it to pieces and put it together again. Adolescent intellectuality seems merely to minister to day-dreams. Even the ambitious phantasies of the pre-pubertal period are not intended to be translated into reality. When a young lad phantasies that he is a great conqueror, he does not on that account feel any obligation to give proof of his courage . . . in real life . . . He [the boy] evidently *derives gratification from the mere process of thinking* . . . His behaviour is determined *by other factors* and is not necessarily influenced by the results of these intellectual gymnastics [pp. 175-176, italics added].

How different is the story of Peter, the boy who left little or nothing of his fantasy world behind him with the passing of puberty.

Explanations of Peter's psychological processes must be tentative pending corroborative findings in similar cases. A hypothesis could be: Nothing of Peter's fantasy world could be abandoned or left behind because every part of it had to be put at the service of an unconscious need, the need to find substitutes for the growing of longer arms. This mechanism of transformation would be part of a never-ending denial of inferiority. And the deformity would be a perpetual stimulus for compensatory strivings.

CHARACTERISTICS OF THE DISABLED

The belief that "as long as one is convinced one can do something, one can do it" has helped many people to worthy achievements. But it can also be conveniently used to feed daydreaming while inhibiting activity which would put the conviction to the test.

So far as physically disabled people are concerned, surface observation shows that, according to their reactions, they can be divided into two categories, the active and the passive ones, the doers and the dreamers. Apparently, in the analytic literature, more attention has been paid so far to the passive than to the active type. Veterans hospitals are still caring for many patients described as "passive-dependent personalities." Typically these patients use their noncongenital handicaps, consciously or unconsciously, as justification for passivity and dependence. They stop striving for attainable achievements and make inaction morally acceptable by considerations of self-pity. The handicap becomes the pivot for a multitude of unfruitful fantasies and excuses for resignation.

These passive individuals preserve the conviction that they could accomplish great things by avoiding test by action. Analogous is the frequently encountered case of the student with poor grades who does not dare work hard for fear he might shatter the gratifying belief that he would be at the head of his class if only he would apply himself. Here again reality is a threat and is sacrificed. Passivity and fantasy leave no room for achievement.

Not so with Peter. He dared to put his "dreams" to the test. For him there was nothing mutually exclusive between the appearance of compensatory fantasies on the one hand and compensatory actual improvements in ego performance on the other. Peter's real achievements were so well integrated, so positively ego-syntonic, that it seems we must look beyond pathological mechanisms for a comprehensive explanation.

Turning passivity into activity is there, but it is only part of the picture. It will be shown later that the fear of passivity played a part in spurring the boy to greater endeavors. But a purely defensive reaction cannot be the sole impetus for so many positive undertakings. If it could, it would produce reaction formations of classic, crystallized structure whereas Peter's behavior approximates much more closely that resulting from sublimation. It might be better to say that Peter's functioning could serve as an illustration of the adaptive function of fantasy life, according to Heinz Hartmann's elaborations of Anna Freud's views on the denial of reality by fantasy. Hartmann (1939) wrote:

> . . . what are the positive adaptive elements of fantasy? . . . It is possible, and even probable, that the relationship to reality is learned by ways of *detours*. There are avenues of reality-adaptations which, at first, certainly lead away from the real situation.

The function of play is a good example . . . Another example is the auxiliary function of fantasy in the learning process: though fantasy always implies an initial turning away from a real situation, it can also be a preparation for reality and may lead to a better mastery of it. Fantasy may fulfill a synthetic function by provisionally connecting our needs and goals with possible ways of realizing them . . . there are fantasies which, while they remove man from external reality, open up for him his internal reality [pp. 17-19].

Peter's condition, furthermore, should not be compared too narrowly to that encountered in certain character disorders and in manic-depressives who exhibit much compulsive, compensatory activity. Peter was all this—and something more. He looked forward while the others looked backward. His progress was more than a reactive defense. He actually achieved increasing emotional security as he went along. His actions and integration regularly operated to reduce the tension between "wanting" and "being able" to do something.

Compulsive work, counterphobic reaction, reactive compensatory mechanisms, all have something static about them. Peter's activity, in contrast, was creative. There seems no doubt that Peter is an excellent example of an "active disabled" person. The people who belong to this category do not usually seek psychiatric help, and their reactions are usually dismissed as "normal." Whether or not Peter's drive toward activity is characteristic of all the individuals who belong to this group, or whether we have to regard him as exceptional, will have to be decided in the future when more detailed analytic studies of such persons are made available.

ARTIFICIAL ARMS AND EGO IDENTITY

Peter had first been provided with artificial arms several years before his analysis. But for the most part he could not be induced to use them with any regularity. By using his own arms he was putting his inborn physical equipment to the test. After all, Peter had always known his body as it was. For him, his body ego was intact. While others may have been shocked by the sight of his arms, Peter himself was not. His body image had been unchanged all through his life. If there were any element of shock for him, it could only be brought about by the disturbing experience of comparing himself to others, an experience bound to jeopardize his security and self-confidence.

If, then, he so consistently refused to use the artificial arms, the reason must have been to valorize those very body parts that threatened most to feed an inferiority complex. His intense motivation toward action and achievement was a measure of this need to prove his own natural body adequate to every challenge. Yet his competition with other children was of a normal kind. The intensity with which he resorted to the mechanism of compensation in displacement was proportional to the intensity of the threat of inferiority and failure in the experiences of competition. The threat to his inner security first posed by his mother's shame served as a trigger for more compensatory performances.

We hope we correctly use Erikson's concepts and terminology (1956) in stating that the artificial arms were completely excluded from the field of Peter's identity. They were not given even the smallest part to play in his drive toward levels of performance adequate to his ideal ego identity. The sense of *self*, of *his* personality, of *his* potentialities, he felt should be based solely on the physical equipment nature gave him.

Peter's first direct reference to his arms after several months of analysis had nothing to do with his desperate wish to see them grow. On the contrary, it was a protest against having anything further done to his arms as they were. The occasion was the relating of a dream of castration anxiety in which he was walking on railway tracks when a train (the analyst) roared up to him too quickly to be avoided, hit him, and mangled his arms.

Peter himself linked this dream to the previous operations he had undergone preparatory to the fitting of artificial arms. Peter had greatly feared that the hospital doctors might decide to cut off the short arms in order to replace them with artificial ones. The surgeons had, in fact, suggested that this might be necessary in order to fit the newest, most improved type of artificial arms. Peter opposed the possibility with intensity.

Obviously such an ablation was conceived of by the boy as a brutal attack from the adult world, a cruel attempt to deprive him of any chance to reach a meaningful sense of identity. It could destroy any possibility of reaching a reconciliation with his body ego. It could be so traumatic an experience as even to pave the way for depression or devastating passivity.

It should be noted here that there was no evidence that self-pity motivated Peter's exploits. He would go out into the streets with his trumpet at Christmas and other times to play tunes and collect money from the passers-by. In this kind of activity where, if anywhere, self-pity could be expected to reveal itself in passive exploitation, Peter's whole objective was to impress people by his performance, not by his handicap.

SEXUALIZATION

The transformation of fantasies into the ego constitution was not achieved without hazard. For the main fantasy, that of becoming a musician, the process at the instinctual level was for a while a precarious one. During one phase, the musical activity was a highly sexualized, aggressive activity which threatened to interfere with Peter's musical training and performances. He enjoyed, for example, playing with the trumpet pointed as "high up in the air" as his arms would permit. When this playing with trumpet raised was accompanied by real erections in the presence of girls during a concert, Peter had to stop playing because of the sexual excitement. The resulting anxiety tended toward inhibition rather than sublimation. Fortunately, the problem was left behind after the phallic content in the activity was interpreted, thus desexualizing it without destroying it. Toward the end of the analysis Dorothy Burlingham summed up this aspect of Peter's progress: "His ego and id seem to be well lodged in his music, which might enable him really to do something with his gift."[5]

REALITY AND DEPRESSION

Two questions which presented themselves again and again during the analysis were: Why did Peter keep his real achievements out of the analytic sessions for so long? Why did he seem to cease being thrilled by anything as soon as it stopped being a fantasy?

[5] Dorothy Burlingham, Co-director, Hampstead Clinic, during a case conference.

One hypothesis is that a coveted object (trumpet) or function (musician) was unconsciously equated to the growing of longer arms. While such objects or functions remained in fantasy, they held great emotional significance for Peter, but the moment they entered the real world, they lost their symbolic meaning. This process of converting fantasy to fact was one of painful disillusionment in that it meant abandoning a "dream" through which Peter could keep alive his deeply cherished hope for normal arms. His unconscious reaction was to devaluate the real object or function. It could be expected that the process would have a depressive effect, and this did, in fact, occur. At times when he had nothing exciting to talk about in the realm of fantasy and thus felt he had to talk about himself (reality), he would become depressed.

Earlier, when the trumpet was still an object of fantasy, Peter had fully expected to receive one as a birthday present. When it failed to arrive, his disappointment was so great that he became depressed, lost interest in eating, could not sleep, and missed sessions. However, as the analysis proceeded, he developed the ability to accept disappointment and the disillusionments of reality without experiencing such deep feelings of depression.

Important also in Peter's personality was an unconscious feeling of incompleteness expressing itself endlessly in attempts to compensate for his deformity. This feeling developed in spite of the strong body ego which made him resist the use of artificial arms. Toward the end of the analysis, it was apparent that Peter would never be able to feel he had achieved full masculine status. Unlike most physically normal men who reach a relatively satisfactory state of equilibrium in their male role, Peter gave indication that he would always need some mechanism to deal with the psychic effects of his deformity. Achievement and success would be needed again and again to bolster his masculine ego.

This mechanism was seen in operation on a number of occasions. For instance, after six successful months as a trumpeter in a band, Peter began talking about forming his own band where he would be the leader, "the boss." But, he emphasized, he had no intention of showing off. This was in contrast to the exhibitionism he had displayed earlier. In talking about "his" band, he said he would not want to make it too obvious that he was the conductor. He would just like to give a discreet signal to start the band playing. Surely the other members of the band would not like him to show off too much and he would not want to make them envy him.

Further, revealing his need to devaluate arms of normal length, Peter commented that he particularly disapproved of the usual behavior of most trumpet players on the stage. He described them as "being foolish with their trumpets . . . showing off by throwing them up in the air . . . and playing in the sky." Peter, of course, could not flourish his trumpet in this fashion. In a matter-of-fact way, he summed up: "A trumpet is meant to play music, not to make a big show."

In the foregoing, Peter's psychic handling of his physical defect might be compared with the way in which young girls typically deal with a castration complex. They depreciate their own bodies but take pride in their pursuits. It is as if they were to say: "My body is of no consequence, but what I do is marvelous." Similarly, Peter's phallic exhibitionism found expression through achievement.

Oedipus Complex, Regression, and Adolescence

One day Peter came to his session fully determined, for the second time, to play the trumpet for his analyst. On the one hand, this was a sign of increasing security and reconciliation with reality. On the other, it revealed strong oedipal rivalry and forewarned of the danger of regression to a passive-masochistic state.

Unconsciously, this performance meant that he could do in front of his analyst something the latter was incapable of doing. It proved to be too daring a show of his phallic superiority as it was followed by nightmares in which his trumpet was broken into pieces and in which he was run over by horses and gorillas. In the nightmares he was reduced to a castrated, female condition. He had many ensuing fantasies, verging into real beliefs, in which his analyst was jealous of him, was unhappy that he had become a musician, and was displeased that he had got a bigger trumpet. (Peter had recently changed his small cornet for a trumpet.)

Earlier in the analysis, the rivalry in the transference and the anxiety accompanying it did not go too deeply and were expressed quite simply. He would say: "I would like to be the boss here, too, and make you talk to me and not only me talking to you . . ." One day, a necessary visit to his dentist provoked a nightmare that was related to the transference relationship: Two very big men seized him and took him by force to the dentist; they were ugly and wanted to take out all his teeth. After relating this dream, he went on without a pause into his own fantasy: "A boy is in the dentist chair; the dentist takes a hammer, hits the boy, and takes out all his teeth. Then the boy wakes up [recovers consciousness], takes the hammer, knocks down the dentist, and takes out all his teeth." This tooth-for-a-tooth fantasy was related with great gusto.

But the feelings which emerged at this later phase presented greater difficulties. Peter was no longer cooperative and said he wished to see the analysis come to an end. He would reiterate that he did not feel like coming any more. He would insist that he was cured, not having wet the bed for so long. His father told him it would be a waste of time to go on. It was obvious that Peter no longer found the analysis exciting. He felt he had nothing more to expect of it. It was now even disappointing. Above all, Peter did not feel like talking about his trumpet. He wanted to keep it to himself, away from the analysis, away from the analyst he was sure was opposed to his becoming independent and grown up with his big trumpet. He was convinced that the analyst was envious and consequently ill-disposed toward him. His resistance at this stage almost reached phobic proportions. He was very anxious in his silences, in his avoidance of any mention of his prized trumpet. Through dreams and fantasies, it became obvious that he was afraid of being deprived of this most exciting possession. He had to keep all his strong feelings about it from the analyst. Symbolically, he was hiding away his pleasurable, exciting erection, and his unconscious fears of castration were expressed in nightmares in which his trumpet was broken while he was on his way to a session.

A little later the masturbation displacement, the guilt, and the castration anxiety became even more dominant in his dreams. In place of the gorillas of previous nightmares there appeared an even more obvious representative of the superego, the policeman. Peter reported the following nightmare: He was playing jazz with his trumpet as a member of a nightclub dance band when several policemen rushed in; he became so upset and frightened that he dropped his trumpet to the floor where it smashed into pieces. He woke up sweating profusely. Following the sessions dealing with this dream, there was a gradual lessening of the sexualization of Peter's musical activity.

Some earlier indications of the intensity of Peter's oedipal strivings were noted during the first phases of the analysis. Peter used to say that he very much liked to act in school plays, "specially the grown-up parts where I can let myself go with rage, telling off the others . . ." He particularly enjoyed making a noise, especially whistling or sounding off with his trumpet. The significance of this can be more readily appreciated when it is known that whistling was forbidden at home during the day in order not to disturb the sleep of the father who worked night shifts. The making of noise was perhaps his favorite way of expressing his opposition to his father. Another cathected area related to his oedipal rivalry was the great temptation to remain awake as late as possible at night; this meant consciously daring to do what his father did.

In the latter part of the analysis, the mother and mother figures came more and more to the foreground. Some ambivalence had first been observed. On the unconscious, negative side, his mother was a bad, orally depriving mother. He dreamed that he had not enough to eat, that she had given him "much less sandwiches" than she had given his father. His father thus "had better chances to grow."

This negative aspect, however, was much less important in the analysis than his febrile desire to impress the mother and win her admiration and love. His yearning for her love and approval came out in a recurring daydream in which the Queen honored him for his fishing abilities by inviting him to dinner and presenting him with £1,000 for fishing equipment. Another revealing daydream found him planning to work and make money to buy a better house for his mother.

An almost incredible feat throws further light on Peter's oedipal strivings. He set himself the task of building a real bicycle without his parents' knowledge. A friend who was in on the scheme let Peter use a shed at the back of his house. Here Peter gradually assembled the parts as he was able to save his money, bit by bit, to buy them.

As the project progressed, Peter's excitement ran high. The analytic sessions were filled with vivid fantasies of how at last he would be able to perform on his bicycle for his mother. One could feel the boy's determination to let nothing stand in the way of the fulfillment of this dream, not even the disapproval he knew he could expect from his parents who had always opposed the idea of bicycle riding for Peter.

As with the trumpet, Peter surprised everyone by achieving his goal. He became a skillful cyclist.

The Mother's Changing Attitude

About halfway through the analysis, there was a significant change in the mother's attitude. She began to tell her therapist how much happier she was feeling about her son. With each of Peter's successive achievements—fishing, playing the trumpet, swimming, lifesaving, diving, and bicycling—she would express surprise and a growing pride and pleasure. More and more he was becoming an indispensable part of her life. She was finding that she liked having him around the house. One time when he was away at camp for a few days, she said how much she was looking forward to having him back and hearing him practice on his trumpet again. His deformity no longer caused her embarrassment and shame.

This change in his mother's attitude was a source of great satisfaction to Peter. As all his hard-won feats had been undertaken basically to win her love and admiration, her pleasure and pride made him very happy and promoted his growing sense of security. Evidence of the oedipal coloring of his strivings and the assurance that he was becoming "the little man" of a proud mother was the simultaneous wish of mother and son for another baby in the family. Previously both parents had maintained that they did not want another child. Now, only the father was still against the idea.

Hazards of Passivity

During the latter phase of the analysis Peter's fight against regression to a masochistic, passive-feminine relationship in the transference became a major issue. Evidence of this struggle had appeared earlier in the form of an unconscious wish to be beaten by the analyst. There was also an earlier dream of a car accident in which he received an injury that left him with an opening into the middle of his body, a condition he equated to the female sexual constitution.

While his determination to achieve independence led him to "cut" several of his sessions and to argue for a reduction from five to two or three sessions a week, the latent wish to become more dependent betrayed him into several slips of the tongue in which his plea for fewer sessions came out as one for more sessions, actually "seven" sessions a week.

The analytic interpretation of Peter's conflict around dependence-independence produced some therapeutic results. These were manifest in his increased self-confidence, and in an easier, freer relationship with his analyst. As should be expected in the analysis of an adolescent, this development resulted in an increasing detachment from the analyst and a decreasing interest in continuing the analysis.

At this point I realized that Peter was no longer talking to me as a patient. He had, as never before, a matter-of-fact way of expressing his intentions; he now had the direct, open manner of an adolescent boy determined to see to his own affairs. With a sense of purpose and self-assurance, he explained how he now felt about the analysis. Reasoning logically, he wanted me to understand that after school he would like to follow his friends rather than attend a session. He wanted to do what the other members of his "gang" or club did at that particular time of day; he wanted to participate in their games; he wanted to go out with girls. The more fully his passive wishes were analyzed, the more urgent became his adolescent self-assertion and revolt. Accordingly we let Peter go on his way toward the independence he was seeking—and that meant the end of the analysis.

TECHNICAL PROBLEMS

As Peter made no mention of his arms in the early analytic sessions, the question as to whether or not the analyst should himself introduce the subject was raised at a case conference. Anna Freud recommended against this, suggesting that the analysis should be conducted like any other, with no topic being avoided or introduced. Interference, she felt, could result in bypassing the full analysis of his personality. She pointed out that the material then being presented concerned Peter's fear of castration. Dealing first with this anxiety would have certain advantages. As castration was not a reality, interpretation of his fears in this area would be more reassuring than interpretation of those having a basis in reality—the malformed arms. She also saw in this procedure a safeguard against Peter's depressive tendencies.

Throughout the entire course of the analysis, the requirements of Peter's ego functioning were respected. And nothing seems to have been lost by following this procedure. His real-life activities and achievements came late but safely into the analysis. After the interpretation of much of the castration material, Peter himself introduced the subject of his arms. This occurred in a depressive context, revealing that he had been harboring the illusion that the analysis would make his arms grow. He had dreamed that he was working in a coal mine with adults; a "big accident happened" and completely cut off their air supply; he fainted and woke up in a hospital, saved from death because he had been given *artificial* air; and he completely recovered. In the dream, the hospitalization was followed by normal life (normal arms). But in real life, his hospital experiences for the fitting of artificial arms were not followed by "real arms." Nor did the analysis bring about the growth of longer arms. There was no magic. At long last he was able to speak of the hopelessness of his wish.

Weathering this critical period of disillusionment, Peter went on to new achievements. Gradually, the enrichment of his real abilities and his growing self-esteem made it seem likely that he would continue to make reasonably satisfactory progress toward adulthood without further help from his analyst.

BIBLIOGRAPHY

Erikson, E. H. (1956), The Problem of Ego Identity. *J. Am. Psa. Assn.*, IV.
Freud, A. (1936), *The Ego and the Mechanisms of Defence.* New York: International Universities Press, 1946.
Hartmann, H. (1939), *Ego Psychology and the Problem of Adaptation.* New York: International Universities Press, 1958.

PSYCHIATRIC IMPLICATIONS OF TEMPORAL LOBE DAMAGE

MARY A. SARVIS, M.D. (Berkeley, Calif.)

The case to be presented is one in which organic brain disease could be detected on psychological grounds at a time when the diagnosis had not yet been made by neurological examination. Because the patient was an unusually perceptive boy, the case afforded a striking opportunity to distinguish between organic and psychological factors in the disturbance. Hugh's temporal lobe symptoms, as they were gradually identified in treatment, could be separated from his psychological problems and identified by the patient as the work of "Mr. 'Cephalitis," his name for the organic lesion. The ways in which the patient handled his organic damage and the body-image problems related to it could be distinguished from the symptoms he developed and the defenses he used with respect to his secondary psychological problems.

PRESENTING SYMPTOMS

The parents of a six-year-old boy asked for a consultation, saying "Ever since Hugh was nine months old he had what people call emotional disturbances . . . They call them temper tantrums but they aren't." These eruptions, Hugh's "mads," consisted of frequent, unpredictable, apparently unmotivated aggressive outbursts of murderous intensity in which the boy attacked anyone near him, striking, biting, scratching, kicking, and screaming. His father was the only family member strong enough to restrain him. Until recently, if he had been ignored in an attack, Hugh had followed family members around the house, striking them.

The explosive outbursts were the parents' chief concern; the mother feared Hugh was psychotic. However, the patient also had many other difficulties. He was bound up in extensive compulsive rituals, particularly around eating and bedtime. It took two or three hours to put him to bed because of his anxiety and his rituals; any interference with the rituals produced marked panic and aggressive outbursts. He had a totem toy tiger which had to be with him, especially in bed. He usually refused to eat with the family and restricted his diet almost entirely to popcorn and mush. His food rituals and inhibitions embarrassed him so much that he avoided social events. He could not play with other children because of his unstable behavior and his own self-consciousness. He felt that children regarded him as crazy. He was frequently absent from school because of recurrent illnesses. When he was able to attend school, he showed the strain by increased explosiveness at home.

The patient had frequent low-grade fevers, often on a respiratory basis: during these bouts his symptoms increased markedly. His gait was clumsy and his motor coordination poor; Thomas shoes (which he refused to wear) had been prescribed, and he wore glasses for a mild visual disturbance. On the basis of skin tests, he was said to have mild allergies. Neurological examinations had been negative. The medical reports indicated that all these physical findings were minimal and that no prescriptions would have been given if the parents had not been so desperate to have something done. The common medical impression was that the boy was spoiled and the mother was overprotective. The mother's extreme anxiety level, with its coercive impact, her demands for absolute medical authority, and her scattered, anxious matching of one doctor's opinion against another's reinforced this impression.

DEVELOPMENTAL HISTORY

Infancy

The patient was the third of four adopted children. They had all come from different families and had been adopted a few days after their birth. None of the other children presented any unusual difficulties. Hugh's early infancy was sufficiently socialized and advanced to earn him the family nicknames "Mr. Jaberwocky" and "Mr. Precocious." In the mother's words, "He drank from the cup early. Solids were taken at six weeks. He had an especially lusty fondness for meats. Until nine months he would clutch his spoon and play with food, mess his hands in it and talk and laugh." His sleep was undisturbed and his developmental skills were normal to superior.

Acute Illness

When Hugh was nine months old, his parents went out for three hours, leaving the children with a housekeeper. They returned to find the baby screaming, unable to recognize them and refusing to let anyone touch him. Shortly thereafter, he developed severe, recurrent diarrhea which lasted until he was three. No etiological agent was found, despite exhaustive medical work-ups. The only positive physical finding was moderate leukocytosis of unknown origin. For this, the patient was maintained on sulfa compounds for two or three years.

His behavior changed abruptly with this illness. The mother said, "After nine months, he clenched his mouth tight to avoid the spoon and hit it and us. He wasted away and looked emaciated. . . He would stare at the nipple for awhile, then cry and push it away or accept it greedily for a few moments, then scream and hit it away again. We discovered that he would drink more if we did not hold him and would hold the bottle through the sides of the crib at arm's length. . . He refused to touch the bottle with his hands, and his former habit of fondling the nipple and bottle changed to striking it away. . . He would hold his hands over his genitals and kick violently and scream whenever diapered. We tried leaving off the diapers, but any sight or odor of B.M. caused a tantrum again." The other children in the family had learned to use the toilet by copying, but the mother said of Hugh that "any suggestion that he use the toilet threw him into screams; so we did not pursue it."

His sleeping changed from normal to "light sleep. . . He screamed and fretted till exhausted then took a short nap and woke crying again day and night until almost two years. He began to improve then. At nine months he began head banging. . . He cried and thrashed around in a jerking motion in his crib so much that the sides had to be padded because his head became bruised. He stayed on his back. At fifteen months, he insisted on having lights and vacuum cleaner on to sleep. We moved his crib against the wall so he could turn the wall switch on—we would hear it click on and off all during the night. He insisted on staring into bright lights; day and night the lights had to be kept on or he would become frantic. By eighteen months, he would turn the vacuum cleaner on with the palm of his hand—he never used his fingers. He had violent tantrums unless the lights were on and the vacuum cleaner running loudly. . . If we entered his room, he would awaken screaming. He jerked in his sleep.

"At nine months, he stopped developing, refused to touch anything with his hands until almost two years. He made almost no effort to turn over, crawl or walk. He walked suddenly and clumsily at fifteen months without much previous attempt at sitting or pulling himself up." During this period of acute illness he would "hold his head and cry, walk into objects and get hurt. . . He would not pick up anything or play with toys. . . Between nine months and two years, Hugh would strike anyone who leaned across him or put their arms around him. He could not be loved in our arms or cuddled in any way. He made a special point of hitting anyone who wore glasses and knocked them off and broke them. Until about five, he had a violent spell if his babyhood was mentioned, tore up his own baby pictures, said, 'I hated being a baby.' He covered his ears and wouldn't listen.

"At eighteen months, Hugh discovered music and became obsessed with listening to records. It worried us that he would listen only to Tschaikovsky and that he refused nursery rhymes, yet it encouraged us to realize that he could recognize certain records. At three, he insisted upon taking music lessons."

During the period of acute illness, the patient reacted with indifference to personal events around him. A new-born (adopted) sister arrived when he was thirteen months old, but "he seemed too ill to notice." He acted as if he were unaware of a two-week separation from his mother at fifteen months. An eccentric housekeeper, who had been in the home since Hugh's birth, was fired when he was twenty-one months old, and he did seem to react favorably to that and to the family's move to the country when he was two; he slept uninterruptedly for the first time and shortly began to move his hands again. However, he continued to be unmoved by deaths of close relatives and friends, regardless of how much these upset the family or how close he had been to the person involved.

Hugh's improvement began at about two. At about three, his

diarrhea abruptly ceased and his behavior rapidly began to shift from a psychotic to a more clearly neurotic pattern. The mother said that he "started voiding outside. . . At three and a half, he conformed to sitting on the toilet or standing there, never wet his pants. Until about three and a half, he would only have a B.M. outside the house. By four years, he stopped complaining about the odor of his B.M.'s and became very proud of his feces. He enjoyed flushing the toilet, expressed admiration over the size of his B.M. He annoyed our other children by demanding to flush *their* toilets. He bullied his little sister by insisting, 'I'm the boss of the toilets.' "

When Hugh was four and a half to five and a half, things improved generally in the family, even though the mother was ill for a year in hospital or at home, and had two major operations (on kidneys and back). The patient continued to improve physically and emotionally. The parents assumed that Hugh's difficulties were completely psychogenic, blaming themselves and a housekeeper. This housekeeper (Hugh called her "the Cooker," "the Spanker") was said to be eccentric and was suspected of aggressive behavior toward the children and sexual abuse of the patient. Between four and a half and five and a half, the patient attended a therapeutically oriented nursery school, where the theory of the housekeeper as prime villain of the piece was developed and the parents' view of the psychogenic nature of the difficulty was consolidated. During this period between four and a half and five and a half, Hugh still hid his genitals in bed and bath, became extremely upset if anyone saw them, and had the aggressive outbursts, compulsive rituals, phobias, and inhibitions already mentioned. He feared having his mother leave him, crying, "What if Cooker beats me?" He screamed at nursery school. He tore up his baby books until he was about five, when he gradually "became very affectionate again, permitted physical comforting and loving . . and began talking about his infancy."

INITIAL EVALUATION AND PROCEDURES

Hugh himself, at the time of the evaluation, was a shy, clinging, meticulous boy whose opening remark to me concerned "the Old Witch" (presumably the housekeeper). He was untalkative but responsive to the playroom situation and to me. He was markedly compulsive and showed particular concern with testing his control over spatial boundaries; for instance, when blocking in a colored area, he painted perpendicularly up to a boundary line rather than parallel to it. The content of his play in the three evaluation sessions was violent: snakes and monsters attacked the people of a family. This play was repetitive and rose to a crescendo: "The snakes won the war!" He became progressively more spontaneous in his play and less shy with me.

Diagnostic Impression

This case at first seemed rather puzzling, partly because the parents' information was presented so unquestioningly within a psychogenic framework, which had been supported by the nursery school teachers. I knew, however, that the personnel of this nursery school were given to rather facile psychogenic assumptions, and it seemed likely that there might be retrospective distortion in the parents' presentation. There seemed to be no doubt that, superficially, the wicked housekeeper was the witch to whom the boy referred in the evaluation interviews. On the other hand, the parents were good observers and attentive to their children; there were older, highly articulate, and confiding children in the family; it did not seem likely that the housekeeper could have abused the children very seriously or very long. I felt that "the Cooker" became the personification of the attacking female as a displacement from the mother. The history told of a period of rather striking autistic symptoms, yet Hugh—though he communicated in an oblique and symbolic way and was rather remote in personal relationships—did not impress one as an autistic child. Nor did the quality of family relationships, either currently or in the developmental story, suggest this.

There were two principal factors which directed one's attention to organic brain disease, presumably originating in the acute illness at nine months.

1. The extreme intensity of the mother's anxiety is hard to convey: she was in a state of continual panic and the quality of this panic reminded one of Goldstein's description of the catastrophic anxiety in patients with organic brain disease who experience their mental processes as strange and unpredictable, as not making sense, and who

no longer feel completely responsible for them—not even unconsciously. In a similar way, this patient's mother reacted to her son's
disease (despite her conscious, verbal assumption of psychogenesis
and responsibility) as if it had this same quality of incongruity, un-
predictability, and natural catastrophe.

2. There were, of course, neurotic characterological interactions
in the family. However, I could see no evidence that the patterning
of family neurotic interactions had any significant causal relationship
to the boy's disturbance.

Therefore, an electroencephalogram was recommended. This
disclosed extensive focal and degenerative lesions in the right temporal lobe.

Initial Hypotheses and Maneuvers

My working assumption at this point was that the aggressive
outbursts were triggered by stimuli from the organically damaged
area of the brain. I assumed that the remainder of the boy's symptoms
represented his efforts to bind the severe anxiety associated with his
organic brain disease, largely by compulsive symptoms, partially by
phobias and inhibitions. I did not anticipate that other symptoms,
like his "mads," might also be a direct result of stimuli from damaged brain areas.

I felt that the medical aspects of the situation should be brought
under control and separated from the psychological management.
If Hugh could be stabilized on anticonvulsive drugs, I hoped it
would lower the intensity of his "actual" anxiety[1] (that associated
with the brain damage) and make his compulsive defenses less crucial
to him psychologically. It was also hoped that this approach would
reduce the level of the mother's anxiety, help her to stay with one
doctor, and give her confidence in beginning to learn to differentiate
her son's "mads" from his psychological problems. It was agreed that
medical stabilization would be begun before the boy returned to me
for psychotherapy.

Hugh was put on Dilantin, which moderated his aggressive behavior but produced intellectual dulling and retardation. A change

---

[1] Namely, anxiety associated with physiological excitation, like Freud's concept of
"actual neurosis," rather than anxiety associated with psychological conflict.

to Hibicon diminished these side effects.[2] However, six months after the initial contact, Hugh developed a fever, and his aggressive-assaultive outbursts increased violently. The mother once more became catastrophically anxious and again began frantically to seek auxiliary medical advice. A family friend suggested phenobarbital, the boy reacted to it with further excitement, the parents persuaded their doctor that there might be fresh encephalopathy, and the patient was put in a hospital for a pneumoencephalogram. Here he remained for four weeks with a low-grade fever before the neurological work-up could be completed. Hugh was a difficult patient to handle and, despite the known organic lesion, was often treated by the medical and nursing staff like a spoiled or naughty boy. The patient himself, alert, anxious, and curious, listened to discussions on rounds, spied on conversations in the nursing station, became thoroughly conversant with his diagnosis and the opinions concerning his current medical status and behavior. No new encephalopathy was found.

He was reluctant to return to see me; as he admitted several months later, he thought I had put him in the hospital and that I could read his mind. Ten months after the initial contact, when he was seven, he agreed to come to psychotherapy once a month.

Meanwhile, I had seen the parents several times. Both were people who functioned well and did not suffer from gross neurotic symptoms. The mother had a hysterical character structure, with notable suppression and repression of hostility; the father was a moderately passive-aggressive, somewhat inhibited man. Psychological testing (Minnesota Multiphasic Personality Inventory) was within statistically normal limits for both, with considerable evidence of symptom suppression (i.e., high K scores).

It seemed crucial in the management of the family situation to reduce their confusion between organic and psychological symptoms, their guilt and their anxious pressure for objective authority. I agreed to see them regularly once a month and at any other time they wished. They always came in together. In our discussions, I strongly supported the validity of their own observations and urged them to act accordingly. For instance, the mother felt that there was a clear relationship between low fever and exacerbations in Hugh's

2 The patient was stabilized eventually on Milontin.

aggressive behavior. This relationship had always been minimized
by doctors because the mother appeared so overprotective. I encouraged the parents to trust their own judgment in this and other
aspects of Hugh's management. Because the mother felt that Hugh
was able to attend school only at great emotional cost, collapsing as
soon as he got home, I asked the school to put him on home instruction, where he remained for a little over a year. Later in treatment,
the parents talked with me at times about transient difficulties with
the other children, asked my advice about infants they thought of
adopting, etc., but the focus of the counseling with the parents was
essentially that described above. I also suggested attitudes and maneuvers designed to diminish the intensity of the mother-child relationship and to strengthen the realistic, positive relationship between
the father and the boy. The mother concurred in this. No attempt
was made to focus on the parents' problems with themselves or each
other.[3]

COURSE IN TREATMENT

When Hugh, now seven years old, came into treatment, the initial
stage was primarily concerned with the working through of his paranoid transference fantasies via repetitive monster play. All the aggressive animals and robots in the playroom and all the decrepit,
mutilated animals were monsters who attacked a child or a whole
family and destroyed them. In the third session (third month of
treatment), the leader of the monsters became a "crabby lady." Hugh
devoted much time to details of the war but always, in an excited,
explosive climax, had the people totally destroyed. He was friendly,
tentative, and taciturn with me. With his mother he was domineering, clinging, demanding, and angry. However, the family reported
progressive stabilization of behavior at home: the clawing, scratching, and fighting had given way in part to verbal assaultiveness. In
the third therapy session, Hugh asked me about my notes (which
had to be made during the sessions for reasons of expediency). He
also referred briefly to the bad lady as a nurse in the hospital.

---

[3] I do not wish to minimize the fact that the parents' psychological problems influenced the meaning of the patient's illness to them and also their handling of it. The
mother's fear of hostility is an obvious case in point. In working with the parents,
however, my efforts were directed largely at *counteracting* these attitudes rather than
interpreting them.

In the fifth month of treatment, he agreed to come in every other week. The monster fantasy theme took on a markedly stereotyped quality with more and more burlesque of a television-type show. The lady villain was sometimes made humorous and the monsters were sometimes defeated. In general, he began to accept himself as a patient, to refer to previous events in the playroom, and to tell me of things that happened at home. I felt there was more modulation in his playroom behavior.

Then during the seventh to ninth month of treatment, Hugh's play shifted markedly to compulsive number play, with great emphasis on boxing in all the numbers and drawings. He became more tense, withdrawn, and uncommunicative. He acted very angry with his mother, hit her, and then spent most of the hour standing at the window to make sure she did not leave the building. I began to discuss his fear that he would be deserted because of his aggressive behavior and the meaning which his hospital experience had had for him. As usual throughout the first phase of treatment, Hugh would not answer such remarks, sometimes turning away or looking angry and stubborn. However, when my comments were appropriate, he would often gradually relax and become involved in play. He continued to be tense, hyperactive, and anxious in the playroom; he refused to come to see me once a week, and he complained of being no good at anything that he tried to do.

His parents reported that he had seen a movie about the cruel Roman emperor, Caligula, had said, "Caligula must have had 'cephalitis like me." He had begun very repetitive, intensive Caligula play at home and induced his parents to read to him at length about this period of Roman history.

I have mentioned his refusal to communicate with me directly. Typically, he would bring up a problem by telling his mother to ask me about something. Cues to his body image and some of his organically determined symptoms had already appeared, though I did not recognize their specificity at the time. Before treatment began, Hugh had complained that at night he feared a tiger jumping out at him in a "bad thought . . a movie in my head." (You will recall the way he fought fire with fire by way of his toy, the totemistic tiger.) He had also described his body as full of little rooms; his illness was always peeking around the corners of the rooms, but he could never catch it. Early in treatment, he asked his parents about his tinnitus and told them to ask me. He talked to his mother about the bad smells he used to smell.

Now in the ninth month of treatment, he told his mother to ask me about my notes. When I took this up with him, he admitted he felt his treatment was not a secret, that I discussed him with other doctors. He also complained to the secretaries of the clinic that I intended to force him back into school. In the next session, he seemed tense and angry. I talked about his feeling that I could read his mind and his paranoid misinterpretations; he admitted his anger at having people tell me about him and went on to discuss his fear in the hospital and his anger about having 'cephalitis. He said he was like Caligula but referred later to "the bad Caligula dream" (see below, "color dreams").[4] He admitted that he had believed I could read his mind and said he tried to think only of Bugs Bunny and not of his worries when he came to see me. Heretofore, he had been unshakable in refusing to listen "officially" to interpretations. By contrast, in this session, he was attentive to my speculations about the meaning of the hospital experience and his relations with me. Two or three times, during pauses, he asked: "Are you thinking?" and let me bring something up. Now after seven months, he agreed to come in once a week. His manner became markedly more relaxed and friendly; his behavior at home and in the waiting room improved dramatically.

In the tenth month, the persecutory play themes shifted to a war between children and adults with the mother as the most frequent malefactor. The essence of this repetitive play was the concept of mothers being deceitful to children—telling them something was for the children's benefit when the real aim was cruelty. Hugh said that the adults "want to make the children horrible people like they are." This play culminated in an almost literal tale of his illness as he saw it: two women put a man on the table, cut his head open, inserted a hydrogen bomb, and sewed him up again, while the bomb ticked. The ensuing explosion killed all the men; all the women escaped unharmed.

Hugh then was willing to tell me, with elaborate diagrams of the

4 The Caligula play waned in the tenth month and ceased with the naming of a Chihuahua pup by that name!

floor plan, about his experiences in the hospital and his confusion about whether he had 'cephalitis or was just bad. His discussion of details of his emotional experiences always was preceded and pointed up by the location of these events on his diagram. He needed to locate himself in space and derive the memory of what happened from this spatial orientation. Shortly thereafter, at his request, I told him about the etiology and course of his illness and how it caused the "mads."

In the next session, he began to discuss his paranoid transference by playing with the doll who previously had been the "crabby lady" who led the monsters, saying, "She is a member of the Bag family who looks something like you." To my question, "The bad lady?" he replied, "Sometimes." He then burlesqued Mrs. Snob-bag and Mrs. Crab-bag, who had just tortured the male members of their families, conversing in a false, mannered, social chit-chat which was a parody of his mother. The next hour he gave me a flower which he said was called either "Heaven in the Mist" or "Devil in the Bush" and asked me which I was. At this time, when his ambivalence and his paranoid fantasies had been expressed, I inquired how long he thought he would have to come. He replied, "Oh, a year, at least!"

During the fifteenth to twenty-fifth months of treatment, his play shifted to problems concerned with his body image and his organic lesion (interpolated with compulsive or smearing activities). His relationship with me was stably positive; he treated me like a benevolent protector (against his phobias), a chum, or a well-liked but a slightly stupid pupil (e.g., in the chess sequence).

Hugh came in with a chess set and insisted that we play. He told me his rules of how each piece was allowed to move but did not disclose the point of the game. After a couple of sessions, I realized that in the game (as described by the patient) the knight seemed to be the only piece that could capture the queen. I said as much and he responded enthusiastically, "Yeah, the knight's called the Queen Killer!" The parents, who did not know what had transpired, told me that until now Hugh had become so upset when his queen was captured in chess that the family had refrained from taking it; now he said it was all right to capture her, the pawn would win her back. The problem was discussed with the patient in terms of its oedipal meaning. The chess ceased in an atmosphere of satiation.

Hugh had also disclosed, through spatial metaphor, his envy of women, saying that the king could only move one space at a time but the queen could move anywhere! The indirect nature of this entire communication was typical.

Early in treatment, certain paintings had suggested the patient's loss of spatial differentiation between his body and the outside world, the merging of figure and ground, and the remote, inhuman feelings connected with it. In white paint on white paper, he drew three paintings: "A Ghostly Gas Station," "Swings in a Snowstorm," and the bubbles which showed on the surface of the water after a swimmer had dived in and disappeared—then the swimmer's track or wake through the water. No figures appeared. These paintings were done in May, 1954, when the patient was seven years old. Hugh's first conventional child's drawing appeared a year and a half later, in October, and his first representational figures—a witch and her cat—at Halloween of that year.

A set of Bender Gestalt figures were presented to the patient in the seventh month of treatment. Hugh's Bender did not give any evidence of his organic brain disease. It did reflect his superior intellectual level and, in its compulsive organization, his concern with enclosing and binding space.

Around the fifteenth month, space binding became the most prominent feature of treatment. The patient diagrammed action drawings of cars and busses with emphasis on danger in space and time; he did a series of elaborate ant-warren diagrams with much accurate detail; he diagrammed a jail, a gas chamber, an electric chair. He spent much time and took elaborate care in boxing in score sheets, constructing boxes for his number work, etc. When he returned to school at the age of eight and a half years, his compulsive activity increased, particularly number play and boxed, compulsive diagrams and drawings. His relationship with me continued to be friendly and he allowed me to explain a pending intravenous pyelogram (after first covering his ears and saying, "No shots!"). Also, for the first time in treatment, he volunteered to tell me about the results of a medical procedure.

About four months followed in which oedipal and castration fears alternated with striking magical, destructive-restitutive play. Hugh drew a "dangerous house"; then he said that since he had made it, he could make it safe and did so, fixing up all the dangerous features. After an earthquake, he drew a skyscraper falling over, then emphasized the body-image meaning by making a sixty-two-story skyscraper (with the stories all counted), showed the top twenty stories falling and called it "Hugh and Co." In this period (after a year and a half of treatment), he came to a session with clear intent to communicate something, drew a witchlike diagram and spent the whole hour removing and interchanging arms, legs, and hat. He gave it a clear personal reference by drawing a box in the brain and describing it as the controlling mechanism. He showed how its connections were wrong when the figure was mutilated; when the figure was put back together correctly, he changed the connection in the brain box to suit. This kind of play was repetitive and persistent. His probable castration fears in the hospital were discussed with him and he elaborated various fearful events in the hospital. Following this period in therapy, he became more direct in his relations to me and less fearful about the clinic. Whereas he had previously insisted that I call for him in the waiting room and escort him back to his mother, and had gone into a panic when he had smeared his clothes or skin lest people laugh at him, he now could get dirty, allowed himself to be called on the public address system, and formally took leave of me at the door to the playroom. It was the next month, the eighteenth, that he drew the witch and her cat—his first "human" forms.

In the next four months of treatment. the patient's body image was explicitly elaborated and it became possible to differentiate symptoms and fantasies which were a result of excitation from damaged brain areas from his other symptoms and problems. I must emphasize again, however, that the parents had reported some body-image concepts (body made up of little rooms) and some symptoms (tinnitus and bad smells) before treatment began; the fact that Hugh would not discuss them explicitly until late in the second year of treatment did not result from repression of a deep nature but from feelings of embarrassment, shame, mistrust, fear of consequences, etc. It seems likely that the body-image concepts and the meaning of the organic symptoms were preconscious, but that the devouring witch fantasies and the paranoid transference had to be worked through before the patient could or would discuss the meaning of the organic disease.

In the organic category, the eating problem was the first symptom to be brought up. The parents and the pediatrician had become increasingly concerned about Hugh's poor diet and loss of weight and had discussed the problem with me. Hugh came in one day looking troubled and tense, seemed anxious to talk about something but unable to do so. Next he brought in a note: "1. I lost 3 pounds. 2. i can't eat good. 3. I only eat mush or popcorn. 4. Lately i can't hardly eat at all." He still could not bring himself to discuss the problem directly. He then requested an extra appointment because of something he had forgotten to show me and brought in a diagram of a "machine" comprising power circuits. I suggested that this had some connection with his fears of food, how food goes through the body (assuming it was related to his protracted diarrhea), etc. Hugh denied this. However, he admitted to fantasies of people in his blood and, when I asked him to paint a diagram of how his brain, heart, and stomach were connected, he readily began to do so.

The body-image drawing was done in three sections on three sheets of newsprint paper in two sessions, a week apart. Though he did not compare the sections, the body outlines were well matched, suggesting a definite spatial concept on the boy's part. The body was outlined in faint pink, while the organs and the "people who live in the blood" were bright red or undiluted black. Hugh drew, on the heart, two stick figures: "The Red King in charge of blood and the Black King in charge of cephalitis." Each King had stick-figure guards around him. Hugh drew a window they could look out of in the head (where the control mechanism was) and had it similarly guarded. "Blood veins" ran from the heart to the head and to the extremities; the soldiers of the Black and Red Kings traveled up and down these. The red and black forces were evenly matched. He omitted the penis; when I commented on this, he said, "Oh yes, the cannon," drew it and described how the guards mounted steps to fire it.

Excited play followed in which a soldier dreamed of a hand with fifty fingers so he could fire more guns at once. Then Hugh did a series of drawings with an erotized theme, in which parts of a boy and girl were interchanged. For the first time, women were defeated;

they ended in a fight and killed each other while the boy escaped unharmed: "He wasn't interested in them anyhow."

A few sessions later, Hugh told of Mr. 'Cephalitis, who lived in one mansion while Hugh lived in another. The mansions, of course, were identically furnished and decorated. He talked first of getting robbers or criminals in jail but having them break out and repeat their crimes, then he said that Mr. 'Cephalitis did the same. He, Hugh, would subdue Mr. 'Cephalitis and make him sign a paper to be good, but Mr. 'Cephalitis would immediately break his word and do it again. Hugh discussed the rooms in his own body where Mr. 'Cephalitis lived: in the arm (big room) and fingers with hall (blood veins) going up to the head. In connection with his trouble in controlling Mr. 'Cephalitis, he said poignantly: "A body has a million rooms."

The eating problem was still troublesome and the family (in response to the pediatrician's urging) was putting pressure on Hugh to overcome it. Presumably in response to this, he returned to play of aggressive women in a number of play sessions. Thinking of the "cannon" he had omitted from his body image, I again discussed his feeling that I had sent him to the hospital, his castration fear, and his fears of women as the aggressor. He talked about his fears of the two housekeepers in the past: one in the home during his mother's illness (when he was four and a half to five and a half), who set no limits, the other (the original witch, "the Cooker"), during his infancy. He called the latter "the Spanker" and said: "I must have thought my mother was the Spanker and she never spanks. I got scared of her." Earlier, he had said, "I didn't know who was the Cooker and who was my mother, so I just hit everybody."

He admitted his paranoid fantasies about his mother (as usual, in spatial terms) in connection with his drug therapy. He told how huge the pills seemed at first and admitted the thought: "What's mother trying to do—fill my mouth to the back and choke me? . . Not really . . . But I thought the pills would swell in my stomach." "And choke your stomach?" "Yeah. . . Now the pills seem small."

Hugh became willing at this point to discuss further the symptoms which—as gradually became clear—were related to excitation from damaged brain areas. You will recall that he had brought up his eating problems, denying fears and fantasies, saying he just didn't like the taste. I had proceeded nonetheless on a psychogenic hypothesis, and requested that he be given a Rorschach, asking particularly about fantasies in this area. The Rorschach interpretation suggested that Hugh did have opposing concepts of "bad-oral aggression" vs. "head-intellectual functioning-control." I told Hugh about this dichotomy; he denied its etiological importance. However, he was willing to discuss his abnormal perceptions. He told me of his nightly bad dreams which were like movies and usually in color. The themes of these bad color dreams all concerned being chased by bad guys, murders, frightening situations, torture dreams, in which some or all of his family were involved. Earlier, he had dreamed of being abandoned himself or lost or given away. Despite the dramatic content, it occurred to me that these dreams had a stereotyped quality reminiscent of organic deliria. Hugh told me, on inquiry, that they all occurred in the early morning and their occurrence in color distinguished them, in his mind, from his other dreams. I wondered if they could originate in excitation from brain-damaged areas and suggested a two-hour delay in the evening dose of Milontin (till bedtime). The dreams promptly ceased and have not recurred.

This called forcibly to my attention the possibility that other symptoms might be related to stimuli from the damaged brain area and I recalled Ostow's article (1955) and Penfield's work (1954) on perceptual disturbances associated with temporal lobe damage. The patient's reaction to my discovery that his bad color dreams seemed to be caused by Mr. 'Cephalitis confirmed his inclusion of them into his damaged body image. He said, "Of course," it was the 'cephalitis causing them—he knew that all the time—if I had wanted to know, why hadn't I asked him?

I asked his mother to keep a diary about his symptoms. Here she described the *déjà vu* phenomena mentioned by Penfield. "Hugh says, 'Sometimes things happen in the day and I think I dreamed them before. Like a man will come to the door and I think it has happened before in my dream. The man will come in the same face and nose and clothes that was in my dream before. But that happens to everybody, doesn't it? . . I know a dream is really a dream because in real life I cannot see my face. If I can see my face then I know it is a dream.' "

On the day he brought in this record, Hugh asked me what further comments I had to make about his food problems. I said I didn't know, except somehow eating seemed to be connected with 'cephalitis. He replied: "Of course it is, by the tongue." I asked: "How does it get to the tongue?" "Well, 'cephalitis is a disease. . . It climbs [to the tongue] by the blood veins." I questioned him further, "You mean tastes are made funny by the 'cephalitis like those sounds[5] you used to hear?" He replied: "Yes . . . They're too strong." He discussed the exacerbation of tastes and how, if the smells are strong, he could not bear to taste the food at all. I suggested that he try holding his nose to see if he could eat more things; this was moderately successful.

The patient talked about certain other symptoms as if they occupied the same place with respect to his body image as the above. He included his hoarse voice which embarrassed him greatly, his clumsiness and incoordination of gait, and his genitourinary difficulties (e.g., his repeated infections and occasional dribbling). The "bladder room" featured prominently in his early discussions of his body image.[6] Periodically Hugh shyly asked me for my thoughts or suggestions on the management of these symptoms.

During the summer in which Hugh was nine years old, the family planned a trip to Europe. In view of the specific relation of some symptoms in the perceptual realm to stimulation from damaged brain areas, I suggested that they consult Penfield, in Montreal, about possible extirpation of focal areas. This obviously traumatizing plan was thoroughly discussed with the patient and, despite an initial phobic reaction, he accepted it calmly. The period before the trip (the last two months of his second year of treatment) was devoted to discussions of this anticipated trauma and to management of Hugh's panic about the shots and other procedures preparatory to the trip. He had a fairly severe regressive, coercive reaction to the shots, but skillful handling by the pediatrician enabled him to get through them.

During the European sojourn, unforeseen difficulties once more

[5] The tinnitus reported by the parents before treatment began.

[6] The patient had been subject to repeated genitourinary infections. All studies, including intravenous pyelograms, were negative and did not disclose any peripheral defect to account for the predisposition.

ensued. Hugh was referred by Penfield to Sir Russell Brain in London, but before he could be worked up neurosurgically, he again developed a refractory genitourinary infection and was hospitalized for several weeks in a children's hospital. The eventual neurosurgical decision was that the brain damage was too extensive for operative intervention. In general, the boy's medical experiences in England were very supportive, in contrast to his previous hospital experience. When his behavior was difficult, a surgeon commented to the mother, "These temporal lobe lesions make it terribly difficult for a little chap, don't they." However, again one surgeon and one nurse told the family that the patient was simply spoiled and they must ignore his complaints. The parents responded with their typical overcompliance to authority and ignored Hugh's complaints of ear-ache until an infection was florid and rupture of the eardrum imminent. During this period, Hugh's aggressive behavior increased.

When Hugh returned to treatment, he did not show direct or indirect resentment of me because of his difficult medical experiences this time. He said, "Well, you told me about it . . and why . . and you couldn't know I'd get bladder trouble." He was readily willing to discuss his hospital experiences in detail. In striking contrast to his previous account of hospitalization, where he had to describe his emotional reactions in relation to the floor plan, he now could focus directly on the interpersonal transactions and his emotional reactions. During the next four months, he continued in a realistic, friendly relationship with me, engaging in nonsymbolic play and using therapy for supportive and ego-oriented purposes. The question of termination was brought up with him at the end of this time because it seemed advisable (for expedient reasons) that further dynamically oriented therapy be deferred. Hugh agreed to a termination date two and a half months in the future.

He promptly began playing with a box of modular blocks which came in five sizes, each about an inch larger than the last. He had never played with these blocks before. At this time in his daily life, Hugh showed little of the incoordination, clumsiness, or perceptual uncertainty which had been characteristic when he was first seen. He had learned to roller skate, to ride a bicycle, and to do reasonably well in all sports save those, like baseball, in which his perceptual difficulties made him uncertain.

However, in his play with the blocks he showed striking retro-gression to much earlier spatial and perceptual confusion. Since he played with nothing else for the remaining months of treatment, it seemed clear that this was a psychologically meaningful change. In every session, he built two-story houses. He showed marked pseudo stupidity in matching the blocks for size, making no effort to use a measuring block or even to look at the blocks carefully. He built by a process of approximation and patching, which at first seemed merely to be far below his current functional and maturational level. After a few times, however, I realized that each two-story edifice, however patched and approximated, was solid except that each one was completed with a definite gap or chink in the second story—very poorly patched, if at all. It then seemed clear that the block play was a recapitulation of Hugh's feelings about his body and his organic damage. I said, "They've all got a hole in the head." He agreed enthusiastically.

In the remaining sessions, he built progressively better and more skillfully erected houses in a clear, magical attempt to create a less damaged body image. He began to select blocks accurately by size, then to use a sample block and lay out enough materials in advance to carry out his plans. Some tendency to improvisation or patching continued until, in the last session, he built a carefully planned, complexly designed, very well-proportioned, perfect building. He was just ten years old when treatment ended.

Progress in Treatment

During the course of treatment, the patient had made remarkable social advances. His aggressive outbursts and his compulsive rituals were strikingly diminished, as was his tormenting demandingness on his family. Hugh himself knew when he needed to increase his drug dosage and could distinguish the symptoms originating from his brain damage from other problems. He still had some eating diffi-culties, fears of shots and medical procedures, and periods of tense, irritable behavior. However, in school, he was performing excel-lently at grade level and had been elected president of his class. His improvement in motor skills has been described. His social relations were good and he was no longer suspicious, withdrawn, or felt that he was crazy.

Dynamically, I believe one can say that Hugh worked out much of the anxiety associated with his brain damage. His basic identification with the female aggressor was only partially modified. This identification represented Hugh's "solution" of the paranoid attitude toward his mother which had resulted from the acute stage of the organic illness. Thus it was ego-syntonic and not as accessible to psychotherapy as his other difficulties. I felt that (1) a continued abatement of the aggressive outbursts and improved social adjustment as a result of medication and psychotherapy might make his identification with the female aggressor less necessary; (2) the consequently improved realistic relationship with his father might enable Hugh later to view the feminine identification as more ego-alien and to work it through with the aid, if necessary, of further formal therapy.

FOLLOW-UP

The parents were retested and Hugh was seen again eight months after termination of treatment. The parents, according to their MMPIs, were relatively unchanged. Not so with Hugh: he presented himself as a strikingly more self-confident and masculine boy who had lost much of the shy, uncertain, indefinably handicapped and somewhat feminine bearing which had characterized him before. He summarized his impression of treatment when I commented that he had "forgotten" some of the dynamic transactions: "Yes . . . but I remember the important problems." To Hugh, these were problems concerning Mr. 'Cephalitis, whom he now demoted to the familiar nickname "Sephy." His previous anger against his father had been repressed; he looked at me in astonishment when I reminded him that he had often written his father notes, saying he hated him; he told me, "I'm a woman hater now." Improved masculine identification had clearly taken place. When I said it looked as if Mr. 'Cephalitis was locked up in jail for good, Hugh smiled broadly and agreed with assurance.

He did another portrait of his body image which showed traces of his previous drawing but also reflected his marked clinical improvement and mastery over aggressive impulses. The Red King in charge of Blood had become the Queen; the Black King in charge of 'Cephalitis had become the Good King, the ruler, and now was blue. The Queen's guards were still red and traces of the connection with the blood remained (e.g., their hospital was in the heart). The King's evil soldiers had become Government Agents (presumably a reflection of ego and superego control over aggression). The control box was gone from the head and the blood veins no longer existed (you will recall that they previously served as "roads" for the conveyance of aggressive impulses and abnormal perceptions). Now, the feet and legs were made repositories for a factory and storehouses containing all kinds of Thanksgiving foods (this was humor, related to the date of the interview). The patient was clearly speaking metaphorically: at first he labeled the kidneys as "filters," then he said, "No, that's what they really are; this is a game; they have to be something different," and made them storehouses for old clothes. Much humor appeared in the drawing. I asked Hugh (recalling the chess sequence) where the knight was. He replied (referring, I believe, to treatment), "Oh, this isn't such olden times!" He had come in with a minor complaint about his hoarse voice (an encephalopathic symptom); probably because of this, he located a dungeon on one side of his neck. This was the only feature of the new body-image drawing done in the original black. Hugh incarcerated Sephy and his guards in it and stated that Sephy was locked up for good there.[7]

His social improvement had continued. His relation with me was friendly, assured, and realistic. His perception of encephalopathic symptoms was unchanged; his memory of psychological attitudes and problems had undergone marked distortion and repression. In contrast to his early fears about confidentiality and his paranoid attitudes, he now was entirely unconcerned to hear that I wanted to write a story about him and Mr. 'Cephalitis to tell to other doctors. I explained the use of a pseudonym; he asked what his would be and,

[7] Further development of a more realistic body image was seen two years after treatment. Hugh made a very aesthetic ceramic paperweight which showed his accurate perception of his organic lesion and his ability to sublimate through creative productivity. He made a semiabstract model of a brain, using coils of clay which were smoothly interwoven and represented the convolutions of the brain. However, precisely in the right temporal area was a distorted, twisted patch of thin, spidery coils. Ends of these coils protruded; the organization and unity shown in the rest of the model were conspicuously lacking in this area. The coils themselves were "deformed" by twisting and unevenness. He had modeled his organic lesion.

when I told him, laughed heartily and said, "That's nothing like my name."

<h2 style="text-align:center">DISCUSSION</h2>

The patient's difficulties can be classified under: (1) the organic factors: the perceptual abnormalities and the aggressive outbursts; (2) the boy's efforts to organize these organic symptoms and his view of his disease (a) in terms of body image and (b) in his fantasies about Mr. 'Cephalitis and how to control him; (3) the psychodynamic problems. This third category includes the distortions of psychosexual development, the fixations and the defensive maneuvers which relate (a) to the nature and timing of the organic onslaught and (b) to the characteristic interpersonal transactions in his family.

The Organic Factors

Let us consider first the part Mr. 'Cephalitis played in the picture—the symptoms caused by stimuli originating in the damaged brain area which comprised widespread degenerative and irritative lesions of the right temporal lobe. Penfield and Jaspar (1954) and Ostow (1955) describe the temporal lobe as a receiving station for olfactory and taste stimuli. Sensations of vertigo and disturbances of equilibrium may be produced by stimulation of the lateral aspects of the temporal lobe (Ostow, p. 388). "Perceptual illusions, dream-like hallucinations, and attempts to repeat the stereotyped automatic behavior were seen. The perceptual illusions included impairment of judgment about the size of a visual object, its distance from the patient, the loudness of noise, the pitch of a voice, or the speed of an event. There was also the well-known *déjà vu*, the illusional impression of familiarity. The hallucinatory sequences might be memories, recent or remote, or dreamlike productions, or actual reproductions of dreams with which the patient was familiar" (Ostow, p. 389). Penfield and Jaspar refer to alimentary seizures, autonomic seizures, etc.: "The attacks from which this patient suffered were obviously in a part of the brain related to the alimentary tract and producing at different times borborygmi, nausea, bad taste, salivation, and sensations referred to stomach, throat, and mouth. Each series of attacks was associated with diarrhea" (Penfield and Jaspar, p. 430).

How do these considerations apply in the case of our patient? In differentiating psychological problems from symptoms directly related to the damaged brain area, my bias was psychogenic: I did not anticipate that temporal lobe damage triggered symptoms other than the aggressive outbursts. Two differentiating criteria seem to apply: (1) Certain symptoms which were described in the literature as occurring with temporal lobe lesions occurred in the patient and, in two of these (the aggressive outbursts and the color dreams), abatement of the symptoms seemed to occur with pharmacological management. (2) The patient's affective-defensive attitude toward certain symptoms seemed to differentiate them from other problems even before the patient became aware of this difference or was willing to tell me which symptoms he felt were related to Mr. 'Cephalitis.

The patient's eating disturbance is a typical example. You will recall that I had proceeded on the assumption that his difficulties were psychogenic, i.e., related to the onset of his illness in the oral stage, the painful diarrhea, and his fantasies of being devoured or torn apart by food and by those who fed him. In actuality, when the issue of hyperreactivity of the perceptual apparatus was raised, Hugh replied that he knew the problem was organic. He said, "Of course . . . 'Cephalitis is a disease. It climbs down the blood veins to the tongue."

Note that this datum was integrated by the patient into his encephalitic body image and taken for granted, not reacted to like a psychological conflict. Schilder (1935) states that organic lesions are perceived by the person as being peripheral rather than central to the ego. "Organic disease and organic change have less to do with the personality than functional disease. A functional disease is connected with the innermost problems of the individual—with the centre of his Ego" (Schilder, p. 156). You have noted that both Hugh and his mother responded to the boy's disease as if it were an external catastrophe which had overwhelmed them.

The symptoms which satisfy the above criteria for organicity include the aggressive outbursts, the bad smells, and the eating disturbance, the tinnitus, the *déjà-vu* experiences, and the color dreams. These can almost certainly be considered as direct results of stimuli from damaged areas of the temporal lobe. Also, it seems likely that certain spatial and visual distortions fall into this category.

Perceptual difficulties in temporal lobe lesions may include impairment of judgment about the size or distance of a visual object, the
speed of an event, etc. The patient's specific fear of baseball, persisting after he had mastered other motor skills involving coordination,
suggests an origin in such disordered perception. His disturbed
perception of the size of his pills may be a neat example of the
fusion between his paranoid feeling that his mother was responsible
and the spatial distortions relating to the temporal lobe damage.

The patient acted as if his hoarse voice and his clumsy gait were
also directly connected with his organic lesion (e.g., he reacted to
them with embarrassment and shame rather than repression or
distortion). Hugh also included his periodic genitourinary disturbances in this category, but, since retrograde pyelography has not
been done, a peripheral cause for these difficulties has not been
completely ruled out. The diarrhea which accompanied Hugh's acute
illness may be an example of the alimentary seizures referred to by
Penfield; at least no peripheral cause was ever discovered.

Hugh's view of all these symptoms is uniform and fits in with
Schilder's concept (that they are peripheral in the ego): he reacts
to them with marked embarrassment and shame but very little guilt.
He is clever in disguising these symptoms. He is afraid of being
sold or abandoned because of his aggression, but he regards all
these difficulties as enemy aliens rather than problems incorporated
into his own psychic economy and condemned by his superego.

Body Image

Loss of Boundaries: Schilder (1935) and Bender (1952) have made
extensive studies of the spatial organization of the world (e.g., sidewalk drawings of children, Bender Gestalt test) as projections of
body image. Hugh, in his rendering both of his own explicit body
image and in his other productions, showed his lack of a firm boundary between his body and the outside world. You remember that,
in his early pictures, he did three in white paint on white paper
which seemed to reflect this lack of differentiation. Later, in his body-
image painting, the interior of his body (showing his conflict with
Mr. 'Cephalitis) was painted in bright red and black, but the outline
of the figure was done in pale pink. He behaved as if the aggressive

outbursts and perceptual distortions had made him literally uncertain of his own spatial boundaries.

Hugh tried to combat this loss of boundaries by preoccupation with binding and enclosing space. During treatment, one of the most prominent features of his graphic productions was repetitive and emphasized boxing in of drawing, numbers, etc. He did drawings in which the danger was that of going too far in space-time. Diagrams of a catacomb type were numerous. His performance on the Bender Gestalt represented a successful effort to conceal his organically determined loss of boundaries by his compulsive and meticulous rendition of the figures (space binding). This boxing in of space did not ebb and flow with other compulsive activities; although certainly an effort to bind anxiety compulsively, it seemed also to be a specific effort to delineate the boundaries of the patient's own body and to contain Mr. 'Cephalitis within that boundary. He typically used spatial metaphor to describe his problems with Mr. 'Cephalitis. He spoke of the body as a series of rooms with a control box in the head representing his disease. He said Mr. 'Cephalitis lived in a mansion with fifty rooms. Efforts to control his aggression were described as putting Mr. 'Cephalitis into jail. In the last phase of treatment, when he was trying to reconstruct a less damaged body image, he did so by repetitively building two-story houses out of blocks. Similarly, he used spatial referrents in describing his own experiences. In his first traumatic hospitalization, for instance, he located his emotional experiences and reactions by reference to a floor plan of his ward. As he improved clinically, Hugh also was less threatened by the loss of spatial boundaries; in his second hospitalization, no floor plan was used to locate or mediate his emotional reactions. His second body-image drawing, likewise, showed his markedly lessened anxiety about his problems of spatial boundaries; now both events inside the body and the outline of the body drawing were equally vivid and definite.

The Autistic Phase

In the light of current discussions of infantile autism, it is particularly interesting to note that such classical autistic symptoms could occur at the most acute stage of Hugh's illness and abate, without formal treatment, as his diarrhea diminished. Physiological varia-bles are highlighted as etiological agents in his autistic reaction.

Hugh did not show the inborn "thin protective barrier against stimuli" described by Bergman and Escalona (1949). His first nine months of development were not only normal but relatively lusty and outgoing. He did suffer a sudden and massive illness at nine months. This illness caused hyperreactivity of the perceptual appa-ratus, which, when it occurs at this critical developmental stage, is a powerful stimulus for autism. His illness, in addition, caused severe recurrent diarrhea, which lasted until he was about three years old. This diarrhea constituted a "maximum developmental insult," that is, it interfered with the developmental modes and zones most highly cathected at that stage. Also, it constituted a proprioceptive insult. Mahler (1952) noted that an autistic child she observed was mark-edly reactive to proprioceptive stimuli, i.e., visceral pain. This was in sharp contrast to the child's lack of response to exteroceptive pain, i.e., a burn on the mouth.

Mahler and Gosliner (1955) describe the critical stage for autistic reactions as that in which the infant is gradually differentiating himself from the mother and establishing the mother as an external object. They feel that this developmental stage is typically "still a very precarious one at twelve to thirty months of age" (p. 195). From Hugh's case, it seems that differentiation of the mother as a hostile external object may occur even earlier than twelve months if some inner or outer source of pain (e.g., diarrhea, an overstimulating mother) forcibly disrupts the infant's symbiotic gratifications.

Hugh reacted to the double assault on him at nine months with the predictable developmental response: since his mother was the primary object, he developed a paranoid reaction to her. The the-oretical implications of this primary rejection of the mother will not be elaborated here, since they are discussed elsewhere (Sarvis and Garcia, 1960). However, it should be noted that the stimulation of the paranoid reaction in this boy was physiological and not related to family psychodynamics. In fact, the family psychodynamics were so strongly organized against a chronic autistic reaction, that Hugh, as soon as his diarrhea abated, began to recover from his autism without any formal psychotherapeutic intervention.

It seems probable that infantile autism is a two-stage process.

Any combination of etiological variables, at the vulnerable developmental stage, may cause a child to reject his mother in a primary autistic reaction. One of these etiological variables may, of course, be the pathology of the mother, but others are clearly physiological, constitutional, etc. Whatever the causes, the child has rejected the mother because, at that age, she is the primary object. Now, the mother has to struggle with her own temptation to counterreject or counterwithdraw from the child. If this counterrejection is marked, it predisposes to the consolidation of the autistic reaction into chronic autistic disease. If the counterrejection is absent, as in the case of Hugh's family, the child's recovery from an autistic reaction is greatly supported.

At times, however, it seems that constitutional variables or physiological assaults may be so overwhelming to the child's ego that no attitude on the part of the mother or the therapist suffices to help the child master an autistic reaction.

BIBLIOGRAPHY

Bender, L. (1952), *Child Psychiatric Techniques.* Springfield, Ill.: Charles C Thomas.
Bergman, P. & Escalona, S. K. (1949), Unusual Sensitivies in Very Young Children. *This Annual,* III/IV.
Mahler, M. S. (1952), On Child Psychosis and Schizophrenia. *This Annual,* VII.
—— & Gosliner, E. J. (1955), On Symbiotic Child Psychosis. *This Annual,* X.
Ostow, M. (1955), A Psychoanalytic Contribution to the Study of Brain Function. Part II. *Psa. Quart.,* XXIV.
Penfield, W. & Jaspar, H. (1954), *Epilepsy and the Functional Anatomy of the Human Brain.* Boston: Little, Brown.
Sarvis, M. A. & Garcia, B. (1960), Etiological Variables in Autism. *Psychiatry* (in press).
Schilder, P. (1935), *The Image and Appearance of the Human Body.* New York: Intertional Universities Press, 1950.

CONTENTS OF PREVIOUS VOLUMES

VOLUME I, 1945

VOLUME II, 1946

VOLUME III/IV, 1949

VOLUME V, 1950

VOLUME VI, 1951

VOLUME IX, 1954

VOLUME X, 1955

VOLUME XI, 1956

VOLUME XII, 1957

VOLUME XIII, 1958

VOLUME XIV, 1959